FROMMER'S

COMPREHENSIVE TRAVEL GUIDE

PARIS '95

W9-ARM-617

by Darwin Porter
Assisted by Danforth Prince

MACMILLAN • USA

FROMMER BOOKS

Macmillan Travel
A Prentice Hall Macmillan Company
15 Columbus Circle
New York, NY 10023

ISBN 0-671-88378-X
ISSN 0899-3203

Design by Robert Bull Design
Maps by Ortelius Design

Manufactured in the United States of America

CONTENTS

LIST OF MAPS

INVITATION TO THE READERS

In researching this book, I have come across many fine establishments, the best of which I have included here. I am sure that many of you will also come across appealing hotels, inns, restaurants, guesthouses, shops, and attractions. Please don't keep them to yourself. Share your experiences, especially if you want to comment on places that I have included in this edition that have changed for the worse. You can address your letters to me:

Darwin Porter
Frommer's Paris '95
c/o Macmillan Travel
15 Columbus Circle
New York, NY 10023

A DISCLAIMER

Readers are advised that prices fluctuate in the course of time, and travel information changes under the impact of the varied and volatile factors that affect the travel industry. The author and the publisher cannot be held responsible for the experiences of readers while traveling. Readers are invited to write to the publisher with ideas, comments, and suggestions for future editions.

SAFETY ADVISORY

Whenever you're traveling in an unfamiliar city or country, stay alert. Be aware of your immediate surroundings. Wear a moneybelt and keep a close eye on your possessions. Be particularly careful with cameras, purses, and wallets, all favorite targets of thieves and pickpockets.

INTRODUCING PARIS

Paris has been celebrated in so many songs, poems, stories, books, paintings, and movies that for millions of people it is an abstraction rather than a city. To French people living in the provinces, Paris is the center of the universe, the place where laws and careers are made and broken. To North American tourists, it is still "Gay Paree" inviting you for a fling, the hub of everything "European," and the epitome of that nebulous attribute known as "chic." Say "Paris" and you produce an instant image of sidewalk cafés and strolling lovers beneath the Eiffel Tower.

To Hemingway, Paris was "a moveable feast" and the city to which "there is never any ending." To me, Paris is by day a stone mosaic of delicate gray and green, by night a stunning, unforgettable sea of lights—white, red, and orange. Broad, tree-lined boulevards open before you, mansions loom tall, ornate, and graceful. Everywhere you look are trees, squares, and monuments. Whether you see it for the first or fiftieth time, the discovery of the city, and making it your own, is and always has been the most compelling reason for coming to Paris.

1. GEOGRAPHY & PEOPLE

GEOGRAPHY The nation's capital lies on both banks of the Seine, near the center of a low-lying region known as the Paris Basin. Rich in history and cultural implications, the river undulates in a gentle S-shaped curve through the city, sheltering amid its currents the pair of islands upon which Paris was born. The river's many bridges (32 in all) gracefully unite the city into a coherent and unusually beautiful whole.

Centuries of city planning have produced some of the most splendid panoramas in the world—which are one of the city's most memorable features. The river's northern part is called the Right Bank (*Rive Droite*) and the southern part (site of a university since the 12th century) the *Rive Gauche*. These designations make sense when you stand on a bridge facing downstream and watch the waters flow toward Normandy and the sea—to your right is the north bank and to your left the south bank.

✓ WHAT'S SPECIAL ABOUT PARIS

Great Neighborhoods
- ☐ The Latin Quarter, precinct of the Sorbonne on the Left Bank, where students meet and fall in love.
- ☐ The Marais, center of fashion and aristocratic Paris in the 17th century.

Monuments
- ☐ Eiffel Tower, with a fabulously dizzying view over a 40-mile radius on a clear day.
- ☐ Arc de Triomphe, the gateway to the Champs-Elysées and a tribute to the glory of France, built to pay homage to the Napoleonic campaigns.

Buildings
- ☐ Notre-Dame, a cathedral for the ages, through which everyone from Napoléon and Joséphine to Quasimodo and his beloved Esmeralda has passed.
- ☐ Conciergerie, the infamous prison of the Revolution that housed Marie Antoinette and others.

Museums
- ☐ The Louvre, the largest single museum in the West, the largest palace in Europe, and repository of some of the masterworks of Western civilization.
- ☐ Musée d'Orsay, a "bridge" between the works in the Louvre and the modern art of Pompidou Center.
- ☐ Pompidou Center, controversial in design, is a modern building dedicated to 20th-century art.

- ☐ Musée Picasso, housing most of this prolific painter's vast works and his favorite art by other masters.

Parks/Gardens
- ☐ Tuileries Gardens, elegantly mapped out by André Le Nôtre, "the king's gardener," in the heart of the Right Bank.
- ☐ Luxembourg Gardens, a 60-acre playground in the center of the Left Bank, saved from Baron Haussmann's greedy wreckers.
- ☐ Bois de Boulogne, beloved by Parisians, is a former royal hunting ground now acclaimed for grand restaurants, such racetracks as Longchamps, and flower gardens.

Events/Festivals
- ☐ The Festival Estival (summertime), with live performances of 700 years of musical tradition in the churches and auditoriums throughout Paris.
- ☐ Paris Auto Show, with all the hype, glamour, and excitement to draw thousands "from everywhere."

For the Kids
- ☐ Montmartre, a walking carnival where kids can sit for a charcoal sketch at place du Tertre, and take a funicular up the hill.
- ☐ Cité des Sciences et de l'Industrie, where everything's like a giant 3-D cinema, with several special exhibitions for the little ones.

PEOPLE If there is one characteristic Parisians share, it is their big-city spirit, the somewhat-aggressive, novelty-addicted, extremely cynical metropolitanism that makes "provincial" the worst insult in their dictionary.

Tolerance, gentleness, and patience are not their strongest points. They don't suffer fools gladly (although they adore eccentrics), and the worst offense a public figure can commit in their eyes is to make himself ridiculous.

The Parisians' behavior stems from their environment. For all its matchless splendor, Paris is a difficult place in which to scramble for a living. Working hours are long, competition murderous, traffic nerve-grinding, accommodations crowded and difficult to get; the pace is hectic and the cost of everything is the highest in France.

But a hard shell often protects a soft center. There is a startling contrast between the face Parisians show to passing strangers and their manner toward anyone with whom they share even the slightest personal rapport.

Compliment a surly bistro owner on his or her cuisine and—9 times out of 10—he or she will melt before your eyes. Admire a Parisian's car or dog and you'll find you have a loquacious companion for the next five minutes. Ask about the correct pronunciation of a French word (before you mispronounce it), and you'll instantly have a language teacher.

Paris is so packed with minority groups that the true natives ironically refer to themselves as the "Parisians of Paris." There are Russians (descendants of the flood of White Russian refugees who poured into Paris after the Bolshevik Revolution), Poles, English, Belgians, Italians, and Spaniards. Here, too, are vast colonies of Vietnamese, Algerians, Moroccans, Lebanese, and West Africans, all mingling with less friction than anyone who's ever heard a UN debate would believe possible.

2. HISTORY & POLITICS

HISTORY

THE ROMANS & THE MEROVINGIANS
Paris emerged at the crossroads of three major traffic arteries on the muddy island that today is known as the Ile de la Cité.

By around 2000 B.C., the island served as the fortified headquarters of the Parisii tribe, who referred to it as Lutetia. The pair of crude wooden bridges that connected the island to the left and right banks of the river were strategically important. In his *Commentaries*, Julius Caesar mentioned how these bridges were burned during the Gallic War of 52 B.C., and how the town on the island was pillaged, sacked, and transformed into a Roman-controlled stronghold.

DATELINE

- **2000 B.C.** Paris (ancient Lutetia) thrives along a strategic crossing of the Seine, the fortified headquarters of the Parisii tribe.
- **52 B.C.** Julius Caesar conquers Paris during the Gallic Wars.
- **A.D. 150** Lutetia flourishes as a Roman colony, *(continues)*

DATELINE

expanding to Paris's Left Bank.

200 Barbarian Gauls force Romans to retreat to the fortifications on Ile de la Cité.

300 "Paris" officially named as such. Roman power weakens in northern France.

350 Beginnings of Paris's Christianization.

400s Frankish invasions of Paris, with social transformation from Roman to Gallo-Roman culture.

466 Birth of Clovis, founder of the Merovingian dynasty, first non-Roman ruler of Paris since the Parisii.

800 Coronation of Charlemagne, founder of the Carolingian dynasty and first Holy Roman Emperor, who rules from Aachen in modern Germany.

987 Hugh Capet, founder of France's foremost early medieval dynasty, rises to power. He and his heirs rule from Paris.

1066 Viking descendants (traditional pillagers of northern France and Paris) invade England at the Battle of Hastings, forever linking the histories of France and England.

(continues)

Within a century, Lutetia had become a full-fledged Roman town, and some of the inhabitants abandoned the frequently flooded island in favor of higher ground on what is today the Left Bank. The Romans laid out their streets and monuments in a standardized format that matched hundreds of other Roman-built towns throughout the Empire. By the year A.D. 200, barbarian invasions increasingly threatened the stability of Roman Gaul, and the populace retreated from the surrounding hills to the fortified safety of the island. A wall almost 8 feet thick was built around the perimeter of the island, its marshes were filled in, and the population grew denser. An excavated milestone carved during the early 300s indicates the name of the city as "Paris" (not Lutetia) for the first time.

Within about 50 years, a Christian community gained a tenuous foothold on the island of Paris. According to legend, St. Denis served as the city's first bishop (beginning around 250), but it took the tenures of eight more bishops until St. Marcel was able to erect a crude wooden church on the Ile de la Cité. Although the political power of the Roman Empire had begun to wane within the Paris region by this time, the cultural and religious attachment of the community to the Christian bishops of Rome grew even stronger.

During the 400s, with the Roman armies in great decline, Germanic tribes from the east (the Salian Franks) invaded Paris and came under the Latin cultural sway, becoming more civilized during the process. The first of these Frankish kings, Clovis (466–511), founder of the Merovingian dynasty, embraced Christianity as his tribe's official religion. Recognizing the easy defensibility and convenience of the Ile de la Cité, he established his capital at Paris, setting a precedent for many succeeding rulers.

CHARLEMAGNE & THE CAROLINGIANS The Merovingian dynasty was replaced by the Carolingians, whose heyday began with the coronation of Charlemagne in 800. Neither Charlemagne nor any other Carolingian ever considered Paris the capital of an empire that sprawled over western Germany and eastern France. Responding to immediate political needs, they moved their capital to more easterly cities, which included Metz,

Reims, Cologne, and—most important—Aachen (Aix-la Chapelle). Despite its loss of political stature, Paris remained a commercial and religious center, sacred to the memory of St. Genevieve, who reputedly protected the city during the Huns' attempted sacks during the final days of the Roman Empire.

The Carolingian dynasty came to an end in 987. Regional loyalties were activated that signaled the political and linguistic divisions between what would eventually become modern France and modern Germany. Hugh Capet (ruling from 987 to 996), count of Paris and duke of France, became the first of a new dynasty, the Capetians, whose kings would rule from Paris throughout the Middle Ages.

THE MIDDLE AGES Around 1100, Paris began to emerge as a great city, with a university established on what is today known as the Left Bank. It attracted scholars from all over Europe. Kings and bishops began building the great Gothic cathedrals of France. The earliest of these, St. Denis and Chartres, were within an easy day's journey of Paris. Their stone and stained-glass grandeur was soon challenged by Paris's Notre-Dame, a soaring ecclesiastical monument rising from the very heart of the city. The population of Paris increased greatly, as did the city's mercantile activity. During the 1200s, a virtual building explosion transformed the skyline with convents and churches (including the jewel-like Sainte-Chapelle, completed within an astonishingly short two years beginning in 1247). During the next century, the increasingly powerful French kings added dozens of monuments of their own.

As time passed, the fortunes of Paris became closely linked to the luck and skill of the French monarchs in assuming power from the disparate and highly competitive feudal entities of the outlying provinces. Civil unrest, a series of plagues (including the famous Black Death), the takeovers of Paris by one warring faction after another, and a dangerous alliance of the English with the powerful rulers of Burgundy during the Hundred Years' War all contributed to the city's problems. To the everlasting humiliation of the French monarchs, the city was invaded by the English army in 1422. Joan of Arc (ca. 1412–31) tried unsuccessfully to reconquer Paris in 1429, two years before being

DATELINE

- **1100** The Université de Paris attracts scholars from throughout Europe.
- **1200s** Construction of cathedrals at St-Denis, Chartres, and Paris. Numerous churches, convents, and royal buildings also built in Paris. Paris's population and power grow, although frequently unsettled by plagues and feudal battles.
- **1422** Paris invaded by England during the Hundred Years' War.
- **1429** Joan of Arc tries unsuccessfully to regain Paris for the French. The Burgundians later capture and sell her to the English, who burn her at the stake in Rouen.
- **1500s** François I, considered first of the French Renaissance kings, embellishes Paris but chooses to maintain court in the Loire Valley.
- **1549** Henri II rules France from Paris. Construction of public and private residences begins, many of them in the Marais neighborhood.
- **1564** Construction of Catherine de Médicis's Tuileries Palace. Building facades in Paris transform from half-timbered to more durable chiseled

(continues)

DATELINE

stonework.

1572 The Wars of Religion reach their climax with the massacre of Protestants on St. Bartholomew's Day.

1598 Henri IV, most eccentric and enlightened monarch of his era, endorses the Edict of Nantes, granting tolerance to Protestants, for which a crazed monk fatally stabs him 12 years later.

1615 Construction of the Luxembourg Palace by Henri IV's widow, Marie de Médicis.

1636 Construction of the Palais-Royal by Richelieu. Soon thereafter, two marshy islands in the Seine are interconnected and filled in to create the Ile St-Louis.

1643 Rise to power of Louis XIV, "the Sun King," the most powerful ruler since the Caesars. He moves his court to newly constructed Versailles.

1776 American Declaration of Independence from Britain, striking a revolutionary chord in France.

1789 Outbreak of the French

(continues)

burned at the stake in Rouen (Normandy) by the English. Paris was reduced to poverty and economic stagnation and its embittered and greatly reduced population turned to banditry and street crime.

THE RENAISSANCE & THE REFORMATION The first of the Renaissance monarchs, François I, began an extensive enlargement of Paris's Louvre to make it suitable as a royal residence. Despite the building's embellishment, and the continued designation of Paris as the French capital, he spent much of his time at other châteaux amid the fertile hunting grounds of the Loire Valley. Intermittently, future monarchs would share his opinion that the narrow streets and teeming commercialism of Paris were unhealthy and upsetting.

The supremacy of Paris within France had been frequently eclipsed by the wishes of several monarchs to live elsewhere. Only the triumphant arrival in Paris in 1549 of Henri II, who successfully ruled France from within the city's borders, cemented Paris as the nation's undisputed capital. Responding to their ruler's initiative, fashionable aristocrats quickly began to build private residences on the right bank, within a marshy low-lying area known as *Le Marais* (the swamp).

Paris as the world knows it today came into existence during this period. The expansion of the Louvre continued, and Catherine de Médicis began building her Tuileries palace in 1564. From the shelter of dozens of elegant urban residences, the aristocracy of France imbued Paris with their sense of architectural and social style, as well as the mores and manners of the Renaissance. Stone quays were added to the banks of the Seine, defining their limits and preventing future flood damage, and royal decrees were passed establishing a series of building codes. To an increasing degree, Paris adopted the planned perspectives and visual grace of the preferred residence of an absolute monarchy.

During the late 1500s and 1600s, Protestantism was persecuted brutally by the French monarchs. Under Henry III the bloodletting reached a high point during the St. Bartholomew's Day massacre in 1572.

Henri III's tragic and eccentric successor,

Henri IV, ended the wars of religion by endorsing the Edict of Nantes (1598, which offered religious freedom to the Protestants of France) and laid out the lines for one of the memorable plazas of Paris—the place des Vosges. His reward for political leniency was to be stabbed by a deranged monk who was infuriated by religious tolerance.

After Henry IV's death, his second wife, Marie de Médicis (acting as regent), planned the Luxembourg Palace (1615), whose gardens have functioned ever since as a rendezvous for Parisians. In 1636, Cardinal Richelieu (who virtually ruled France during the minority of Louis XIII) built the sprawling premises of the Palais-Royale.

Under Louis XIII (1601–43) two uninhabited islands in the Seine were joined together with landfill, connected to the Ile de la Cité and also to the mainland with bridges, and renamed the Ile St-Louis. Also laid out were the Jardin des Plantes, whose flowers and medicinal herbs were arranged according to their scientific and medical category.

LOUIS XIV & THE FRENCH REVOLUTION

Louis was crowned king of France when he was only 9 years old. The government in Paris was almost completely dominated during Louis's minority by his Sicilian-born chief minister, Mazarin (1602–61).

This era marked the emergence of the French kings as absolute monarchs. As if to symbolize their power, the face of Paris was embellished with many of the monuments that still serve as symbols of the city. These included new alterations to the Louvre, and construction of the Pont-Royal, the quai Peletier, the place des Victoires, the place Vendôme, the Champs-Elysées, and the Hôtel des Invalides. Meanwhile, Louis XIV preferred to absent himself from the city center, constructing—at staggering expense—the palace at Versailles, 13 miles southwest of Paris. Today, its echoing and sometimes tiresome splendor is the single most visible monument to the most flamboyantly ostentatious era of French history.

Meanwhile the rising power of England, particularly its navy, represented a serious threat to France, which was otherwise the most powerful nation in the world. One of the many theaters of

DATELINE

Revolution.

- **1793** Louis XVI and his Austrian-born queen, Marie Antoinette, are publicly guillotined.
- **1799** Napoléon Bonaparte crowns himself Master of France. Paris is further embellished with neoclassical splendor.
- **1803** Napoléon abandons French overseas expansion and sells Louisiana to America.
- **1812** Defeat of Napoléon in the Russian winter campaign.
- **1814** Aided by a military coalition of France's enemies, especially England, the Bourbon monarchy, under Louis XVIII, is restored.
- **1821** Death of Napoléon Bonaparte.
- **1824** Death of Louis XVIII; Charles X accedes.
- **1830** Charles X is deposed, the more liberal Louis-Philippe is elected king. Paris prospers as it industrializes.
- **1848** Violent working-class revolution deposes Louis-Philippe, who is replaced by autocratic Napoléon III. Forced redesigning of Paris's landscapes by Baron Haussmann.
- **1863** Birth of impressionism.
- **1870** Franco-
  (continues)

DATELINE

Prussian War ends
in the defeat of
France; Paris is
threatened with
bombardment by
Prussian cannons
placed on the
outskirts of the
city. A revolution in
the aftermath of
this defeat
destroys the
Tuileries Palace
and overthrows the
government. Rise
of the Third
Republic and its
elected president,
Marshal
MacMahon.

- **1878–1937** A
series of
international
expositions adds
many enduring
monuments to the
Paris skyline,
including the Eiffel
Tower.
- **1914–18** World
War I
- **1940** German
troops invade
Paris. The official
French govern-
ment, under Pétain,
evacuates to
Vichy, while the
French Resistance
under de Gaulle
maintains symbolic
headquarters in
London.
- **1944** Paris
liberated by U.S.
troops. De Gaulle
returns from
London in triumph.
- **1948** Revolt in
French colony of
Madagascar costs
80,000 French
lives. France's
empire continues
to collapse in
Southeast Asia and
Equatorial Africa.

(continues)

the Anglo-French conflict was the war for American independence, during which the French kings had supported the American revolutionaries in their struggle against the crown. Ironically, within 15 years the same revolutionary fervor would cross the Atlantic and destroy the French monarchy.

None of this occurred within a philosophical vacuum. For years before the outbreak of hostilities between the American revolutionaries and the British, the Enlightenment and its philosophers, usually formulating their views within the sophisticated salons of Paris, had been fostering a new generation of thinkers who opposed absolutism, religious fanaticism, and superstition. Revolution had been brewing for almost 50 years, and after the French Revolution's explosive and world-shaking events, Europe was completely changed.

Beginning in 1789 with moderate aims, the Revolution soon became dominated by the radical Jacobins, led by Robespierre.

On August 10, 1792, troops from Marseilles, aided by a Parisian mob, threw Louis XVI and his Austrian-born queen, Marie Antoinette, into prison. Several months later, after countless humiliations and a bogus trial, they were guillotined at the place de la Revolution (later renamed the place de la Concorde) on January 21, 1793. The Reign of Terror continued for another 18 months, with Parisians of all political persuasions fearing for their lives.

THE RISE OF NAPOLEON It required the militaristic fervor of Napoléon to unite France once again. Considered then and today a genius with almost limitless ambition, he restored to Paris and to France a national pride that had been diminished during the horror of the Revolution. In 1799 at the age of 30, after many impressive political and military victories, he entered Paris and crowned himself First Consul and Master of France.

A brilliant politician, Napoléon moderated the atheistic rigidity of the early adherents of the Revolution by establishing peace with the Vatican. Soon thereafter, the legendary love of Parisians for their amusements began to revive; the boulevard des Italiens became the rendezvous point of the fashionable, while the boulevard du Temple, which housed many of the capital's vaudeville and cabaret theaters, became the favorite watering hole of the working class. In his self-appointed role as a French Caesar, Napoléon continued to alter the face of Paris with the construction of the neoclassical arcades of the rue de Rivoli (1801), the triumphal arches of the Arc du Carrousel and the place de l'Etoile, and the neoclassical grandeur of the Church of the Madeleine. On a less grandiose scale, the city's slaughterhouses and cemeteries were sanitized and moved away from the center of town, and new industries began to crowd workers from the countryside into the cramped slums of a newly industrialized Paris.

Napoléon's victories had made him the envy of Europe, but his infamous retreat from Moscow during the winter of 1812 reduced his formerly invincible army to tatters as 400,000 Frenchmen lost their lives. After a complicated series of events that included his return from exile, Napoléon was defeated at Waterloo by the combined armies of the English, the Dutch, and the Prussians. Exiled to the British-held island of St. Helena in the remote reaches of the South Atlantic, he died in 1821, probably the victim of an unknown poisoner. Some time later, his body was interred within a massive porphyry sarcophagus within Louis XIV's monument to the ailing and fallen warriors of France, Les Invalides in Paris.

In the power vacuum that followed the expulsion and death of Napoléon, Paris became the scene of intense lobbying concerning the future fate of France. The Bourbon monarchy was soon reestablished, but with reduced powers. In 1830 the regime was overthrown. Louis-Philippe, duke of Orléans and the son of a duke who had voted in 1793 for the death of Louis XVI, was elected king under a liberalized constitution. His calm, prosperous reign lasted for 18 years, during which England and France more or less collaborated on matters of foreign policy.

Paris reveled in its new prosperity, grateful for the funds and glamour that had elevated it to one of the top cultural and commercial centers of the world. As a fringe benefit of France's campaigns in the Egyptian desert, Paris received the Luxor obelisk as a gift from the caliphs of Egypt. Transporting it across the Mediterranean and reerecting it on a granite plinth in the place de la Concorde was considered a major triumph of engineering in 1836. Paris received its first railway line in 1837 (running from the center

DATELINE

- **1954–62** War in and eventual loss of Algeria. Paris is flooded with refugees, the nation bitterly divided over its North African policies.
- **1958** France's Fourth Republic collapses. General de Gaulle is called out of retirement to head the Fifth Republic.
- **1968** General revolt by Paris's students and factory workers. The French government is overhauled in the aftermath.
- **1981** François Mitterrand is elected France's first socialist president since the 1940s. Reelected in 1988.
- **1989** Paris celebrates the Bicentennial of the French Revolution.
- **1990–91** France joins the U.S., Britain, and other Allies in a successful war against Iraq's invasion of Kuwait.
- **1992** Euro Disney opens on Paris's outskirts.

of town to a suburb near St-Germain), and shortly thereafter the first gas-fed streetlights.

THE SECOND EMPIRE This was a time of wealth, grace, and the expansion of the arts for some French people, although the industrialization of certain working-class districts of Paris produced horrible poverty. The era also witnessed the development of French cuisine to the high art form that still prevails, while a newly empowered *bourgeoisie* reveled in its attempts to create the good life.

In 1848 a series of revolutions spread from one European capital to the next. The violent upheaval in Paris revealed the increasing dissatisfaction of many members of the working class. Fueled by a financial crash and scandals within the government, the revolt forced Louis-Philippe out of office. That year, on the dawn of the Second Republic, Emperor Napoléon's nephew, Napoléon III, was elected president by moderate and conservative elements. Appealing to the property-owning instinct of a nation that hadn't forgotten the violent revolution of less than a century before, he established a right-wing government and eventually assumed complete power—as emperor—in 1851.

In 1853, Napoléon III undertook the largest urban redevelopment project in the history of Europe. He commissioned Baron Haussmann (1809–91) to redesign the city of Paris. Haussmann created a vast network of boulevards interconnected with a series of squares (*places*) that cut across old neighborhoods. While this redesigning greatly enhanced the capital and gave it the look for which it is famous today, screams of outrage could be heard throughout most of France.

By 1866 the entrepreneurs of an increasingly industrialized Paris began to regard the Second Empire as a hindrance to its development. In 1870, during the Franco-Prussian War, the Prussians defeated Napoléon III at Sedan and held him prisoner along with 100,000 of his soldiers. Paris was threatened with bombardments from German cannon—by far the most advanced of their age—that were set up on the city's eastern periphery.

Agitated diplomacy encouraged a Prussian withdrawal, although the event's legacy of international humiliation and perceived military incompetence sparked a revolt in Paris. One of the immediate effects of the revolt was the burning of one of Paris's historic palaces, the Tuileries. Today, only the sprawling gardens of this once-great palace remain. The aftereffects of the events of 1870 ushered in the Third Republic and its elected president, Marshal Mac-Mahon, in 1873.

Peace and prosperity gradually returned; Paris regained its glamour. A series of Universal Expositions held in 1878, 1889, 1900, and 1937 was the catalyst for the construction of such enduring Paris monuments as the Trocadéro, the Palais de Chaillot, the Eiffel Tower, both the Grand and the Petit Palais des Champs-Elysées, and the neo-Byzantine church of Sacré-Coeur in Montmartre. Simultaneously, the *réseau métropolitain* (the Métro, or Paris subway) was constructed, providing a model for subsequent subway systems throughout Europe.

WORLD WARS I & II International rivalries and conflicting alliances led to World War I, which, after decisive German victories for two years, degenerated into the mud-slogged horror of trench warfare. Industrialization during and after the war transformed Paris and its outlying boroughs into one vast interconnected whole, by now one of the largest metropolitan areas in Europe and undisputed ever since as the center of France's intellectual and commercial life.

Immediately after the Allied victory, grave economic problems, coupled with a populace demoralized from years of fighting, encouraged the rise of socialism and the formation of a Communist party. The headquarters for both of these reigned undisputed within Paris. Also from Paris, the French government, led by the almost obsessively vindictive Clemenceau, occupied Germany's Ruhr Valley, then and now one of the most profitable and industrialized regions of Germany, and demanded every centime of reparations it could wring from its humiliated neighbor, a policy that contributed to the outbreak of World War II.

Thanks to an array of alliances, France had no choice but to declare war on Germany in 1939 when Germany invaded France's ally, Poland. Within only a few months, on June 14, 1940, Nazi armies marched arrogantly down the Champs-Elysées. Newsreel cameras recorded the French openly weeping at the sight. The city suffered little from the war materially, but for four years it survived in a kind of half-life, cold, dull, and drab, fostering scattered pockets of fighters who resisted sometimes passively, and sometimes with active sabotage.

During the Nazi occupation of Paris, the French government, under Marshal Pétain (1856–1951), moved to the quiet and isolated resort of Vichy and cooperated (or actually collaborated, depending on your point of view) with the Nazis. Tremendous internal dissension, the memory of which still simmers today, pitted many factions against one another. The Free French Resistance fled for its own safety to London, where it was headed by Charles de Gaulle (1880–1970).

POSTWAR PARIS Despite its gains in both prestige and prosperity after the end of World War II, Paris was rocked many times by internal dissent as domestic and international events embroiled the French government in dozens of controversies. In 1951 Paris forgot its cares by celebrating the 2,000th anniversary of the founding of the city, and poured much of its energy into rebuilding its image as a center of fashion, lifestyle, and glamour. Paris became internationally recognized as both a touristic staple in the travel diets of many North Americans and as a beacon for art and artists. The War of Algerian Independence (1954–58) was an anguishing event, more devastating than the earlier loss of France's colonies. Algeria had previously been considered a *département* (an integral extension of the French nation). The population of France (and Paris in particular) ballooned immediately as French citizens, fleeing with few possessions and much bitterness, escaped from Algeria. In 1958, as a result of the enormous loss of lives, money, and prestige in the Algerian affair, France's Fourth Republic collapsed, and de Gaulle was called out of retirement to form a new government. The Fifth Republic was launched. In 1962 the Algerian war of liberation ended with victory for Algeria, as France's colonies in Central and Equatorial Africa became independent one by one. The sun had finally set on an empire that had transformed Paris, during the period of its most spectacular construction, into a mighty city.

In 1968 a general revolt by students in Paris turned the capital into an armed camp, causing a near-collapse of the national government and the very real possibility of total civil war.

Paris today struggles with additional social unrest in Corsica and from Muslim fundamentalists residing both in and outside of France. In 1981 François Mitterrand (with a very close vote of 51%) was elected the first socialist president of France since World War II. The flight of massive amounts of capital held by French millionaires slowed somewhat after initial jitters, although many wealthy Parisians still prefer to invest their money elsewhere. Although much feared by the rich, Mitterrand was reelected in 1988 and (according to many of his critics) soon thereafter adopted a kind of imperial demeanor better suited to a French monarch than to a duly elected president.

In 1989 Paris celebrated the bicentennial of the French Revolution with much fanfare. In the winter of 1990–91, France joined with the United States, Great Britain, and other Allies in a successful war against Iraq, in response to that country's invasion of Kuwait. On the architectural front, new and daring designs (including Pei's iconoclastic addition of a glass pyramid within the courtyard of the Louvre, and the construction of a series of new museums and urban attractions) continued to give Paris the controversial zest for which it has traditionally been famous.

The postwar passion for exhibiting French culture has included the opening or redesigning of such museums as the Musée d'Orsay, the Centre Pompidou at the place Beaubourg, and the Musée Picasso; the newly renovated Orangerie of the Tuileries; construction of the Opéra Bastille, the newly gentrified Marais district; the Forum des Halles; and the Cité des Sciences et de l'Industrie at La Villette.

POLITICS

France is a republic. Its parliament, chosen through free elections, consists of the National Assembly and the Senate. The National Assembly makes the laws. The president of the republic is elected by a simple majority and serves a term of seven years. After that, he or she can be elected once more. The president, who represents France in international negotiations, is considered the representative of the most "permanent and immutable interests of the state." Political parties are not always well organized in France on a national level; their views range from the far right to socialist to the extreme left (exemplified by the most militant Communists). Sometimes loose and temporary coalitions among several political parties are formed, but these alliances tend to be weak and can easily break up over a given issue.

3. FAMOUS PARISIANS

Josephine Baker (1906–75) Although born in an African-American ghetto in St. Louis, this singer and cabaret entertainer became the toast of *tout Paris*. The French called her "La Baker."

Honoré de Balzac (1799–1850) This French novelist dropped out of law school and became the greatest portrayer of the mores and values of 19th-century French society. Always in debt, he produced more than 350 lengthy works. Among his most famous works—collectively called *La Comédie humaine*—are *Eugénie Grandet*, *La Cousine Bette*, and *Père Goriot*.

Charles Baudelaire (1821–67) The work of this French impressionist poet was condemned by mainstream critics as obscene and decadent. Considered one of the world's first modern poets, he ended his life in abject poverty, hopelessly addicted to opiates. His most famous work is *Les Fleurs du mal* (Flowers of Evil, 1857).

Simone de Beauvoir (1908–86) A French essayist and novelist, she was the leading female writer of the existentialist movement and the on-again, off-again lover of Jean-Paul Sartre. Awarded the Prix Goncourt in 1945 for her novel *The Mandarins*, she was also one of the most articulate spokespersons for the postwar feminist movement. Her most influential feminist books are *The Second Sex*, and *La Vieillesse* (Old Age). *Memoirs of a Dutiful Daughter* amounts to an autobiography.

Louis Braille (1809–52) French musician and educator of the blind, he invented the reading and writing system for the blind using a system of embossed dots. Himself blind from the age of three, Braille became a noted organist and cellist and was far more famous as a musician during his lifetime than as the inventor of braille. Braille died impoverished and alone.

Gabrielle ["Coco"] Chanel (1883–1971) This French image-maker and designer created chic, simple women's clothing, the classic lines of which have endured longer than those of any other designer in the world. Establishing her career from a shop on the boardwalk of Deauville, she promoted small and pert hats to replace the garlands of fruit, swaths of veils, and masses of straw or linen that were fashionable during the Edwardian age. In the 1950s she introduced her famous "little black dress."

Jean Cocteau (1889–1963) A multimedia French artist, Cocteau was a style-setter and *enfant terrible*. After experimenting in the surrealistic and avant-garde movements of the 1910s and 1920s, Cocteau wrote novels, poems, film scripts, essays, and scenarios for plays; painted church murals; designed restaurant menus; invented costumes; choreographed parties; and directed films. *Blood of a Poet*, *Beauty and the Beast*, and *Orphée* are three of his best-known films. His important writings include *Les Enfants terribles*, *Journal d'un inconnu*, and *La Difficulté d'être*. He was buried with full honors from the Académie Française.

Marie Curie (1867–1934) A French physicist and chemist, born Marie Slodowska in Poland, she and her French-born husband, Pierre Curie, discovered radium and determined its radioactive properties in 1898. Winner of two Nobel prizes for her experimentation with the curative effects of radiation, she died in 1934, worn out and exhausted, from radium poisoning.

Georges Jacques Danton (1759–94) A revolutionary and political philosopher, his policies of relative moderation evoked the rage of more radical factions, who had him guillotined. At his most powerful he served as minister of justice and president of the Committee of Public Safety shortly after the fall of Louis XVI.

Honoré Daumier (1808–79) Cartoonist, caricaturist, and painter, Daumier was the most acerbic and accurate cartoonist of the 19th century, exposing in his more than 4,000 cartoons the smugness, corruption, arrogance, and silliness of the 19th-century French bourgeoisie.

Christian Dior (1905–57) This fashion designer helped revolutionize the French fashion industry with the "New Look" after establishing his own couture business in 1947. The recognition, prestige, and money his work brought to a France ravaged by the traumas of World War II eventually earned him membership in the French Legion of Honor.

Jean-Honoré Fragonard (1732–1806) His paintings, more than anyone else's, capture the illusionary sweetness of upper-class life during the ancien régime. His best-known work, *The Swing*, is an unabashedly rococo portrayal full of ribbons, flowers, and blue satin, of fey and perhaps fickle young lovers joyously appreciating the airborne rhythms of a swing in a highly idealized garden.

Yves Montand (1921–91) The last of the great French entertainers, Montand symbolized every American's idea of a debonair Frenchman, even though he was born in Italy. He had great success in such films as *The Wages of Fear* in the 1950s and later there was Costa-Gavras's *Z*. His scandalous love affair with Marilyn Monroe during the filming of *Let's Make Love* attracted international publicity, since he was married to actress Simone Signoret. Signoret died of cancer in 1985. In 1991 Montand was buried next to her at Père-Lachaise Cemetery.

Edith Piaf (1915–63) The quintessential Parisian singer, who could move listeners to tears, was born Edith Gassion, the daughter of a circus acrobat. She was raised by her grandmother, who owned and operated a brothel. Piaf began singing in the streets at age 15 and later began appearing in cafés. Beautiful only when her plain features were illuminated while singing, Piaf was nicknamed "The Little Sparrow" by her ardent admirers. Companion of pimps, thieves, prostitutes, and drug addicts, she led a life filled with tragedy, illness, despair, and lost love. Her best-loved songs include "Milord," "A quoi ça sert, l'amour," "La Foule," and "La Vie en Rose."

Cardinal Richelieu (Armand Jean du Plessis, duc de Richelieu; 1585–1642) A French financier and prelate, Richelieu effectively controlled France after the death of Louis XIII's mother, Marie de Médicis. Merciless in his hatred and persecution of Protestants, Richelieu starved and destroyed the Huguenot strongholds of France, most notably La Rochelle. He founded the Académie Française to impose linguistic and grammatical rules on the then loosely defined language that we now know as French.

Marquis de Sade (Donatien Alphonse Françoise, comte de Sade; 1740–1814) A French soldier and libertine, his sexually explicit novels, *Justine* and *Juliette*, so outraged the religious and political authorities of his era that he was thrown into prison and mental asylums for most of his life. He was, in modern times, the first to advocate formally inflicting pain on others for the enhancement of self-pleasure. The psychological tendencies and the sexual acts that he encouraged were called *sadism* after him.

Madame de Staël (Anne-Louise-Germaine Necker, baronne de Staël-Holstein; 1766–1817) This French writer maintained the most sought-after salon in Paris prior to, during, and after the French Revolution. She popularized and praised German romanticism in her most widely read book, *De l'Allemagne*, which, although at first suppressed by Napoléon, later encouraged the Romantic movement in France.

4. ART & ARCHITECTURE

ART   Paris's true artistic flowering began around 1150, when the city's active trade, growing population, and struggles for political and ecclesiastic power added dozens of new buildings to the city's skyline. Between 1200 and 1400, the city flowered into the Gothic explosion whose legacy includes the city's architectural symbol—the Cathedral of Notre-Dame—as well as the Cathedral of St-Denis on the city's eastern outskirts. In these and other Gothic buildings, the medieval sculptures on the facades and inside the buildings became less incidental to the structures they adorned and more fully developed as artistic expressions in their own right. Secondary crafts, such as the manufacture and installation of stained glass (as represented by the windows in Paris's Sainte-Chapelle), became an art form in their own right, French glass of this age attaining an intensity of blues and reds that has never been duplicated.

Gothic painters became adept at the miniaturization of religious and secular scenes that art lovers (in an era without corrective lenses for myopia) could richly appreciate close at hand. The most famous of these, Pol de Limbourg's *Les très riches heures du duc de Berri* and Fouquet's *Heures d'Etienne Chevalier*, showed occasional scenes of medieval Paris in a charmingly idealized celebration of the changing of the seasons. Around 1360, Paris provided the setting for the painting of what is usually credited by art historians as the first (known) portrait, that of Jean le Bon (artist unknown), and the weaving of one of the most famous tapestries in history, the *Angers Apocalypse*.

The evolution of French art slowed during much of the 1400s. By the 1500s, however, Paris enjoyed a great rebirth in the arts, thanks to a military campaign into Italy and the subsequent fascination with all things Italian. Two of that era's main sculptors, who embellished the facades and fountains of Paris, were Jean Goujon (1510–85), whose inspiration came mainly from the ancient Greeks as reinterpreted by Renaissance themes, and Germain Pilon (1535–90), whose carvings at St-Denis of the French kings followed mostly religious, rather than neoclassical, themes. By the late 1500s, under the auspices of the Renaissance king François I, the royal château at Fontainebleau, 37 miles south of Paris, became a caldron of the arts, eventually producing a style of painting known later as the school of Fontainebleau.

The arts in and around Paris during the 1600s so permeated French culture that the century has been known ever since as "Le Grand Siècle" (the grand century). France's monarchy by now was so entrenched and society sufficiently stable and centralized that the arts flowered as Paris was embellished with hundreds of aristocratic mansions within Le Marais district. Important painters included Philippe de Champaigne (1602–74), famous for his severe portraits, Charles le Brun (1619–90), who painted the Galerie d'Apollon at the Louvre, and his rival Pierre Mignard (1610–95), painter of the interior of the cupola in the church of Val-de-Grâce. Simultaneously, the art of tapestry weaving was given a tremendous boost thanks to the establishment and royal patronage of the Manufacture Royale des Gobelins.

During the early 1700s, the taste for the grandiose in France was profoundly influenced by the personality of the Sun King,

IMPRESSIONS

He gazed at me with lowered lids, his eyes blazing, and then, with the same expression that he had before his works, he came toward me. He ran his hands over my neck, breast, stroked my arms and ran his hands over my hips, my bare legs and feet. He began to knead my whole body as if it were clay.
—Isadora Duncan, on meeting Rodin

Louis XIV. His construction and furnishing of Versailles called for mind-boggling quantities of art and decoration, giving lavish commissions to sculptors and craftsmen of every kind. In furnishing the thousands of salons and apartments within the palace, the techniques of fine cabinetmaking reached their apogee under such cabinetmakers as André-Charles Boulle (1642–1732). Boulle's writing tables, secretaries, and *bombé*-fronted chests, either ebonized or inlaid with tortoiseshell, mother-of-pearl, and gilded bronze ornaments (ormolu), are today considered among the finest pieces of cabinetry in European history, and command appropriately stratospheric prices. Boulle was supplanted by Crescent and Oeben, under Louis XV, who were themselves replaced by such neoclassic-inspired masters as Weisweiler and Kiesner during the reign of Louis XVI.

Painters from the era of Louis XIV and XV include Largillière and Rigaud and the skilled portraitists La Tour (1704–66) and Perronneau (1715–88), whose coloring techniques have been likened to those used by the impressionists more than a century later. Also noteworthy, both as an artist and a sociological phenomenon, was the female artist Vigée-Lebrun (1755–1842), whose lavish but natural style won her a position as Marie Antoinette's preferred painter. Especially famous paintings from this era are those of Fragonard (1732–1806) and Boucher (1703–70), whose canvasses captured the sweetness and whimsy of aristocratic life during the ancien régime.

In sculpture, painting, and furniture, the 18th century in Paris began with an allegiance to the baroque curve and a robustly sensual kind of voluptuousness, and ended with a return to the straight line and the more rigid motifs of the classical age. Especially indicative of this return to sobriety was Houdon (1741–1828), who is especially remembered for his extraordinarily lifelike portrait busts such as that of Voltaire.

The French Revolution, whose first violence had erupted in 1789, brought a new politicization to the arts. Noteworthy was David (1748–1825), whose painting *Oath of the Horatii* has been credited as one of the most revolution-inducing catalysts in the history of Europe. To reward his zeal, David was appointed director of the Arts of the Revolution, an incentive that helped produce such richly idealized paintings as *The Murder of Marat*. Always in control of his own political destiny, David was later appointed court painter to Napoléon.

Meanwhile, as France grew wealthy from the fruits of the industrial revolution and the expansion of its colonial empire, Paris blossomed with the paintings of Ingres (1780–1867) and his bitter rival, Delacroix (1798–1863). Primary among their academic disputes were allegiances to the beauty of line (Ingres) and the subtleties of color (Delacroix).

Between 1855 and 1869, the partial demolition of medieval Paris and its reconstruction into the series of panoramic plazas and monuments that the world today knows as the City of Light was engineered by Napoléon III's chief architect, Baron Haussmann.

The birth of impressionism generally began with the exhibition, in Paris in 1863, of the *Salon des Refusés*. There, the works of such painters as Manet—rejected by the mainline art establishment—were shown. One of the most memorable paintings seen there was Manet's then-scandalous and still-riveting *Déjeuner sur l'herbe*. Prior to that, the subtle colorings of the landscape artist Corot (1796–1875) had presaged impressionism by several years. Soon after, such artists as Sisley, Pissarro, Degas, Renoir, and the immortal Monet painted in the open air, often evoking the everyday life and cityscapes of Paris and its surroundings.

Later, the best scenes ever painted of Paris would be credited to Utrillo (1883–1955) and, to a lesser degree, Marquet (1875–1947). Utrillo in particular concentrated on the unpretentious, often working-class neighborhoods (especially Montmartre) rather than the city's more famous monumental zones. Marquet, whose work helped to establish the definition of the fauve school of painting, often executed his stylized and brightly colored works from the balcony of his Paris apartment.

Though many of them never made a career out of painting Paris itself, other 20th-century painters who for the most part made Paris their home included Vlaminck, Derain, Vuillard, Bonnard, Braque, Picasso, Dufy, and Matisse.

Among sculptors, Paris's greatest contribution to the art of the late 19th century was Auguste Rodin (1840–1917), whose figures added new dimensions to the human form. Especially famous was the raw power emanating from his rough-surfaced sculptures *The Thinker* and *The Kiss*.

ARCHITECTURE Despite its role as an outpost of ancient Rome, the development of Paris into a bustling community of traders, merchants, and clerics didn't really come to pass until the 1100s. Historians cite the abandonment of Romanesque building techniques within the Ile de France at around 1150. Because of that, the city has surprisingly few Romanesque buildings, good examples of which are more common in such French provinces as Burgundy. Identified by their thick walls, barrel vaults, and groined vaults, small windows, and minimal carvings, the city's most important Romanesque buildings include the churches of St-Germain-des-Prés, St-Pierre-de-Montmartre, St-Martin des Champs, and—in the suburbs—the Church of Morienval.

The genius of Paris's architects, however, flowered during the Gothic age, which was signaled early in the 1200s with the construction of the cathedrals of St-Denis, in Paris's eastern suburbs; Chartres, 60 miles to the city's southwest; and Notre-Dame of Paris, situated on the Ile de la Cité. Before the mid-15th century, Gothic architecture would transform the skyline of Paris as dozens of new churches, chapels, and secular buildings outdid their neighbors in lavishness, beauty, and intricacy of design.

Although Gothic architecture was firmly rooted in the principles of the Romanesque, it differs from its predecessor in the complicated patterns of vaulting and columns, and walls that became increasingly thinner as the weight of ceilings and roofs were transferred onto newly developed systems of abutment piers (flying buttresses). Because of the thinner walls, larger openings became architecturally feasible. Churches became filled with light filtered

IMPRESSIONS

*Paris (in each shape and gesture and avenue and cranny of her being)
was continuously expressing the humanness of humanity. Everywhere I
sensed a miraculous presence, not of mere children and women and
men, but of living human beings.*
—E.E. CUMMINGS

Paris is a sphinx. I will drag her secret from her.
—MIRABEAU

through stained glass, and enormous rose windows awed their observers with the delicate tracery of their stonework.

During the Renaissance, beginning around 1500, influences from
Italy rendered the Gothic style obsolete. In its place arose the
yearning for a return to the aesthetics of ancient Greece and Rome.
Massive arcades, often decorated with bas-relief sculpture of symbols of triumph, as well as Corinthian, Doric, and Ionic pediments,
added grandeur to the Paris of the Renaissance kings. All links of
royal residences to feudal fortresses vanished as the aristocrats of
Paris competed with one another to construct elegant town houses
and villas filled with sunlight, tapestries, paintings, music, and fine
furniture.

During the early 17th century, many of Paris's distinctive
Italianate baroque domes were created. Louis XIV employed such
Italian-inspired architects as Le Vau, Perrault, both Mansarts, and
Bruand for his buildings and Le Nôtre for the rigidly intelligent lay-
outs of his gardens at Versailles. Paris and the surrounding region
flourished with the construction of the lavishly expensive château
of Vaux-le-Vicomte and the even more lavish royal residence of
Versailles. Meanwhile, wealthy entrepreneurs encouraged the development of new expressions of artistic and architectural beauty from
the many literary and artistic salons sprouting up throughout the city.

By the early 19th century, a newly militaristic Paris, flushed
with the titanic changes of the Revolution and the subsequent victories of Napoléon, returned to a restrained and dignified form of
classicism. Modeling their urban landscape on an idealized interpretation of imperial Rome, buildings such as the Church of
the Madeleine evoked the militaristic rigidity and grandeur of the
classical age.

By 1850, enjoying a cosmopolitan kind of prosperity, Paris grew
bored with things Greek and Roman. Despite a brief flirtation with
Egyptology (based on Napoléon's campaign in the Egyptian desert
and the unraveling of the secrets of the Rosetta stone) a new
school of eclecticism added controversial but often elegant touches
to the Paris landscape. Among them were the voluptuous lines of
the art nouveau movement, whose aesthetic was inspired by the
surging curves of the botanical world. Stone, cast iron, glass, and
wood were carved or molded into forms resembling orchids, vines,
laurel branches, and tree trunks, each richly lyrical and based on
new building techniques made possible by the Industrial Age.
Youthful and creative architects began to specialize in the use of
iron as the structural support of bridges, viaducts, and buildings—
such as the National Library (1860). These techniques opened the
way for Gustav Eiffel to design and erect the most frequently
slurred building of its day, the Eiffel Tower, for the Paris Exposition of 1889

During the 1920s and 1930s, a newly simplified aesthetic was highly refined and greatly appreciated within Paris. Art deco, a style reflecting the newly developed materials and decorative techniques of the machine age, captured sophisticated sensibilities around the world. After Braque defined cubism, the angular simplicity of the new artistic movement influenced architectural styles as well. Le Corbusier, a Swiss-born architect who settled in Paris in 1917, eventually developed his jutting, gently curved planes of concrete, opening the doors for a new, but often less talented, school of modern French architects.

In recent years, critics have not been kind to the exposed, rapidly rusting structural elements of Paris's Centre Pompidou, and the new Opéra Bastille has also aroused opposition. The most recent controversial structure in a city where everyone presumably has an architectural opinion is undoubtedly I. M. Pei's glass pyramid in the courtyard of the Louvre.

Despite the dozens of often captivating architectural influences that have converged upon Paris, all but a handful of buildings constructed in the center within the past 150 years have been designed at roughly the same height, giving the city an evenly spaced skyline and helping to justify its claim to be the most beautiful city in the world.

5. FOOD & DRINK

Volumes have been written about French gastronomy—my comments are meant to be a brief introduction only. First, as any French person will tell you, French food is the best in the world. That's as true today as it was in the days of the great Escoffier. More than ever, young *chefs de cuisine* are making creative statements in the kitchen, and never in the history of the country has there been such an emphasis on superfresh ingredients. One chef I know in Paris has been known to shut down his restaurant for the day if he can't find exactly what he wants in the marketplace that morning.

Of course, you may want to ask, "What will it cost?" Paris has gained a reputation as being an extremely expensive city for dining out. True, its star-studded, internationally famous establishments—such as Tour d'Argent—are very expensive indeed. In such culinary cathedrals, you pay not only for superb decor and regal service but also for the art of celebrated chefs on ministerial salaries.

There is also a vast array of expensive restaurants in Paris that cater almost exclusively to the tourist trade. Their food may be indifferent or downright bad, but they'll also have ice water and ketchup to anesthetize your taste buds, trilingual waiters, and quadrilingual menus. Luckily, there are others—hundreds of others. Paris, which is said to have more restaurants than any other city on earth, has many good, reasonably priced ones. And they aren't hard to find. I've counted 18 of them on a single, narrow Left Bank street.

MEALS & DINING CUSTOMS French restaurants by law add a service charge of 12% to 15% to your bill: Your bill will say *service compris*, which means that the tip is included. However, it's customary to leave a little something extra.

In many of the less expensive establishments described in this guide, the menu will be handwritten, in French only. Don't let that intimidate you. Nor should you be timid about ordering dishes without knowing precisely what they are. You'll get some delightful surprises. I know a woman who wouldn't have dreamed of asking for escargots if she'd realized they were snails cooked in garlic sauce. As it was, she ate this appetizer in a spirit of thrift rather than adventure—and has been addicted to it ever since. As for vegetables, the French regard them as a separate course and eat them apart from the meat or poultry dishes. But I wouldn't advise you to order them specially unless you're an exceptionally hearty eater. Most main courses come with a small helping, or *garni*, of vegetables anyway.

You'll find a large number of specific dishes explained in the glossary of menu terms in the appendix as well as in the restaurant descriptions themselves. No one, however, can explain the subtle nuances of flavor that distinguish them. Those you have to taste for yourself.

As a rule, it's better to order an apéritif—often the house will have a specialty—rather than a heavy drink such as a martini before a classic French dinner. Vodka or scotch can assault your palate, destroying your taste buds for the festive repast to come.

Allow plenty of time for a gourmet dinner. Orders are often prepared individually, and it takes time to absorb the wine and the flavors. Sometimes sorbet (a sherbet) is served midway in your meal to cleanse the palate.

Making reservations is important, and please try to show up on time. Too many Americans make reservations and then become a "no-show," which creates ill will, especially since many nine-table restaurants must be filled completely every night in order to make a profit. If you're window-shopping for a restaurant, you'll find the menu most often displayed outside. Parisians read it like a book. It's there for you to study and ponder—so read it in anticipation. Most French people have their main meal during the day; you, too, may want to follow that custom, dining more lightly in the evening.

Most meals consist of several small courses. You can begin, for example, with hors d'oeuvres or a light potage (soup). The classic restaurant used to serve a small order of fish after the appetizer, then the meat or poultry course, but nowadays it's likely to be either fish or meat. A salad follows the main course, then a selection of cheese (there are 365 registered French cheeses) and a dessert (often a fruit concoction or a sorbet). In this book, prices are given for fixed-price or à la carte meals. The price for an à la carte meal is based on a three-course meal.

If you find the food "too rich, with too many sauces," that may be because you've been overdoing it. Elaborately prepared gourmet banquets should not be consumed for both lunch and dinner, or even every day. Sometimes an omelet or a roast chicken can make a delightful light meal, and you can "save up" for your big dining experience.

THE CUISINE   The revolution against Escoffier has been raging for so long that many of the early rebels are now returning to the old style of cookery, as exemplified by the boeuf bourguignon, the blanquette de veau, and the pot-au-feu.

The battle between haute cuisine and nouvelle cuisine didn't begin in Paris. One would like to imagine that it started when Michel

Guérard's beautiful Christine murmured in his ear, "*Tu sais*, Michel, if you would lose some weight, you'd look great."

For a man who loved food as much as Guérard, this was a formidable challenge. But he set to work and, ultimately, invented "cuisine minceur," which is a way to cook good French food without the calories. The world now makes its way to Guérard's restaurant, at Eugénie-les-Bains in the Landes, just east of the Basque country. His *Cuisine minceur* became a best-seller in North America, and food critic Gael Greene hailed Guérard as "the brilliant man who is France's most creative chef." Cuisine minceur is more a diet cuisine than nouvelle cuisine, which, despite the fact that it is no longer *nouvelle*, remains a viable part of the Paris dining scene.

The "new cuisine," like cuisine minceur, represents a major break with haute cuisine, while still being based on the classic principles of French cookery. Rich sauces, for example, have been eliminated. Cooking times that can destroy the best of fresh ingredients have been reduced. The aim is to release the natural flavor of food without covering it with heavy layers of butter and cream. New flavor combinations in this widely expanding repertoire are often inspired.

Many chefs, including some of the finest in Paris, dislike the word "nouvelle" when applied to cuisine. They call theirs "moderne" instead—a blend of the finest dishes of the classic repertoire with those of the nouvelle kitchen. Broadly defined, moderne means paying homage to the integrity of ingredients—certainly fresh ones—and working in the kitchen to bring out natural flavors and aromas.

There is really no such thing as Parisian cuisine. The capital of France borrows from the other provinces, all of which have distinctive cuisines. Even if you don't venture outside the city limits, you can get a good sampling of the diversified regional cooking of France, because all French kitchens are represented in Paris. Some restaurants specialize in one cuisine—such as that of Normandy— while others offer various dishes that might range from Brittany to Provence.

WINE French cookery achieves palate perfection only when accompanied by wine, which is not considered a luxury or even an addition, but rather an integral part of every meal. Certain rules about wine drinking have been long established in France, but no one except traditionalists seems to follow them anymore. "Rules" would dictate that if you're having a roast, steak, or game, a good burgundy should be your choice. If it's chicken, lamb, or veal, you would choose a red from the Bordeaux country, certainly a full-bodied red with cheese such as Camembert, and a blanc-de-blanc with oysters. A light rosé can go with almost anything, especially if enjoyed on a summer terrace overlooking the Seine.

Let your own good taste—and sometimes almost as important, your pocketbook—determine your choice of wine. Most wine stewards, called sommeliers, are there to help you in your choice, and only in the most dishonest of restaurants will they push you toward the most expensive selections. Of course, if you prefer only bottled water or perhaps a beer, then be firm and order either without embarrassment. In fact, bottled water might be a good idea at lunch if you're planning to drive later. Some restaurants include a beverage in their menu rates (*boisson compris*), but that's only in the cheaper places. Nevertheless, some of the most satisfying wines I've drunk in Paris came from unlabeled house bottles or carafes, called a *vin de la maison*. In general, unless you're a real connoisseur, don't worry about labels and vintages.

When in doubt, you can rarely go wrong with a good burgundy or bordeaux, but you may want to be more adventurous than that. That's when the sommelier can help you, particularly if you tell him or her your taste in wine (semidry or very dry, for example). State frankly how much you're willing to pay and what you plan to order for your meal. If you're dining with others, you may want to order two or three bottles with an entire dinner, selecting a wine to suit each course. However, Parisians at informal meals—and especially if there are only two persons dining—select only one wine to go with all their platters, from hors d'oeuvres to cheese. As a rule of thumb, expect to spend about one-third of the restaurant tab for wine.

Wine Labels Since the latter part of the 19th century, French wines sold in France (and sometimes elsewhere) have been labeled. The general labeling term is *appellations contrôlées*. These controls, for the most part, are by regions such as Bordeaux and the Loire. The wines so labeled are the simple, honest wines of the district. They can be blended from grapes grown at any place in the region. Some are composed of the vintages of different years.

In most cases, the more specific the label, the better the wine. For example, instead of a bordeaux, the wine might be labeled "Médoc" (pronounced *May*-doc), which is the name of a triangle of land extending some 50 miles north from Bordeaux. Wine labels can be narrowed down to a particular vine-growing property, such as a Château Haut-Brion, one of the most famous and greatest of red wines of Bordeaux (this château produces only about 10,000 cases a year).

On some burgundies, you are likely to see the word *clos* (pronounced *cloe*). Originally, that meant a walled or otherwise enclosed vineyard, as in Clos-de-Bèze, which is a celebrated Burgundian vineyard producing superb red wine. *Cru* (pronounced *croo*, and meaning "growth") suggests a wine of superior quality when it appears on a label as *vin-de-cru*. Wines and vineyards are often divided into crus. A grand cru or premier cru should, by implication, be an even superior wine.

Labels are only part of the story. It's the vintage that counts. Essentially vintage is the annual grape harvest and the wine made from those grapes. Therefore, any wine can be a vintage wine unless it is a blend. But there are good vintages and bad vintages. The variation between wine produced in a "good year" and wine produced in a "bad year" can be great, and even noted by the neophyte.

Finally, champagne is the only wine that can be correctly served through all courses of a meal—but only to those who can afford its astronomical cost.

IMPRESSIONS

I am the man who accompanied Jacqueline Kennedy to Paris, and I have enjoyed it
—JOHN F. KENNEDY, 1961

6. RECOMMENDED BOOKS & FILMS

BOOKS

Becoming more familiar with France before you go can greatly enhance your trip. There are numerous books on all aspects of French history and society—ranging from the very general, such as the section on France in the *Encyclopedia Americana*, International Edition (Grolier, 1989), which presents an excellent, illustrated overview of the French people and their way of life, to the very specific, such as Judi Culbertson and Tom Randall's *Permanent Parisians: An Illustrated Guide to the Cemeteries of Paris* (Chelsea Green, 1986), which vividly depicts the lives of many famous French and foreign people who are buried in Paris. The books I have selected below are grouped into four categories: history, biography, the arts, and fiction.

HISTORY A broad overview of French history can be found in many encyclopedias and general history books. A comprehensive history with illustrations and plenty of obscure but interesting facts is *History of France* by Guillaume de Bertier de Savigny and David H. Pinkney (Forum Press, 1983).

Two books that present French life and society in the 17th century are Warren Lewis's *The Splendid Century* (William Morrow, 1978) and Madame de Sévigné's *Selected Letters*, edited by Leonard W. Tancock (Penguin, 1982), which contains imaginative and witty letters written to her daughter during the reign of Louis XIV.

Simon Schama's *Citizens* (Alfred A. Knopf, 1989) is "a magnificent and electrifyingly new history of the French Revolution"—long, but very enjoyable.

Moving into the 20th century, *Pleasure of the Belle Epoque: Entertainment and Festivity in Turn-of-the-Century France*, by Charles Rearick (Yale University Press, 1985), depicts public diversions in the changing and troubled times of the Third Republic. *Paris Was Yesterday, 1925–1939* (Harcourt Brace Jovanovich, 1988) is a fascinating collection of excerpts from Janet Flanner's "Letters from Paris" column of *The New Yorker*. Larry Collins and Dominique Lapierre have written a popular history of the liberation of Paris in 1944 called *Is Paris Burning?* (Warner Books, 1991).

Two unusual approaches to French history are Rudolph Chleminski's *The French at Table* (William Morrow, 1985), a funny and honest history of why the French know how to eat better than anyone else and how they go about it; and *Paris: A Century of Change, 1878–1978*, by Norman Evenson (Yale University Press, 1979), a notable study of the urban development of Paris. *The Fall of Paris: June 1940*, by Herbert R. Lottmann (HarperCollins, 1992), was written by the biographer of Colette, Flaubert, and Pétain. It's a riveting account of one of the saddest events of World War II.

BIOGRAPHY You can get a different look at history by reading biographies of historical figures. Hugh Ross Williamson brings to life Catherine de Médicis in his *Catherine de Medici* (Viking Press,

1973) by combining text and magnificent illustrations from the art of the 16th century. This queen of France was the dominant personality during her nation's religious wars and mother of three kings of France, a queen of Spain, and a queen of Navarre.

Representing a very different era are *A Moveable Feast* (Collier Books, 1987), Ernest Hemingway's recollections of Paris during the 1920s, and Morley Callaghan's *That Summer in Paris: Memories of Tangled Friendships with Hemingway, Fitzgerald and Some Others* (Penguin Books, 1979), an anecdotal account of the same period. Another interesting read is *The Autobiography of Alice B. Toklas,* by Gertrude Stein (Vintage Books, 1990). It's not only the account of 30 years in Paris, but also the biography of Gertrude Stein.

Simone de Beauvoir, by Deirdre Bair (Summit Books, 1990), was described by one critic as a biography "*à l'americaine*—that is to say, long, with all the warts of its subject unsparingly described." The story of the great feminist intellectual was based in part on tape-recorded conversations and unpublished letters. *Colette: A Life,* by Herbert R. Lottman (Little, Brown, 1991), is a painstakingly researched biography of the celebrated French writer and her fascinating life—which included not only writing novels and appearing in cabarets but also dabbling in lesbianism and, on the darker side, perhaps even collaborating with the enemy during the Nazi occupation.

You See, I Haven't Forgotten, by Yves Montand, with Hervé Hamon and Patrick Rotman (Alfred A. Knopf, 1992), is a fine biography of one of France's most beloved showmen. Montand may not have been the actual author, but he cooperated fully on the biography, granting 200 hours of interviews.

In *Madame du Barry: The Wages of Beauty* (Grove Weidenfeld, 1992), Joan Haslip narrates the story of the convent-educated prostitute who at the age of 25 became the last mistress of Louis XV. Surviving the king and going on to other lovers, Madame du Barry met her fate at the guillotine during the Reign of Terror.

The Divine Sarah: A Life of Sarah Bernhardt, by Arthur Gold and Robert Fizdale (Alfred A. Knopf, 1991), is the life story of the woman still acclaimed as the world's greatest actress—her triumphs and tragedies, her love affairs, her friends and foes, all enlivened by journals, letters, and comments from contemporaries.

ART & ARCHITECTURE Much of France's beauty can be found in its art. Three excellent books that approach France from this perspective are *The History of Impressionism,* by John Rewald (Museum of Modern Art, 1973), which is a collection of documents, both writings and quotations of the artists, clearly illuminating this valuable period in the history of art; *The French Through Their Films,* by Robin Buss (Ungar, 1988), an exploration of the history and themes of more than 100 widely circulated films; and *The Studios of Paris: The Capital of Art in the Late Nineteenth Century,* by John Milner (Yale University Press, 1988). In the last, Milner presents the dynamic forces that made Paris one of the most complex centers of the art world in the early modern era.

Nightlife of Paris: The Art of Toulouse-Lautrec, by Patrick O'Connor (Universe, 1992), is an enchanting 80-page book with lively anecdotes about the hedonistic luminaries of belle époque Paris, with paintings, sketches, and lithographs by the artist.

Olympia: Paris in the Age of Manet, by Otto Friedrich (HarperCollins, 1992), takes its inspiration from the celebrated artwork in the Musée d'Orsay in Paris. From here the book takes off on an anecdote-rich gossipy chain of historical associations, tracing the rise of the impressionist school of modern painting, but incorporating social commentary too, such as the pattern of prostitution and venereal disease in 19th-century France.

Paris: An Architectural History, by Anthony Sutcliffe (Yale University Press, 1993), offering 250 illustrations, is perhaps the best study to date on this subject, and it's by a leading historian who links the city's fabled beauty to its architecture.

FICTION The *Chanson de Roland,* edited by F. Whitehead (2nd ed.; Basil Blackwell, 1942), written between the 11th and 14th centuries, is the earliest and most celebrated of the "songs of heroic exploits." *The Misanthrope* and *Tartuffe* (Harcourt, Brace and World, 1965) are two masterful satires on the frivolity of the 17th century by the great comic dramatist Molière. François-Marie Arouet Voltaire's *Candide* (Bantam Classics, 1981) is a classic satire attacking both the philosophy of optimism and the abuses of the ancien régime.

A few of the masterpieces of the 19th century are *Madame Bovary,* by Gustave Flaubert (Random House, 1982), in which the carefully wrought characters, setting, and plot attest to the genius of Flaubert in presenting the tragedy of Emma Bovary; Victor Hugo's *Les Misérables* (Modern Library, 1983), a classic tale of social oppression and human courage set in the era of Napoléon I; and the collection *Selected Stories* by the master of short stories, Guy de Maupassant (New American Library, 1984).

Honoré de Balzac's *La Comédie humaine* (1830–50) depicts life in France from the fall of Napoléon to 1848. Henry James's *The Ambassadors* (Oxford University Press, 1985) and *The American* (Houghton, Mifflin, 1985) both take place in Paris. *The Vagabond,* by Colette (1910, translated in 1955) evokes the colorful life of the French music hall performer (Ballantine, 1982).

Tropic of Cancer (Modern Library, 1934) is the semiautobiographical story of Henry Miller's early years in Paris. One of France's leading thinkers, Jean-Paul Sartre, shows individuals struggling against their freedom in *No Exit and Three Other Plays* (Random House, 1955). Finally, writer Georges Simenon and illustrator Frederick Franck combined to create *Simenon's Paris* (1970), a beautifully illustrated book of Simenon's Paris stories.

FILMS

Although Americans understood—very quickly, too—the commercial wealth to be made from films, the French are credited with the scientific and technical inventions that made them possible. French physicists had laid the groundwork for a movie camera as early as the mid-1880s, and the world's first movie was shown in Paris on December 28, 1895. Its makers were the Lumière brothers, who considered filmmaking a scientific oddity and stubbornly confined its use to the production of international newsreels. Later, a vaudevillian actor and illusionist, Georges Méliés, used film to convey plot and drama.

Charles Pathé and Léon Gaumont were the first to exploit filmmaking on a grand scale. Beginning in 1896, they produced and distributed their own films, building their company into a giant before World War I. When Gaumont made his first film, he enlisted his secretary, Alice Guy-Blanché, to create the plot, design the scenery, and direct it. She proved so successful that she was eventually promoted to the head of Paris's largest studio and became the world's first female director.

Before World War I the many talented actors arriving *en scène* included Max Linder, a popular French comic, whose style influenced Charlie Chaplin and helped him develop his keen sense of timing. By the 1920s the French began to view filmmaking as an art form and infused it with surreal and dada themes. Examples include Man Ray's *Le Retour à la raison* (1923), Fernand Léger's *Le Ballet mécanique* (1924), and Jean Cocteau's *Le Sang d'un poète* (1930).

The golden age of the French silent screen on both sides of the Atlantic was 1927–29. Actors were directed with more sophistication, and technical abilities reached an all-time high. One of my favorite films—despite its mind-numbing length—is Abel Gance's sweepingly evocative masterpiece *Napoléon* (1927); its grisly battle scenes are easily as chilling as any war film made today. Other highlights from this era included René Clair's *Un Chapeau de paille d'Italie* (An Italian Straw Hat, 1927), Carl Dreyer's *La Passion de Jeanne d'Arc* (1928), and an adaptation of Emile Zola's *Thérèse Raquin* (1928) by Jacques Feyder.

Experiments with the early productions of "talkies" were less successful. One popular film director, Pagnol, declared that the role of films was to publicize to the masses the benefits of the theatrical stage. During this period, many of the counterculture's most gifted directors either left France (as did René Clair, who immigrated to England in 1934) or died (Jean Vigo, *Zéro de conduite*).

In 1936 the Cinémathèque Française was established to find and preserve old (usually silent) French films. By that time, French cinematographers had divorced themselves completely from the value systems of the stage and had found a style of their own. An average of 130 films a year were made in France, by (among others) Jean Renoir, Charles Spaak, and Marcel Carne. This was also the era that brought such French luminaries as Claudette Colbert and Maurice Chevalier to Hollywood.

During World War II, the best known (to Americans) of the French directors fled to Hollywood. Those who remained were heavily censored by the Vichy government. Despite that, more than 350 French films, many relating to distant past events (which were thus not controversial) were produced. Exceptions were Carne's *Les Enfants du paradis* (Children of Paradise, 1945).

In 1946 France slapped a heavy quota system onto the importation of foreign (especially American) films. A semigovernmental film authority (Le Centre National du Cinéma Français) financed independent French film companies and encouraged liaisons between the French and Italian film industries. Many directors who had supported the Vichy government's Nazi collaboration were soon accepted back into the cinematic community.

Two strong traditions—film noir and a return to literary traditions—flourished. Film noir included such existentially inspired nihilistic themes as André Cayatte's *Nous sommes tous des assassins* (We Are All Assassins, 1952) and Yves Allegret's *Dedée d'Anvers* (1948). Examples of the literary tradition include Bresson's *Journal d'un curé de campagne* (Diary of a Country Priest, 1951) and a film rendition of Stendahl's *Le Rouge et le noir* (The Red and the Black, 1954) by Autant-Lara. By the 1950s comedy adopted a new kind of genre with Jacques Tati's *Les Vacances de Monsieur Hulot* (Mr. Hulot's Holiday). By the mid-1950s French filmmaking ushered in an era of enormous budgets, à la Hollywood, and the creation of such frothy potboilers as *And God Created Woman*, which helped make Brigitte Bardot a penthouse name around the world.

By the late 1950s François Truffaut, widely publicizing his *auteur* theories, rebelled with a series of films (including the most famous—*The 400 Blows*, 1959), which was financed partly by government funds and partly by wealthy benefactors. With Jean-Luc Godard (*A Bout de souffle*, or Breathless) and Claude Chabrol (*Le beau Serge*, 1959), they pioneered one of the most publicized movements in 20th century French art—*la nouvelle vague*. In the early 1960s dozens of new directors joined the movement, furiously making films, some of which are considered classics while others were quickly forgotten. Enthusiastically endorsed by the counterculture on both sides of the Atlantic, these directors included Resnais (*Muriel*), Roger Vadim, Agnès Varda (*Le Bonheur*), Jacques Demy (*Les Parapluies de Cherbourg*), Godard (*Pierrot-le-Fou*), Louis Malle, Chris Marker, and Marguerite Duras (*Détruire, dit-elle*).

After a switch to political themes (Costa-Gavras's *Z*) during the 1968 rebellions (and a politically motivated abandonment of the film festival at Cannes by at least a dozen prominent French directors), French Cinema turned to comedy in the early 1970s. Examples include Buñuel's *Le Charme discret de la bourgeoisie* (1972) and Yanne's *Tout le monde il est beau, tout le monde il est gentil* (1972).

Claude Sautet's *Un Coeur en hiver* (A Heart in Winter, 1993) was hailed by some critics as one of the finest French films in years. The *New York Times*, in particular, cited its "atmosphere of intelligence and precision."

Krzysztof Kieslowski's *Blue*, the Polish director's most recently acclaimed French film, is the first in a planned trilogy that will eventually include *White* and *Red*. It tells the story of Julie, as portrayed by Juliette Binoche, who closes her country house and seeks anonymity by moving to Paris where, among other things, she has a strange confrontation with a rat and learns that her husband's devotion is suspect.

PLANNING A TRIP TO PARIS

This chapter is devoted to the where, when, and how of your trip—the advance-planning issues required to get it together and take it on the road.

After deciding where to go, most people have two fundamental questions: "What will it cost?" and "How do I get there?" This chapter will answer both those questions and also provide data to help you with such issues as deciding when to go, what insurance coverage is necessary, and where to obtain more information about your destination.

The chapter also presents various alternative and specialty travel options and includes tips for special travelers such as the disabled or senior citizens.

1. INFORMATION, ENTRY REQUIREMENTS & MONEY

SOURCES OF INFORMATION

Your best source of information before you go—besides this guide—is the **French Government Tourist Office,** which can be reached at the following addresses.

In **the U.S.:** 628 Fifth Ave., New York, NY 10020; 645 N. Michigan Ave., Suite 630, Chicago, IL 60611; 2305 Cedar Springs Blvd., Dallas, TX 75201; 9454 Wilshire Blvd., Beverly Hills, CA 90212-2967. To request information, call the **France on Call** hot line (tel. 900/990-0040); each call costs 50¢ per minute.

In **Canada,** write to Maison de la France/French Government Tourist Office at 1981 av. McGill College, Suite 490, Montréal, PQ H3A 2W9 (tel. 514/288-4264); or 30 St. Patrick St., Suite 700, Toronto, ON M5T 3A3 (tel. 416/593-6427).

In **Great Britain,** write to Maison de la France/French Government Tourist Office at 178 Piccadilly, London, W1V 0AL (tel. 071/491-7622).

In **Australia,** write to the French Tourist Office, B.N.P. Building, 12th floor, 12 Castlereagh St., Sydney, NSW 2000 (tel.02/231-5244).

In **Ireland,** write to the Maison de la France/French Government Tourist Office at 35 Lower Abbey St., Dublin 1, Ireland (tel. 01/703-4046).

At present there is no representative in New Zealand, so New Zealanders should write to the representative in Australia.

IN PARIS You need never be totally alone in Paris. There's always someone who speaks your language standing ready to provide assistance, give you information, and help you solve problems. **Office de Tourisme et des Congrès de Paris** (or Welcome Offices) in the center of the city will give you free maps, informative booklets, and "Paris Monthly Information," an English-language listing of all current shows, concerts, and theater. At 127 Champs-Elysées, 8e (tel. 49-52-53-54), you can get information regarding both Paris and the provinces. The office is open daily except May 1 from 9am to 8pm. Métro: Charles de Gaulle–Etoile.

ENTRY REQUIREMENTS

DOCUMENTS In recent years Americans and Canadians traveling to France were required to obtain a visa in advance. However, since July 1989 only special groups, such as journalists on assignment and students enrolling in French schools, must still obtain visas. For tourism or business visits of less than 90 days, all you need now is a valid passport.

With today's ever changing political climate, it's always a good idea to confirm the situation. Contact the French Embassy (4101 Reservoir Rd. NW, Washington, DC 20007; tel. 202/944-6000), or the French Consulate (934 Fifth Ave., New York, NY 10021; tel. 212/606-3653).

Canadian, Swiss, and Japanese citizens and citizens of E.C. countries, such as Britain and Ireland, are exempt from any visa requirement, but check with your nearest French consulate because the situation can change overnight. Citizens of Australia need a visa to enter France, but citizens of New Zealand require only a valid passport.

U.S. and Canadian **driver's licenses** are valid in France, but if you're touring Europe by car, you may want to invest in an International Driver's License just to be on the safe side. Apply at a branch of the American Automobile Association (AAA). You must be 18 years old and include two 2-by-2-inch photographs, a $10 fee, and your valid U.S. driver's license with your application. If AAA doesn't have a branch in your hometown, send a photograph of your driver's license (both the front and the back) with the fee and photos to AAA, 1000 AAA Dr., Heathrow, FL 32746-5063 (tel. 407/444-4300). You should always carry your original license with you to Europe, however.

In Canada, you pay $10 Canadian and apply to CAA (Canadian Automobile Association), 2 Carlton St., Toronto, ON M5B 1K4 (tel. 416/964-3111).

You must also have an **international insurance certificate,** called a green card (*carte verte* in French), to drive. The car-rental agency will provide one if you're renting.

CUSTOMS Customs restrictions differ for citizens of the European Community and for citizens of non-E.C. countries. Non-E.C. nationals can bring in duty free 200 cigarettes or 100 cigarillos or 50 cigars or 250 grams of smoking tobacco. This amount is doubled if you live outside Europe. You can also bring in 2 liters of wine and either 1 liter of alcohol over 38.80 proof or 2 liters of wine under 38.80 proof. In addition you can bring in 50 grams (1.75 oz.) of perfume, ¼ liter of eau de toilette, 500 grams (1 lb.) of coffee, and 200 grams (½ lb.) of tea. Visitors 15 years of age and over may also bring in other goods totaling 300F ($52.50), while the allowance for those 14 and under is 150F ($26.30). (Customs officials tend to be lenient about general merchandise, realizing that the limits are unrealistically low.)

Visitors from E.C. countries can bring in 300 cigarettes or 150 cigarillos or 75 cigars or 400 grams (14 oz.) of smoking tobacco. The maximum for "spirits" is 5 liters of table wine, and either 1½ liters of alcohol over 38.80 proof or 3 liters of alcohol under 38.80 proof. Visitors can also bring in 75 grams (2.6 oz.) of perfume, ⅜ of a liter of eau de toilette, 1,000 grams (2 lb.) of coffee, and 80 grams (2.8 oz.) of tea. Visitors over 15 can bring in other goods totaling 2,800F ($490); the allowance for those 14 and under is 700F ($122.50).

Items for personal use, including bicycles and sports equipment already in use, whether or not packed in personal luggage, are admitted providing that these goods do not appear to be intended for sale. Such goods cannot be sold or given away in France and must be reexported.

MONEY

CASH/CURRENCY French currency is based on the **franc (F),** which consists of 100 **centimes (c).** Coins come in units of 5, 10, 20, and 50 centimes; and 1, 2, 5, and 10 francs. Notes come in denominations of 20, 50, 100, 500, and 1,000 francs.

All banks are equipped for foreign exchange, and you will find exchange offices at the airports and airline terminals. Banks are open from 9am to noon and 2 to 4pm Monday through Friday. Major bank branches also open their exchange departments on Saturday between 9am and noon.

When converting your home currency into French francs, be aware that rates vary. Your hotel will probably offer the worst rate of exchange. In general, banks offer the best rate, but even banks charge a commission for the service, often $2 or $3, depending on the transaction. Whenever you can, stick to the big banks of Paris, like Crédit Lyonnais, which usually offer the best exchange rates and charge the least commission. Always make sure you have enough francs for the weekend.

TRAVELER'S CHECKS Before leaving home, purchase traveler's checks and arrange to carry some ready cash (usually about $250, depending on your habits and needs). Most large banks sell traveler's checks, charging fees that average between 1% and 2% of the value of the checks you buy. If your bank wants

CONVERTING MONEY

For American Readers   At this writing $1=approximately 5.70F (or 1F=17.5¢), and this was the rate of exchange used to calculate the dollar values given in this book.

For British Readers   At this writing £1=approximately 8.57F (or 1F=11.6p), and this was the rate of exchange used to calculate the pound values in the table below.

Note: Because the exchange rate fluctuates from time to time, this table should be used only as a general guide:

F	US$	UK£	F	US$	UK£
1	.18	.12	75	13.13	8.75
2	.35	.23	100	17.50	11.66
3	.53	.35	125	21.88	14.58
4	.70	.47	150	26.25	17.49
5	.88	.58	175	30.63	20.41
6	1.05	.70	200	35.00	23.32
7	1.23	.82	225	39.38	26.24
8	1.40	.93	250	43.75	29.15
9	1.58	1.05	300	52.50	34.98
10	1.75	1.16	350	61.25	40.81
15	2.63	1.75	400	70.00	46.64
25	4.38	2.92	450	78.75	52.47
50	8.75	5.83	500	87.50	58.30

more than a 2% commission, it may be worthwhile to call the traveler's check issuers directly for the address of outlets where the commission will be less.

American Express (tel. toll free 800/221-7282 in the U.S. and Canada) is one of the largest and most immediately recognized issuers of traveler's checks. No commission is charged to members of the American Automobile Association or to holders of certain types of American Express credit cards. The company issues checks denominated in U.S. dollars, Canadian dollars, British pounds, Swiss francs, French francs, German marks, and Japanese yen.

Citicorp (tel. toll free 800/645-6556 in the U.S. and Canada, or 813/623-1709, collect, from anywhere else in the world), issues checks in U.S. dollars, British pounds, German marks, and Japanese yen.

Thomas Cook (tel. toll free 800/223-9920 in the U.S. or 609/987-7300, collect, from other parts of the world) issues MasterCard traveler's checks denominated in U.S. dollars, French francs, German marks, Dutch guilders, Spanish pesetas, Australian dollars, Japanese yen, and Hong Kong dollars.

Interpayment Services (tel. toll free 800/221-2426 in the U.S. or Canada, or 800/453-4284 from most other parts of the world) sells VISA checks sponsored by Barclays Bank and/or Bank of America at selected branches around North America. Traveler's checks are denominated in U.S. or Canadian dollars, British pounds,

Swiss francs, French francs, German marks, and Japanese yen.

Each of these agencies will refund your checks if they are lost or stolen, provided you can produce sufficient documentation. Of course, your documentation should be carried in a safe place—never in the same place as your checks. When purchasing checks from one of the banks listed, ask about refund hot lines; American Express and Bank of America have the most offices around the world. Purchase checks in a variety of denominations—$20, $50, and $100.

Sometimes you can purchase traveler's checks in the currency of the country you're planning to visit, thereby avoiding a conversion fee, which could amount to as much as $5. Note, also, that you always get a better rate if you cash traveler's checks at the institutions that issued them: VISA at Barclays, American Express at American Express, and so forth.

WHAT THINGS COST IN PARIS	U.S.$
Taxi from Charles de Gaulle Airport to the city center	35.00
Taxi from Orly Airport to the city center	28.00
Public transportation for an average trip within the city from a Métro *carnet* (packet) of 10	.65
Local telephone call	.20
Double room at the Ritz (very expensive)	586.30
Double room at Lord Byron (moderate)	157.50
Double room at Hotel Opal (budget)	91.00
Lunch for one, without wine, at Chez Georges (moderate)	35.00
Lunch for one, without wine, at Le Drouot (budget)	16.00
Dinner for one, without wine, at Le Grand Véfour (very expensive)	131.30
Dinner for one, without wine, at Chez André (moderate)	40.00
Dinner for one, without wine, at Aux Charpentiers (budget)	25.00
Glass of wine	3.00
Coca-Cola	3.50
Cup of coffee	3.00
Roll of ASA 100 film, 36 exposures	7.00
Admission to the Louvre	6.00
Movie ticket	7.50
Theater ticket (at the Comédie-Française)	25.00

CREDIT CARDS Credit cards are useful in France. Both **American Express** and **Diners Club** are widely recognized. The French equivalent for VISA is Carte Bleue. If you see the **Eurocard** sign on an establishment, it means it accepts MasterCard.

You may purchase something with a credit card thinking you will be charged at a certain exchange rate, only to find the dollar has declined by the time your bill arrives, and so you're actually paying more than you had bargained for, but those are the rules of the game. It can also work in your favor if the dollar should rise after you make your purchase.

Some **automatic-teller machines** in Paris accept U.S. bank cards such as VISA or MasterCard. The exchange rates are often good, and the convenience of obtaining cash on the road is without equal. Check with your credit-card company or bank before leaving home.

2. WHEN TO GO—CLIMATE, HOLIDAYS & EVENTS

In August Parisians traditionally leave for their annual holiday and put the city on a skeleton staff to serve visitors. Now, July has also become a popular vacation month, with many a restaurateur shuttering up for a month-long respite.

From May through September, the city is swamped with tourists, and you must write well in advance for hotel reservations. Try to avoid the first two weeks in October, when the annual motor show attracts thousands of boy-at-heart enthusiasts.

The best time to come to Paris is off-season, in the early spring or late autumn, when the tourist trade has trickled to a manageable flow and everything is easier to come by—motel rooms, Métro seats, even good-tempered waiters.

THE CLIMATE Balmy weather in Paris has probably prompted more popular songs and love ballads than weather conditions in any other city in the world. The main characteristic of the city's weather is its changeability. Rain is much more common than snow throughout the winter, prompting many longtime residents to complain about the occasional bone-chilling dampness.

In recent years, Paris has had only about 15 snow days a year, and there are only a few oppressively hot days (that is, over 86° F) in midsummer. Perhaps the most disturbing aspect of Parisian weather is the blasts of rapidly moving air—perhaps the result of a wind tunnel effect caused by the city's long boulevards being bordered by buildings of uniform height. Other than the occasional winds and rain (which add an undeniable drama to many of the city's panoramas), Paris offers one of the most pleasant weather conditions of any capital in Europe, with a highly tolerable average temperature of 53°F.

Paris's Average Daytime Temperature & Rainfall

	Jan	Feb	Mar	Apr	May	June	July	Aug	Sept	Oct	Nov	Dec
Temp (°F)	38	39	46	51	58	64	66	66	61	53	45	40
Rain(inches)	3.2	2.9	2.4	2.7	3.2	3.5	3.3	3.7	3.3	3.0	3.5	3.1

HOLIDAYS In France, holidays are known as *jours fériés*. Shops and banks are closed, as well as many (but not all) restaurants and museums. Major holidays include January 1, Easter, Ascension Day (40 days after Easter), Pentecost (seventh Sunday after Easter), May

1, May 8 (V-E Day), July 14 (Bastille Day), August 15 (Assumption of the Virgin Mary), November 1 (All Saints' Day), November 11 (Armistice Day), and December 25 (Christmas).

PARIS CALENDAR OF EVENTS

JANUARY

- □ **The Boat Fair** (Le Salon International de la Navigation de Plaisance). One of Europe's largest boat shows. Parc des Expositions, Porte de Versailles, Paris, 15e (Métro: Porte de Versailles).
- □ **International Ready-to-Wear Fashion Shows** (Le Salon International de Prêt-à-Porter). Parc des Expositions, Porte de Versailles, Paris, 15e (Métro: Porte de Versailles). Various couture houses, such as Lanvin and Courrèges, have their own shows at their respective headquarters. Mid-January to mid-February.

MARCH

- □ **Foire du Trône,** Neuilly Lawn of the Bois de Vincennes, a mommoth amusement park, operates from end of March through May daily from 2pm to midnight.

MAY

- □ **French Open Tennis Championship,** Stade Roland-Garros. May 24 to June 6.
- □ **Paris Marathon.** Runners compete from around the world. Second weekend.
- □ **Illuminated fountains at Versailles.** May to September.
- □ **Festival de Versailles.** Features opera, concerts, theater, and ballet. Call 30-21-20-20 for information. Late May to late June.
- □ **Festival de Musique de St-Denis.** Music in the church. Call 42-43-72-72 for information. Late May through late June.
- □ **Festival de Paris,** 38 rue des Blancs-Manteaux, 4e. An assemblage of some of the world's leading orchestras and choruses. Tickets cost 50F to 500F ($8.80 to $87.50). Call 40-26-45-34 for information. Mid-May to late June.

JUNE

- □ **Paris Air Show,** at Le Bourget Airport. Early June in alternate years only (next air show is 1995).
- □ **Grand Steeplechase de Paris,** in the Bois de Boulogne, Auteuil racetrack. Mid-June.
- □ **Grand Prix de Paris,** at Longchamp raceway. Late June.
- □ **Festival du Marais.** Many events—theater, exhibitions, classical and jazz music—are presented in renovated Renaissance buildings and courtyards. For details, contact Festival du Marais, 68 rue François Minon, 75004 Paris (tel. 48-87-60-08). Mid-June to mid-July.

❖ **BASTILLE DAY** *The nation's festivities reach their peak in Paris with street fairs, pageants, fireworks, and feasts. The day begins with a parade down the Champs-Elysées and ends with fireworks at Montmartre. Wherever you are, before the end of the day you'll hear Piaf warbling "La Foule" (The Crowd), the song that celebrated her passion for the stranger whom she met and later lost in a crowd on Bastille Day.*

When: July 14. Where: Bars, restaurants, streets, and private homes throughout Paris. How: Hum the Marseillaise; outfit yourself with a beret, a pack of Gauloises, and a bottle of cheap wine; leave your hotel; and stamp around the neighborhood.

□ **Festival Estival (Summertime Festival),** with music at churches and concert halls throughout Paris. For details, write to Festival Estival de Paris, 20 rue Geoffroy l'Asnier, 75004 Paris (tel. 48-04-98-01). Mid-July to late September.
□ **Le Grand Tour de France.** Europe's most visible bicycle race decides its winner at a finish line drawn across the Champs-Elysées. Late July.

□ **Festival Estival.** All month.

□ **Festival Estival.** Through late September.
□ **Festival d'Automne.** Concentrating mainly on modern music, ballet, theater, and modern art, it's the most eclectic of the festivals. For details, write to the Festival d'Automne, 156 rue de Rivoli, 75001 Paris (tel. 42-96-12-27). Late September until just before Christmas.

□ **Festival d'Automne.** All month.

❖ **PARIS AUTO SHOW** *Glistening metal, glitzy women, lots of hype, and the latest models from world auto makers, this is the showcase for European car design.*

Where: Parc des Expositions, near the Porte de Versailles in western Paris. When: 10 days in early October. How: Check Pariscope for details or contact the French Government Tourist Office (see the addresses and telephone numbers in "Information, Entry Requirements, and Money," above).

□ **Prix de l'Arc de Triomphe.** France's answer to the horsey set at Ascot is the country's most prestigious horse race. Early October.

NOVEMBER

☐ **Festival d'Automne.** All month.
☐ **Armistice Day,** celebrated with a military parade from the Arc de Triomphe to the Hôtel des Invalides. November 11.

DECEMBER

☐ **Festival d'Automne.** Through late December.
☐ **Fête de St-Sylvestre** (New Year's Eve). It's best celebrated in the *quartier latin* around the Sorbonne. At midnight, the city explodes. Strangers kiss strangers, boulevard St-Michel becomes a virtual pedestrian mall, as does the Champs-Elysées.

3. HEALTH & INSURANCE

HEALTH You aren't required to have any particular inoculations to enter France (except for yellow fever, and then only if you're arriving from an infected area). Paris should not pose any major health hazards, although many travelers suffer from diarrhea. This is generally caused by the overly rich cuisine—heavy cream sauces, butter, and wine. Take along some antidiarrhea medicine, moderate your eating habits, and even though the water in Paris is considered safe, consume mineral water only. Sometimes travelers find that a change of diet leads to constipation. If this occurs, eat a high-fiber diet and drink plenty of mineral water. Avoid large lunches and dinners with wine. Consult your pharmacist about taking an over-the-counter drug such as Colace (a stool softener) or Metamucil.

Take along an adequate supply of any prescription drugs that you need and a prescription that specifies the generic name of the drug (not just the brand name).

If you're subject to motion sickness on a plane or train, remember to bring along motion-sickness medicine.

Of course, carry all your vital medicine and drugs (the legal kind) with you in your carry-on luggage, in case your checked luggage is lost.

If you suffer from a chronic illness, talk to your doctor before taking the trip. For such conditions as epilepsy, diabetes, or a heart condition, wear a **Medic Alert Identification Tag,** which will immediately alert any doctor to your condition and provide the number of Medic Alert's 24-hour hot line so that a foreign doctor can obtain medical records for you. For a lifetime membership, the cost is $35, $40, or $60. The cost depends on the metal that goes into the tag. Contact the Medic Alert Foundation, P.O. Box 1009, Turlock, CA 95381-1009 (tel. toll free 800/432-5378 in the U.S.).

Before you leave home, you can obtain a list of English-speaking doctors in Paris from the **International Association for Medical Assistance to Travelers (IAMAT)**—in the United States at 417 Center St., Lewiston, NY 14092 (tel. 716/754-4883); in Canada at 40 Regal Rd., Guelph, ON N1K 1B5 (tel. 519/836-0102). In Europe, the address is 57 Voirets, 1212 Grand-Lancy-Geneva, Switzerland.

INSURANCE Insurance needs for the traveler abroad fall into three categories: (1) health and accident, (2) trip cancellation, and (3) lost luggage.

First, review your present policies before traveling abroad—you may already have adequate coverage between them and what is offered by credit-card companies.

Many credit-card companies insure their users in case of a travel accident, if the plane ticket was purchased with their card. Sometimes fraternal organizations have policies that protect members in case of sickness or accidents abroad.

Incidentally, don't assume that Medicare is the answer to illness in France. It covers U.S. citizens who travel to Mexico or Canada, but it does not cover travel in Europe. Canadians, though, are generally protected with health-insurance plans from their individual provinces.

Many homeowners' insurance policies cover theft of luggage during foreign travel and loss of documents—your Eurailpass, your passport, or your airline ticket, for instance. To submit a claim on your insurance, remember that you'll need police reports or a statement from a medical authority that you did in fact suffer the loss or experience the illness for which you are seeking compensation. Such claims, by their very nature, can be filed only when you return from France.

Some policies (and this is the type you should have) provide cash advances or transfer of funds so that you won't have to dip into your precious travel funds to settle medical bills.

If you've booked a charter flight, you will probably have to pay a cancellation fee if you cancel a trip suddenly, even if it is because of an unforeseen crisis. It's possible to get insurance against such a possibility from some travel agencies, and often flight insurance against a canceled trip is written into tickets paid for by credit cards from such companies as VISA and American Express. Many tour operators or insurance agents also provide this type of insurance.

Among the companies offering such policies are the following:

Travel Guard International, 1145 Clark St., Stevens Point, WI 54481 (tel. toll free 800/826-1300), offers a comprehensive insurance package that covers basically everything, including lost luggage, emergency assistance, accidental death, trip cancellation and interruption, and medical coverage abroad. There are restrictions, however, which you should understand before you buy the policy.

Travelers Insurance Company, Travel Insurance Division, One Tower Square, 10 NB, Hartford, CT 06183-5040 (tel. toll free 800/243-3174 in the U.S.). Travel accident and illness coverage starts at $10 for 6 to 10 days; $500 worth of coverage for lost, damaged, or delayed baggage costs $20 for 6 to 10 days; and trip cancellation costs $5.50 for $100 worth of coverage. Written approval is necessary for cancellation coverage above $10,000.

Mutual of Omaha, Mutual of Omaha Plaza, Omaha, NE 68175 (tel. toll free 800/228-9792 in the U.S.). This company offers insurance packages priced from $113 for a three-week trip. Included in the packages are travel-assistance services; and financial protection against trip cancellation, trip interruption, flight and baggage delays, accident-related medical costs, accidental death and/or dismemberment, and medical evacuation coverage. Application for insurance can be taken over the phone for major credit card holders.

Wallach and Co., 107 W. Federal St., Middleburg, VA

22117-0480 (tel. 703/687-3166, or toll free 800/237-6615 in the U.S.), offers coverage for 10 to 120 days at $3 per day; this policy includes accident and sickness coverage to the tune of $100,000. Medical evacuation is also included, along with a $25,000 accidental death and dismemberment compensation. Provisions for trip cancellation and lost or stolen luggage can also be written into this policy at a nominal cost.

Access America, 6600 W. Broad St., Richmond, VA 23230 (tel. 804/285-3300, or toll free 800/284-8300 in the U.S.), offers a comprehensive travel insurance and assistance package, including medical expenses, on-the-spot hospital payments, medical transportation, baggage insurance, trip cancellation/interruption insurance, and collision-damage insurance for a car rental. Their 24-hour hot line connects you to multilingual coordinators who can offer advice and help on medical, legal, and travel problems. Packages begin at $27.

In the United Kingdom, contact **Columbus Travel Insurance Ltd.** (tel. 071/375-0011) or, for students, **Campus Travel** (tel. 071/730-3402). If you're not sure who provides what kind of insurance and offers the best deal, contact the **Association of British Insurers,** 51 Gresham St., London EC2V 7HQ (tel. 071/600-333).

4. WHAT TO PACK

Parisians are both stylish *and* conservative; city clothes are in order here. Pack what you might wear to visit San Francisco or New York. Unlike the British, the French tend to dress down rather than up, but always with style. Parisian women go to work, restaurants, or the theater wearing beautifully cut and tailored pants suits. While ties for men are advisable in the posh places, they are seldom required in more moderate restaurants. Even churches don't insist that women wear head coverings—that is up to you.

Always pack as light as possible. Sometimes it's hard to get a porter or a baggage cart in rail and air terminals. Also, airlines are increasingly strict about how much luggage you can bring aboard, not only carry-on items, but checked suitcases as well. This is particularly true when flights are fully booked. Checked baggage should not measure more than 62 inches (width plus length plus height) and shouldn't weigh more than 70 pounds. Carry-on luggage shouldn't measure more than 45 inches (width plus length plus height) and must fit under your seat or in the bin above.

Whatever the season, bring a raincoat and umbrella to Paris, just to be on the safe side.

The general rule of packing is to bring four of everything. For men that means four pairs of socks, four pairs of slacks, four shirts, and four sets of underwear. At least two of these will always be either dirty or in the process of drying. Women could follow the same rule, four of each of the "basics," such as undergarments and stockings.

Take at least one outfit for chilly weather and one outfit for warm weather, especially if you plan to tour the rest of France after visiting Paris. Always take two pairs of shoes for walking Paris streets during the day. You may get your shoes soaked and need that extra pair.

5. TIPS FOR THE DISABLED, SENIORS, SINGLES, FAMILIES & STUDENTS

FOR THE DISABLED Facilities for the disabled are certainly above the world average. The French government every year does more and more to help ease life for the disabled in the public facilities of the country.

If you're considering a trip to Paris, contact one of the French Government Tourist Offices abroad (see "Information," in Section 1, above). You'll be sent a publication with an English glossary, called **Touristes Quand Même.** It provides a province-by-province overview of the facilities for the disabled in the French transportation system and at monuments and museums. There is a special emphasis on Paris.

Nearly all modern hotels in Paris now have rooms designed especially with the disabled in mind. Older hotels, unless they've been renovated, may not provide such important features as elevators, special toilet facilities, or ramps for wheelchair access. For a list of hotels in Paris offering facilities for the disabled, contact the **Association des Paralysés de France,** 22 rue du Père Guérin, 75013 Paris (tel. 44-16-83-83). The cost of its guide, *Où ferons-nous étape?* is 100F ($17.50).

For more detailed information, try **MossRehab,** 1200 W. Tabor Rd., Philadelphia, PA 19141 (tel. 215/456-9603); this service is not a travel agency. For assistance with your travel accessibility needs, call the number above. MossRehab provides information to telephone callers only.

You can also obtain a copy of *Air Transportation of Handicapped Persons,* published by the U.S. Department of Transportation. It's free if you write to Free Advisory Circular No. AC12032, Distribution Unit, U.S. Department of Transportation, Publications Division, M-4332, Washington, DC 20590.

You may also want to consider joining a tour for disabled travelers. The names and addresses of such tour operators can be obtained from the **Society for the Advancement of Travel for the Handicapped,** 347 Fifth Ave., Suite 610, New York, NY 10016 (tel. 212/447-7284). Yearly membership in this society is $45 ($25 for senior citizens and students). Send a self-addressed stamped envelope.

FEDCAP Rehabilitation Services (formerly, the Federation of the Handicapped), 211 W. 14th St., New York, NY 10011 (tel. 212/727-4268), operates summer tours to Europe and elsewhere for its members. Membership costs $6 a year.

For the blind, the best source to contact is the **American Foundation for the Blind,** 15 W. 16th St., New York, NY 10011 (tel. 212/620-2000, or toll free 800/232-5463 in the U.S.), which has information on travel. For those who are legally blind, it also issues identification cards for $6.

In France, most high-speed trains can deal with wheelchairs. Guide dogs ride free. Older trains have special compartments built for wheelchair boarding. On the Paris Métro, handicapped persons can sit in wider seats provided for their comfort. Some stations don't have escalators or elevators, however, and this may present problems.

In the United Kingdom, **British Rail** offers discounts of up to 50% on certain fares to anyone using a wheelchair, and one companion. RADAR (Royal Association for Disability and Rehabilitation) publishes two annual holiday guides for the disabled: "Holidays and Travel Abroad" and "Holidays in the British Isles." It also serves as a clearinghouse for travel information for and with disabled persons. There is a nominal charge for all publications, which can be ordered by calling 071/637-5400 or by writing RADAR, 25 Mortimer St., London W1N 8AB.

Another unusual clearinghouse for pertinent information for elderly or infirm travelers is the **Holiday Care Service,** 2 Old Bank Chambers, Station Rd., Horley, Surrey RH6 9HW (tel. 0293/774-535).

FOR SENIORS Many discounts are available for seniors—that is, men and women who have reached, as the French say, "the third age." Be advised, however, that you must be a member of an association to obtain certain discounts. The French domestic airline, **Air Inter,** offers seniors 25% to 50% reductions on its regular, nonexcursion flights, but there are restrictions. At any railway station, seniors (men and women 60 years or older) can obtain a **Carte Vermeil (Vermilion Card)** for 230F ($40.30). This card is valid for one year and entitles you to a 50% discount on train fares in both first- and second-class compartments (but not during peak periods) as well as a 10% reduction on all rail excursions. Carte Vermeil also offers reduced prices on certain regional bus lines, on about 20 weekly Air France flights to Nice, and on theater tickets, as well as half-price admission to state-owned museums. A more limited card, offering discounts on just four trips, is available for 130F ($22.80). For more information, contact a French Government Tourist Office (see "Information, Entry Requirements, and Money," above).

For information before you go, obtain a copy of *Tips for the Mature Traveler*, available from Grand Circle Travel, 347 Congress St., Suite 3A, Boston, MA 02210 (tel. 617/350-7500, or toll free 800/248-3737 in the U.S.).

One of the most dynamic travel organizations for seniors is **Elderhostel,** 75 Federal St., Boston, MA 02110 (tel. 617/426-7788), which arranges numerous courses throughout Europe, including France. Most courses, lasting around three weeks, represent good value since they include airfare, accommodations in student dormitories or modest inns, all meals, and tuition. The courses involve no homework, are ungraded, and often focus on the liberal arts. They're not luxury vacations, but they are fun and fulfilling. Participants must be 60 years or older (for couples, only one member needs to be over 60). Write or call for their free newsletter and a list of upcoming courses and destinations.

The **AARP Travel Experience** from American Express, 400 Pinnacle Way, Suite 450, Norcross, GA 30071 (tel. toll free 800/927-0111 in the U.S. for land arrangements; 800/745-4567 for cruises; or 800/659-5678 for TTD), arranges travel for members of the American Association of Retired Persons, 601 E St. NW, Washington, DC 20049 (tel. 202/434-AARP). Travel Experience offers members a wide variety of escorted, hosted, go-any-day packages and cruises to most parts of the world.

Information is also available from the nonprofit **National Council of Senior Citizens,** 1331 F St. NW, Washington, DC 20004-1171 (tel. 202/347-8800). For an annual charge of $12 per person/couple, you'll receive a regular magazine that includes travel tips; you'll also qualify for discounts on hotels and auto rentals.

In the United Kingdom, **Wasteels,** Victoria Station, opposite Platform 2, London SW1V 1JY (tel. 071/836-8541), currently provides a Rail Europe Senior Card for those over 60. Its price is £5 for any British citizen with government-issued proof of age, and £19 for anyone with a certificate of age not issued by the British government. With this card, discounts are often available on trains within Britain and the rest of Europe. There are coach tours for seniors; an excellent operator, **Cosmos Tourama,** 17 Holmsdale Rd., Bromley, Kent BR2 9LX (tel. 081/464-3477), offers a wide range of trips all over Europe.

FOR SINGLE TRAVELERS A recent census found that 77 million Americans over 15 years of age are single. The travel industry, however, tends to be geared toward double occupancy of hotel rooms. One company that has made heroic efforts to match single travelers with like-minded companions is now the largest and best-recommended company in the United States. **Jens Jurgen,** the German-born founder, charges $36 to $66 for a six-month listing in his well-publicized records. New applicants who want to find a suitable travel companion fill out a form stating their preferences and needs. Then they receive a minilisting of potential travel partners. Companions of the same or opposite sex can be requested. Since Jens Jurgen's listings are extensive, it's quite likely that you could find a travel companion. A sample copy of his newsletter, filled with travel tips for singles and 300 to 400 listings of others who are seeking partners, is available postpaid for $4. For an application and more information, write to Jens Jurgen, Travel Companion, P.O. Box P-833, Amityville, NY 11701 (tel. 516/454-0880).

In the United Kingdom, for single people who prefer to travel with groups composed largely of singles, there is **Explore, Ltd.** (tel. 0252/344-161). About 50% of those in its tour groups are unattached, and the company has a well-deserved reputation for offering unusual tours. Groups rarely include more than 16 participants, and children under 14 are not accepted.

FOR FAMILIES Advance planning is the key to a successful overseas family vacation. If you have very small children you should discuss your vacation plans with your family doctor and take along such standard supplies as children's aspirin, a thermometer, Band-Aids, and the like.

Families Welcome!, 21 W. Colony Place, Suite 140, Durham, NC 27705 (tel. 919/489-2555, or toll free 800/326-0724), a travel company specializing in worry-free vacations for families, offers "City Kids" packages to Paris, featuring accommodations in family-friendly hotels or apartments. Some hotels include a second room for children free, at a reduced rate during certain periods. Packages, which can include car rentals, train and ferry passes, and special air prices, are individually tailored for each family. A welcome kit is provided, with "insider's information" for families traveling in Paris—reliable babysitters, where to buy Pampers, and other such details. A list of restaurants that can be enjoyed with children is also included.

In the United Kingdom, the best deals for families are often package tours arranged by some of the giants of the British travel

industry. Foremost among these is **Thomsons Tour Operators.**
Through its air/land packages to Europe, a prearranged number of
airline seats are reserved free for children under 18 who accompany
their parents. To qualify, parents must book airfare and hotel
accommodations for two weeks or more, and as far in advance as
possible. Savings for families with children can be substantial.

FOR STUDENTS   Students can usually obtain a number of
travel discounts. The most wide-ranging travel service for students
is **Council Travel,** a subsidiary of the Council on International
Educational Exchange (CIEE), 205 E. 42nd St., New York, NY
10017 (tel. 212/661-1450), which provides details about budget
travel, study abroad, work permits, and insurance. It also publishes
a variety of helpful materials and issues an International Student
Identity Card (ISIC) for $16 to bona fide students. For a copy of
its *Student Travels* magazine, with information on all of the
council's services and CIEE's programs and publications, send $1 in
postage. Council Travel offices are located throughout the United
States. Call toll free 800/GET-ANID to find out where the closest
office is to you. There is also a Council Travel Office in France at
51 rue Dauphine, 75006 Paris (tel. 43-26-79-65).

For true budget travelers it's worth joining **Hostelling/Interna-
tional/IYHF** (International Youth Hostel Federation). For information write: Hostelling International American Youth Hostels
(HI-AYH), 733 15th St. NW, No. 840, Washington, DC 20005
(tel. 202/783-6161). Membership costs $25 annually; for those
under 18 it is $10; and for those over 54, $15.

In the United Kingdom, **Campus Travel,** 52 Grosvenor
Gardens, London SWIW 0AG (tel. 071/730-3402), provides information for student travelers. The International Student Identity
Card (ISIC), which is recognized internationally, will entitle you to
savings on flights, sightseeing, food, and accommodations throughout Europe and the world. It costs only £5 and is well worth the
money. **Youth hostels** are the place to stay if you're a student or
traveling on a shoestring. You'll need an International Youth Hostels Association Card, which you can purchase from the youth hostel store at 14 Southampton St., London (tel. 071/836-8541), or at
Campus Travel (see above).

6. ALTERNATIVE/ADVENTURE TRAVEL

EDUCATION/STUDY TRAVEL   The **Alliance Française,**
101 bd. Raspail, 75270 Paris CEDEX 06 (tel. 45-44-38-28)—
a state-appointed, nonprofit organization with a network of 1,300
establishments in more than 127 countries—offers French-language
courses to some 385,000 students. The international school in Paris
is open all year, and you can enroll for a minimum of a month-long
session. Fees tend to be reasonable, and the school offers
numerous activities and services. Write for information and applica-
tion forms at least one month before your departure for Paris.

The **National Registration Center for Studies Abroad**
(NRCSA), 823 N. 2nd St., Milwaukee, WI 53203 (tel. 414/278-
0631), has a catalog ($2) of schools in France, including the

Sorbonne in Paris. They will register you at the school of your choice, arrange for room and board, and make your airline reservations, all for no extra charge. Contact them and ask for a (free) copy of their newsletter.

COOKING SCHOOLS In a nation devoted to the pursuit of gastronomic excellence, you'll find a wide array of chefs (skilled and otherwise) eager to impart a few of their culinary insights—for a fee. A knowledge of at least rudimentary French is a good idea before you enroll, although a visual demonstration of any culinary technique is often more valuable than reading or hearing about it. The cooking schools listed below will send you information in English or French if you write to them in advance; their courses might be attended by professional chefs and serious or competitive connoisseurs.

Ritz-Escoffier Ecole de Gastronomie Française, 75001 Paris (tel. 42-60-38-30, or toll free 800/966-5758 in the U.S.). Famed for his titanic rages within the kitchens of the French and English aristocrats who engaged him to prepare their banquets, and also for his well-publicized culinary codifications, Georges-Auguste Escoffier (1846–1935) taught the Edwardian Age how to eat. Today, the Ritz Hotel, site of many of Escoffier's meals, maintains a school that articulates the conservative doctrines of the master's techniques. Courses last from 1 to 12 weeks and are taught in French and English.

Le Cordon Bleu, 8 bis, rue Léon Delhomme, 75015 Paris (tel. 48-56-06-06, or toll free 800/457-2433 in the U.S.). Originally established in the 1890s, this is probably the most famous French cooking school and the one with the most sophisticated marketing techniques (call the toll free number in the U.S. and the school will send you its brochures on request). Cordon Bleu's most famous courses last for 10 weeks, at the end of which certificates of competence are issued that are highly sought after within the restaurant world. Many readers of this guidebook, however, prefer either the four- or five-day program (usually held during Easter and Christmas), or the two-hour demonstration classes. Enrollment in these programs is available on a first-come, first-served basis, and the cost is around 200F ($35) each; these programs sometimes offer unexpected insights into the culinary subculture of Paris.

SAILING UP THE SEINE The river that winds through the heart of Paris is the third longest of the four great rivers of France, yet its role within French history is probably greater than that of the other three waterways combined. Sailing between its banks, with the architecture of what is probably the most beautiful city in the world passing on either side of you, is probably one of the most rewarding experiences in France.

For a description of the glass-sided *bateaux-mouches* that offer short-term river excursions through the monumental zone of Paris, see Chapter 6. Some visitors, however, prefer longer excursions along the river that gave rise to the French nation. **Paris Canal** (tel. 42-40-96-97) requires advance reservations for three-hour waterborne tours that begin either at the quays in front of the Musée d'Orsay (Métro: Solférino) or in front of the Musée des Sciences et de l'Industrie at Parc de la Villette (Métro: Porte de la Villette). Excursions negotiate the waterways and canals of Paris, including the Seine, an underground tunnel below the place de la Bastille, and the Canal St-Martin. The cost is 90F ($15.80) per person, and tours are offered daily only from March through November.

HOME EXCHANGES For home exchanges, which can be fun and save you money, contact the following:

Intervac U.S. is part of the largest worldwide home exchange network. It publishes three catalogs a year, listing more than 9,000 homes in more than 36 countries. Members contact each other directly. The $62 cost, plus postage, entitles you to receive all three of the company's catalogs, as well as include your own listing in whichever individual catalogs you choose. If you want to publish a photograph of your home, it costs $11 extra. Hospitality and youth exchanges are also available. The organization can be contacted at P.O. Box 590594, San Francisco, CA 94119 (tel. 415/435-3497, or toll free 800/756-HOME in the U.S.).

Vacation Exchange Club, P.O. Box 650, Key West, FL 33041 (tel. 305/294-3720, or toll free 800/638-3841 in the U.S.), will send you four directories a year—in one of which you are listed—for $60.

7. GETTING THERE

BY PLANE FROM NORTH AMERICA

The flying time to Paris from New York is about 7 hours; from Chicago, 9 hours; from Los Angeles, 11 hours; from Montréal, about 6½ hours; and from Toronto, about 7½ hours.

THE MAJOR AIRLINES

One of the best choices for passengers flying to Paris from both the southeastern United States and the Midwest is **Delta Airlines** (tel. toll free 800/241-4141), whose network greatly expanded after its acquisition of some of the former Pan Am routes. From such cities as New Orleans, Phoenix, Columbia (S.C.), and Nashville, Delta flies to Atlanta, connecting every evening with a nonstop flight to Orly Airport in Paris. Delta also operates a daily nonstop flight to Orly from both Cincinnati and New York's JFK. Both of these leave late enough in the day to permit easy transfers from much of Delta's vast North American network.

Another excellent choice for Paris-bound passengers is **United Airlines** (tel. toll free 800/538-2929), with nonstop flights from Chicago, Washington, D.C., Los Angeles, and San Francisco to Paris's Charles de Gaulle Airport. United also offers attractive promotional fares—especially in the low and shoulder seasons—to London's Heathrow from at least six major North American hubs. From London, it's an easy train and Hovercraft connection to Paris, a fact that tempts many passengers to spend a weekend in London either before or after their visit to Paris.

Another excellent choice is **Continental Airlines** (tel. toll free 800/231-0856) which services the Northeast and much of the Southwest through its busy hubs in Newark and Houston. From both of those cities, Continental provides nonstop flights to Charles de Gaulle Airport. Flights from Newark depart daily, while flights from Houston depart between four and seven times a week, depending on the season.

TWA (tel. toll free 800/221-2000) operates daily nonstop service to Charles de Gaulle Airport from Boston, New York's JFK, and

Washington, D.C.'s Dulles airports. TWA also offers three-times-per-week nonstop service to Paris from St. Louis, although the flights touch down briefly in either Boston, Washington, D.C., or New York.

American Airlines (tel. toll free 800/221-2000) provides daily nonstop flights to Paris (Orly) from Dallas/Fort Worth, Raleigh/Durham, Chicago, Miami, and New York's JFK.

USAir (tel. toll free 800/428-4322) offers daily nonstop service from Philadelphia International Airport to Paris's Orly Airport.

Aircraft of the French-nationalized **Air France Group** (tel. toll free 800/237-2747) also cross the Atlantic. Today's company was formed by a merger in the late 1980s of the nation's largest government-owned airlines: Air France, UTA (Union des Transports Aériens), and France's domestic airline, Air Inter. The conglomerate flies daily nonstop from Newark to Orly. The airline also offers daily or several-times-a-week flights from San Francisco, New York's JFK, Dallas, Miami, Chicago, Mexico City (via Houston), Toronto, Montréal, and Los Angeles to Charles de Gaulle Airport. The nonstop flights from Los Angeles originate in Papeete, French Polynesia.

Canadians usually choose **Air Canada's** (tel. toll free 800/776-3000 from the U.S. and Canada) flights to Paris from Toronto and Montréal. Nonstop flights from Montréal depart every evening for Paris, while flights from Toronto to Paris are nonstop six days a week, and direct (with a touchdown in Montréal en route) one day a week. Two of the nonstop flights from Toronto are shared with Air France, and feature Air France aircraft.

REGULAR AIRFARES Fares and conditions for the flights of each of the airlines listed above are highly competitive. All of them offer a consistently popular **advance-purchase excursion (APEX)** fare that requires a seven-day advance payment and a minimum stay of between 7 and 30 days. Usually this ticket, although reasonably priced, is nonrefundable or only partially refundable; you must pay a penalty if you change flight dates or destination.

Delta Airlines offers a "7-day Advance Purchase" fare from New York to Paris costing $844 on weekdays in high season and $518 on weekdays in low season. (Flights on Friday through Sunday carry a supplemental charge of $50 to $60, depending on the season.)

Most airlines divide their year into seasonal slots, with the least expensive fares offered between November 1 and March 14. Shoulder season, which includes April, May, and October, is only slightly more expensive; many veteran tourists consider this the ideal time to visit Paris.

A regular one-way economy-class ticket between New York and Paris on Delta, for example, is priced year-round at about $972 (subject to change, of course), plus tax. With this ticket you can literally catch any flight, depending on seat availability, without regard to advance-booking requirements or penalty for last-minute changes in your itinerary.

Business class offers wider seats, more legroom, and sometimes—but not always—the advantages of first class. Currently, Delta's year-round one-way fares from Atlanta to Paris are from $1,735 in business class and $2,842 in first class. These fares carry a surcharge of about $30 for taxes and security fees.

OTHER GOOD-VALUE CHOICES Proceed with caution through the next grab bag of suggestions. What constitutes "good value" keeps changing in the airline industry. It's hard to keep up, even if you're a travel agent. Fares change all the time, and what was the lowest possible fare one day can change the very next day when a new promotional fare is offered. So be aware of how volatile the situation is.

U.S. Bucket Shops The name originated in the 1960s, when mainstream airlines gave the then-pejorative term to resellers of blocks of unsold tickets consigned to them by major transatlantic carriers. "Bucket shop" has stuck as a label, but it might be more polite to refer to them as "consolidators." In the purest sense, a bucket shop acts as a clearinghouse for blocks of tickets that airlines discount and consign during normally slow periods of air travel.

Charter operators (see below) and bucket shops used to perform separate functions, but their offerings in many cases have been blurred recently. Many outfits perform both functions.

Tickets are discounted anywhere from 20% to 35% of the full fare. Terms of payment can vary, anywhere from 45 days before departure to last-minute sales offered in a final attempt by an airline to fill a semiempty craft.

Consolidators abound from coast to coast, but just to get you started, here are some names. Look also for their small one-column ads in your local newspaper's travel section.

One of the biggest U.S. consolidators is **Travac,** 989 Sixth Ave., New York, NY 10018 (tel. 212/563-3303, or toll free 800/TRAV-800), which offers discounted seats throughout the United States to most cities in Europe, including Paris, on such airlines as TWA, Continental, United, Delta, and USAir.

UniTravel, 1177 N. Warson Rd., St. Louis, MO 63132 (tel. toll free 800/325-2222), offers tickets from many of the U.S.-based carriers to Paris and elsewhere in Europe at prices that could be lower than what a customer would pay if he or she phoned the airlines directly. As is true at any consolidator, the offered discount could be undermined if any airline suddenly initiated a new range of promotional prices. UniTravel is best suited to providing discounts for passengers who decide (or need) to get to Paris on short notice.

One final option is suitable only for clients with extremely flexible travel plans—**Airhitch,** 2790 Broadway, Suite 100, New York, NY 10025 (tel. toll free 800/326-2009). It offers a rare service: prospective travelers notify Airhitch of any five consecutive days in which they're available to fly to Europe. Airhitch then agrees to fly them within those five days from any of three regions in the United States: the East Coast, the West Coast, or the Midwest/Southeast. Attempts will be made to fly passengers to and from the cities of their choice, but there are no guarantees. A client might land at a city as far flung as Barcelona or Düsseldorf from a departure city as widely separated as Boston or Philadelphia. Travelers on the West Coast should contact Airhitch's California office at 1341 Ocean Ave., Suite 62, Santa Monica, CA 90401 (tel. toll free 800/397-1090).

Since dealing with unknown consolidators could be somewhat risky, it would be advisable to call the Better Business Bureau in your area to see if any complaints have been filed against the company from which you plan to purchase a ticket.

Ⓕ FROMMER'S SMART TRAVELER: AIRFARES

1. Shop all the airlines that fly to your destination.
2. Always ask for the lowest-priced fare, not just for a discount fare.
3. Keep calling the airline—availability of cheap seats changes daily. Airline managers would rather sell a seat than have it fly empty. As the departure date nears, additional low-cost seats become available.
4. Ask about frequent-flyer programs to gain bonus miles when you book a flight.
5. Check "bucket shops" for last-minute discounts even cheaper than their advertised "slashed" fares.
6. Check about discounted land arrangements. Sometimes these are cheaper when booked with an air ticket.
7. Check "standby" fares, if any.
8. Fly free or at a heavy discount as a "courier."
9. Look for special promotional fares offered by major carriers or airlines struggling to gain a foothold in the market.

Charter Flights For reasons of economy—never for convenience—some travelers choose charter flights to France or to one of the countries bordering it.

Jet Vacations, 1775 Broadway, New York, NY 10019 (tel. 212/247-0999, or toll free 800/538-0999), is a wholly owned subsidiary of Air France and an obvious charter-line choice for Paris. Committed to filling as many seats on Air France flights as possible, and operating from many cities including New York's JFK, Newark, Boston, Washington, D.C. (Dulles), Chicago, Miami, Houston, Los Angeles, and San Francisco, it has no objections to selling one-way tickets to Paris, space available, up until a few days before departure for any given flight. One-way tickets from New York to Paris, with many restrictions attached, range in price from $233 to $325, depending on the season. Cancellations prior to nine days before your anticipated departure require a penalty of $50 in each direction, while cancellations within eight days or less of your takeoff entail the complete forfeiture of your ticket. Be warned in advance that the telephones for this company (open Monday through Friday from 9am to 8pm) tend to be extremely busy. If you're interested, it's probably best to phone in the morning.

If you're visiting other countries in Europe, there are other possibilities.

For example, you might use **Balair Ltd,** 608 Fifth Ave., Suite 803, New York, NY 10020 (tel. 212/581-3411, or toll free 800/322-5247), the charter-airline subsidiary of Swissair. It runs charter flights to Zurich from Orlando, San Francisco, Miami, Halifax (Nova Scotia), and Anchorage, Alaska. Flights to Zurich from Miami range from $512 to $700, round-trip, with many restrictions, depending on the season. From Zurich, you have a wide choice of trains, which run frequently, to Paris.

DER Tours, 9501 W. Devon Ave., Rosemont, IL 60018 (tel.

toll free 800/782-2424), sells seats to Paris at discounted prices, usually from the unsold inventories of major international carriers. Some of the flights to Paris require the added inconvenience, however, of a transfer through London.

Another possibility is **Europa Travel Service,** 911 E. 185th St., Cleveland, OH 44119 (tel. 216/481-3612, or toll free 800/677-1313). Especially tailored to the needs of clients in Canada and the Midwest, it offers discounted tickets (almost all of which require a transfer in Newark or Houston) to Paris, as well as other cities.

Another organization that arranges charters is the **Council on International Educational Exchange (Council Travel),** 205 E. 42nd St., New York, NY 10017 (tel. 212/661-0311, or toll free 800/800-8222). It also provides low-cost student airfares in Europe, as well as discounted rail and ferry tickets.

Rebators To make the situation even more confusing, rebators also compete in the low-cost airfare market. These outfits pass along to the passenger part of their commission, although many of them assess a fee for their service. Most rebators offer discounts that range from 10% to 25% (but this could vary from place to place), plus a $25 handling charge. They are not the same as travel agents, although they sometimes offer similar services including discounted land arrangements and car rentals. Their advertisements appear in small one-column ads in local newspapers.

Rebators include **Travel Avenue,** 641 W. Lake St., Suite 201, Chicago, IL 60606-3691 (tel. 312/876-6866, or toll free 800/333-3335 in the U.S.); and **The Smart Traveller,** P.O. Box 330010, 3111 SW 27th Ave., Miami, FL 33133 (tel. 305/448-3338, or toll free 800/448-3338).

Travel Clubs Another possibility of low-cost air travel is the travel club, which supplies an unsold inventory of tickets offering discounts in the usual range of 20% to 60%.

After you pay an annual fee, you are given a "hot line" number to call to find out what discounts are available. Many of these discounts become available several days in advance of actual departure, sometimes as long as a week and sometimes as much as a month. It all depends. Of course, you're limited to what's available, so you have to be fairly flexible.

Some of the best of these clubs include the following:

Moment's Notice, 425 Madison Ave., New York, NY 10017 (tell. 212/486-0500), has a member's 24-hour hot line (regular phone toll charges) and a yearly fee of $45 per family.

Sears Discount Travel Club, 3033 S. Parker Rd., Suite 1000, Aurora, CO 80014 (tel. toll free 800/255-1487), offers members, for $49, a catalog (issued four times a year), maps, discounts at select hotels, and a 5% cash bonus on purchases.

BY PLANE FROM THE U.K.

From London, **Air France** (tel. 081/742-6600), **British Airways** (tel. 081/897-4000), and **Caledonian Airways** (tel. 0293/36321), a charter division of BA, fly regularly and frequently from London to Paris (trip time is only one hour). Air France and British Airways alone operate up to 17 flights daily from Heathrow, one of the busiest air routes in Europe. Air France also flies four or five times a day from Gatwick to Charles de Gaulle Airport. Many commercial travelers also use regular flights originating from the

London City Airport in the Docklands. There are also direct flights to Paris from such major cities as Manchester, Birmingham, Glasgow, Edinburgh, and Southampton.

Flying from England to France is often quite expensive, even though the distance is short. That's why most Brits rely on a good travel agent to get them the lowest possible airfare. Good values are offered by a number of companies, including **Nouvelles Frontières,** 1–2 Hanover St., London W14 9WB (tel. 071/629-7772). One of the least expensive tickets offered by this company is a Caledonian Airways flight from Gatwick to the town of Beauvais, 46 miles north of Paris, where rail connections can easily be made to the French capital.

There are no hard and fast rules about where to get the best deals for European flights, but do bear the following points in mind. (1) Daily papers often carry advertisements for companies offering cheap flights. Highly recommended companies include **Trailfinders** (tel. 071/937-5400), which sells discounted fares, and **Avro Tours** (tel. 081/543-0000), which operates charters. (2) In London, there are many **bucket shops** in the neighborhood of Earl's Court and Victoria Station that offer cheap fares. For your own protection, make sure that the company you deal with is a member of the IATA, ABTA, or ATOL. (3) **CEEFAX,** a British television information service (received by many private homes and hotels), presents details of package holidays and flights to Europe and beyond.

BY TRAIN

If you're already in Europe, you might decide to travel to Paris by train, especially if you have a **Eurailpass.** Even if you don't, the cost is relatively low. For example, the one-way fare from London to Paris by train (including the Channel crossing) is $180 in first class and $138 in second class; from Rome to Paris, the fare is $187 in first class and $121 in second class; and from Madrid to Paris the fare is $158 in first class and $105 in second class.

Visitors from London may want to consider a British/French joint rail pass, linking the two most popular vacation spots in Europe—Britain and France. Called **BritFrance Railpass,** it is available to North Americans, providing unlimited train travel in Britain and France, plus a one-way ticket to cross the English Channel by Hovercraft. You may choose a total of any five days of any 10 days of unlimited rail travel during any one-month period on both the British and French rail networks. Adult first-class fares for the less comprehensive of the above-mentioned options cost $359 in first class and $259 in second class. Youth second-class fares (for ages 12 to 25) are $220 for any five days within any month-long period. Children from 4 to 12 travel for half the adult fare, and those below 4 travel free. The pass is activated the first time you use it. Rail passes as well as individual rail tickets within Europe are available at most travel agencies, at any office of RailEurope (tel. toll free 800/848-7245 in the U.S.), or at BritRail Travel International (tel. 212/575-2667 in New York City).

In London, an especially convenient place to buy railway tickets to virtually anywhere is just opposite Platform 2 in Victoria Station, London SW1V 1JY. **Wasteels, Ltd.** (tel. 071/834-7066) will provide railway-related services and discuss the pros and cons of various types of fares and rail passes; its staff will probably spend more than the usual amount of time with a client while planning an itinerary. Depending on circumstances, Wasteels sometimes charges a £5 fee for its services, but for the information provided, the fee might be worth it. Some of the most popular passes, including Inter-Rail and EuroYouth, are available only to those under 26 years of age for unlimited second-class travel in 26 European countries.

BY BUS

Bus travel to Paris is available from London as well as many other cities throughout the Continent. Just before press time, the French government established strong incentives for long-haul buses not to drive into the center of Paris. The arrival and departure point for Europe's largest bus operators, **Eurolines France,** is a 35-minute Métro ride from central Paris, at the terminus of Métro line 3 (Métro: Gallieni), in the eastern suburb of Bagnolet. Despite this inconvenience, many people prefer bus travel. Eurolines France is located at 28 av. du Général de Gaulle, 93541 Bagnolet (tel. 1/49-72-51-51).

Long-haul buses are equipped with toilets and stop every four hours for rest and refreshment. At press time, the price of a round-trip ticket between Paris and London was 530F ($92.80); between Paris and Rome, 820F ($143.50); between Paris and Stockholm, 1,400F ($245) for a two-day trip each way.

Because Eurolines does not have a U.S.-based sales agent (at press time), most people wait until they reach Europe to buy their tickets. Any European travel agent can arrange for these purchases. If you're traveling to Paris from London, you can contact Eurolines U.K., Victoria Coach Station (the continental check-in desk) or call 0582/40-45-11 for information, or 071/73-03-499 for credit-card sales. In Frankfurt, contact L'Agence Wasteels, Am Hauptbahnhof 18, 6000 Frankfurt (tel. 069/232385).

BY FERRY FROM ENGLAND

For many visitors, crossing the English Channel offers a highly evocative insight into European culture and history. If your plans call for water travel to France, there are three main carriers. The most frequently used are **Sealink** (conventional ferryboat service) and **Hoverspeed** (travel on motorized catamarans—Seacats—which skim along a few inches above the surface of the water). Cars can usually be taken on both types of vessel, although the rates are probably cheaper for conventional ferryboats. The shortest and busiest route between London and Paris is the one from Dover to Calais. By ferryboat, the trip takes about 90 minutes, although a Seacat can make the run in about 35 minutes. The Seacat also crosses from Folkestone to Boulogne in about 55 minutes. Each crossing is carefully timed to coincide with the arrival and departure of trains from London and Paris, which disgorge passengers and their luggage a short walk from the piers. The U.S. sales agent for the above-mentioned lines is Britrail (tel. 212/575-2667).

Another opportunity to travel by ferryboat from England to France (including the vital link between Dover and Calais)—is offered by **P&O Channel Lines.** Their U.S. representative is Scots-American Travel, 26 Rugen Dr., Harrington Park, NJ 07640 (tel. 201/768-5505).

If you plan to take a rented car across the Channel, check carefully about license and insurance requirements with the rental company before you leave.

BY LE SHUTTLE FROM THE U.K.

Opened in the summer of 1994, **Le Shuttle** is a train that transports motorists beneath the English Channel, completing the 31-mile journey between France and Great Britain in just 35 minutes.

Le Shuttle accommodates passenger cars, charter buses, taxis, and motorcycles through a tunnel under the English Channel between Folkestone, England, and Calais, France. Le Shuttle operates 24 hours a day, 365 days a year, running every 15 minutes during peak travel times and at least once an hour during the night. Tickets may be purchased in advance or at the tollbooth. With Le Shuttle, gone are weather-related delays, seasickness, and the need for reservations.

Motorists drive onto a half-mile-long train and travel through an underground tunnel built beneath the seabed through a layer of impermeable chalk marl and sealed within a reinforced concrete lining.

Before boarding Le Shuttle, motorists stop at a tollbooth and then pass through immigration for both countries at one time. During the ride, motorists stay in bright, air-conditioned carriages, remaining inside their cars or stepping outside to stretch their legs. When the trip is completed, motorists simply drive off toward their destinations. Total travel time between the French and English highway systems is about one hour.

Stores selling duty-free goods, restaurants, and service stations are available to travelers on both sides of the Channel. A bilingual staff is on hand to assist people at both the British and French terminals.

PACKAGE TOURS

Some people prefer to have a tour operator make all their travel arrangements. Many companies operate tours to France, each offering transportation to and within France, prearranged hotel space, and such extras as a bilingual tour guide and lectures geared more or less to your general interests.

Some of the best values in the tour industry can be had when air transportation and hotel accommodations are arranged simultaneously; this can be done by the booking agencies within a major airline (for example, Delta). Their staffs, through volume purchases of hotel rooms, can arrange affordable visits to Paris (and elsewhere in Europe) that are geared to either first-timers or seasoned travelers. (Tours range from the fully escorted variety with trained guides to independent travel where the airline provides phone help in case of confusion or emergencies, but allows visitors maximum freedom to explore on their own.)

An eight-day tour that includes Paris and the Ile de France, with visits to Versailles and Chartres, plus six nights at a well-recommended hotel in Paris, can cost from $800 to $1,200 per person, double occupancy, depending on the season. Breakfast is usually included, as well as a pass to many of Paris's museums. Other add-ons may be available for excursions to the Riviera, Geneva, and the rest of Europe at prices that are lower (sometimes significantly lower) than if you had made your own arrangements.

The French Experience, 370 Lexington Ave., New York, NY 10017 (tel. 212/986-3800), offers several fly-drive programs using different types and price categories of hotels. They also take reservations for about 50 hotels in Paris, arrange short-term apartment rentals there, and offer prearranged package tours of various regions of France. Any of these can be adapted and altered to suit your individual needs.

American Express Vacations (as represented by Certified Vacations, Inc.), P.O. Box 1525, Fort Lauderdale, FL 33302 (tel. toll free 800/446-6234 in the U.S. and Canada), is perhaps the most instantly recognizable tour operator in the world. Their offerings in France and the rest of Europe are probably more comprehensive than those of many other companies. If you have a clear idea of what you want (and it is not already available), they can arrange an individualized itinerary through specific regions for you.

GETTING TO KNOW PARIS

Ernest Hemingway referred to the many splendors of Paris as a "moveable feast" and wrote, "There is never any ending to Paris, and the memory of each person who has lived in it differs from that of any other." It is this personal discovery of the city that has always been the most compelling reason for coming to Paris. And perhaps that's why France has been called *le deuxième pays de tout le monde*—everybody's second country.

The Seine not only divides Paris into a Right Bank *(Rive Droite)* and a Left Bank *(Rive Gauche)*, but it also seems to split the city into two vastly different sections and ways of life. Depending on your time, interest, and budget, you may quickly decide which section of Paris interests you the most.

1. ARRIVING

BY PLANE

Paris has two major international airports: **Aéroport d'Orly** (tel. 49-75-15-15), 8½ miles south, and **Aéroport Roissy–Charles de Gaulle** (tel. 48-62-22-80 or 43-20-14-55), 14¼ miles northeast of the city. A shuttle operates between the two airports about every 30 minutes, taking 50 to 75 minutes to make the journey. At Orly catch this bus at Exit B.

CHARLES DE GAULLE AIRPORT At Charles de Gaulle Airport, foreign carriers use Aérogare 1, and Air France uses Aérogare 2. From Aérogare 1, you take a moving walkway to the passport checkpoint and the Customs area. The two terminals are linked by a shuttle bus *(navette)*.

The **shuttle bus** connecting Aérogare 1 with Aérogare 2 also transports passengers to the Roissy rail station, from which fast **RER trains** leave every 15 minutes to such Métro stations as Gare du Nord, Châtelet, Luxembourg, Port-Royal, and Denfert-Rochereau. The typical fare is 35F ($6.10).

You can also take an **Air France shuttle bus**—to the Arc de Triomphe, for example—for 42F ($7.40). That ride, depending on traffic, takes less than 45 minutes. The shuttle departs about every 12 minutes between 5:45am and 11pm.

Taxis into the city will cost about 200F ($35). At night (from 8pm to 7am), fares are 35% higher.

Buses *to* Charles de Gaulle Airport leave from the terminal in the basement of the Palais des Congrès at Port Maillot every 15 minutes to Aérogare 2 and every 20 minutes to Aérogare 1. The trip takes about 30 minutes, but during rush hours allow another half hour.

ORLY AIRPORT   Orly also has two terminals—Orly Sud (south) for international flights and Orly Ouest (west) for domestic flights. They are linked by a shuttle bus.

Air France buses leave Orly Sud every 12 minutes between 5:45am and 11pm from Exit 1, heading for Gare des Invalides. At Exit D, you can board bus 215 for place Denfert-Rochereau in the south of Paris.

A **shuttle bus** leaves Orly about every 15 minutes for the **RER train** station, Pont-de-Rungis/Aéroport-d'Orly, from which RER trains take 30 minutes into the city center. A trip to Les Invalides, for example, costs 30F ($5.30).

You can also take a **shuttle bus** from Orly Sud to the Orly train station, where high-speed RER trains leaving every 15 minutes will take you to all the central stops along the Seine. En route you can transfer to any Métro line.

A **taxi** from Orly to the center of Paris costs about 160F ($28) and is higher at night. Don't take a meterless taxi from Orly Sud— it's much safer to get a metered cab from the line, which is under the scrutiny of a police officer.

Buses *to* Orly Airport leave from the Invalides terminal to either Orly Sud or Orly Ouest every 15 minutes, taking about 30 minutes.

BY TRAIN

There are six major train stations in Paris: **Gare d'Austerlitz,** 55 quai d'Austerlitz, 13e (servicing the southwest with trains to the Loire Valley, the Bordeaux country, and the Pyrénées); **Gare de l'Est,** place du 11 Novembre 1918, 10e (servicing the east, with trains to Strasbourg, Nancy, Reims, and beyond to Zurich, Basel, Luxembourg, and Austria); **Gare de Lyon,** 20 bd. Diderot, 12e (servicing the southeast with trains to the Côte d'Azur, Provence, and beyond to Geneva, Lausanne, and Italy); **Gare Montparnasse,** 17 bd. Vaugirard, 15e (servicing the west, with trains to Brittany); **Gare du Nord,** 18 rue de Dunkerque, 15e (servicing the north with trains to Holland, Denmark, Belgium, and the north of Germany); and **Gare St-Lazare,** 13 rue d'Amsterdam, 8e (servicing the northwest with trains to Normandy).

For **general train information** and to make **reservations,** call 45-82-50-50 from 7am to 10pm daily. Buses operate between stations.

Note: The stations and the surrounding areas are usually seedy and frequented by pickpockets, hustlers, prostitutes, and drug addicts. Be alert, especially at night.

Each of these stations also has a Métro stop, making the whole city easily accessible. Taxis are also available at every station at designated stands. Look for the sign that says TETE DE STATION.

BY BUS

Most buses arrive at **Gare Routière Internationale du Paris-Gallieni,** avenue du Général de Gaulle, Bagnolet (tel. 49-72-51-51; Métro: Gallieni). For more information about bus routes, call 40-38-93-93.

BY CAR

Driving a car in Paris is definitely not recommended. Parking is difficult and traffic is dense. If you do drive, remember that Paris is encircled by a ring road called the *périphérique*. Always obtain detailed directions to your destination, including the name of the exit on the périphérique (exits are not numbered). Avoid rush hours.

Few hotels, except the luxury ones, have garages, but the staff will usually be able to direct you to one nearby.

The major highways into Paris are the A1 from the north (Great Britain and Benelux); the A13 from Rouen, Normandy, and other points of northwest France; the A109 from Spain, the Pyrénées, and the southwest; the A7 from the French Alps, the Riviera, and Italy; and the A4 from eastern France.

TOURIST INFORMATION

The main **Paris tourist information office** is at 127 Champs-Elysées, 8e (tel. 49-52-53-54), where you can secure information about both Paris and the provinces. The office is open daily except May 1 from 9am to 8pm.

Welcome Offices in the city center will also give you free maps, brochures, and *Paris Monthly Information,* an English-language listing of all current events and performances.

CITY LAYOUT

Paris is surprisingly compact. Occupying 432 square miles (6 more than San Francisco), it is home to more than 10 million people. As mentioned, the River Seine divides Paris into the **Right Bank** (Rive Droite) to the north and the **Left Bank** (Rive Gauche) to the south. These designations make sense when you stand on a bridge and face downstream, watching the waters flow out toward the sea—to your right is the north bank, to your left the south. Thirty-two bridges link the Right and Left banks, some providing access to the two small islands at the heart of the city, **Ile de la Cité**—the city's birthplace and site of Notre-Dame—and **Ile St-Louis,** a moat-guarded oasis of sober 17th-century mansions. These islands can cause some confusion to walkers who think they've just crossed a bridge from one bank to the other, only to find themselves caught up in an almost medieval maze of narrow streets and old buildings.

MAIN ARTERIES & STREETS Between 1860 and 1870 Baron Haussmann forever changed the look of Paris by creating the legendary **boulevards:** boulevards St-Michel, St-Germain, Haussmann, Malesherbes, Sébastopol, Magenta, Voltaire, and Strasbourg.

The "main street" on the Right Bank is, of course, the **Champs-Elysées,** beginning at the Arc de Triomphe and running to the place de la Concorde. Haussmann also created avenue de l'Opéra (as well as the Opéra), and the 12 avenues that radiate starlike from the Arc de Triomphe, giving it its original name, place de l'Etoile (renamed place Charles-de-Gaulle following the general's death). Today it is often referred to as place Charles-de-Gaulle–Etoile.

Haussmann also cleared Ile de la Cité of its medieval buildings, transforming it into a showcase for Notre-Dame. Finally, he laid out the two elegant parks on the western and southeastern fringes of the city: **Bois de Boulogne** and **Bois de Vincennes.**

FINDING AN ADDRESS   Paris is divided into 20 municipal wards called *arrondissements,* each with its own mayor, city hall, police station, and central post office. Some even have remnants of market squares. Most city maps are divided by arrondissement, and all addresses include the arrondissement number (written in Roman or Arabic numerals and followed by "e" or "er"). Paris also has its own version of a zip code. Thus the proper mailing address for a hotel is written as, say, 75014 Paris. The last two digits, 14, indicate that the address is in the 14th arrondissement, in this case, Montparnasse.

Numbers on buildings running parallel to the River Seine usually follow the course of the river—that is, east to west. On perpendicular streets, numbers on buildings begin low closer to the river.

ARRONDISSEMENTS IN BRIEF

Each of Paris's 20 arrondissements possesses a unique style and flavor. You will want to decide which district appeals most to you and then find accommodations there. Later on, try to visit as many areas as you can.

1st Arr.   Located on the Right Bank, the 1st has the most popular attractions, including the Louvre, the Forum des Halles (now transformed into a modern shopping mall), Sainte-Chapelle, Conciergerie, and the Jardin des Tuileries. Two of the most prestigious addresses are place Vendôme (site of the Hôtel Ritz) and Palais Royal, a section of elegant buildings and galleries surrounding the gardens to the north.

2nd Arr.   Home to the Bourse, or stock exchange, the 2nd is in fact primarily a working-class district. Highlights include rue de la Paix, a traditional street of goldsmiths and furriers, and the Bibliothèque National. The Right Bank district lies mainly between the Grands Boulevards and the rue Etienne Marcel.

3rd Arr.   This embraces much of Le Marais (the swamp), one of the best-loved Right Bank neighborhoods of Paris. Many of the buildings date from the Middle Ages, and much of the old has been saved and restored. Highlights include the Musée Picasso.

4th Arr.   This area contains the Hôtel de Ville (city hall) and such major attractions as Notre-Dame (on Ile de la Cité), the Centre Pompidou, and place des Vosges, site of the Musée Victor Hugo. It also includes Ile St-Louis with its aristocratic town houses, courtyards, and antiques shops.

5th Arr.   Known as the Latin Quarter, its attractions include the Sorbonne, the Panthéon, the Musée de Cluny, and the Jardin des Plantes. When people refer to the Left Bank they usually mean the 5th and 6th arrondissements—an area filled with students, cafés, bistros, and street life.

6th Arr.   This is the heartland of Paris publishing and, for some, the most colorful part of the Left Bank. Waves of earnest young artists can be seen emerging from the Ecole des Beaux-Arts. This is one of the best areas for good budget hotels and restaurants. Highlights include the Jardin du Luxembourg and place St-Germain-des-Prés.

7th Arr.   The home of the Eiffel Tower is primarily an upscale

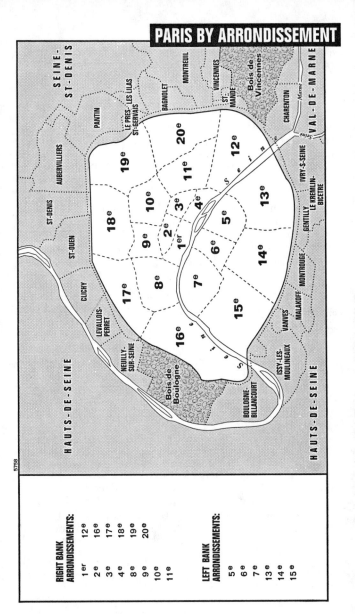

PARIS BY ARRONDISSEMENT

SEINE-ST-DENIS

VAL-DE-MARNE

HAUTS-DE-SEINE

HAUTS-DE-SEINE

MONTREUIL

VINCENNES

Bois de Vincennes

ST-MANDE

BAGNOLET

CHARENTON

PANTIN

LE PRÉS-LES LILAS ST-GERVAIS

AUBERVILLIERS

IVRY-S-SEINE

LE KREMLIN-BICÊTRE

GENTILLY

MONTROUGE

MALAKOFF

VANVES

ISSY-LES-MOULINEAUX

BOULOGNE-BILLANCOURT

NEUILLY-SUR-SEINE

LEVALLOIS-PERRET

CLICHY

ST-OUEN

ST-DENIS

Bois de Boulogne

19ᵉ 20ᵉ 11ᵉ 12ᵉ 18ᵉ 10ᵉ 3ᵉ 4ᵉ 13ᵉ 9ᵉ 2ᵉ 1ᵉʳ 5ᵉ 8ᵉ 6ᵉ 17ᵉ 7ᵉ 14ᵉ 16ᵉ 15ᵉ

5758

RIGHT BANK ARRONDISSEMENTS:

1ᵉʳ 12ᵉ
2ᵉ 16ᵉ
3ᵉ 17ᵉ
4ᵉ 18ᵉ
8ᵉ 19ᵉ
9ᵉ 20ᵉ
10ᵉ
11ᵉ

LEFT BANK ARRONDISSEMENTS:

5ᵉ
6ᵉ
7ᵉ
13ᵉ
14ᵉ
15ᵉ

Left Bank residential and government-diplomatic area. Other highlights include Napoléon's Tomb, the Invalides Musée de l'Armée, and the Musée d'Orsay.

8th Arr. The 8th is the heart of the Right Bank and its prime showcase is the Champs-Elysées, linking the Arc de Triomphe with the delicate obelisk on place de la Concorde. Here you'll find the fashion houses, the most elegant hotels, expensive restaurants and shops, and the most fashionably attired Parisians. Other landmarks include the Palais de l'Elysée, home of the French president; the church of the Madeleine; the Faubourg St-Honoré; and the Parc de Monceau.

9th Arr. Visited primarily because of its Grands Boulevards, such as boulevard des Capucines and boulevard des Italiens, the 9th also includes the Quartier de l'Opéra and the strip joints of Pigalle (the infamous "pig alley" for the GIs of World War II). Other major attractions include the Folies Bergère.

10th Arr. The Gare du Nord and Gare de l'Est are both in this commercial district. Movie theaters and porno houses often dot this area.

11th Arr. Increasingly fashionable, this is the site of place de la Bastille and the new Opéra Bastille. For many decades, it has been a working-class district, attracting immigrants from all over the world.

12th Arr. Very few tourists come here, but when a famous French chef opened the restaurant Au Trou Gascon *tout le monde* showed up (see "Paris Dining," Chapter 5). Its major attraction is the Bois de Vincennes, a popular patch of woodland with boating lakes, a racecourse, and a zoo. The Gare de Lyon is located here, too.

13th Arr. This primarily working-class district emerged around the famous Gobelins tapestries works (which can still be visited today—see Chapter 6). The Gare d'Austerlitz is a landmark.

14th Arr. Montparnasse, home of the "lost generation," is well known to tourists. Stein, Toklas, Hemingway, and other American expatriates gathered here in the 1920s. After World War II it ceased to be the center of intellectual life in Paris, but the memory lingers on in its cafés.

15th Arr. Beginning at Gare Montparnasse, the 15th stretches all the way to the Seine. In landmass and population, it's the largest quartier of Paris, but it attracts few tourists and has few attractions, except for the Parc des Expositions and the Institut Pasteur. In the early 20th century, many artists—Chagall, Léger, and Modigliani—lived in this arrondissement in "The Beehive."

16th Arr. Originally the village of Passy, where Benjamin Franklin lived during most of his time in Paris, this district is still reminiscent of Proust's world. Highlights include the Bois de Boulogne; the Jardin du Trocadéro; the Musée de Balzac, the Musée Guimet (famous for its Asian collections); and the Cimetière de Passy, resting place of Manet, Talleyrand, Giraudoux, and Debussy.

17th Arr. Although partly in the 8th, Parc Monceau flows into the 17th. This is the home of the Palais des Congrès and Porte Maillot Air Terminal.

18th Arr. The 18th is the most famous outer *quartier* of Paris, embracing Montmartre, associated with such legendary names as the Moulin Rouge, the Basilica of Sacré-Coeur, and the place du Tertre. Utrillo was its native son, Renoir lived here, and Toulouse-Lautrec adopted the area as his own. The most famous enclave of artists in Paris, the Bateau-Lavoir, of Picasso fame, gathered here. Max Jacob, Matisse, and Braque all came and went from here.

Today, place Blanche is known for its prostitutes, and Montmartre is filled with honky-tonks and terrible restaurants. Go for the attractions and the *mémoires*. The most famous flea market, Marché aux Puces de St-Ouen, is another landmark.

19th Arr. Today, visitors come to what was once the village of La Villette to see the new Cité des Sciences et de l'Industrie, a spectacular science museum and park. The district also includes Les Buttes–Chaumont, a park where kids can enjoy puppet shows and donkey rides.

20th Arr. Its greatest landmark is Père-Lachaise Cemetery, resting place of Edith Piaf, Marcel Proust, Oscar Wilde, Isadora Duncan, Sarah Bernhardt, Gertrude Stein, Colette, and many, many others.

MAPS

If you're staying more than two or three days, purchase an inexpensive, pocket-size book that includes the "plan de Paris" by arrondissement available at all major newsstands and bookshops. Most of these guides provide you with a Métro map, a foldout map of the city, and indexed maps of each arrondissement, with all streets listed and keyed.

2. GETTING AROUND

Paris is a city for strollers whose greatest joy in life is rambling through unexpected alleyways and squares. Given a choice of conveyance, make it your own two feet whenever possible. Only when you're dead tired and can't walk another step, or in a roaring hurry to reach an exact destination, should you consider the following swift and prosaic means of urban transport.

BY PUBLIC TRANSPORTATION

DISCOUNT PASSES You can purchase a *Le Paris-Visite* pass, a tourist pass valid for three or five days on the public transportation system, including the Métro, city buses, even RER (Réseau Express Régional) trains. (The RER has both first- and second-class compartments, and the pass lets you travel in first class.) As a special bonus, the funicular ride to the top of Montmartre is also included. The cost is 90F ($15.80) for three days or 145F ($25.40) for five days. The card is available at RATP (Régie Autonome des Transports Parisiens), tourist offices, or at the main Métro stations.

There are other discount passes as well. *Formule 1,* costing 27F ($4.70) per day, is for travel on the Métro, buses, and RER trains within Paris. A *coupon vert* at 59F ($10.30) and a *carte orange* at 208F ($36.40) are also available. The former is good for a week of travel on all buses and the Métro, and the *carte orange* is good for a month. You'll need to produce an ID-type photo, however.

BY SUBWAY

The **Métro** (tel. 43-46-14-14 for information) is the most efficient

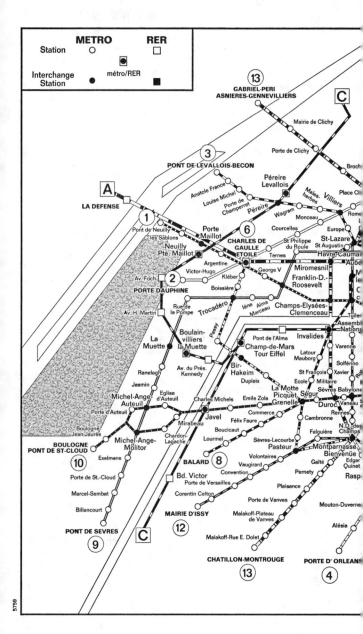

means of transportation, and it's easy to use. Each line is numbered and the final destination of each is clearly marked on subway maps, on the trains themselves, and in the underground passageways. Most stations display a map of the system at the entrance. Figure out the route from where you are to your destination, noting the stations where you will have to change. To make sure you catch the right train, find your destination, then

visually follow the line it's on to the end of the route and note its name. This is the *direction* you follow in the stations and see on the train. Transfer stations are known as *correspondances*. (Note that some require long walks—Châtelet is the most notorious.)

Most trips will require only one transfer. Many of the larger stations have maps with push-button indicators that will help you plot your route more easily by lighting up automatically when you press the button for your destination. A ride on the urban lines costs the same to any point.

On the Sceaux, the Noissy-St-Léger, and the St-Germain-en-Laye lines serving the suburbs, fares are based on distance. One ticket costs 16F ($2.80). A *carnet* (ticket book) is the best buy—or 10 tickets for 36.50F ($6.40).

At the turnstile entrances to the station, insert your ticket in the turnstile and pass through. At some exits tickets are checked, so hold on to your ticket. There are occasional ticket checks on the trains, platforms, and passageways, too.

If you are changing trains, get out and determine which *direction* (final destination) on the next line you want, and follow the bright-orange CORRESPONDANCE signs until you reach the proper platform. Don't follow a SORTIE sign, which means "exit," or else you'll have to pay another fare to resume your journey.

The Métro starts running daily at 5:30am and closes around 1:15am. It's reasonably safe at any hour, but beware of pickpockets.

BY BUS

Bus travel is much slower than the subway. Most buses run from 7am to 8:30pm (a few operate until 12:30am, and 10 operate during the early-morning hours). Service is limited on Sunday and holidays. Bus and Métro fares are the same and you can use the same *carnet* tickets on both. Most bus rides require one ticket, but there are some destinations requiring two (never more than two within the city limits).

At certain bus stops, signs list the destinations and numbers of the buses serving that point. Destinations are usually listed north to south, and east to west. Most stops along the way are also posted on the sides of the buses. To catch a bus, wait in line at the bus stop. Signal the driver to stop the bus and board in order. During rush hours you may have to take a ticket from the dispensing machine, indicating your position in the line.

If you intend to use the buses frequently, pick up a RATP bus map at the office on place de la Madeleine, 8e; at the tourist offices at RATP headquarters, 53 bis, quai des Grands Augustins, 75006 Paris, or write to them ahead of time. For detailed information on bus and Métro routes, call 43-46-14-14.

BY TAXI

It's impossible to get one at rush hour, so don't even try. Taxi drivers are organized into an effective lobby to keep their number limited to 14,300.

Watch out for the common rip-offs. Always check the meter to make sure you're not paying the previous passenger's fare. Beware of cabs without meters, which often wait for tipsy patrons outside nightclubs—always settle the tab in advance. Regular cabs can be hailed on the street when their signs read LIBRE. Taxis are easier to find at the many stands near Métro stations.

The flag drops at 16F ($2.80), and you pay 2.79F (50¢) per kilometer (.6 mile). At night, expect to pay 4.35F (80¢) per kilometer.

On airport trips you don't have to pay for the driver's empty return ride, but you'll pay 4.35F (80¢) extra to be taken to railroad stations.

You are allowed several small pieces of luggage free if they're transported inside and do not weigh more than 5 kilograms (11 lb.). Heavier suitcases carried in the trunk cost 6F ($1.10). Tip 12% to 15%—the latter usually elicits a *merci.* For radio cabs, call 42-41-50-50, 42-70-41-41, or 47-39-47-39, although you'll be charged from the point where the taxi begins the drive to pick you up.

BY CAR

Don't even think about driving a car in Paris. The streets are narrow and parking is next to impossible. Besides, most visitors don't have the nerve, skill, and ruthlessness required.

If you insist on ignoring my advice, here are a few tips: Get an excellent street map and ride with a copilot because there's no time to think at intersections. "Zone Bleue" means that weekdays and Saturdays you can't park without a parking disc, obtainable from garages, police stations, and hotels. Parking is unrestricted in these zones Sundays and holidays. Attach the disc to your windshield, setting its clock to show the time of your arrival. Between 9am and noon and from 2:30 to 5pm you may park for one hour, from noon to 2:30pm for 2½ hours.

Watch for the gendarmes, who lack patience and consistently countermand the lights. Horn-blowing is absolutely forbidden except in dire emergencies.

RENTALS The major car-rental companies usually try to match one another's price schedules and rental conditions. Of the major worldwide competitors, the cheapest weekly arrangements, as of this writing and subject to change, are offered by Budget and Hertz, followed (often in hot pursuit) by Avis and National. These relative advantages change (sometimes radically) as the type of car becomes more luxurious, but usually always the best deal is a weekly rental with unlimited mileage and an advance reservation *made from North America,* generally two business days in advance. Shop around before you commit yourself, knowing that it pays to ask questions. *Warning:* All car-rental bills in France are subject to an 18.6% tax, one of the highest in Europe. In some cases, the tax will be factored into the rate quoted to you over the phone. Be sure to ask.

Renting a car in Paris (and France) is easy. All you need is a valid driver's license, a passport, and (unless the rate is prepaid in dollars in North America) a valid credit card. Usually it isn't obligatory, but small companies may require an international driver's license as well. To rent the cheapest cars, Budget requires that drivers be at least 23; Hertz, at least 25; Avis and National, at least 21.

Unless it's already factored into the rental contract, an optional collision-damage waiver (CDW) carries an additional charge of 70F to 80F ($12.30 to $14) a day for the least expensive cars. Buying this additional insurance will usually eliminate all except 1,000F ($175) of your responsibility in the event of theft or accidental damage to the car. Because most newcomers are not familiar with local driving customs and conditions, it's a good idea to buy the

CDW, although certain credit-card issuers will compensate a renter for any accident-related liability to a rented car if the imprint of their card appears on the original rental contract.

At all four car-rental companies, the least expensive car will probably be either a Ford Fiesta, a Renault 5, a VW Polo, or a Fiat Uno, usually with manual transmission and few frills. Depending on the company and the season, prices may range from $170 to $225 per week, with unlimited mileage (but not including tax or CDW). Discounts are usually granted for rentals of two weeks or more. Automatic transmission is regarded as a luxury in Europe, so if you want it, you'll probably have to pay dearly for it. All of the agencies allow clients to prepay their rentals in U.S. dollars.

Budget Rent-a-Car (tel. toll free 800/527-0700) maintains about 30 locations inside Paris. Cars can be picked up in one French city and dropped off in another with no additional charge. Drop-offs in cities within an easy drive of the French border (including Geneva, Zurich, and Frankfurt, for example) incur no additional charges either; however, drop-offs in other non-French cities can be arranged for a surcharge. Its rates are among the most competitive and its cars well maintained, but be aware that Budget does not allow its French cars to be driven anywhere in Britain.

Hertz (tel. toll free 800/654-3001) maintains about 15 locations in Paris, including the city's airports. The company's main office is at 27 rue St-Ferdinand, 17e (tel. 45-74-97-39). Be sure to ask about any promotional discounts the company might be offering.

Avis (tel. toll free 800/331-1084) has offices at both city airports, as well as an inner-city headquarters at 5 rue Bixio, 7e (tel. 44-18-10-50), near the Eiffel Tower.

National Car Rental (tel. toll free 800/227-3876) is represented in Paris by Europcar, whose largest office is at 145 av. Malakoff, 16e (tel. 45-00-08-06). It also has offices at both of the Paris airports and at about a dozen other locations throughout the city. Any of its offices can rent you a car on the spot, but to qualify for the cheapest rates, it is usually best to reserve in advance from North America.

Gasoline Gasoline—or *essence,* as it's known in France—is extraordinarily expensive for the visitor who's used to North American prices. All except the cheapest European cars require an octane rating that the French classify as *super,* which costs around 5.65F ($1) per liter, which works out to around 21.35F ($3.70) per North American gallon. Depending on your car, you'll need either unleaded gasoline (*sans plomb*), or—less frequently—leaded gasoline (*avec plomb*). What this means is that filling up the tank of a medium-sized car can cost between $40 and $65. Plan your finances accordingly.

Driving Rules Everyone in the car, in both the front and back seats, must wear seat belts. Children under 12 must ride in the back seat. Drivers are supposed to yield to the car on their right, except where signs indicate otherwise, for instance, at traffic circles. If you violate the speed limits, expect a large fine. Speed limits are usually 130 kmph (80 mph) on expressways, about 100 kmph (60 mph) on major national highways, and 90 kmph (56 mph) on small country roads. In towns, don't exceed 60 kmph (37 mph).

Maps Before setting out from Paris on a tour of that city's environs, pick up a good regional map of the district you plan to explore. If you're visiting a town, ask at the local tourist office for a town plan. They are usually given away free.

For France as a whole, most motorists prefer the Michelin map 989. For regions, Michelin publishes a series of yellow maps that are quite good. Large travel bookstores in North America carry these maps, but they are commonly available in France and at lower prices. One useful feature of the Michelin map (in this age of congested traffic) is its designations of alternative *routes de dégagement,* which let you skirt big cities and avoid traffic-clogged highways.

Breakdowns/Assistance A breakdown is called *une panne* in France, and it is just as frustrating there as anywhere else. Call the police at 17, anywhere in France, and they will put you in touch with the nearest garage. Most local garages have towing services. If your breakdown should occur on an expressway, find the nearest roadside emergency phone box, pick up the phone, and put a call through. You'll be connected immediately to the nearest break-down service facility.

BY BICYCLE

To ride a bicycle through the streets and parks of Paris, perhaps with a *baguette* tucked under your arm, might have been a fantasy of yours since you saw your first Maurice Chevalier film. If the idea appeals to you, you won't be alone: The city in recent years has added many miles of right-hand lanes specifically designated for cyclists, and hundreds of bike racks. (When these aren't available, many Parisians simply chain their bike to the nearest available fence or lamp post.) Cycling is especially popular within Paris's larger parks and gardens.

One of the largest companies in Paris for renting a bicycle is the **Bicy-Club,** 8 place de la Porte-de-Champerret, 17e (tel. 47-66-55-92; Métro: Porte-de-Champerret); it maintains at least a half-dozen rental outlets within the parks and gardens of the Paris region, usually on weekends and holidays between March and November. Two of the company's most popular outlets include a kiosk behind the Relais du Rois, route de Suresnes, in the Bois de Boulogne, and another kiosk in the Bois de Vincennes near the entrance to the Parc Floral, near the Esplanade du Château. Rates are 25F ($4.40) per hour, or from 100F ($17.50) per day. Deposits from 1,000F to 2,000F ($175 to $350) must be posted. Bikes are rented July through September daily from 9am to 7pm; October through June, Monday through Friday, from 9am to 7pm, and on Saturday from 9am to 1pm and 2 to 7pm.

FAST FACTS: PARIS

Airport See "Arriving" above in this chapter.

American Express Offices are located at 11 rue Scribe, 9e (tel. 47-77-79-79), which is close to the Opéra (also the Métro stop). Hours are 9am–5:30pm Mon–Fri. The bank window is open Sat 9am–5pm, but you can't pick up mail until Mon. Other offices are at 5 rue de Chaillot, 16e (tel. 47-23-61-20; Métro: Alma-Marceau), 83 bis, rue de Courcelles, 17e (tel. 47-66-03-00; Métro: Courcelles), and 38 av. de Wagram, 8e (tel. 42-27-58-80; Métro: Ternes).

Area Code   Paris's telephone area code is 1, followed by the eight-digit number. No other provinces have area codes. However, to dial long distance anywhere within France, you must first dial 16.

Auto Clubs   The Association Française des Auto Clubs, 9 rue Anatole-de-la-Forge, 75017 (tel. 42-27-82-00), provides limited information to members of U.S. auto clubs such as AAA.

Babysitters   Institut Catholique, 21 rue d'Assas, 6e (tel. 45-48-31-70), offers a service with its students. The price is 32F ($5.60) an hour. The main office is open from 9am–noon and 2–6pm Mon–Sat only. **Tip:** It is advisable to verify that the sitter and your child speak the same language before you commit yourself.

Banks   American Express may be able to meet most of your banking needs. If not, banks in Paris are open 9am–4:30pm Mon–Fri. A few are open on Sat. Ask at your hotel for the location of the bank nearest to you. Shops and most hotels will cash your traveler's checks, but not at the advantageous rate a bank or foreign exchange office will give you, so make sure you've allowed enough funds for *le weekend*.

Bookstores   Paris has several English-language bookstores carrying American and British books and maps and guides to the city and other destinations. Try Brentano's, 37 av. de l'Opéra, 2e (tel. 42-61-52-50; Métro: Opéra), open Mon–Sat 10am–7pm; or Galignani, 224 rue de Rivoli, 1e (tel. 42-60-76-07; Métro: Tuileries), open Mon–Sat 10am–7pm. Most famous of all is Shakespeare and Company, 37 rue de la Bûcherie, 5e (no phone; Métro or RER: St-Michel). It's open daily 11am–midnight.

Business Hours   French business hours are erratic, as befits a nation of individualists. Most **museums** close one day a week (often Tues). They are generally closed on national holidays. Usually hours are 9:30am–5pm. Some museums, particularly the smaller and less-staffed ones, close for lunch from noon–2pm. Most French museums are open Sat; many are closed Sun morning but are open Sun afternoon. Again, refer to the individual museum listings. Generally, **offices** are open Mon–Fri 9am–5pm, but don't count on it. Always call first. **Stores** are open from 9 or 9:30am (often 10am) to 6 or 7pm without a break for lunch. Some shops, particularly those operated by foreigners, open at 8am and close at 8 or 9pm. In some small stores the lunch break can last three hours, beginning at 1pm.

Cameras and Film   See "Photographic Needs," below.

Car Rentals   See "Getting Around" above in this chapter.

Cigarettes   Bring in as many as Customs will allow if you're addicted to a particular brand, because American cigarettes are very expensive in France. A possible solution is to learn to smoke French cigarettes. Don't expect them to taste anything like your familiar brand, but you may acquire a liking for the exotic. One of the most popular French cigarettes is called Gauloise Bleu.

Climate   See "When to Go" in Chapter 2.

Currency   See "Information, Entry Requirements, and Money" in Chapter 2.

Currency Exchange   For the best exchange rate, cash your traveler's checks at banks or foreign-exchange offices, not at shops and hotels. Most post offices will also change traveler's checks or convert currency. Currency exchanges are also found at

Paris airports and train stations. One of the most central currency-exchange branches in Paris is at 154 av. des Champs-Elysées, 8e (tel. 42-25-93-33; Métro: George-V). It's open Mon–Fri 9am–5pm and Sat–Sun 10:30am–6pm. A small commission is charged.

Dentists If a toothache strikes you at night or in the early hours of the morning (and doesn't it always?), telephone 43-37-51-00 anytime 8pm–8am Mon–Fri. On Sat, Sun, and holidays, you can call this number day or night. You also can call or visit the American Hospital, 63 bd. Victor-Hugo, Neuilly (tel. 46-41-25-25). A bilingual (English-French) dental clinic is on the premises. Métro: Pont de Levallois or Pont de Neuilly. Bus: 82.

Doctors Some large hotels have a doctor attached to their staff. If yours doesn't, I recommend the American Hospital, 63 bd. Victor-Hugo, Neuilly (tel. 46-41-25-25). The emergency room is open 24 hours daily with 43 outpatient and inpatient specialists housed under one roof. Métro: Pont de Levallois or Pont de Neuilly. Bus: 82.

Documents Required See "Information, Entry Requirements, and Money" in Chapter 2.

Driving Rules See "Getting Around" above in this chapter.

Drug Laws A word of warning: Penalties for illegal drug possession in France are more severe than those in the United States or Canada. You could go to jail or be deported immediately. By law, the police can stop you and search you at will. *Caveat:* Drug pushers often turn in their customers to the police.

Drugstores Go to the nearest *pharmacie*. If you need a prescription during off-hours, have your concierge get in touch with the nearest Commissariat de Police. An agent there will have the address of a nearby pharmacy open 24 hours a day. French law requires that the pharmacies in any given neighborhood designate which one will remain open all night. The address of the one that will stay open for that particular week will be prominently displayed in the windows of all other drugstores. One of the most centrally located pharmacies is 24-hour Pharmacy les Champs, 84 av. des Champs-Elysées, 8e (tel. 45-62-02-41). Métro: George-V.

Electricity In general, expect 200 volts, 50 cycles, although you'll encounter 110 and 115 volts in some older establishments. Adapters are needed to fit sockets. Many hotels have two-pin (in some cases, three-pin) sockets for electric razors. It's best to ask at your hotel before plugging in any electrical appliance.

Embassies and Consulates If you lose your passport or have some such emergency, the consulate can usually handle your individual needs. An embassy is more often concerned with matters of state between France and the home country represented. Hours and offices of the various foreign embassies and consulates follow. **United States:** The embassy at 2 av. Gabriel, 75008 Paris (tel. 42-96-12-02), is open Mon–Fri 9am–6pm. Passports are issued at its consulate at 2 rue St-Florentine (tel. 42-96-12-02, ext. 2531), which is situated off the northeast section of place de la Concorde (Métro: Concorde). To get a passport replaced costs $55. In addition to its embassy and consulate in Paris, the United States also maintains the following consulates: 22 cours du Maréchal-Foch, 33080 Bordeaux (tel. 56-52-65-95); 12 bd. Paul-Peytral, 13286 Marseille (tel. 91-54-92-00); and 15 av. d'Alsace, 67082 Strasbourg (tel. 88-35-31-04). **Canada:** The embassy is at 35 av. Montaigne, 75008 Paris (tel. 44-43-29-00), open Mon–Fri 9am–noon and

2–5pm. The Canadian consulate is located at the embassy (Métro: F. D. Roosevelt or Alma-Marceau). **Great Britain:** The embassy is at 35 rue du Faubourg St-Honoré, 75383 Paris (tel. 42-66-91-42), open Mon–Fri 9:30am–1pm and 2:30–6pm (Métro: Concorde or Madeleine). The U.K. consulate is at 9 av. Hoche (tel. 42-66-91-42), near Parc Monceau (Métro: Charles-de-Gaulle–Etoile). Hours are Mon–Fri 9am–noon and 2–5pm. **Australia:** The embassy is at 4 rue Léonard-de-Vinci, 75016 Paris (tel. 45-00-24-11), open Mon–Fri 9am–1pm and 2:30–5:30pm (Métro: Victor-Hugo).

Emergencies For the police, call 17, to report a fire, 18. For an ambulance, call the fire department at 45-78-74-52; a fire vehicle rushes cases to the nearest emergency room. S.A.M.U. (tel. 45-67-50-50) is an independently operated, privately owned ambulance company. You can reach the police at 9 bd. du Palais, 4e (tel. 42-60-33-22; Métro: Cité).

Etiquette If you make a reservation at a restaurant, keep it or call in good time to cancel. Always refer to your waiter as *"monsieur,"* not *"garçon."* When entering a shop or café, nod and greet strangers with a "Monsieur" or "Madame." Be aware of your voice level in public places—the French are. Refrain from smoking between courses in restaurants. Avoid discussing money, salaries, size of houses, and horsepower of U.S. cars compared with French cars. Discussions about World War II, the Algerian revolution, religion, or politics can sometimes spark violent controversy, especially at gatherings of extended families.

Eyeglasses Lissac Brothers (Frères Lissac) is one of the city's largest chains, with at least 18 branches in greater Paris. On the Right Bank, go to 112–114 rue de Rivoli, 1e (tel. 42-33-44-77; Métro: Châtelet), and on the Left, to 207 bd. St-Germain, 7e (tel. 45-48-16-76; Métro: Rue du Bac). There's a surcharge for same-day service. Always carry an extra pair.

Hairdressers and Barbers In France, they're known as *coiffeurs.* One of the best is Alexandre de Paris, 3 av. Matignon, 8e (tel. 42-25-57-90; Métro: F. D. Roosevelt). Everybody from crowned heads to French film stars comes here for that elegant look. Always call for an appointment. Harlow, 24 rue St-Denis, 1er (tel. 42-33-61-36; Métro: Châtelet), is also good. As one satisfied customer put it, "Harlow is with it and yet not too far out." The team specializes in coiffeurs calling for minimum care. An appointment is needed.

Holidays See "When to Go" in Chapter 2.

Hospitals The American Hospital, 63 bd. Victor-Hugo, Neuilly (tel. 46-41-25-25), operates 24-hour emergency service. The direct line to its emergency service is 47-47-70-15. Métro: Pont de Levallois or Pont de Neuilly. Bus: 82.

Hot Lines See "Networks and Resources," below.

Information See "Information, Entry Requirements, and Money" in Chapter 2.

Language In the wake of two world wars and many shared experiences, not to mention the influence of English-language movies, TV, and records, the English language has made major inroads and is almost a second language in some parts of Paris. An American trying to speak French might even be understood. The world's best-selling phrase books are published by Berlitz—*French for Travelers* has everything you'll need.

Laundry and Dry Cleaning Ask at your hotel for the nearest laundry or dry-cleaning establishment. Expensive hotels provide this service, but it costs. Instead, consult the yellow pages under *laveries automatiques*. For dry cleaning, look under *nettoyage à sec*. If you're staying in the Latin Quarter, take your clothes for cleaning or pressing to Moderne des Ecoles, 34 rue des Ecoles, 5e (tel. 46-33-47-13, Métro: Maubert-Mutualité), open Mon–Sat 8:30am–7:30pm. Another well-located laundry in the same quarter is St-Germain Lav' Club, 9 rue Lobineau, 6e (Métro: Mabillon). Don't call—just show up, dirty laundry in hand. It's open daily 7am–10pm.

Libraries There are many. The American Library, 10 rue du Général Camou, 7e (tel. 45-51-46-82; Métro: Alma-Marceau), founded in 1920, allows nonmembers to read for 50F ($8.80) per day. Bibliothèque Publique Information, Centre Pompidou, place Georges-Pompidou, 4e (tel. 44-78-12-33; Métro: Rambuteau), has books in English. There are also records, videos, CDs, a software library, and a data-base service. You can read on the premises but can't check out books. Hours are Mon and Wed–Fri noon–10pm, Sat–Sun 10am–10pm. Closed Tues.

Legal Aid This may be hard to come by in Paris. The French government advises foreigners to consult their embassy or consulate (see "Embassies and Consulates," above) in case of a dire emergency, such as an arrest. Even if a consulate or embassy declines to offer financial or legal help, they will generally offer advice as to how you can obtain help locally. For example, they can furnish a list of attorneys who might represent you. Most arrests are for illegal possession of drugs, and the U.S. embassy and consulate officials cannot interfere with the French judicial system in any way on your behalf. A consulate can only advise you of your rights.

Liquor Laws Visitors will find it easier to get a drink—wine, beer, or other spirits—in France than in England or some other countries. Supermarkets, grocery stores, and cafés sell alcoholic beverages. The legal drinking age is 16. Persons under that age can be served an alcoholic drink in a bar or restaurant if accompanied by a parent or legal guardian. Wine and liquor are sold every day of the week all year round.

Hours of cafés vary throughout the country and with local restrictions. Some open at 6am, serving drinks until 3am; others are open 24 hours a day. Bars and nightclubs may stay open as they wish.

The Breathalyzer test is in use in France, and a motorist is considered "legally intoxicated" with 0.8 grams of alcohol per liter of blood. (The more liberal U.S. law is 1 gram per liter.) If convicted, a motorist faces a stiff fine and a possible prison term of two months to two years. If bodily injury results, the judge might throw the book at a convicted person.

Lost Property Frankly, there isn't much chance of retrieving lost property in Paris. Go to (don't call) the Bureau des Objets Trouvés, 36 rue des Morillons, 15e (tel. 45-31-14-80; Métro: Convention), open Fri–Mon 8:30am–5pm, Tues–Thurs 8:30–8pm, and Wed 8:30am–5pm.

Luggage Storage and Lockers Your best bet is your hotel, especially if you plan to return to Paris after a tour of the provinces. Otherwise try the *consignes* at the railroad stations.

Mail Most post offices in Paris are open Mon–Fri 8am–7pm and Sat 8am–noon. Allow five to eight days to send or receive mail from your home. To send an *aerogramme* to the U.S. or Canada costs 4.20F (70¢). To send a letter weighing 20 or 30 grams (about an ounce) costs 6.90F ($1.20). A postcard to the U.S. or Canada is 3.70F (60¢). Letters to the U.K. cost 2.50F (40¢) for up to 20 grams.

If you don't have a hotel address in Paris, you can receive mail c/o American Express (see above). However, you may be asked to show an American Express card or traveler's check when you go to pick up your mail.

Another option is to send your mail *poste restante* (general delivery) in care of the major post office in whatever town you plan to visit. You'll need to produce a passport to pick up mail, and you may be charged a small fee for the service. You can also exchange money at post offices.

Many hotels sell stamps.

Maps See "Getting Around" above in this chapter.

Medical Emergencies If you are ill and need medicine at night and on Sun, the local Commissariat de Police will tell you the location of the nearest drugstore that's open or the address of the nearest doctor on duty. The police or fire department will also summon an ambulance if you need to be rushed to a hospital. Seek assistance first at your hotel desk if language is a problem. Or call the "hot line" (tel. 47-47-70-15) of the American Hospital (see "Hospitals," above).

Money See "Information, Entry Requirements, and Money" in Chapter 2.

Newspapers and Magazines English-language newspapers are available at nearly every kiosk (newsstand) in Paris. Published Mon through Sat, the *International Herald-Tribune* is the most popular paper with visiting Americans and Canadians. Kiosks are generally open daily 8am–9pm.

Passports See "Information, Entry Requirements, and Money" in Chapter 2.

Pets If you have certificates from a vet and proof of antirabies vaccination, you can bring most house pets into France.

Photographic Needs All types of film are available in Paris at fairly modest prices. Unless you're going to be in France for an extended period, I don't recommend that you process your film here, for it takes time. Ask at your hotel for the nearest camera shop.

Police Call 17. The principal prefecture is at 7 bd. du Palais, 4e (tel. 42-60-33-22; Métro: Cité).

Post Office The main post office (P.T.T.) for Paris is Bureau de Poste, 52 rue du Louvre, 75001 Paris (tel. 40-28-20-00; Métro: Louvre). Your mail can be sent here *poste restante* (general delivery) for a small fee. Take an ID, such as a passport, if you plan to pick up mail. It's open daily 8am–7pm for most services, 24 hours a day for telegrams and phone calls. Stamps can be purchased also at your hotel reception desk (usually) and at *café-tabacs* (tobacconists).

Radio and TV The major TV channels in France are Antenne 2, TF1, FR3, La Cinq, and M6. All programs are broadcast in French. However, after a day of sightseeing, you might be able to catch a foreign film late at night in English with French subtitles. In the summer months, the domestic radio France-Inter broadcasts daily news and important traffic conditions in English. Broadcast times are (usually) 8am and 1 and 7pm. Short- or medium-wave radios allow you to tune in to BBC programs.

Religious Services France is a predominantly Roman Catholic country, and churches of this faith are found in every city and town. Many churches in Paris conduct services in English: The interdenominational American Church in Paris, 65 quai d'Orsay, 7e (tel. 47-05-07-99; Métro: Invalides); the First Church of Christ, Scientist, 36 bd. St-Jacques, 14e (tel. 47-07-26-60; Métro: St-Jacques); Second Church of Christ, Scientist, 58 bd. Flandrin, 16e (tel. 45-04-37-74; Métro: Dauphine); and the Third Church of Christ, Scientist, 45 rue La Boétie, 8e (tel. 45-62-19-85; Métro: St-Augustin). The Great Synagogue is at 44 rue de la Victoire, 9e (tel. 42-85-71-09; Métro: La Peletier). An English-speaking Roman Catholic church is St. Joseph's, 50 av. Hoche, 8e (tel. 42-27-28-56; Métro: Charles-de-Gaulle–Etoile).

Restrooms If you are in dire need, duck into a café or brasserie to use the lavatory. It's customary to make some small purchase if you do so. Paris Métro stations and underground garages usually have public lavatories, but the degree of cleanliness varies. France still has many "hole-in-the-ground" toilets, so be forewarned.

Safety Whenever you're traveling in an unfamiliar city or country, stay alert. Be aware of your immediate surroundings. Wear a moneybelt and keep a close eye on your possessions. Be particularly careful with cameras, purses, and wallets, all favorite targets of thieves and pickpockets.

In Paris, be especially aware of child pickpockets. They roam the French capital, preying on tourists around sights such as the Louvre, Eiffel Tower, and Notre-Dame, and they usually like to pick your pockets in the Métro, sometimes blocking you off from the escalator. A band of these young thieves can clean your pockets even while you try to fend them off. Their method is to get very close to a target, ask for a handout (sometimes), and deftly help themselves to your money or passport.

Shoe Repairs Ask at your hotel for a nearby repair shop or try Central Crepins, 48 rue de Turbigo, 3e (tel. 42-72-68-64; Métro: Etienne-Marcel), which performs at least some of its sewing by hand and does very competent repair work. It's open Mon–Fri 8am–2:30pm and 3:30–7pm Sat 8am–1pm. Or try La Cordonnerie Pulin, 5 rue Chaveau-LaGarde, 8e (tel. 42-65-08-57; Métro: Madeleine), open Mon–Sat 9am–7pm.

Taxes Watch it: You could get burned. As a member of the European Community, France routinely imposes a value-added tax (VAT) on many goods and services—currently 6% or 33.3%. You can get a tax refund on purchases over 2,000F ($350). Ask the shopkeepers to make out an export sales invoice (*bordereau*), which you show to the French Customs officer when you leave the country (at the airport, on the train, at the highway border post). In a number of weeks the shop will send you a check for the amount of the refund. Not all shops participate in the program. Ask before you buy.

Taxis See "Getting Around" above in this chapter.

Telegrams, Telex, and Fax Telegrams may be sent from any Paris post office during the day (see "Post Office," above) and anytime from the 24-hour central post office. In sending telegrams to the United States, the address is counted in the price, there are no special rates for a certain number of words, and night telegrams cost less. If you're in Paris and wish to send a telegram in English, call 42-33-44-11. The 24-hour public telex office in Paris is at 103 rue de Grenelle, 7e (tel. 45-50-34-34; Métro: Rue du Bac). By phone, you can dictate a telex by calling 42-47-12-12. You can also send telex and fax messages at the main post office in each arrondissement of Paris.

Telephone Public phone booths are found in cafés, restaurants, Métro stations, post offices, airports, and train stations and occasionally on the streets. Some of these booths work with tokens called *jetons,* which can be purchased at the post office or from the cashier at any café. (It's usually customary to give a small tip if you buy them at a café.) Pay telephones accept coins of ½, 1, 2, and 5F; the minimum charge is 1F (20¢). Pick up the receiver, insert the *jeton* or coins, and dial when you hear the tone, pushing the button when there is an answer. The French also use a *télécarte,* a telephone debit card, which can be purchased at rail stations, post offices, and other places. Sold in two versions, it allows callers to use 50 or 120 charge units by inserting the card in a phone booth. They cost 40F ($7) and 96F ($16.80), respectively.

If possible, avoid making calls from your hotel, which might double or triple the charges.

When you're calling long distance within France, dial 16, wait for the dial tone, and then dial the eight-digit number of the person or place you're calling. To reach Paris from one of the provinces, dial 16 and 1, then the eight-digit number. To call the U.S. or Canada, first dial 19, listen for the tone, then slowly dial 1, the area code, and the seven-digit number. To place a collect call to North America, dial 19-33-11, and an English-speaking operator will assist you. Dial 19-00-11 for an American AT&T operator.

For information, dial 12.

Television See "Radio and TV," above.

Time French summer time lasts from around April to September, and runs one hour ahead of French winter time. Depending on the time of year, France is six or seven hours ahead of eastern standard time in the United States.

Tipping Tipping is practiced with flourish and style in France, and, as a visitor, you're expected to play the game. All bills, as required by law, show *service compris,* which means the tip is included; customary practices of additional gratuities are as follows.

Cloakroom attendants: Often the price is posted; if not, give at least 2F to 4F (40¢ to 70¢).

Guides: In museums, guides expect 5F to 10F (90¢ to $1.80).

Hairdressers: The service charge is most often included; otherwise, tip at least 15%, more in swankier places.

Hotels: The service charge is added, but tip the bellboy extra—from 5F to 10F (90¢ to $1.80) per bag (more in deluxe and first-class hotels). A lot depends on how much luggage he has carried and the class of the establishment. Tip the concierge based entirely on how many requests you've made. Give the maid about 20F ($3.50) if you've stayed for three or more days. The doorman who summons a cab expects another 5F (90¢), likewise your room-service waiter, even though you've already been hit for 15% service.

Incidentally, most small services around the hotel should be rewarded with a 5F (90¢) tip.

Porters: Usually a fixed fee is assessed, about 5F to 10F (90¢ to $1.80) per piece of luggage. You're not obligated to give more; however, many French people do, ranging from 1F to 2F (20¢ to 40¢).

Theater Ushers: Give at least 2F (40¢) for seating up to two persons.

Waiters: In restaurants, cafés, and nightclubs, service is included; however, it is customary to leave something extra, especially in first-class and deluxe establishments, where 10% to 12% extra is often the rule. In inexpensive places, 8% to 10% will suffice.

Toilets See "Restrooms," above.

Transit Info For information on the city's public transportation, stop in at either of the two offices of the Services Touristiques de la RATP—at 53 bis, quai des Grands-Augustins, 6e (tel. 40-46-42-12; Métro: St-Michel), or at place de la Madeleine, 8e (tel. 43-46-14-14; Métro: Madeleine).

Useful Telephone Numbers Police, 17; fire, 18; emergency medical assistance, 15.

Visas See "Information, Entry Requirements, and Money" in Chapter 2.

Water Drinking water is generally safe, although it has been known to cause diarrhea. If you ask for water in a restaurant it will be bottled water (for which you'll pay) unless you specifically request tap water (*l'eau du robinet*).

Weather Call 36-69-00-00.

Yellow Pages As in North America, the yellow pages are immensely useful. Your hotel will almost certainly have a copy, but you'll need the help of a French-speaking resident before tackling the French Telephone Company's (PTT's) yellow pages.

Some words aren't too different from the English. *Pharmacie* (pharmacy), *antiquités* (antiques), *théâtres* (theaters), and *objets d'art* may be easy to decipher. But other words, such as *cordonniers* (shoemakers and shoe-repair shops) and *horlogerie* (watch-repair shop), might be less obvious. Ask someone at the reception desk of your hotel for translations if needed.

Don't ever assume that someone on the other end of the phone speaks English. You may have to ask a French-speaking person to make the call for you.

3. NETWORKS & RESOURCES

FOR STUDENTS One privately run establishment catering most of the year to students is the **Maison d'Etudiants J. de Ruiz de Lavison,** 18 rue Jean-Jacques Rousseau, 75001 Paris (tel. 45-08-02-10). It offers inexpensive lodgings for about 50 male students, ages 18 to 23, for three to six months during the scholastic year.

In summer, from late May to early October, it opens its doors to nonstudents, male and female, and houses them in simple rooms with one to four beds. (In summer, about 80 beds are available, and the minimum stay is reduced to three days.) With breakfast included, overnight rates are 120F ($21.60) per person per night. Advance reservations are essential. The building is owner-managed and has a small but charming garden in the back. Métro: Louvre.

From June through September, temporary housing (60 beds) for students, male and female, ages 18 to 26, is available at the **Association des Etudiants Protestants de Paris,** 46 rue de Vaugirard, 75006 Paris (tel. 43-54-31-49), on the Left Bank. They have a library and various cultural activities. Rates, including a continental breakfast and showers, are 68F ($11.90) daily in a dormitory (four to six beds), or 81F ($14.20) per person in a double. The single rate is 88F ($15.40) per person. In summer, bookings must be for a minimum of four weeks. Métro: Luxembourg, St-Sulpice, Odéon, or Mabillon.

FOR GAY MEN, LESBIANS & BISEXUALS "Gay Paree," with one of the world's largest homosexual populations, has dozens of clubs, restaurants, organizations, and services. Other than publications (see below), one of the best sources of information on gay and lesbian activities is **Maison des Homosexualités,** 25 rue Michel-le-Compte, 3e (tel. 42-77-72-77; Métro: Rambuteau); this cultural center is open Monday through Saturday from 3 to 8pm only. The Parisian gay hot line (English spoken) receives calls at 48-06-19-11 Monday through Friday from 6 to 10pm only.

Another helpful source is **La Maison des Femmes,** 8 Cité Prost, 11e (tel. 43-79-61-91; Métro: Charonne), offering information about Paris for lesbians and bisexual women. It sponsors Friday dinners from 8pm to midnight costing 50F ($8.75). Call for further information.

A publication, Gai Pied's *Guide Gai* (revised annually) is the best source of information on gay and lesbian clubs, hotels, organizations, and services—even restaurants. Women or bisexual women might also like to pick up a copy of *Lesbia,* to check ads if for no other reason. These publications and others are available at **Les Mots à la Bouche,** 6 rue Ste-Croix-de-la Bretonnerie, 4e (tel. 42-78-88-30), the leading gay and lesbian bookstore of Paris. Hours are Monday through Saturday from 11am to 11pm.

FOR WOMEN The leading feminist bookstore of Paris is **La Librairie des Femmes,** 74 rue de Seine, 6e (tel. 43-29-50-75; Métro: Odéon), open Monday through Saturday from 10am to 7pm. It features a vast collection of women's literature, much of it in English.

In 1993, the French government initiated a nationwide service for counseling women and children who have experienced domestic violence. This **Numéro Violence Conjugale** (tel. 40-02-02-33) is staffed Monday to Friday from 10am to 8pm. Someone there can refer callers to additional women's services within France's individual **départements.** The country's rape crisis center is **SOS Viol** (tel. 05-05-95-95), which offers counseling and both legal and medical advice Monday through Friday from 10am to 6pm.

PARIS ACCOMMODATIONS

Paris offers more than 1,500 hotels—of which a handful at the top of the price scale are world famous. But many modest hotels also provide decent value. Their only drawback is that they are well known among shrewd travelers and are likely to be booked, especially in summer. I suggest reserving rooms a full month in advance at *any* time of the year and as far as six weeks ahead during the busiest season from early May through mid-October. You may want to send a one-night deposit just to be sure.

The majority of Parisian hotels share a common problem—noise. I'd heartily recommend that late sleepers request rooms at the back of their hotel.

If you crave smartness in your surroundings, choose a Right Bank hotel. That puts you close to all the most elegant shops—Dior, Cardin, Saint-Laurent—and within walking distance of such important sights as the Arc de Triomphe, the place de la Concorde, the Tuileries Gardens, and the Louvre. And for relaxing after sightseeing during the day or for an apéritif at night, you have all the glittering cafés along the Champs-Elysées.

The best Right Bank hotels are in the 8th arrondissement, and many first-class ones are found in the 16th and 17th arrondissements. If you'd like to be near the place Vendôme, then try for a hotel in the 1st arrondissement.

Other Right Bank hotel sections include the increasingly fashionable Marais and Bastille districts, comprising the 3rd and 4th arrondissements, and Les Halles/Beaubourg, mainly in the 3rd arrondissement, which is the site of the Centre Pompidou and Les Halles shopping mall, site of the former marketplace of Paris.

If you'd like to live more informally with more of a flavor of the Latin Quarter, then head for the Left Bank, where prices are traditionally lower. Hotels here are mainly in the 5th and 6th arrondissements, which is the area of the Sorbonne, café life, and bookstores. Many hotels in this district cater to students. The 7th arrondissement provides a touch of the life of St-Germain.

If they were so inclined, the French could ask a riddle going something like "When is a hotel not a hotel?" The answer is when it's another kind of building. The world *hôtel* in French has several meanings. It means a lodging house for transients, of course, but it also means a large mansion or town house, such as the Hôtel des Invalides, once a home for disabled soldiers, now the most important military museum in the world. Hôtel de Ville means town hall; Hôtel des Postes refers to the general post office; and Hôtel-Dieu is a hospital. So watch that word.

It is important to remember that the last two numbers of the postal code indicate the arrondissement. A postal code of 75008 Paris means that the hotel lies in the 8th arrondissement; 75005 indicates the hotel is in the 5th arrondissement.

In general, the following price categories have been used: "Very Expensive," doubles from 2,600F ($455); "Expensive," 1,200F to 2,600F ($210 to $455); "Moderate," 800F to 1,200F ($140 to $210); "Inexpensive," anything under 800F ($140). *Note:* There are many exceptions to this general rule of thumb, however, since Paris hotels—especially the older ones—have a wide selection of different types of rooms, often at very different prices. Service and tax (value-added tax) are included in the rates unless otherwise specified. Hotels in France must also charge a tax ranging from 1F to 7F (18¢ to $1.20) per person per night for each room rented.

Hotel breakfasts are fairly uniform and include your choice of coffee, tea, or chocolate, a freshly baked croissant and roll, plus limited quantities of butter and jam or jelly. It can be at your door moments after you call down for it, and can be served at almost any hour requested. When a breakfast charge is given for an individual listing, it is always a continental breakfast. Breakfasts with eggs, bacon, ham, or other items will have to be ordered from the à la carte menu. For a charge, larger hotels serve the full breakfast—called "English breakfast"—but smaller hotels typically serve only the continental variety.

If you like bed-and-breakfast establishments in the United States, Canada, the United Kingdom, or even Scandinavia and Germany, this can be arranged in Paris as well, although you may have to use a booking agency. **Bed & Breakfast,** 7 rue Campagne Première, 74014 (tel. 43-35-11-26; fax 40-47-69-20), offers rooms in private homes (a two-day minimum); most homes are close to a Métro station. An attempt is made at personalized matching of hosts and visitors. With breakfast included, charges range from 250F to 360F ($43.80 to $63) for a single and from 290F to 460F ($50.80 to $80.50) for a double. Fully equipped apartments (two-week minimum) are also available, costing from 350F to 700F ($61.30 to $122.50) a day. A reservation fee of 50F ($8.80) per person is assessed. A VISA credit card is accepted.

1. 8TH ARRONDISSEMENT

VERY EXPENSIVE

HOTEL DE CRILLON, 10 place de la Concorde, 75008 Paris. Tel. 44-71-15-00. Fax 44-71-15-02. 120 rms, 43 suites. A/C MINIBAR TV TEL **Métro:** Concorde.

$ Rates: 2,450F–2,700F ($428.80–$472.50) single; 3,100F–3,950F ($542.50–$691.30) double; from 6,500F ($1,137.50) suite. Breakfast 140F ($24.50) extra. AE, DC, MC, V.

The Crillon offers the most dramatic setting in Paris, overlooking the place de la Concorde, where the guillotine claimed the lives of such celebrated victims as Louis XVI,

Marie Antoinette, Madame du Barry, Madame Roland, and Charlotte Corday. Designed by the famed Gabriel, the building was the former home of the duke of Crillon. Although more than 200 years old, it has been a hotel only since 1909. As such, it accommodated Woodrow Wilson during his stay in Paris following World War I. More recent guests have included Meryl Streep, Tom Cruise, Madonna, and Debra Winger.

The colonnaded exterior is so discreet you won't think it is a hotel at first—it rather looks like the headquarters of a governmental minister. The hotel encircles a large, formal courtyard, one of the ideal places in Paris for those of refined taste to order afternoon tea. The formal 18th-century courtyard is surrounded by flowers and plants.

Massively restored, the hotel still evokes the 18th century, with parquet floors, crystal chandeliers, sculpture, 17th- and 18th-century tapestries, gilt moldings, antiques, and paneled walls. If you get a room at the front, you'll be treated to a view of one of the most beautiful plazas in the world. Tranquillity seekers should ask for a room opening onto an inner courtyard. The rooms, for the most part, are generous in size and classically furnished. All the bathrooms are fresh and well maintained, lined with travertine or pink marble.

Dining/Entertainment: Guests can dine at the elegant Les Ambassadeurs, or the more informal L'Obélisque. Les Ambassadeurs offers a businessperson's lunch Monday to Friday only, priced at 330F ($57.80). The *menu dégustation* is served at lunch on weekends and every evening, and costs 590F ($103.30). At L'Obélisque, the fixed-price menu is 250F ($43.80).

Services: 24-hour room service, secretarial and translation services.

Facilities: Meeting and conference rooms, garden-style courtyard with restaurant service, elevators, shops.

GEORGE V, 31 av. George V, 75008 Paris. Tel. 47-23-54-00. Fax 47-20-40-00. 245 rms, 53 suites. A/C MINIBAR TV TEL **Métro:** George-V.
$ Rates: 2,345F–2,650F ($410.40–$463.80) single; 2,910F–3,925F ($509.30–$686.90) double; from 5,700F ($997.50) suite. Breakfast 120F–($21) extra. AE, DC, MC, V.

The George V is affectionately called "George Sank" by the bustling expense-accounters who crown its ornate lobby. Midway between the Champs-Elysées and the Seine, it is luxurious (reportedly, the management keeps a "black file" on the mysterious "whims and preferences" of its habitués) and often is referred to as "the French Waldorf-Astoria." The service is excellent, beginning with registration at the Empire-style reception desk and continuing in your room, where you just press a buzzer and servants attend to your every whim.

The public lounges are adorned with tapestries and 100- and 200-year-old paintings. Inlaid marble walls in the Pompeian style add a touch of staid dignity. The preferred rooms overlook the courtyard; those with terrace balconies are also the height of perfection. The hotel is now a far cry from what it was in 1944, when General Eisenhower made it his headquarters during the liberation of Paris.

Dining/Entertainment: In good weather, haute cuisine luncheons are served in the courtyard's garden-style outdoor café/restaurant.

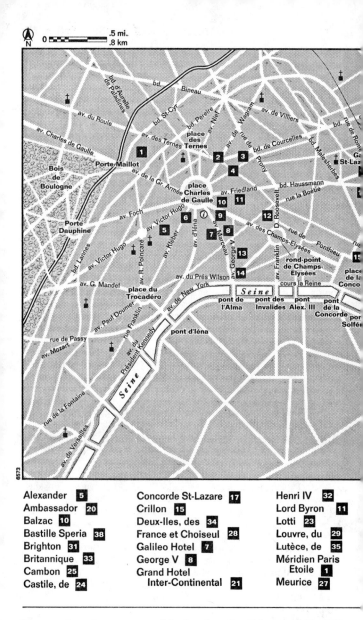

The two formal restaurants of the hotel are Les Princes and Le Grill. The cheapest fixed-price menu at Les Princes begins at 350F ($61.30), and à la carte meals at Le Grill start at 180F ($31.50).

Services: Concierge, 24-hour room service, CBS news service, in-room movies, laundry, valet.

Facilities: Beauty salon, seven conference rooms, tearooms, florist, gift shop.

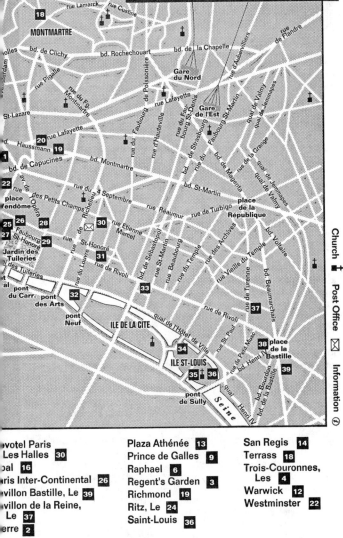

Church ✝   Post Office ⊠   Information ⓘ

ovotel Paris
  Les Halles **30**
oal **16**
aris Inter-Continental **26**
villon Bastille, Le **39**
villon de la Reine,
  Le **37**
erre **2**

Plaza Athénée **13**
Prince de Galles **9**
Raphael **6**
Regent's Garden **3**
Richmond **19**
Ritz, Le **24**
Saint-Louis **36**

San Regis **14**
Terrass **18**
Trois-Couronnes,
  Les **4**
Warwick **12**
Westminster **22**

**PLAZA ATHENEE, 23–27 av. Montaigne, 75008 Paris. Tel.
47-23-78-33.** Fax 47-20-20-70. 211 rms, 42 suites. A/C MINIBAR
TV TEL **Métro:** F. D. Roosevelt.

$ Rates: 2,660F ($465.50) single; 2,920F–3,330F ($511–$582.80)
double; from 6,270F ($1,097.30) suite. Breakfast 120F ($21) extra.
AE, DC, MC, V.

⭐ The Plaza Athénée was known to Mata Hari; it's also been
known to about half of all the visiting celebrities of Paris.

Between the Seine and the Champs-Elysées, it is a veritable palace of gilded luxury set in the midst of embassies (the rich ones) and the temples of haute couture, from which it draws many of its guests. It is said that there are two employees for each guest in this citadel dedicated to the good life. Arched windows and ornate balconies evoke the pre–World War I style. A liveried attendant stands under a glass shelter waiting to help you out of your taxi. When you check in, the reception staff seats you at a Louis XVI marquetry desk that faces an antique Flemish painting.

The style of the hotel is exemplified by the Montaigne Salon, with its mellow wood-grain paneling and marble fireplace. In the courtyard, tables are sheltered by parasols, and climbing vines and borders of flowers add a touch of gaiety. The preferred bedrooms overlook this courtyard. The well-maintained units each have a private tile bath that is especially large, with double basins and shower. Other amenities such as ample closet space and taffeta draperies make the rooms elegant, comfortable places to stay.

Dining/Entertainment: Meals are an occasion. The preferred choice for dining is La Régence, a room of handsome hand-carved oak paneling, its large curvy-topped windows opening onto the garden courtyard. It is known for its lobster soufflé. With it bright colors and decoration, the Grill Relais Plaza is the meeting place of *tout Paris*, especially at lunch, drawing dress designers and personalities from the world of publishing, cinema, and art. The Bar Anglais is a favorite spot for a late-night drink (it's open until 1:30am).

Services: 24-hour room service, concierge, laundry, Reuters telex with international stock quotes.

Facilities: Conference rooms, beauty parlor and hair dresser, massage parlor.

PRINCE DE GALLES, 33 av. George V, 75008 Paris. Tel. 47-23-55-11. Fax 47-20-96-92. 140 rms, 30 suites. A/C MINIBAR TV TEL **Métro:** George-V.

$ Rates: 2,000F–2,600F ($350–$455) single; 2,200F–2,800F ($385–$490) double; from 2,900F ($507.50) suite. Breakfast 95F ($16.60) extra. AE, DC, MC, V.

When this hotel was constructed in 1927, the cognoscenti of the era's social life adopted the Prince de Galles's art deco/neo-Byzantine courtyard as their preferred rendezvous spot. In the 1950s diarist and composer Ned Rorem recorded the trysts and trials of the "unapproachable innermost snob-life of Paris" that transpired within the hotel walls. Eras change but the allure of the "Prince of Wales" remains.

The hotel occupies a platinum location only a short stroll from the Champs-Elysées, the Arc de Triomphe, and the glamorous boutiques of the avenue Montaigne. Guests are greeted at the door with a smile by a team of uniformed attendants, who quickly arrange for baggage to be sent to one of the plushly upholstered, very spacious accommodations. A cluster of bench sofas and armchairs is grouped around bouquets of flowers, complementing the Regency detailing of the six-sided lobby.

Each of the high-ceilinged accommodations has an ultra-comfortable bathroom, the surfaces of which repeat the Edwardian/art deco tilework that so successfully adorns the hotel's facade. The elegantly furnished bedrooms are equipped with in-room movies, radios, and plenty of sunny space. A well-trained staff seems eager to respond to queries and requests, and to safeguard the complete privacy that many of this hotel's well-heeled guests demand.

Dining/Entertainment: The paneled bar, with its leather replicas of 18th-century armchairs, is one of the great hotel bars of Paris. The paneled dining room overlooks the garden-style courtyard, which has restaurant service.

Services: 24-hour room service, concierge, babysitting.

Facilities: Conference rooms, elevator, in-room movies.

EXPENSIVE

HOTEL BALZAC, 6 rue Balzac, 75008 Paris. Tel. 45-61-97-22. Fax 42-25-24-82. 70 rms. A/C MINIBAR TV TEL **Métro:** George-V.

$ Rates: 1,600F ($280) single; 1,830F ($320.30) double; 3,000F $525) suite. Breakfast 90F ($15.80) extra. AE, DC, MC, V.
Parking: 150F ($26.30).

Possibly the most successful renovation in this part of Paris, Hôtel Balzac opened late in 1985 in a neighborhood well acquainted with 19th-century grandeur.

When they created it, a team of French and Lebanese designers added well-studied touches of the best decors of England, Italy, and France to a sophisticated series of public rooms that include elements of art deco, Palladian revival, and neo-Byzantine. A recessed alcove in the lobby is covered with hand-painted tendrils and vines, which seem to grow into the white marble of a sun-flooded atrium. Kilim carpets, plum-colored upholstery, burnished paneling, and antique oil portraits add to the allure.

Accommodations are reached through a glass-walled elevator that glides past Turkish-patterned carpeting. Each bedroom is outfitted with a marble bathroom, thick upholstery, and tasteful decors.

Dining/Entertainment: The hotel's Italian restaurant, Bice, is recommended separately in Chapter 5.

Services: Laundry, 24-hour room service, babysitting.

HOTEL CONCORDE ST-LAZARE, 108 rue St-Lazare, 75008 Paris. Tel. 40-08-44-44, or 212/752-3900 in New York State, toll free 800/888-4747 in the U.S. and Canada; 071/630-1704 in London. Fax 42-93-01-20. 277 rms, 23 suites. A/C MINIBAR TV TEL **Métro:** St-Lazare.

$ Rates: 1,050F–1,350F ($183.80–$236.30) single or double; from 1,950F–2,450F ($341.30–$428.80) suite. Breakfast from 100F ($17.50) extra. AE, DC, MC, V. **Parking:** 100F ($17.50).

One of the most historic hotels in its neighborhood, the St-Lazare was originally built in 1889 as lodging for the thousands of visitors who flocked to Paris's *Exposition Universelle*. Situated across from the newly completed St-Lazare railway station (at the time, one of the world's busiest), the hotel combined easy access with some of the most richly ornate public rooms anywhere. Inspired by British and Spanish models, the hotel's architects designed a turn-of-the-century palace suited to the travel tastes of France's emerging merchant class. They combined gilded-age luxury with white marble, mirrors, Scottish granite, bronze, mosaics, a soaring ceiling, and the newfangled inventions of electricity and telephones.

In the 1990s, the St-Lazare's main lobby (a carefully protected historic monument) was richly restored under the supervision of the Concorde chain. The bedrooms were elevated to modern standards of maintenance and comfort, redecorated, and soundproofed. Today, the accommodations are elegant, high-ceilinged, very French, accented with flowered fabrics in tones of blue and yellow; and well cared for.

Dining/Entertainment: The hotel has a gilt-and-russet room worthy of J. P. Morgan, which is devoted exclusively to French billiards—the only room of its kind in any hotel in Paris. An American bar, Le Golden Black, bears Sonia Rykiel's signature decor of black lacquer with touches of gold and amber. The Café Terminus, accessible directly from the nearby railway station, bristles with turn-of-the-century accessories and daily brasserie service from noon to 11pm.

Services: 24-hour room service, babysitting, laundry/valet, concierge, currency exchange.

HOTEL SAN REGIS, 12 rue Jean-Goujon, 75008 Paris. Tel. 43-59-41-90. Fax 45-61-05-48. 33 rms, 12 suites. A/C MINIBAR TV TEL **Métro:** F. D. Roosevelt.

$ Rates: 1,525F–2,275F ($266.90–$398.10) single; 2,000F–2,275F ($350–$398.10) double; from 5,000F ($875) suite. Breakfast 100F ($17.50) extra. AE, DC, MC, V.

A fashionable town house until 1922, the San Régis is located in a neighborhood of embassies and exclusive boutiques (Christian Dior is across the street), enjoying, in a quiet and modest way, its position as one of the best hotels in Paris in its price bracket. It is right off the Champs-Elysées, and just a short walk from the Seine. Guests here find it much like a private club. There is a small and attentive staff that quickly learns your whims and fancies and makes you feel at home. Each room is unique and decorated with discretion and taste. All units have music and a private bath, a few have a separate sitting room, and many overlook a side garden. Thirty-five are air-conditioned.

Dining/Entertainment: The hotel has an elegantly decorated restaurant in the classic style, serving formal French cuisine. There is also a winter garden.

Services: 24-hour room service, laundry/valet, babysitting.
Facilities: Car-rental desk.

HOTEL LE WARWICK, 5 rue de Berri, 75008 Paris. Tel. 45-63-14-11. Fax 45-63-75-81. 127 rms, 21 suites. A/C MINIBAR TV TEL **Métro:** George-V.

$ Rates: 2,030F ($355.30) single; 2,560F ($448) double; from 3,020F ($528.50) suite. Breakfast 105F ($18.40) extra. Children under 12 stay free in parents' room. AE, DC, MC, V. **Parking:** 80F ($14.)

The Warwick, which opened in 1981, occupies a desirable location near the upper end of the Champs-Elysées. It is a bastion of comfort and convenience, with elegant, contemporary decor. Perhaps because it is owned by investors from Hong Kong, many of the lacquered accents in the public rooms are of deep Chinese red, alternating with mirrors and an abundance of plants. Even the young staff is attired, as is the establishment's facade, in shades of maroon.

About 30% of the bedrooms have evergreen-covered terraces with views of the Eiffel Tower and the 18th-century buildings across the street. Business travelers from North and South America, along with such celebrities as Boy George and Grace Jones, appreciate the soundproof windows; the opulent marble-covered baths; the bronze, bordeaux, and peach accents; the 24-hour video on the color TVs; and the attractively concealed minibars.

Dining/Entertainment: On the ground floor is the Swann Bar, named after the character in a literary work of Marcel Proust, with live piano music and views into the hotel's elegant restaurant, La Couronne.

Services: 24-hour room service, laundry and valet, babysitting.
Facilities: Limousine rentals, car rentals, shopping boutiques.

MODERATE

GALILEO HOTEL, 54 rue Galilée, 75008 Paris. Tel. 47-20-66-06. Fax 47-20-67-17. 27 rms (all with bath). A/C MINIBAR TV TEL **Métro:** George-V.

$ Rates: 800F ($140) single; 950F–980F ($166.30–$171.50) double. Breakfast 50F ($8.80) extra. AE, MC, V.

Located about two blocks from the Arc de Triomphe and a block from the Champs-Elysées, this is a streamlined, modern, and very comfortable 1992 restoration of a gracefully elegant older building. Its facade has all the neoclassical carved-stone details and ornate wrought iron you'd expect in the neighborhood, but the inside is well lit, warmly decorated, and comfortably modern. There's a small garden on the premises; the soothing color scheme inside consists of neutral ambers and beiges. Breakfast, served in the basement-level breakfast room, is the only meal offered.

RESIDENCE LORD BYRON, 5 rue de Chateaubriand, 75008 Paris. Tel. 43-59-89-89. Fax 42-89-46-04. 31 rms (all with bath), 6 suites. MINIBAR TV TEL **Métro:** George-V.

$ Rates: 650F–720F ($113.80–$126) single; 800F–900F ($140–$157.50) double; from 1,250F ($218.80) suite. Breakfast 50F ($8.80) extra. MC, V.

Just off the Champs-Elysées on a curving street of handsome buildings, the Lord Byron sports fine antique reproductions and framed prints of butterflies and of scenes in France. The bathrooms are as attractively decorated as they are functional. If you choose to have breakfast at the hotel, you can order it in the dining room or in a shaded inner garden. Six suites with two beds and two baths are available.

INEXPENSIVE

HOTEL OPAL, 19 rue Tronchet, 75008 Paris. Tel. 42-65-77-97. Fax 49-24-06-58. 36 rms (all with bath or shower). MINIBAR TV TEL **Métro:** Madeleine.

$ Rates: 465F–520F ($81.40–$91) single; 520F–575F ($91–$100.60) double. Breakfast 40F ($7) extra. AE, MC, V. **Parking:** 120F ($21).

In the heart of Paris, behind the Madeleine church and within an easy walk of the Opéra, this rejuvenated hotel is a real find. Decorated with style and taste, it offers entirely renovated but small bedrooms. Some people especially enjoy the closet-size bedrooms on the top floor, reached by a narrow staircase. These are really attic rooms, but some have skylights opening onto the rooftops of Paris.

2. 16TH & 17TH ARRONDISSEMENTS

VERY EXPENSIVE

RAPHAEL, 17 av. Kléber, 75116 Paris. Tel. 45-02-16-00, or toll free 800/223-5695 in the U.S. Fax 45-01-21-50. 53 rms, 35 suites. MINIBAR TV TEL **Métro:** Kléber/Charles de Gaulle–Etoile.
$ Rates: 1,600F–2,700F ($280–$472.50) single; 2,300F–3,900F ($402.50–$682.50) double; from 6,000F ($1,050) suite. Breakfast 110F ($19.30) extra. AE, DC, MC, V.

The Raphaël enjoys special patronage from the Italian-American movie world as well as other world celebrities. Near the Arc de Triomphe, it is an oasis of stately dignity. When you pay your bill, you can admire an original Turner (the orange-and gold painting to the right of the cashier). The tone of the hotel is set by the main hallway, with its dark-paneled walnut walls, oil paintings framed in gilt, and lavish bronze torchères. The rich wood paneling continues into the music salon, with its opera-red carpeting and marble fireplace. The bedrooms are impressive, luxuriously furnished with brass-trimmed chests, tables of inlaid wood, armoires, and silk draperies. Some units are air-conditioned. Prices depend on the view.

Dining/Entertainment: Be sure to have a meal in the formal dining room, La Salle à Manger, with its gold-and-red carpeting, white paneled walls, and arched windows with rich draperies, or enjoy your favorite drink in the wood-paneled English Bar.

Services: Room service, laundry, babysitting.

Facilities: Car-rental desk.

EXPENSIVE

LE MERIDIEN PARIS ETOILE, 81 bd. Gouvion-St-Cyr, 75017 Paris. Tel. 40-68-34-34. Fax 40-68-31-31. 989 rms, 17 suites. A/C MINIBAR TV TEL **Métro:** Porte Maillot.
$ Rates: 1,150F–1,450F ($201.30–$253.80) single or double; from 3,800F ($665) suite. Breakfast 85F ($14.90) extra. AE, DC, MC, V. **Parking:** 100F ($17.50).

The largest hotel in France, under the aegis of Air France, the Méridien is the first of its kind in Paris, opened in the '80s, catering to groups as well as to individuals. The location is opposite the air terminal at the Port-Maillot Métro stop on the Neuilly-Vincennes line. The setting of the hotel is contemporary French, and the overscale lobby chandelier is an eye-catcher. Bedrooms are designed to provide convenience and comfort, and often you get a good view as well.

Dining/Entertainment: The four restaurants feature everything from traditional French cuisine (Le Clos Longchamp) to Japanese specialties (Yamato). Other dining choices include La Maison Beaujolaise and Le Café Harlequin. There's a musical apéritif hour at 6pm and a 10pm jazz session at the Lionel Hampton Jazz Club.

Services: Laundry, babysitting, room service, express check-out.

Facilities: Foreign-currency exchange, business office with English-language secretarial services, photocopies.

MODERATE

ALEXANDER, 102 av. Victor-Hugo, 75016 Paris. Tel. 45-53-64-65. Fax 45-53-12-51. 57 rms (all with bath), 3 suites. MINIBAR TV TEL **Métro:** Victor-Hugo.

$ Rates: 830F–1,090F ($145.30–$190.80) single; 1,190F ($208.30) double; from 1,870F ($327.30) suite. Breakfast 70F ($12.30) extra. AE, DC, MC, V. **Parking:** 100F ($17.50) across the street.

This is really the perfect bourgeois hotel, the kind you might send an elderly relative to on a first trip to Paris. It's correct and conservative with a few elegant touches, such as chandeliers in each room. A wrought-iron stairwell winds around the elevator. Rooms are carpeted and rather frilly, half of them facing a well-planted, quiet courtyard. One-day laundry service is provided, and room service is available daily from 7am to 9pm.

HOTEL PIERRE, 25 rue Théodore-de-Banville, 75017 Paris. Tel. 47-63-76-69. Fax 43-80-63-96. 50 rms (all with bath), MINIBAR TV TEL **Métro:** Ternes.

$ Rates: 770F ($134.80) single; 830F ($145.30) double. Breakfast 60F ($10.50) extra. AE, DC, MC, V.

The Pierre was named as a facetious counterpoint to the owner's favorite North American hotel, the Pierre in New York City. To create it, the owners combined a trio of 19th-century buildings into a clean, modern hotel with art deco styling. Opened in 1986, it sits at the end of a residential street a short walk from the Arc de Triomphe. Each stylish accommodation has a TV with video movies, a safe with a combination lock, and is outfitted in restful shades of pastel.

HOTEL REGENT'S GARDEN, 6 rue Pierre-Demours, 75017 Paris. Tel. 45-74-07-30. Fax 40-55-01-42. 39 rms (all with bath). MINIBAR TV TEL **Métro:** Ternes or Charles-de-Gaulle–Etoile.

$ Rates: 660F–855F ($115.50–$149.60) single; 710F–960F ($124.30–$168) double. Breakfast 40F ($7) extra. AE, DC, MC, V. **Parking:** 50F ($8.80).

The Regent's Garden has a proud heritage: Napoléon III built this stately château for his physician. It's near the convention center and minutes from the Arc de Triomphe. There are two gardens, one with ivy-covered walls and umbrella tables—a perfect place to meet other guests. The interior resembles a country house with classic touches. The entryway has fluted columns, and the lobby has a casual mixture of comfortable furniture. The rooms are outfitted with French flower prints on the walls and bedspreads; the furniture is mostly traditional French. The tall French windows are soundproof and have light, airy curtains. Hairdryers are thoughtfully provided.

TIVOLI-ETOILE, 7 rue Brey, 75017 Paris. Tel. 42-67-12-68. Fax 47-64-01-21. 30 rms (all with bath). MINIBAR TV TEL **Métro:** Charles-de-Gaulle–Etoile.

$ Rates (including continental breakfast): 530F–730F ($92.80–$127.80) single; 575F–835F ($100.60–$146.10) double. AE, DC, MC, V.

Rue Brey is a side street branching off avenue de Wagram, one of the spoke avenues of the Etoile. This street has a number of moderately priced hotels (all of which seem to be full all year), but the

---

Ⓕ FROMMER'S COOL FOR KIDS: HOTELS

Novotel Paris Les Halles *(see p. 91)* Every room is suitable for a family "doubling up," and the location overlooks Les Halles shopping complex. Kids love the carousel there.

Hôtel le Warwick *(see p. 82)* For the affluent family seeking a smart Right Bank address, this first-class hotel is inviting. Management welcomes children (in English) and lets those under 12 stay free in their parents' room.

Hôtel de Castille *(see p. 88)* At this Right Bank address, near the place Vendôme and the place de la Concorde, baby cots are provided and babysitting can be arranged. Parents can walk with their children over to the Jardins des Tuileries for amusements.

Tivoli-Etoile offers the best value for its mid-city location. The hotel has a contemporary lobby with a mural and a quiet inner patio. The bedrooms are all equipped with radios, modern furnishings, hairdryers, and individual safes.

INEXPENSIVE

LES TROIS COURONNES, 30 rue de l'Arc de Triomphe, 75017 Paris. Tel. 43-80-46-81. Fax 46-22-53-96. 20 rms (all with bath). MINIBAR TV TEL **Métro:** Charles-de-Gaulle–Etoile.
$ Rates: 400F–590F ($70–$103.30) single or double. AE, DC, MC, V. **Parking:** 75F ($13.10).

This older hotel near the Etoile was renovated by Jean-Louis and Paul Lafont in 1983. The decor is a blend of art deco and art nouveau and includes personal objects they've collected over the years. A 19th-century carved oak mantelpiece flanked with bearded statues has been turned into a reception desk. There also are a narrow marble fireplace that came from a private house in Versailles and a winding staircase with a light forged-iron balustrade. An up-to-date security system protects the many treasures. Rooms are cheerfully decorated, with elmwood trim. An elevator takes you to a vaulted breakfast room. Laundry service is available.

---

3. 1ST ARRONDISSEMENT

VERY EXPENSIVE

HOTEL MEURICE, 228 rue de Rivoli, 75001 Paris. Tel. 44-58-10-10. Fax 44-58-10-15. 148 rms (all with bath), 36 suites. A/C MINIBAR TV TEL **Métro:** Tuileries or Concorde.
$ Rates: 2,200F ($385) single; 2,500F ($437.50) double; from 6,000F ($1,050) suite. Breakfast 130F ($22.80) extra. For stays of two or more nights (including breakfast): 1,800F ($315) single; 2,200F ($385) double; AE, DC, MC, V. **Parking:** 90F ($15.80)

The Meurice offers romantic 18th-century surroundings with a French aura. Its gilded salons were copied from those at the château at Versailles, complete with monumental crystal chandeliers, ornate tapestries, and furnishings from the periods of Louis XIV, XV, and XVI. Built in 1907, the hotel is just off rue de Rivoli and the Tuileries Gardens and within walking distance of the Louvre (you can see the Louvre from the upper floors). The lounge has a circular "star"-studded ceiling.

Rooms are soundproof and richly furnished with some period and modern pieces. Fit for a king, they are more likely to house diplomats, industrialists, and successful authors. The self-proclaimed "mad genius" Salvador Dalí made the Meurice his headquarters, occupying Suite 108, which was once used by the deposed and exiled king of Spain, Alfonso XIII. Suite 108 also served as the office of German General von Choltitz, who was in charge of Paris during the Nazi occupation.

Dining/Entertainment: The Meurice Restaurant serves true French haute cuisine. The Pompadour cocktail lounge is ideal for cocktails and tea, and the elegantly renovated Meurice Bar offers drinks in a warm atmosphere.

Services: 24-hour room service, telex, fax, "solve-everything" concierge, laundry/valet.

Facilities: Six meeting rooms, summer outdoor patio.

PARIS INTER-CONTINENTAL, 3 rue de Castiglione, 75001 Paris. Tel. 44-77-11-11, or toll free 800/327-0200 in the U.S. and Canada. Fax 44-77-14-60. 424 rms.

$ Rates: 2,000F–2,500F ($350–$437.50) single or double; from 3,100F ($542.50) suite. Breakfast 150F ($26.30) extra. AE, DC, MC, V.

The Inter-Continental is a mixture of French tradition, Gallic know-how, and 20th-century modernism. This belle époque hotel is along rue de Rivoli, across from the Tuileries Gardens. Opened in 1878 as "The Continental," it has welcomed many famous guests, including the Empress Eugénie of France and Jean Giraudoux. In 1883, Victor Hugo was the guest of honor at a luncheon. The great inner courtyard known as "La Cour d'Honneur" is paved with white marble, with a splashing circular fountain and an 1864 statue by Cunny.

The main lounge has Persian carpets, period furnishings, bronze sconces, and marble cocktail tables. The colonnaded front entrance has a pair of bronze candelabra from a palace in St. Petersburg. The rooms and suites are among the finest in Paris. The decor is classic French with many antiques, including Louis XVI reproductions. Each chamber has paneled walls, crystal, fine fruitwoods, bronze hardware, desks, and tables. A one-color theme creates a salon effect. A radio and in-room movies also are provided.

Dining/Entertainment: The Terrasse Fleurie is an elegant gourmet restaurant in the interior courtyard. It's landscaped to depict the four seasons. The belle époque Café Tuileries serves breakfasts, snacks, light meals, informal suppers, cocktails, and French pastries (open until midnight). In fair weather, luncheon, tea, and drinks are served in the courtyard under a canopy. There's also a coffee shop.

Services: 24-hour room service, concierge, secretarial service, fax, CNN news service.

Facilities: Conference rooms, underground parking, Jacuzzis in some suites.

LE RITZ, 15 place Vendôme, 75001 Paris. Tel 42-60-38-30.
Fax 42-60-23-71. 142 rms (all with bath), 45 suites. A/C MINIBAR TV TEL **Métro:** Opéra.

$ Rates: 2,450F–3,200F ($428.80–$560) single; 3,350F–4,150F ($586.30–$726.30) double; from 4,500F ($787.50) suite. Breakfast 170F ($29.80) extra. AE, DC, MC, V. **Parking:** 150F ($26.30)

⭐ The Ritz is the greatest hotel in Europe. This enduring symbol of elegance and chic is located on one of the most beautiful and historic squares in Paris. César Ritz, the "little shepherd boy from Niederwald," converted the Lazun Mansion into a luxury hotel that opened in 1898. With the help of culinary master Escoffier, the Ritz became a miracle of luxury living, attracting some of the great names of the world, including Edward VII of England.

In 1979 the Ritz family sold the hotel to Egyptian businessman Mohamed Al Fayed, who refurbished it and added a cooking school. Two town houses were annexed, joined by a long arcade lined with miniature display cases representing 125 of the leading boutiques of Paris. The hotel's drawing rooms, salons, three gardens, and courtyards were preserved. The salons are furnished with museum-caliber antiques: gilt pieces, ornate mirrors, Louis XV and Louis XVI furniture, hand-woven tapestries, and 10-foot-high bronze candelabra. The decor of the bedrooms is impeccably French, with wood and marble, antique chests, desks with bronze hardware, and crystal lighting. Every convenience imaginable has been installed.

Dining/Entertainment: The Espadon grill room is one of the finest in Paris. The Ritz Club includes a bar, a salon with a fireplace, a restaurant, and a dance floor. Drinks can be ordered amid the paneling and garden view of one of the world's most elegant bars, Le Bar Vendôme.

Services: Concierge, 24-hour room service, laundry, valet.

Facilities: Luxury health club with swimming pool and massage parlor, florist, shops, three meeting rooms.

EXPENSIVE

HOTEL CAMBON, 3 rue Cambon, 75001 Paris. Tel. 42-60-38-09. Fax 42-60-30-59. 43 rms (all with bath). A/C MINIBAR TV TEL **Métro:** Concorde.

$ Rates: 1,800F ($315) single; 1,480F–1,880F ($259–$329) double. AE, MC, V. Breakfast 75F ($13.10) extra. **Parking:** Nearby lot 150F ($26.30) per 24-hour period.

Conveniently located on a stylish street in the heart of Paris's monument zone, this stone-fronted 19th-century building recently was completely renovated with comfortable contemporary decor. The public rooms are richly furnished with 19th- and 20th-century sculptures and paintings, including the cozy street-level bar, where guests can usually converse with the genial owners, the Simeone family. Bedrooms are each individually decorated, usually with fabric wallcoverings, marble-sheathed bathrooms, and much exposed wood. The staff here seems especially helpful; many of them speak English.

HOTEL DE CASTILLE, 37 rue Cambon, 75001 Paris. Tel. 44-70-24-24, or toll free 800/949-7562 in the U.S., 0800/220761 in the U.K. 70 rms, 3 junior suites, 14 duplexes. A/C MINIBAR TV TEL **Métro:** Madeleine.

$ Rates: 1,300F–1,900F ($227.50–$332.50) single or double; 2,200F ($385) junior suite; 2,500F ($437.50) duplex suite. English breakfast 115F ($20.10) extra. AE, DC, MC, V. **Parking:** 150F ($26.30) extra.

Hôtel de Castille is a renovated hotel near the headquarters of Chanel and across the street from the "back door" of the Ritz. The Castille is quiet and only a few minutes' walk from place Vendôme, place de la Concorde, and place de la Madeleine. During fashion shows hotel prices rise and the rooms fill up quickly.

A series of beige marble panels and large mirrors, wall sconces, and a black-trimmed elevator bank grace the lobby area. The sunny rooms are painted in a variety of pastel colors and outfitted in a streamlined art deco style, featuring clean white baths with gray marble sinks.

Dining/Entertainment: Regional cuisine is served in the hotel's Italian restaurant, Il Cortile, opening onto a conservatory area. Two lunch menus are offered at 140F ($24.50) and 180F ($31.50), with a fixed-price dinner costing 180F ($31.50).

Services: 24-hour room service, shoe cleaning, secretarial services, babysitting, laundry and dry cleaning, doctor and dentist on request.

Facilities: No-smoking rooms, car rental.

HOTEL DE FRANCE ET CHOISEUL, 239 rue St-Honoré, 75001 Paris. Tel. 42-61-54-60. Fax 40-20-96-32. 104 rms (all with bath), 16 suites. MINIBAR TV TEL **Métro:** Concorde, Tuileries, Opéra, or Madeleine.

$ Rates: 900F ($157.50) single; 1,490F ($260.80) double; from 1,900F ($332.50) suite. Breakfast 90F ($15.80) extra. AE, DC, MC, V. **Parking:** 90F ($15.80).

The France et Choiseul is a remake of a gracious 1720 town house, just off the place Vendôme. Actually, it's been a hotel since the 1870s, and became a fashionable oasis in fin-de-siècle Paris. In the mid 1980s, it was completely remodeled. The bedrooms—most of which open onto the inner courtyard—were entirely gutted, then turned into bandbox-size accommodations that are, nevertheless, attractively decorated. All sorts of conveniences are offered as compensation for the lost belle époque glamour, including radios, dressing tables, and decorative tile baths with all the latest gadgets. A few minisuites have been installed on the top floor under the mansard roof, with a staircase leading up to twin beds on a balcony.

Dining/Entertainment: There is a charming salon, La Lafayette, opening onto the inner courtyard, on the site of the historic salon where Lafayette received the subsidies to participate in the American War of Independence. It serves breakfast only.

Services: Room service, babysitting, laundry/valet.

HOTEL LOTTI, 7–9 rue de Castiglione, 75001 Paris. Tel 42-60-37-34, or toll free 800/221-2626 in the U.S., 800/247-1277 in New York State, 800/237-0319 in Canada, 0800/282729 in the U.K. Fax 40-15-93-56. 131 rms, 2 suites. A/C MINIBAR TV TEL **Métro:** Opéra or Tuileries.

$ Rates: 1,400F–1,900F ($245–$332.50) single; 1,900F–2,600F ($332.50–$445) double; from 4,900F ($857.50) suite. Breakfast 120F ($21) extra. AE, DC, MC, V. **Parking:** 150F ($26.30).

Located just off the historic place Vendôme, the Lotti is known as a "junior Ritz." Inside its doors an elegant French world of marble and gilt, tapestries and crystal, unfolds. The bedrooms' decorators turned to the 19th century for inspiration, using reproductions of furnishings of that era. Rosewood and mahogany, gilt and silk damask, even tambour desks, re-create the ambience of an elegant town house bedroom. Some of the upper-story rooms were probably used at one time by servants of wealthy clients; each room has its own garret-like style.

Dining/Entertainment: The hotel has a distinguished restaurant, Le Lotti, serving classic French cuisine, with meals costing from 240F ($42).

Services: Laundry, babysitting, room service.

HOTEL DU LOUVRE, place André Malraux, 75001 Paris. Tel. 44-58-38-38, or toll free 800/888-4747 in the U.S. Fax 44-58-38-01. 178 rms, 22 suites. A/C MINIBAR TV TEL **Métro:** Louvre.

$ Rates: 1,200F–1,900F ($210–$332.50) single; 1,300F–2,000F ($227.50–$350) double; from 2,500F ($437.50) suite. Breakfast 90F–140F ($15.80–$24.50) extra. Midwinter promotions available, single or double, with breakfast included, 980F ($171.50). AE, DC, MC, V.

When this hotel was inaugurated in 1855 by Napoléon III, French journalists described it as "A palace of the people, rising adjacent to the palace of kings." In 1897 Camille Pissarro moved into one of its rooms, using the view to inspire many of his Parisian landscapes. Today, the hotel's aristocratic position between the Louvre and the Palais-Royal is one of the most disconcertingly centralized in Paris; its soaring marble, bronze, and gilt decor is a logical extension of the grandeur of the Right Bank monuments that flank it. The bedrooms are quintessentially Parisian—cozy, recently renovated, soundproofed against the roar of the outside traffic, and filled with souvenirs of *la belle époque.* Although the views of the inner courtyard have their own understated charm, the sweeping panoramas down the avenue de l'Opéra are among the best in the world.

Dining/Entertainment: Le Bar is a cozy, luxurious, and masculine hideaway, with mahogany trim, overtones of Scotland, an impeccably trained staff, and a worthy collection of single-malt whiskeys. A pianist plays after dusk. There's also an elegant bistro (La Brasserie du Louvre) designed in the style of the French Empire, whose tables extend during fine weather to the terrace beneath the hotel's sandstone arcades. A favorite of the neighborhood's business community, it serves elegant but rapid lunches, and more leisurely dinners, for around 160F ($28) each.

Services: Concierge, 24-hour room service, babysitting, laundry/valet, and tap water that is filtered before its arrival in the bathrooms.

Facilities: Business center with translation facilities, conference facilities.

MODERATE

HOTEL BRIGHTON, 218 rue de Rivoli, 75001 Paris. Tel. 42-60-30-03. Fax 42-60-41-78. 70 rms (all with bath or shower), 1 suite. MINIBAR TV TEL **Métro:** Louvre.

$ Rates (including continental breakfast): 465F–900F ($81.40–$157.50) single; 600F–935F ($105–$163.60) double; 1,380F ($241.50) suite. AE, DC, MC, V.

Despite its English name, the Brighton is a very French hotel, and a good one at that. You're in the heart of one of the major shopping streets of Paris, right across from the Louvre. In fact, if you're lucky enough to snare a front room, you'll look out on not only this world-famous art museum but the Tuileries as well. A scattering of accommodations open onto tiny balconies; on a clear day, you can see the Seine and the Eiffel Tower in the distance. Each of the clean, comfortable rooms is furnished in a traditional style, often with brass beds.

NOVOTEL PARIS LES HALLES, place Marguerite-de-Navarre, 75001 Paris. Tel. 42-21-31-31. Fax 40-26-05-79. 271 rms. 14 suites. MINIBAR TV TEL **Métro:** Les Halles.

$ Rates: 830F ($145.30) single; 900F ($157.50) double; 1,200F–1,500F ($210–$262.50) suite. Buffet breakfast 58F ($10.20) extra. AE, DC, MC, V.

Situated at the edge of the beaux-arts lattices of the place des Halles, this is one of the best Novotels in its worldwide network. Its cubist-inspired, mirror-sheathed facade and sloping skylights mimic the most daring of the Beaubourg neighborhood's futuristic architecture. Built in 1986, the hotel has a sunny lobby and a small-scale copy of the Statue of Liberty, along with an alluring and stylish bar on a dais above the ground floor.

Each room offers a no-nonsense but comfortable and efficient decor, with one double bed and one single (which can serve as a couch or a bed), and a streamlined private bath. All units have the same floor plan and furnishings, but the most sought-after rooms overlook Le Forum des Halles, with its fountains, shrubbery, and carousel. The greenhouse restaurant, Le Sun Deck, opens onto the ancient church of St-Eustace on the opposite side of the square.

INEXPENSIVE

BRITANNIQUE, 20 av. Victoria, 75001 Paris. Tel. 42-33-74-59. Fax 42-33-82-65. 40 rms (all with bath). MINIBAR TV TEL **Métro:** Châtelet.

$ Rates: 570F ($99.80) single; 680F–790F ($119–$138.30) double. Breakfast 50F ($8.80) extra. AE, DC, MC, V. **Parking:** 80F ($14).

After a complete renovation, the Britannique has been rated three stars by the government. It's in the heart of Paris, within easy reach of Les Halles, the Centre Pompidou, and Notre-Dame. The rooms are small but clean, comfortable, and adequately equipped. The TV satellite receiver picks up programs from the United States and United Kingdom.

BUDGET

HOTEL HENRI IV, 25 place Dauphine, 75001 Paris. Tel 43-54-44-53. 22 rms (none with bath). **Métro:** Pont-Neuf.

$ Rates (including continental breakfast): 105F–140F ($18.40–$24.50) single; 165F–195F ($28.90–$34.10) double. No credit cards.

Four hundred years ago the printing presses for the edicts of Henri IV filled this narrow building. Today the orderly rows of trees in the square outside help make this one of the loveliest locations in Paris. This hotel attracts a loyal clientele of budget-conscious academicians, journalists, and Francophiles. The low-ceilinged lobby, one flight above street level, is cramped and a bit bleak. But that is dispelled by the friendliness of Monsieur and Madame Maurice

Balitrand. The bedrooms, reached by a winding stairwell, saw better days under Clemenceau, but many devotees consider them romantically threadbare. None of the rooms has its own bath, shower, or toilet, but each has a sink. The real allure of this place, aside from its dramatic location, is the price. Book well in advance.

4. 2ND & 9TH ARRONDISSEMENTS

VERY EXPENSIVE

LE GRAND HOTEL INTER-CONTINENTAL, 2 rue Scribe, 75009 Paris. Tel. 40-07-32-32, or toll free 800/327-0200 in the U.S. and Canada. Fax 42-66-12-51. 494 rms, 20 suites. A/C MINIBAR TV TEL **Métro:** Opéra.

$ Rates: 1,750F–2,300F ($306.30–$402.50) single; 2,000F–2,900F ($350–$507.50) double; from 4,500F ($787.50) suite. Breakfast 145F ($25.40) extra. AE, DC, MC, V. **Parking:** 95F ($16.60).

In the 1860s, as the bourgeoisie of France flexed its economic and empire-building muscles, The Grand Hotel was conceived as an appropriate neighbor for the Paris opera house, whose foundation was already being laid across the street. Its first visionary was Napoléon III, who had admired the massive hotels of London and wanted to duplicate their size and grandeur in a redesigned Paris. Financed by the Perière brothers (collaborators of Haussmann, the architect of Paris's controversial new street plan), the hotel rose in beaux-arts glory, one of the few in Paris to fill an entire city block, and noteworthy because of its massive size. (Its cost at the time, translated into today's currency, exceeded $60 million.) Work proceeded on the hotel day and night, with pre-cut and carefully numbered building blocks shipped in from quarries 36 miles away. The finished building incorporated 2 acres of mirrors, more than 4 miles of corridors, and most of the aspirations of the French Empire. Inaugurated by the empress Eugénie, its first clients were envoys from the emperor of Japan, the empress Carlota of Mexico, Gordon Bennett, Jr. (who financed Henry Stanley's search for Livingstone and the source of the Nile), and Emile Zola (who paid 12 francs a day for one of the hotel's best rooms).

Since then, the hotel has been an intricate part of the history and culture of Paris, housing the victors and the vanquished—sometimes in rapid succession—through decades of war and peace. After it was purchased by Japan's Seibu Group in the 1980s and came under management of the Inter-Continental Hotels, the Grand embarked on a campaign to eliminate many decades of abuse and "modernization." Millions of dollars' worth of steel, marble, gilt, and fabrics were used in restoring the hotel to its original style. Today, the hotel combines hard-nosed business acumen and luxury, receiving large numbers of guests with French style amid a shimmering Second Empire elegance. The bedrooms are luxurious, high-ceilinged, filled with plush upholstery and comforts, decorated in pastel colors, and equipped with all the electronic amenities needed for a business trip. Some feature spectacular views of the nearby opera house, whose lavish facade and copper domes almost seem close enough to touch.

Dining/Entertainment: The hotel's premier restaurant, Le Restaurant Opéra, is recommended separately in Chapter 5, "Paris Dining." Less formal is the Café de la Paix—the celebration site for countless cultural and military victories since its construction in the 1860s (see Chapter 5, "Paris Dining"). Perfect for breakfast, light lunch, afternoon tea, and conversation over drinks, La Verrière is sheltered from street noise in what was originally planned as an open courtyard.

There's also a small-scale but very comfortable bar decorated like something from a paneled and elegantly upholstered private club.

Services: 24-hour room service, laundry/dry cleaning, beauty parlor, tour desk, and a concierge who can navigate through many of Paris's bureaucracies.

Facilities: Le Gym Club offers exercise equipment and a view over the copper-sheathed domes of the adjacent Opéra that is almost mystical. A business center offers all related services, including secretarial and translation.

EXPENSIVE

HOTEL AMBASSADOR, 16 bd. Haussmann, 75009 Paris. Tel. 48-00-06-38, or toll free 800/888-4747 in the U.S. or Canada. Fax 42-22-08-74. 289 rms, 9 suites. MINIBAR TV TEL
Métro: Richelieu-Drouot or Chaussée d'Antin.
$ Rates: 1,200F–1,600F ($210–$280) single or double; from 1,800F ($315), suite. Breakfast 35F–90F ($6.10–$15.80). AE, DC, MC, V.
Parking: 90F ($15.80).

This hotel was originally built in 1927, just in time to host the reception that welcomed Charles Lindbergh to Paris the evening following his historic flight across the Atlantic. (After the reception, an exhausted Lindbergh retired to spend the night at the U.S. ambassador's residence.) When the hotel opened with 600 rooms, it was the biggest and most modern in Paris, with seven elevators and all-electric amenities, an anchor on the legendary *grands boulevards*. In World War II, the hotel housed Nazi officers during the occupation of Paris. Later in the 1940s, half of the enormous, and by then, run-down premises were sold to an insurance company, and the walls in the remaining section were removed between the rooms, enlarging each of them into comfortable and tasteful areas of calm and quiet. Today, many rooms still have their original art deco built-in wardrobes, as well as floral curtains and pastel-colored carpets and upholstery that were upgraded in the early 1990s. About three-quarters of the rooms are air-conditioned. The display cases in the hotel's public rooms exhibit some of the most exotic memorabilia in Paris, much of it connected with notable events in show biz from the theater next door—the Olympia.

Dining/Entertainment: The hotel contains an award-winning restaurant, Venantius, which is recommended in Chapter 5, "Paris Dining." There's also an appealingly nostalgic bar, Le Bar des Aigles, in a cubbyhole at one end of the grandly eclectic hotel lobby.

Services: 24-hour room service, concierge, babysitting, laundry, dry cleaning.

Facilities: Some of the largest conference and convention facilities in Paris, business center with translation services.

HOTEL WESTMINSTER, 13 rue de la Paix, 75002 Paris.
   Tel. 42-61-57-46. Fax 42-60-30-66. 102 rms, 18 suites. A/C
   MINIBAR TV TEL **Métro:** Opéra.
$ Rates: 1,800F ($315) single; 2,000F ($350) double; 3,600F ($630)
   suite. Breakfast 110F ($19.30) extra. AE, DC, MC, V.

The Westminster, situated between the Opéra and the place
Vendôme, is the sibling of the contemporary Le Warwick. The
Westminster is traditional but, following a massive renovation, en-
joys all the modern comforts as well.

The hotel was originally built during Baron Haussmann's redesigning of Paris in 1846 and incorporated an old convent. By 1907,
it had been declared a national monument and is today a landmark. At the turn of the century the hotel was purchased by Monsieur Bruchon, who renovated it and installed a famous collection
of clocks, which today is one of the attractions of the hotel. In
1981 it was acquired by Warwick International Hotels, which completely renovated it.

Guest rooms are each individually decorated. Pastel colors blend
with rich paneling, molded ceilings, and marble-top fireplaces.
Many antiques, mainly from the Louis XIV era, are found in both
the public and private guest rooms. Each accommodation has its
own luxurious private bath, a radio, and color TV.

Dining/Entertainment: There is an atmospheric bar and
gourmet restaurant, Le Celadon.

Services: 24-hour room service, babysitting, laundry/valet.

INEXPENSIVE

HOTEL RICHMOND, 11 rue du Helder, 75009 Paris. Tel.
   47-70-53-20. Fax 48-00-02-10. 63 rms (all with bath). MINIBAR
   TV TEL **Métro:** Opéra.
$ Rates (including continental breakfast): 600F ($105) single; 750F
   ($131.50) double; 915F ($160.10) triple. AE, DC, MC, V.

This three-star hotel is a short walk from the Opéra, near American Express, the Café de la Paix, and many fine shops. Behind the
attractive facade is a pleasant lounge with sofas, marble columns,
and a Roman-style fountain—all contributing to an old-world feel.
The rooms are comfortably and traditionally furnished in Louis XV
style, with hairdryers and personal safes.

5. 12TH ARRONDISSEMENT

MODERATE

LE PAVILLON BASTILLE, 65 rue de Lyon, 75012 Paris.
   Tel. 43-43-65-65. Fax 43-43-96-52. 23 rms, 1 suite A/C
   MINIBAR TV TEL **Métro:** Bastille.
$ Rates: 925F ($161.90) single or double; from 1,375F ($240.60)
   suite. Breakfast 78F ($13.70) extra. AE, DC, V.

Opened in 1991, this hotel lies within a garden-fronted white-sided
building about a block south of place de la Bastille. Despite the
17th-century fountain that graces one wall of the hotel's cobble-
covered courtyard, the hotel incorporates a postmodern aesthetic
that mixes baroque elements with modern accessories and lighting.

The establishment's theme colors are blue and yellow, which appear along with marble, leather, glass, and both black and beige granite throughout both the public rooms and the bedrooms. The rooms provide twin or double beds, mirrors, and comfortable contemporary built-in furniture. The English-speaking staff offer personalized service.

Dining/Entertainment: Bar; breakfast room set beneath the ceiling vaults of the cellar.

Services: Room service, babysitting, laundry/valet.

6. 5TH ARRONDISSEMENT

MODERATE

HOTEL LE COLBERT, 7 rue de L'Hôtel-Colbert, 75005 Paris. Tel. 43-25-85-65. Fax 43-25-80-19. 38 rms (all with bath). 2 suites. TV TEL **Métro:** Maubert-Mutualité or St-Michel.
$ Rates: 995F ($174.10) single or double; 1,600F–1,900F ($280–$332.50) suite. Breakfast 50F ($8.80). AE, V.

How can you miss by staying at this little centuries-old inn? Not only is it on the Left Bank, a minute from the Seine, but it provides a fine view of Notre-Dame from many of its rooms as well. There's even a small courtyard, setting the hotel apart from the bustle of Rive Gauche life.

You enter a tastefully decorated lobby area, with marble floors, antique furniture, and a view of the wrought-iron fence separating the evergreen trees of the courtyard from the narrow street outside. A sunny bar area is filled with gilt-accented French furniture. The rooms are well designed and tailored. Most of them provide comfortable chairs and a breakfast area. The baths have been recently renovated, the beds are inviting, and units include plenty of towels and efficient maid service.

HOTEL MODERNE ST-GERMAIN, 33 rue des Ecoles, 75005 Paris. Tel. 43-54-37-78. Fax 43-29-91-31. 45 rms (all with bath). TV TEL **Métro:** Maubert-Mutualité or St-Michel.
$ Rates (including continental breakfast): 530F–720F ($92.80–$126) single; 590F–840F ($103.30–$147) double. AE, DC, MC, V.

Near Notre-Dame and the Panthéon, the Grand Hotel Moderne is a successful blend of the Paris of yesterday and that of today. It was completely renovated in 1992. Located in the heart of the Latin Quarter, this hotel provides a warm welcome by its charming owner, Madame Gibon. She rents comfortably furnished bedrooms that are spotlessly maintained. There are double-glazed aluminum windows in the rooms fronting the rue des Ecoles, which create a quieter atmosphere.

INEXPENSIVE

AGORA ST-GERMAIN, 42 rue des Bernardins, 75005 Paris. Tel. 46-34-13-00. Fax 46-34-75-05. 39 rms (all with bath or shower). MINIBAR TV TEL **Métro:** Maubert-Mutualité.
$ Rates: 580F–600F ($101.50–$105) single; 680F ($119) double. Breakfast 40F ($7) extra. AE, DC, MC, V. **Parking:** 100F ($17.50).

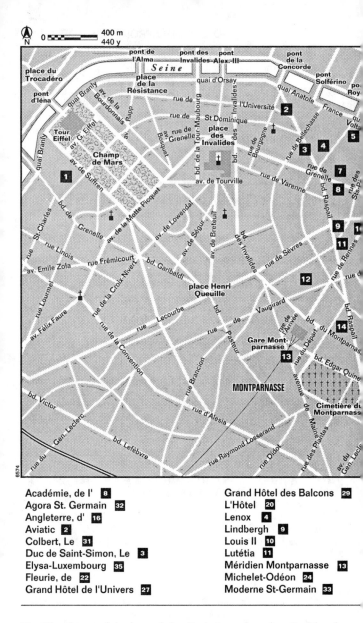

Considered one of the best of the district's moderately priced hotels, Agora St-Germain was originally built in the early 1600s, probably to house a group of guardsmen protecting the brother of the king at his lodgings in the nearby rue Monsieur-le-Prince. The hotel offers compact but soundproof rooms, each comfortably furnished and equipped with an alarm clock, hairdryer, and safety box. Room service is provided every morning, from 7:30 to 10:30am.

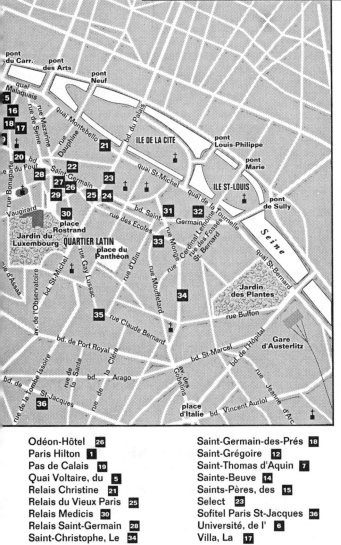

LEFT BANK ACCOMMODATIONS

Odéon-Hôtel **26**	Saint-Germain-des-Prés **18**
Paris Hilton **1**	Saint-Grégoire **12**
Pas de Calais **19**	Saint-Thomas d'Aquin **7**
Quai Voltaire, du **5**	Sainte-Beuve **14**
Relais Christine **21**	Saints-Pères, des **15**
Relais du Vieux Paris **25**	Select **23**
Relais Medicis **30**	Sofitel Paris St-Jacques **36**
Relais Saint-Germain **28**	Université, de l' **6**
Saint-Christophe, Le **34**	Villa, La **17**

HOTEL ELYSA-LUXEMBOURG, 6 rue Gay-Lussac, 75005 Paris. Tel. 43-25-31-74. Fax 46-34-56-27. 30 rms (all with bath or shower). MINIBAR TV TEL **Métro:** Luxembourg.

$ Rates: 530F–620F ($92.80–$108.50) single; 580F–720F ($101.50–$126) double. Breakfast 45F ($7.90) extra. AE, DC, MC, V. **Parking:** 50F ($8.80).

One of the best choices in the heart of the Latin Quarter is near the Luxembourg Gardens. The completely renovated rooms here are charming, spacious, and soundproof. Some accommodations are reserved for nonsmokers. Guests may use the sauna.

HOTEL RESIDENCE SAINT-CHRISTOPHE, 17 rue Lacépède, 75005 Paris. Tel. 43-31-81-54. Fax 43-31-12-54. 31 rms (all with bath). MINIBAR TV TEL **Métro:** Place Monge.

$ Rates: 650F ($113.80) single or double. Breakfast 40F ($7) extra. AE, DC, MC, V.

Warmly accommodating and comfortable, this hotel has a gracious, English-speaking staff and is located in one of the least publicized but charming districts of the *quartier Latin*—a short walk east of the Botanical Gardens (Jardin des Plantes). It was created in 1987 by combining a derelict hotel with an adjacent butcher shop. After spending millions of francs on restoration, the resulting accommodation is clean, charming, friendly, and well upholstered with traditional furniture and wall-to-wall carpeting. The hotel (whose name derives from the son of a long-ago owner) serves only breakfast, although the staff offer good advice about neighborhood restaurants. Each room is equipped with a hairdryer, radio, and tall, sunny windows.

SELECT, 1 place de la Sorbonne, 75005 Paris. Tel. 46-34-14-80. Fax 46-34-51-79. 69 rms (all with bath), 1 suite. TV TEL **Métro:** St-Michel.

$ Rates (including breakfast): 650F–780F ($113.80–$136.50) single or double; 1,250F ($218.80) suite. AE, DC, MC, V.

Built by Le Mercier between 1635 and 1642, this hotel is the only one on this square dominated by the Church of the Sorbonne. Try to get a room overlooking the fountain in this plaza. Nearby, there are cafés on the busy "boul Mich." The rooms, occupying six floors of a building that covers the angle of the place de la Sorbonne and a side street, come in a wide variety of sizes and shapes. There's a bar on the premises (but no restaurant). Guests help themselves from a self-service breakfast buffet.

7. 6TH ARRONDISSEMENT

EXPENSIVE

L'HOTEL, 13 rue des Beaux-Arts, 75006 Paris. Tel. 43-25-27-22. Fax 43-25-64-81. 24 rms, 3 suites. A/C MINIBAR TV TEL **Métro:** St-Germain-des-Prés.

$ Rates: 950F–1,200F ($166.30–$210) small double; 1,700F–2,300F ($297.50–$402.50) large double; from 3,800F ($490) suite. Breakfast 90F ($15.80) extra. AE, DC, MC, V.

⭐ L'Hôtel was a 19th-century "fleabag" called the Hôtel d'Alsace, and its major distinction was that Oscar Wilde, broke and in despair, died here. In one of the upstairs rooms he wrote to the author, Frank Harris, asking him to send "the money you owe me." However, today's guests aren't exactly on poverty row. Through the lobby of what is known only as L'Hôtel march many show business and fashion personalities.

L'Hôtel is the love-hobby creation of French actor Guy-Louis Duboucheron. He's responsible for establishing this intimate atmosphere of supersophistication in a hotel that's been called a "jewel box." A Texas architect, Robin Westbrook, was hired to gut the core of the Alsace, creating a circular courtyard and an interior that reminds one of the tower of Pisa.

You'll feel like a movie star yourself when you take a bath in your tub of rosy-pink imported Italian marble. At the edge of your tub will be a delicate vase holding a single rose. Throughout the building antiques are used with discretion, an eclectic collection that includes pieces from the periods of Louis XV and Louis XVI, as well as Empire and Directoire.

For nostalgia buffs, the ideal rooms are the re-creation of Wilde's original bedchamber and that of Mistinguett, the legendary star of the French stage. In the latter room, the star's original furniture—designed by Jean-Gabriel Domergue—has been installed. Celebrities from Katharine Hepburn to Mick Jagger have enjoyed these rooms.

Dining/Entertainment: Breakfast is served in a stone cellar, which in the evening becomes a tavern for intimate dinners. Le Bélier is a luxurious piano bar/restaurant.

Services: Concierge, 24-hour room service, babysitting, laundry/valet.

HOTEL LUTETIA-PARIS, 45 bd. Raspail, 75006 Paris. Tel. 49-54-46-46, or toll free 800/888-4747 in the U.S. Fax 49-54-46-00. 247 rms, 28 suites. A/C MINIBAR TV TEL **Métro:** Sèvres-Babylone.

$ Rates: 1,250F–1,650F ($218.80–$288.80) single or double; from 3,000F ($525) suite. Breakfast 115F ($20.10) extra. AE, DC, MC, V. **Parking:** 110F ($19.30).

This is the largest and one of the most unusual hotels on the Left Bank, richly associated with Paris's literary history, and restored in 1983 to its original grandeur. It was built in 1910 in the grandest of the art deco styles to provide lodgings for shoppers in the neighborhood's then-innovative department stores. Despite numerous renovations, the hotel deliberately maintains much of its original lobby furniture, including jazz age accessories and a collection of valuable almost-kitsch sculptures, chandeliers, and furniture. Early in its history, the hotel attracted such luminaries as Cocteau, André Gide, Picasso, and Charles de Gaulle, who spent part of his honeymoon at the Lutétia. More recently, the hotel served as the discreet hideaway of Pierre Berger (the business savvy behind Yves Saint-Laurent), Sonia Rykiel (who designed many of the public rooms), and filmmaker Louis Malle. Today, the hotel offers comfortable and not-outrageously priced lodgings, and a distinct flavor of the Roaring '20s; it attracts a knowledgeable clientele of repeat visitors. Bedrooms are tastefully subdued, high-ceilinged, and sound-proofed.

Dining/Entertainment: The hotel's most famous restaurant, Le Paris, has a black-lacquer and amber-colored decor designed by Sonia Rykiel, who was inspired by the great days of the transatlantic ocean liners. Less expensive is the old-fashioned Brasserie Lutétia, where waiters wear black vests and aprons and carry steaming platters of well-flavored bistro food. The Bar Lutèce lies within a darkened but amiable cubbyhole adjacent to the art deco nostalgia of the main lobby.

Services: 24-hour room service, babysitting, laundry/dry cleaning, concierge.

Facilities: Business center, private conference facilities.

RELAIS CHRISTINE, 3 rue Christine, 75006 Paris. Tel 43-26-71-80. Fax 43-26-89-38. 38 rms, 13 duplex suites. A/C MINIBAR TV TEL **Métro:** Odéon.

$ Rates: 1,520F–2,200F ($266–$385) single or double; 2,100F–2,600F ($367.50–$455) duplex suite. Breakfast 95F ($16.60) extra. AE, DC, MC, V, **Parking:** Free.

✪ Relais Christine welcomes an international clientele into what was formerly a 16th-century Augustinian cloister. This is really one of the most unusual hotels in this part of town. You enter from a narrow cobblestone street, first into a symmetrical courtyard and then an elegant reception area dotted with baroque sculpture, plush upholsteries, and a scattering of Renaissance antiques. The Auvergne-based Bertrand family converted the building from a warehouse of a nearby publishing company into this elegant hotel in 1979.

You will not have experienced the hotel until you go down into the vaulted breakfast room on the lower level, the ancient well of which is spotlit from within and the massive central stone column having witnessed all the activity in what used to be the cloister's kitchen. Each bedroom is individually decorated with antiques or antique reproductions and plenty of flair. Accents might include massively beamed ceilings and plush wall-to-wall carpeting.

Dining/Entertainment: Just off the reception area is a paneled sitting room and bar area ringed with 19th-century portraits and comfortable leather chairs.

Services: 24-hour room service, laundry, babysitting.

RELAIS MEDICIS, 23 rue Racine, 75006 Paris. Tel 43-26-00-60. Fax 40-46-83-39. 16 rms (all with bath). A/C MINIBAR TV TEL **Métro:** Odéon.

$ Rates (including breakfast): 1,380F ($241.50) single; 1,190F–1,480F ($208.30–$259) double. AE, DC, MC, V.

Until its radical overhaul in 1991, this place was a well-worn two-star hotel favored by students, indigent artists, and visiting professors from abroad. Today, the establishment is a lavishly decorated and romantic hideaway situated next to the Théâtre de l'Odéon, near the Luxembourg Gardens. The bedrooms are small (sometimes even cramped), but richly upholstered, and include fabric-covered walls, private safes, cable TVs, and a stylishly cluttered and old-fashioned patina you'd otherwise find in a family homestead in Provence. There's a small bar near the antique oil portraits and lithographs of the public rooms; except for breakfast, no meals are served.

RELAIS SAINT-GERMAIN, 9 carrefour de l'Odéon, 75006 Paris. Tel. 43-29-12-05. Fax 46-33-45-30. 20 rms, 4 suites. A/C MINIBAR TV TEL **Métro:** Odéon.

$ Rates (including breakfast): 1,250F ($218.80) single; 1,450F–1,580F ($253.80–$276.50) double; from 1,880F ($329) suite. AE, DC, MC, V.

The Saint-Germain is an oasis of charm and comfort. But keep it a secret. A tall, slender hotel adapted from a 17th-century building, its decor is a happy medley of traditional and modern. Of course, all the necessary amenities were tucked in under the beams as well, including soundproofing, private safe, and hairdryer. Four bedrooms feature a kitchenette, and two of the suites are complete with a terrace.

HOTEL DES SAINTS-PERES, 65 rue des Sts-Pères, 75006 Paris. Tel 45-44-50-00. Fax 45-44-90-83. 37 rms (all with bath), 3 suites. MINIBAR TV TEL **Métro:** St-Germain-des-Prés or Sèvres-Babylone.

$ Rates: 450F–950F ($78.80–$166.30) single or double; from 1,500F ($262.50) suite. Breakfast 50F ($8.80) extra. AE, MC, V.

The best recommendation for this old favorite just off boulevard St-Germain is the long list of habitués, including Edna St. Vincent Millay, who enjoyed the camellia-trimmed garden. The hotel, designed by Louis XIV's architect, is decorated in part with antique paintings, tapestries, and mirrors. The most sought-after room is the *chambre à la fresque,* which has a 17th-century painted ceiling. The modernized bedrooms face the courtyard, where breakfast is served, weather permitting.

RELAIS-HOTEL DU VIEUX PARIS, 9 rue Gît le Coeur, 75006 Paris. Tel 43-54-41-66. Fax 43-26-00-15. 13 rms (all with bath), 7 suites. MINIBAR TV TEL **Métro:** St-Michel.

$ Rates: 1,070F–1,270F ($187.30–$222.30) single or double; from 1,470F ($257.30) suite. Breakfast 50F ($8.80) extra. AE, MC,V.

Tucked away within a maze of medieval streets in the heart of Paris, this stone and timbered building was erected in 1480 as the home of the ducs de Luynes. Later, it was the elegantly appointed home of Pierre Séguier—the *real* marquis d'O—one of Richelieu's advisers. In the 1600s, it was notorious as a hideaway for Henri IV and one of his mistresses. In the 1950s, such members of the Beat Generation as Allen Ginsberg, W. S. Burroughs, and Jack Kerouac made it their Paris headquarters when it was a simple (relatively battered) two-star hotel.

None of them would recognize the place today. In 1991 it was upgraded and restored, and now, though listed as a three-star hotel, it offers many amenities and comforts found in Paris's more expensive four-star properties. The rooms are elegantly furnished with upholstered walls and copies of 19th-century antiques, and about 15 have the massive beams and timbers of the building's original construction. Each accommodation is furnished with a "massage shower," hairdryers, individual safes, and trouser presses. Two of the suite have a mezzanine overlooking the rooftops of Paris, and some of the rooms offer views of the Conciergerie.

MODERATE

HOTEL D'ANGLETERRE, 44 rue Jacob, 75006 Paris. Tel. 42-60-34-72. Fax 42-60-16-93. 29 rms (all with bath). TV TEL **Métro:** St-Germain-des-Prés.

$ Rates: 600F ($105) single; 1,000F ($175) double. Breakfast 40F ($7) extra. AE, DC, V.

Situated amid antique shops and art galleries, this quaint building, constructed in 1650, once housed the British embassy. Despite the antique plumbing, the Angleterre has long been favored by such illustrious guests of yesteryear as Anne Morrow Lindbergh and Ernest Hemingway, who stayed here once while he was ill. Shut off from street traffic, most of its rooms open onto an exposed courtyard and garden, where tables are set for breakfast in summer.

ODEON-HOTEL, 3 rue de l'Odéon, 75006 Paris. Tel 43-25-90-67. Fax 43-25-55-98. 34 rms (all with bath). TV TEL **Métro:** Odéon.

$ Rates: 700F–850F ($122.50–$148.80) single; 850F–1,100F ($148.80–$192.50) double. Breakfast 55F ($9.60) extra. AE, DC, MC, V.

Conveniently located near both the Théâtre de l'Odéon and boulevard St-Germain, the hotel stands on what was, in 1779, the first street in Paris to have pavements and gutters. By the turn of this century this area, which housed the bookshop Shakespeare and Company at no. 12, began attracting such writers as André Gide, Paul Valéry, James Joyce, T. S. Eliot, F. Scott Fitzgerald, Ernest Hemingway, and Gertrude Stein. Today, with its exposed beams, rough stone walls, high crooked ceilings, tapestries, oak-and-bookbinder wallpaper mixed in with bright contemporary fabrics, mirrored ceilings, and black leather furnishing, the Odéon-Hôtel is reminiscent of a modernized Norman country inn. After modern plumbing was installed, each room was individually redesigned.

HOTEL LE SAINTE-BEUVE, 9 rue Ste-Beuve, 75006 Paris. **Tel. 45-48-20-07.** Fax 45-48-67-52. 23 rms (all with bath), 1 suite. MINIBAR TV TEL **Métro:** Vavin.

$ Rates: 680F ($119) single; 950F ($166.30) double; from 1,250F ($218.80) suite. Breakfast 75F ($13.10) extra. AE, MC, V.

This is the answer to your dreams: a small, tastefully restored hotel in Montparnasse, with its many memories of long gone but still fabled personalities. Situated around the corner from Rodin's famous statue of Balzac, Sainte-Beuve is a charmer. Its decor was conceived by the celebrated decorator David Hicks, and that means a warm, cozy atmosphere, aglow with rose-colored chintz. Breakfast can be served in bed, and you can also enjoy the intimate lobby bar with a fireplace. The hotel is decorated mainly with provincial pieces. Each accommodation has an individual safe.

HOTEL ST-GERMAIN-DES-PRES, 36 rue Bonaparte, 75006 Paris. Tel. 43-26-00-19. Fax 40-46-83-63. 28 rms (all with bath), 2 suites. MINIBAR TV TEL **Métro:** St-Germain-des-Prés.

$ Rates: 750F–950F ($131.30–$166.30) single or double; 1,300F ($227.50) suite. Breakfast 50F ($8.80) extra. V.

Much of this hotel's attraction comes from its enviable location in the Latin Quarter—behind a well-known Left Bank street near many shops. Janet Flanner, the legendary correspondent for *The New Yorker* in the 1920s, lived here for a while. Each of the bedrooms is small but charming, each capped with antique ceiling beams and outfitted with a private safe. Public areas are severely elegant, with dentil moldings, Louis XIII furnishings, and exposure of the building's original stonework. Air-conditioning is available in most of the bedrooms upon payment of a 100F ($17.50) daily supplement.

HOTEL LE SAINT-GREGOIRE, 43 rue de l'Abbé-Grégoire, 75006 Paris. Tel. 45-48-23-23. Fax 45-48-33-95. 20 rms (all with bath or shower), 1 suite. TV TEL **Métro:** St-Placide.

$ Rates: 760F–890F ($133–$155.80) single or double; 1,290F ($225.80) suite. Breakfast 65F ($11.40) extra. AE, DC, MC, V. **Parking:** 50F ($8.80).

The Saint-Grégoire is a sparkler that opened in 1989. A restored town house–style structure, the well-run hotel is rated three stars. All of its bedrooms are handsomely furnished; some have private terraces as well. Lighting is subtle in the vaulted breakfast room (breakfast is the only meal served). In winter, there's a cozy fire in the sitting room.

LA VILLA, 29 rue Jacob. 75006 Paris. Tel. 43-26-60-00.
Fax 46-34-63-63. 28 rms (all with bath), 4 suites. A/C MINIBAR TV
TEL **Métro:** St-Germain-des-Prés.

$ Rates: 800F–1,600F ($140–$280) single or double; 1,950F
($341.30) suite. Breakfast 90F ($15.80) extra. AE, MC, V.

La Villa is a small but elegant choice that was developed in 1988
from the crumbling core of an older hotel, the Hôtel d'Isly. Located
on the corner of a street where Richard Wagner lived from 1841
to 1842, it offers a bar and a jazz club (La Villa), which opens
most nights around 10pm to an enthusiastic crowd of jazz-loving
night owls. The bedrooms and suites are warmly and stylishly designed by well-known Parisian decorator Marie-Christine Dorner.

INEXPENSIVE

**AVIATIC, 105 rue de Vaugirard, 75006 Paris. Tel. 45-44-
38-21.** Fax 45-49-35-83. 43 rms (all with bath). MINIBAR TV TEL
Métro: Montparnasse-Bienvenue.

$ Rates (including continental breakfast): 470F–650F ($82.30–
$113.80) single; 560F–780F ($98–$136.50) double. AE, DC, MC, V.
Parking: 120F ($21)

This is a bit of old Paris, with a modest inner courtyard and a
vine-covered lattice on the walls. It's been a family-run hotel of
character and elegance for a century. The reception lounge, with its
marble columns, brass chandeliers, antiques, and petit salon, provides an attractive traditional setting. Completely remodeled, the
hotel is situated in an interesting center of Montparnasse, with its
cafés frequented by artists, writers, and jazz musicians. The staff
speaks English.

**HOTEL DE FLEURIE, 32–34 rue Grégoire-de-Tours, 75006
Paris. Tel. 43-29-59-81.** Fax 43-29-68-44. 29 rms (all with bath).
A/C MINIBAR TV TEL **Métro:** Odéon.

$ Rates: 590F–780F ($103.30–$136.50) single; 780F ($136.50)
double; 1,150F ($201.30) deluxe double. Children under 12 stay free
in parents' room. Breakfast 50F ($8.80) extra. AE, DC, MC, V.

Just 70 feet off the boulevard St-Germain on a colorful little Left
Bank street, the Fleurie is one of the best of the "new" old hotels.
Restored to its former glory in 1988, the facade is studded with
statuary that is spotlit by night, recapturing its 17th-century
elegance. The stone walls have been exposed in the reception salon,
with its refectory desk where guests check in. It has latticework,
and an exposed beamed ceiling. An elevator takes you to the well-
furnished, modern bedrooms; a spiral staircase leads down to a
breakfast room.

**GRAND HOTEL DE L'UNIVERS, 6 rue Grégoire-de-Tours,
75006 Paris. Tel. 43-29-37-00.** Fax 40-51-06-45. 35 rms (all
with bath). MINIBAR TV TEL **Métro:** Odéon.

$ Rates: 590F ($103.30) single; 750F ($131.30) double. Breakfast
35F ($6.10) extra. AE, DC, MC, V.

This venerable and historic building was originally built in the
1400s as the Paris home of a member of the then-emerging bourgeoisie, who probably chose its location because of its nearness to
the Luxembourg Palace. Today, the massive ceiling beams, thick
stone walls, and the facade's incised "logo" of a loincloth-clad barbarian with a club have been carefully retained by the present owners. Some of the pleasantly renovated rooms enjoy a panoramic

view over the crooked rooftops of the surrounding neighborhood, and all are equipped with satellite TV reception and a hairdryer. One of the most amusing rooms is La Bonbonnière, an all-pink concoction whose name translates as "the candy box." Breakfast, the only meal served, is served beneath the 500-year-old stone vaults of a well-decorated cellar.

HOTEL LOUIS II, 2 rue St-Sulpice, 75006 Paris. Tel 46-33-13-80. Fax 46-33-17-29. 22 rms (all with bath). MINIBAR TV TEL **Métro:** Odéon.

$ Rates: 510F–720F ($89.30–$126) single or double; 880F ($154) triple. Breakfast 44F ($7.70) extra. AE, DC, MC, V.

One of the most skillful, charming renovations on the Left Bank transformed the interiors of a run-down pair of 18th-century building into a chintz-covered rustic fantasy. Its decorators exposed as many of the hand-hewn beams as they could, so that in each of the cozy bedrooms wide expanses of mellowed patina contrast pleasantly with flowered wall coverings and plush carpeting. Many repeat visitors request one of the romantic rooms beneath the slope of the building's eaves for an upgraded version of *La Bohème*.

Morning coffee and afternoon drinks are served in an elegant reception salon, where gilt-framed mirrors, bouquets of fresh flowers, and well-oiled antiques add to a refreshingly provincial allure.

HOTEL DU PAS-DE-CALAIS, 59 rue des Sts-Pères, 75006 Paris. Tel. 45-48-78-74. Fax 45-44-94-57. 41 rms (all with bath). TV TEL **Métro:** St-Germain-des-Prés or Sèvres-Babylone.

$ Rates (including continental breakfast): 630F ($110.30) single; 760F ($133) double. MC, V.

Pas-de-Calais is in a historic building with literary connections that has been smartly updated. The five-story structure was built in the 17th century by the Lavalette family and inhabited by Chateaubriand from 1811 to 1814. Possibly its most famous guest was Jean-Paul Sartre, who struggled away with the play *Dirty Hands* in room no. 41 during the hotel's prerestoration days.

Today the hotel retains its elegant facade, complete with its massive wooden doors. Its modern rooms have large baths, color TVs, safety boxes, and hairdryers. The inner rooms surround a modest courtyard, with two garden tables and several green trellises. Off the somewhat sterile lobby is a comfortable, carpeted sitting room with TV.

MICHELET-ODÉON, 6 place de l'Odéon, 75006 Paris. Tel. 46-34-27-80. Fax 46-34-55-35. 42 rms (all with bath). TV TEL **Métro:** Odéon.

$ Rates: 380F ($66.50) single; 450F ($78.80) double; 610F ($106.80) triple. Breakfast 40F ($7) extra. AE, MC, V.

Conveniently located on place de l'Odéon, the Michelet-Odéon owes its theatrical clientele to the nearby Théâtre de l'Europe. Parts of the building date from the 1600s. The hotel, with classic columns and a cozy lounge, is comfortable and reasonably priced. Guests will find the more modern accommodations on the fourth and fifth floors; the lower floors, although renovated, maintain a classic decor.

BUDGET

GRAND HOTEL DES BALCONS, 3 rue Casimir-Delavigne, 75006 Paris. Tel. 46-34-78-50. Fax 46-34-06-27. 55 rms (all with bath). TV TEL **Métro:** Odéon.

$ Rates: 320F ($56) single; 410F–465F ($71.80–$81.40) double. Breakfast 40F ($7) extra. MC, V.

This is perhaps the best buy on this little street off the Odéon. The lobby is rust-colored and decorated with art nouveau panels. An unpretentious two-star hotel, it once sheltered Endre Ady (1877–1919), Hungary's greatest lyric poet.

The compact rooms, each with background music, have been renovated by the owners. Ask for rooms above the street level for greater comfort and security.

8. 7TH & 15TH ARRONDISSEMENTS

EXPENSIVE

LE DUC DE SAINT-SIMON, 14 rue de St-Simon, 75007 Paris. Tel. 45-48-35-66. Fax 45-48-68-25. 29 rms (all with bath), 5 suites. TEL **Métro:** Rue du Bac.

$ Rates: 1,300F–1,450F ($227.50–$253.80) single or double; from 1,750F ($306.30) suite. Breakfast 70F ($12.30) extra. No credit cards

Set on a quiet residential street on the Left Bank, this small villa has a tiny front garden and an 1830s decor with *faux-marbre* trompe-l'oeil panels and a frescoed elevator. The vaulted cellar, formerly reserved for coal storage, accommodates an intimate bar with an adjacent Louis XIII–style breakfast room. Each bedroom is unique, though sure to include at least one antique. The service, perhaps the best reflection of the owner's extensive training, is helpful but reserved.

PARIS HILTON, 18 av. Suffren, 75015 Paris. Tel. 42-73-92-00, or toll free 800/225-9290 in the U.S. Fax 47-83-62-66. 455 rms. 28 suites. A/C MINIBAR TV TEL **RER:** Champ-de-Mars.

$ Rates: 1,490F–2,150F ($260.80–$376.30) single; 1,590F–2,300F ($278.30–$402.50) double; from 3,500F ($612.50) suite. Breakfast 20F ($3.50) extra. **Parking:** 130F ($22.80).

On a tract of land near the Eiffel Tower in the 15th arrondissement, Hilton built one of the city's most impressive modern hotels, shattering the Right Bank's monopoly on grand hotels. Today, it has become a focal point of social life in this part of the city.

Built in the Hilton style of maximum comfort, with strong doses of Parisian flavor and virtually every convenience and efficiency, this 11-story hotel is designed around window-walls and contemporary gadgets, backed up by a professional staff along with a computer-age security system.

Each of the well-furnished, soundproof bedrooms has a generous bathroom covered with a tinted series of marble slabs, an oversize sink, and dozens of square yards of towels, terrycloth bathrobes, and plenty of toilet articles. The emphasis throughout the hotel is on personal service and such amenities as readily available ice cubes.

Dining/Entertainment: A breakfast buffet is served on La Terrasse (one of the best in Paris). There are three bars and Le Western, a steak house with a cowboy theme and a definite sense of humor.

Services: Babysitting, same-day laundry and dry cleaning, travel services, beauty parlor, 24-hour room service.

Facilities: Nearby underground garage (most valuable in Paris), several chic boutiques.

MODERATE

HOTEL DE L'ACADEMIE, 32 rue des Sts-Pères, 75007 Paris. Tel. 45-48-36-22. Fax 45-44-75-24. 34 rms (all with bath). MINIBAR TV TEL **Métro:** St-Germain-des-Prés.

$ Rates: 490F–840F ($84.80–$147) single or double. Breakfast 45F ($7.90) extra. AE, DC, MC, V.

The exterior walls and the old ceiling beams are all that remain of this 17th-century residence for the private guards of the duc de Rohan. In 1983 it was completely renovated to include an elegant marble-and-oak reception area, Second Empire–style chairs, and an English-speaking staff. The comfortably up-to-date rooms have Directoire beds, an "Ile de France" decor in soft colors, radios, alarm clocks, and views over the 18th- and 19th-century buildings in the immediate neighborhood.

HOTEL DE L'UNIVERSITE, 22 rue de l'Université, 75007 Paris. Tel. 42-61-09-39. Fax 42-60-40-84. 28 rms (all with bath). TV TEL **Métro:** St-Germain-des-Prés.

$ Rates: 600F–650F ($105–$113.80) single; 800F–1,300F ($140–$227.50) double. Breakfast 45F ($7.90) extra. V.

This has rapidly become the favorite little hotel of those who want to stay in a St-Germain-de-Prés atmosphere. Unusually fine antiques furnish this 300-year-old converted town house. It's the love child of Madame Bergmann, who has a flair for restoring old places and a collector's nose for assembling antiques. She's renovated l'Université completely.

A favorite room is no. 54, all in shades of Gainsborough blue, with a rattan bed and period pieces as well as a marble bath. No. 35, opening onto the courtyard, is another charmer—there's a fireplace and a large provincial armoire decorated in shades of orange. A small breakfast room, in the bistro style, opens onto a tiny courtyard with a fountain. Everything is personal—and reservations are imperative. It's not cheap, but it's well worth the money if you want a glamorous setting.

INEXPENSIVE

HOTEL LENOX, 9 rue de l'Université, 75007 Paris. Tel. 42-96-10-95. Fax 42-61-52-83. 30 rms (all with bath or shower), 2 duplex suites. TV TEL **Métro:** Rue du Bac.

$ Rates: 580F–770F ($101.50–$134.80) single or double; 820F–950F ($143.50–$166.30) duplex suite. Breakfast 45F ($7.90) extra. AE, DC, MC, V.

The Lenox has been a long-standing favorite for those seeking a reasonably priced and desirable nest in St-Germain-des-Prés. Once this was a rather basic little pension. In 1910, in those halcyon years before the Great War, T. S. Eliot spent a hot summer here on "the old man's money." Today this much-improved hotel offers comfortably furnished bedrooms, small and snug, some with elaborate ceiling moldings. The lobby, with its helpful staff and marble fireplace, sets the tone, and a convivial bar off the main reception area is open daily from 5:30pm to 1:30am. Many returning guests request the attic duplex with its tiny balcony and skylight.

HOTEL LINDBERGH, 5 rue Chomel, 75007 Paris. Tel. 45-48-35-53. Fax 45-49-31-48. 26 rms (all with bath or shower). TV TEL **Métro:** Sèvres-Babylone or St-Sulpice.

$ Rates: 440F–550F ($77–$96.30) single or double; 670F ($117.30) triple; 740F ($129.50) quad. Breakfast 35F ($6.10) extra. AE, DC, MC, V. **Parking:** 150F ($26.30).

Hôtel Lindbergh honors the late American aviator whose nonstop solo flight across the Atlantic electrified Paris and the world in 1927. Not long ago, this establishment looked as if nothing had changed since that day, but now it has a modern, elegant exterior and is completely renovated inside. On a somewhat hidden-away Left Bank street two minutes' walk from St-Germain-des-Prés, it's next to a good budget restaurant, off boulevard Raspail. Breakfast is the only meal served.

SAINT-THOMAS-D'AQUIN, 3 rue du Pré-aux-Clercs, 75007 Paris. Tel. 42-61-01-22. Fax 42-61-41-43. 21 rms (all with bath or shower). TV TEL **Métro:** St-Germain-des-Prés or Rue du Bac.

$ Rates (including continental breakfast): 500F–580F ($87.50–$101.50) single; 620F ($108.50) double. AE, DC, MC, V.

The Saint-Thomas-d'Aquin has been entirely renovated and redecorated. Behind a cream-colored facade with shutters and balconies, the hotel stands on a relatively traffic-free street between the busy boulevard St-Germain and rue de l'Université. The staff speaks English and gives you a warm welcome. Bedrooms are fresh and modern, with flowery French wallpaper. The rooms have insulated windows and are serviced by an elevator.

HOTEL DU QUAI VOLTAIRE, 19 quai Voltaire, 75007 Paris. Tel. 42-61-50-91. Fax 42-61-62-26. 32 rms (all with bath or shower). TV TEL **Métro:** Rue du Bac.

$ Rates: 450F–550F ($78.80–$96.30) single; 550F–690F ($96.30–$120.80) double. Breakfast 40F ($7) extra. AE, DC, MC, V. **Parking:** 80F ($14) nearby.

This is an inn with a past and one of the most magnificent views in all Paris. The hotel occupies a prime site on the Left Bank quays of the Seine, halfway between the pont Royal and the gracefully arched pont du Carrousel. Twenty-nine of its rooms—many of them renovated—gaze over the Louvre, directly across the tree-shaded river. Living here through the year have been Charles Baudelaire, Jean Sibelius, Richard Wagner, and Oscar Wilde. Photos of Wagner and Baudelaire are enshrined in the small, plush sitting room inside the main door. The rooms are pleasantly appointed, but the focal point of every front room is that view—seen through floor-to-ceiling double French windows.

9. 14TH ARRONDISSEMENT

EXPENSIVE

HOTEL MERIDIEN MONTPARNASSE, 19 rue du Commandant-Mouchotte, 75014 Paris. Tel. 44-36-44-36. Fax 44-36-

49-00. 928 rms, 25 suites. A/C MINIBAR TV TEL **Métro:** Montparnasse-Bienvenue.

$ Rates: 1,250F–1,750F ($218.80–$306.30) single or double; from 3,500F ($612.50) suite. Breakfast 115F ($20.10) extra. AE, DC, MC, V. **Parking:** 10F ($1.80) per hour.

This is the largest hotel on the Left Bank, its 25-story skyscraper tower dominating Montparnasse. The rooms are soundproof and color-coordinated, all with views of the city, color cable TVs, and alarm clocks.

Dining/Entertainment: Montparnasse '25 on the building's uppermost observation platform serves high-level French cuisine and takes its look from the 1920s (black lacquered furniture, gold-leaf sculptures, and reproductions of works by Modigliani and van Dongen). Glass-enclosed Restaurant Justine overlooks the gardens and serves both a buffet and à la carte specialties. Justine is open daily from 7am to 11pm, its lunch or dinner buffets costing 200F ($35.). Before-dinner drinks are available in the Platinum Bar and Café Atlantic in the lobby.

Services: Babysitting, 24-hour room service, laundry/valet.

Facilities: Shopping boutiques.

SOFITEL PARIS ST-JACQUES, 17 bd. St-Jacques, 75014 Paris. Tel. 40-78-79-80. Fax 45-88-43-93. 797 rms, 14 suites. A/C MINIBAR TV TEL **Métro:** St-Jacques.

$ Rates (including continental breakfast): 1,230F ($215.30) single; 1,360F ($238) double; from 2,040F ($357) suite. AE, DC, MC, V. **Parking:** 50F ($8.80).

Sofitel Paris St-Jacques is a 14-story glass-and-steel hotel, refreshingly stylish and very French. The main lobby has been upgraded with a marble fountain in the middle. Not only are the public rooms attention-getting, but the bedrooms have color-coordinated textures and fabrics. They come complete with refrigerators, radios, and TVs. The tile bathrooms have both showers and tubs, plus a separate toilet area.

Dining/Entertainment: Le Français is a re-creation of a turn-of-the-century brasserie, with bentwood chairs, 1890s posters, potted palms, and belle époque lighting fixtures.

Services: Laundry/valet, babysitting, 24-hour room service.

Facilities: Business center, shopping boutiques.

---

10. 3RD & 4TH ARRONDISSEMENTS

EXPENSIVE

LE PAVILLON DE LA REINE, 28 place des Vosges, 75003 Paris. Tel. 42-77-96-40. Fax 42-77-63-06. 30 rms (all with bath), 23 suites. A/C MINIBAR TV TEL **Métro:** Bastille.

$ Rates: 1,300F ($227.50) single; 1,500F ($262.50) double; from 1,950F ($341.30) suite. Breakfast 85F ($14.90) extra. AE, DC, MC, V. **Parking:** Free.

 Lovers of Le Marais long lamented the absence of a hotel on this square where Victor Hugo lived, but the inauguration of this hotel in 1986 changed all that. The entrance is through a tunnel leading under the northern side of the square. At the end of the tunnel, flanked with vine-covered lattices and a small formal garden, is a cream-colored villa, the simple neoclassical facade of which blends perfectly into the neighborhood. The hotel of the Bertrand-Chevalier family is relatively new, but it harmonizes with the landscape so well that you can't tell.

Inside, the Louis XIII decor evokes the heyday of place des Vosges. Wing chairs with flame-stitched upholstery, coupled with iron-banded Spanish antiques, create a feeling of relaxed hospitality. Each bedroom is unique; some are duplexes with sleeping lofts set above a cozy salon, and all feature weathered beams, reproductions of famous paintings, and a marble-sheathed bathroom.

MODERATE

HOTEL DES DEUX-ILES, 59 rue St-Louis-en-l'Ile, 75004 Paris. Tel. 43-26-13-35. Fax 43-29-60-25. 17 rms (all with bath). TV TEL **Métro:** Pont-Marie.
$ Rates: 700F ($122.50) single; 800F ($140) double. Breakfast 45F ($7.90) extra. No credit cards.

Hôtel des Deux-Iles is a restored 17th-century mansion on this most charming of Seine islands. The interior decorator, Roland Buffat, was so successful with his other hotel on the same street (Hôtel de Lutèce) that he decided to open his most elaborate establishment to date. The tropical garden of plants and flowers sets the tone, suggesting the charm and taste level provided by this highly recommended spot. Bamboo and reed are used extensively in both the public and private rooms. Monsieur Buffat suggests a touch of whimsy with his cage of white doves. The favorite meeting place is the rustic-style tavern on a lower level, where guests gather in cool weather around the open fireplace.

HOTEL DE LUTECE, 65 rue St-Louis-en-l'Ile, 75004 Paris. Tel 43-26-23-52. Fax 43-29-60-25. 23 rms (all with bath). TV TEL **Métro:** Pont-Marie.
$ Rates: 660F ($115.50) single; 795F ($139.10) double; 970F ($169.80) triple. Breakfast 42F ($7.40) extra. No credit cards.

★ This is like a drink of sparkling champagne—a hotel located on the historic Ile St-Louis, where everybody seemingly wants to live, although there just isn't enough room. You pass through glass entrance doors into what appears to be the attractive and inviting living room of a Breton country house. All this is the creation of the interior designer Roland Buffat. The all-purpose reception salon and lounge focuses on a stone fireplace surrounded by downy couches and armchairs. Tall plants and modern paintings add the new look, while antique tables and crude tile floors pay homage to the traditional. Each of the bedrooms is uniquely decorated, many with antiques interspersed with tasteful reproductions.

INEXPENSIVE

HOTEL BASTILLE SPERIA, 1 rue de la Bastille, 75004 Paris. Tel. 42-72-04-01. Fax 42-72-56-38. 42 rms (all with bath). MINIBAR TV TEL **Métro:** Bastille.
$ Rates: 498F–529F ($87.20–$92.60) single; 529F–590F ($92.60–$103.30) double; 712F ($124.60) triple. Breakfast 40F ($7) extra. AE, DC, MC, V.

The Bastille Speria occupies a seven-story cream-colored building on a corner near the Bastille, the Opéra Bastille, and the Marais. Its completely renovated interior is far more modern than its mansard exterior implies, thanks to a complete overhaul of the building in the late 1980s. Each of the bedrooms contains an acoustical ceiling and simple, but comfortable, furniture.

HOTEL SAINT-LOUIS, 75 rue St-Louis-en-l'Ile. 75004 Paris. Tel. 46-34-04-80. Fax 46-34-02-13. 21 rms (all with bath or shower). TEL **Métro:** Pont-Marie
$ Rates: 665F–765F ($116.40–$133.90) single or double. Breakfast 45F ($7.90) extra. MC, V.

 Hôtel Saint-Louis is a small hotel, fashionably and romantically positioned on the historic Ile St-Louis. Guy Record discovered this hotel and did a good job of conversion. Along with his wife, Andrée, he maintains a charming family atmosphere that is becoming harder and harder to find in Paris. Many of the upper-level accommodations reached by elevator offer views over the rooftops of Paris. I prefer the rooms on the fifth floor, which have the most atmosphere and are decorated with old wood and selections of attractive furniture. Pleasant accessories decorate the rooms, and there are antiques in the small reception lounge. The breakfast room lies in the cellar near a tiny residents' lounge beneath stone vaulting dating from the 14th century.

11. 18TH ARRONDISSEMENT

MODERATE

TERRASS HOTEL, 12–14 rue Joseph-de-Maistre, 75018 Paris. Tel. 46-06-72-85. Fax 42-52-29-11. 91 rms, 10 suites. MINIBAR TV TEL **Métro:** Place de Clichy or Blanche.
$ Rates: 880F ($154) single; 1,050F ($183.80) double; 1,500F ($262.50) suite. AE, DC, MC, V.
Originally built in 1913, and richly renovated into a plush but traditional style in 1991, this is the only four-star hotel on the Butte Montmartre. Graciously staffed with English-speaking employees and its owner-managers, it offers a large, marble-floored lobby ringed with blond oak paneling and accented with 18th-century antiques and even older tapestries. The bedrooms are high-ceilinged, cozy, well upholstered, and very French, often with views. Throughout, the hotel is permeated with good-natured elegance and a firm sense of its location amid the former haunts of Paris's most celebrated artists.

Dining/Entertainment: An elegant street-level restaurant, and a seventh-floor garden/terrace with bar and food service and sweeping views over many of the most important monuments of Paris. For colder weather, a corner bar with its own fireplace offers charm and discretion.

Services: Foreign exchange, car rentals, tour desk, laundry/dry cleaning.

Facilities: Conference facilities.

CHAPTER 5

PARIS DINING

Everything you've ever heard about French cooking is true—it's absolutely superb, and Paris is where you'll find French cuisine at its best. Only in Paris can you turn onto the nearest side street, enter the first ramshackle hostelry you see, sit down at the bare and wobbly table, glance at an illegibly hand-scrawled menu—and get a memorable meal.

In the gastronomic capital of the world, with more than 15,000 restaurants to choose from, it's difficult to list all the noteworthy ones. I have opted to include many favorites, in a wide range of prices. Some of the restaurants are famous throughout the world; others are not well known but still deserve the visitor's attention.

Brasserie and bistro customers beware: Granted, Lasserre and Taillevent are fine French restaurants that serve haute cuisine, but there are also restaurants that serve rather ordinary food under the guise of haute cuisine and get away with it because of the city's culinary reputation. Don't be wooed by a fancy atmosphere or intimidated by haughty maître d's. Use your traveler's common sense: If the locals flock to a particular restaurant, it's probably a good choice.

Paris restaurants by law add a service charge of 12% to 15% to your bill (*service compris*), which means you don't have to leave a tip. But it is customary to leave something extra. Some restaurants include beverage in their menu rates (*boisson compris*).

DINING WITH CHILDREN Meals at the grand restaurants of Paris are rarely suitable for young children. Nevertheless, many parents drag their children to these deluxe citadels, often to the annoyance of other diners. If you want to dine at a fancy restaurant, consider leaving the kids with a babysitter. However, if you prefer to dine with your children, then you may have to make some compromises. Perhaps you'll have to dine earlier than most Parisians. **Hotel dining rooms** can be another good choice for family dining. They usually have children's menus, or at least one or two plats du jour cooked for children, such as spaghetti with meat sauce.

If you take your child to one of the moderately priced or budget restaurants, ask if the restaurant will serve a child's plate. If not, order a *plat du jour* or *plat garni*, which will be suitable for most children, particularly if a dessert is to follow.

Most **cafés** welcome children throughout the day and early evening. At a café, children always seem to like the sandwiches (try a croque-monsieur), the omelets, and especially the pommes frites (crispy french fries). Although we have listed a number of cafés later in this chapter (see Section 15), one that particularly appeals to children and offers a scenic view over the city is **La Samaritaine,** 75 rue de Rivoli (tel. 45-08-33-33; Métro: Pont-Neuf).

Les Drug Stores also welcome children, especially in the early evening, as do most **tearooms,** and you can tide the kids over with pastries and ice cream if dinner will be late. Try a **picnic** in the park. Also, there are lots of fast-food eateries, such as **Pizza Hut** and **McDonald's,** you will see these chains all over the city.

For a rundown of more kid-friendly establishments, see "Frommer's Cool for Kids: Restaurants (Section 14).

WHAT THE LISTINGS MEAN Restaurants classified as "Very Expensive" charge from $100 to $125, or even beyond, plus drinks, for dinner. That's per person, too. In "Expensive" restaurants, dinner ranges from $75 to $100; "Moderate," $50 to $75. Anything under $50 per person is considered "Inexpensive," although such a price tag is luxurious dining in most parts of the world. Any meal for less than $25 is considered "Budget" by Parisian standards.

In the addresses listed, such designations as "1er" and "12e," which follow the name of the street, refer (in French form) to the arrondissement in which the establishment is located.

In France lunch (as well as dinner) tends to be a full-course meal with meat, vegetables, salad, bread, cheese, dessert, wine, and coffee. It may be difficult to find a restaurant that serves the type of light lunch that North Americans are accustomed to. Cafés, however, may be the answer since they offer sandwiches, soup, and salads in a relaxed setting.

Coffee, in France, is served after the meal and carries an extra charge. The French consider it absolutely barbaric to drink coffee during the meal, and, unless you specifically order it with milk (*au lait*), the coffee will be served black. In the more conscientious establishments, it is prepared as the traditional *filtre*, a rather slow but rewarding filter style that takes a bit of manipulating.

---

1. 8TH ARRONDISSEMENT

VERY EXPENSIVE

LASSERRE, 17 av. Franklin D. Roosevelt, 8e. Tel. 43-59-53-43.
 Cuisine: FRENCH. **Reservations:** Required. **Métro:** F. D. Roosevelt
$ Prices: Appetizers 185F–590F ($32.40–$103.30); main courses 205F–420F ($35.90–$73.50). AE, MC V.
 Open: Lunch Tues–Sat 12:30–2:30pm; dinner Mon–Sat 7:30–10:30pm. **Closed:** July 31–Aug. 30.

This elegant restaurant was a simple bistro before World War II—a "rendezvous for chauffeurs." Then along came Rene Lasserre, who bought the dilapidated building and set out to create his dream. His dream turned into a culinary paradise, attracting gourmets from around the world.

Two white-painted front doors lead to the dining rooms and a reception lounge with Louis XVI–style furnishings and brocaded walls. The main salon is two stories high; on each side is a mezzanine. Draped with silk, tall arched windows open onto the street. At a table set with fine porcelain, crystal glasses edged in gold, a silver candelabrum, even a silver bird and a ceramic dove, you sit on a Louis XV– style salon chair and carefully study the menu.

Overhead, the ceiling is painted with lamb-white clouds and a cerulean sky, but in fair weather the staff slides back the roof to reveal the real sky, either moonlight or sunshine.

The food is a combination of French classicism and originality. The presentation of dishes is one of the most winning and imaginative aspects of Lasserre. Always count on high drama.

The appetizers are among the finest in Paris, including an unusual serving of a bouillabaisse in gelatin or a salad of truffles. You might also be tempted by a trio of terrines of the house. The fish selections are excellent, including lobster from Brittany or a sole soufflé. A hallmark dish is fillets de sole Club de la Casserole. Meat and poultry selections are also outstanding, including veal kidneys flambé, and steak de Charolais au Bourgueil, one of the most tender and succulent choices of beef offered in Paris. Desserts are also spectacular and can include soufflés or a soothing sabayon. The cellar, with some 180,000 bottles of wine, is among the most remarkable in Paris; red wines are decanted into silver pitchers or ornate crystal.

MAXIM'S, 3 rue Royale, 8e. Tel. 42-65-27-94.

Cuisine: FRENCH. **Reservations:** Required. **Métro:** Concorde.
$ Prices: Appetizers 90F–790F ($15.80–$138.30); main courses 200F–400F ($35–$70). AE, DC, V.
Open: Lunch daily 12:30–2pm; dinner daily 7:30–11:30pm.
Closed: Sun July–Aug.

Maxim's is the world's most legendary restaurant. It preserves the era of belle époque, and was a favorite of Edward VII, then the prince of Wales. He enjoyed the slightly decadent atmosphere, far removed in spirit from the rigid London ruled by his stern mother, Victoria.

The restaurant is known to many North American moviegoers who have never been to Paris. It was the setting for *The Merry Widow*, where John Gilbert dipped and swayed with Mae Murray. You can always be sure the orchestra will play that tune at least once each evening. Much later in film history, Louis Jourdan—at that time called "the handsomest man in the world"—took Leslie Caron to the restaurant "the night they invented champagne" in the musical *Gigi*.

Over the years, Maxim's has carried on, though the big names of yesterday—Callas, Onassis, and the like—are long gone. Today, tourists from around the world are likely to occupy once-fabled tables. Clothing-industry giant Pierre Cardin took over the restaurant in 1981. The kitchen has a staff of some of the finest and most talented young cooks in France. Many of them train at Maxim's before going on to open a restaurant of their own. One of the finest soups I've had anywhere—and it's a great opener to a meal at Maxim's—is Billi-By Soup, made with mussels, white wine, cream (of course), chopped onions, celery, and parsley, as well as coarsely ground pepper. Another favorite, the sole Albert, named after the late famous maître d'hôtel, is flavored with chopped herbs

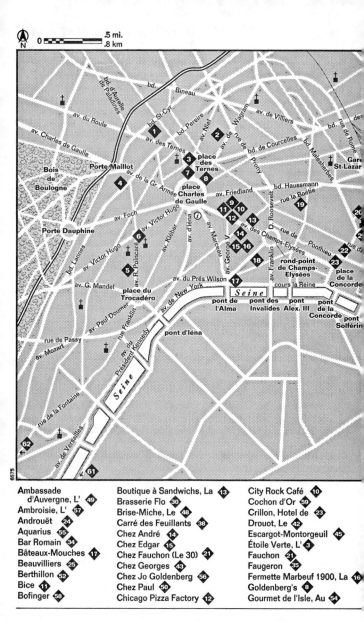

and breadcrumbs, plus a large glass of vermouth. For dessert, try the tarte Tatin.

Arrive slightly early so you can have a drink at the Imperial Bar upstairs. Formal dress is de rigueur on Friday. It's fashionable to have an after-theater supper here, listening or dancing to the music.

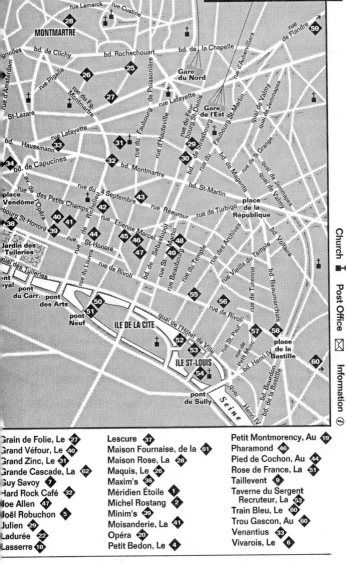

RIGHT BANK DINING

Church ☩ Post Office ⊠ Information ⓘ

Grain de Folie, Le 27	Lescure 37
Grand Véfour, Le 40	Maison Fournaise, de la 61
Grand Zinc, Le 31	Maison Rose, La 28
Grande Cascade, La 62	Maquis, Le 26
Guy Savoy 7	Maxim's 36
Hard Rock Café 32	Méridien Étoile 1
Joe Allen 47	Michel Rostang 2
Joël Robuchon 5	Minim's 39
Julien 29	Moisanderie, La 41
Ladurée 22	Opéra 20
Lasserre 18	Petit Bedon, Le 4

Petit Montmorency, Au 19
Pharamond 46
Pied de Cochon, Au 44
Rose de France, La 51
Taillevent 9
Taverne du Sergent Recruteur, La 53
Train Bleu, Le 60
Trou Gascon, Au 60
Venantius 33
Vivarois, Le 6

TAILLEVENT, 15 rue Lamennais, 8e. Tel. 45-63-39-94.
   Cuisine: FRENCH. **Reservations:** Required weeks, even
   months, in advance for both lunch and dinner. **Métro:**
   George-V.
$ Prices: Appetizers 180F–280F ($31.50–$49); main courses
   220F–380F ($38.50–$66.50). AE, DC, MC, V.

Open: Lunch Mon–Fri noon–2:30pm; dinner Mon–Fri 7–10pm.
Closed: Aug.

⭐ Taillevent dates from 1946, when the restaurant was founded by the father of present owner Jean-Claude Vrinat. It has climbed steadily in the ranks of excellence since then, and today it is recognized as arguably the most outstanding all-around dining place in Paris.

The setting is a grand 13th-century town house off the Champs-Elysées, once inhabited by the duc de Morny, with paneled rooms and crystal chandeliers. The name of the restaurant honors a famous chef of the 14th century who was the author of one of the oldest known books on French cookery. The place is not huge, but that is as the owner wishes, since it permits him to give personal attention to every facet of the operation, seeing to the continuation of the discreet club atmosphere he so carefully maintains.

You might begin with aspic de foie gras (diced liver and veal sweetbreads in aspic jelly with very finely diced carrots and truffles). Menu choices include a minestrone of crayfish, a boudin (sausage) of lobster, scallop salad, aiguillette de bar, red mullet served with baby vegetables, and a creamy black olive sauce, and Scottish salmon cooked in sea salt with a sauce of olive oil and lemons. Desserts might include a nougatine glacé with pears, or grilled small cherries with vanilla ice cream and bitter cherry sauce. Taillevent's wine list is one of the best in the city. Although Monsieur Vrinat likes Americans, it isn't always easy for visitors from the States and other countries to book a table, since the owner prefers for about 60% of his clients to be French.

EXPENSIVE

AU PETIT MONTMORENCY, 26 rue Jean Mermoz, 8e. Tel. 42-25-11-19.
   Cuisine: FRENCH. **Reservations:** Required. **Métro:** F. D. Roosevelt.
$ Prices: Appetizers 80F–350F ($14–$61.30); main courses 110F–240F ($19.30–$42). MC,V.
   Open: Lunch Mon–Fri noon–2:15pm; dinner Mon–Fri 7:30–10:15pm.
   Closed: Aug.

Before Daniel Bouché and his wife, Nicole, opened this establishment, Bouché trained at a number of restaurants, including Maxim's in Chicago. But he seems to have charted his own culinary course and turns out a delicate and subtle cuisine—hot oysters with a Pomerol sauce and wild-mushroom toast; haddock and watercress with fresh salmon toast; Bresse chicken with wild mushrooms; and, in season, such game as hare, venison, partridge, and pheasant.

For dessert, I recommend le grande dessert au chocolat (bitter chocolate) or one of an assortment of different chocolate cakes served with a small, hot pistachio soufflé and a coffee sauce.

The French wines are well selected, including some choice but little publicized ones.

MODERATE

ANDROUET, 41 rue d'Amsterdam, 8e. Tel. 48-74-26-93.
   Cuisine: FRENCH. **Reservations:** Required. **Métro:** St.-Lazare or Liège.

$ Prices: Appetizers 45F–95F ($7.90–$16.60); main courses 90F–185F ($15.80–$32.40); *dégustation des fromages* 250F ($43.80); fixed-price lunch 175F–230F ($30.60–$40.30); fixed-price dinner 195F–230F ($34.10–$40.30) AE, DC, MC, V.

Open: Lunch Mon–Sat noon–3pm; dinner Mon–Sat 7:30–10pm.

Cheese is king here. Time was when an invitation to taste the cheese in Monsieur Androuët's cellars was a badge of honor. Now half of Paris and three-quarters of all visiting foreigners who love cheese have probably made their way to this unique restaurant up the street from the St-Lazare railway station. On the lower level is a luscious shop selling every conceivable variety of cheese from all regions of France. Some of the fixed-price menus include dishes that focus on cheese; others are well prepared and traditional.

For a first course, the ravioles de chèvre frais (ravioli stuffed with fresh goat cheese) is a fine choice. A good main dish is filet de boeuf contentin (beef fillet with Roquefort sauce flambéed with calvados). Other menu listings include a "trio de canard" containing foie gras de canard, magret de canard, and cuisse de canard en confit.

CHEZ ANDRE, 12 rue Marbeuf, 8e. Tel. 47-20-59-57.

Cuisine: FRENCH. **Reservations:** Recommended. **Métro:** F. D. Roosevelt.

$ Prices: Appetizers 25F–100F ($4.40–$17.50); main courses 85F–140F ($14.90–$24.50). AE, DC, MC, V.

Open: Daily 11:30am–1am.

On the corner of rue Clément-Marot is one of the neighborhood's favorite bistros. A discreet red awning stretches over an array of shellfish on ice; inside, an art nouveau decor includes etched glass and masses of flowers. You'll probably be seated elbow to elbow with someone whose picture you have seen in a magazine. The old-fashioned menu is hand-scrawled and includes a very French collection of such dishes as pâté of thrush, Roquefort in puff pastry, several kinds of omelets, calves' head vinaigrette, a potage du jour, and an array of fresh shellfish, along with several reasonably priced wines. Desserts might include rum baba, chocolate cake, or a daily pastry.

CHEZ EDGARD, 4 rue Marbeuf, 8e. Tel. 47-20-51-15.

Cuisine: FRENCH. **Reservations:** Required. **Métro:** F. D. Roosevelt.

$ Prices: Appetizers 40F–80F ($7–$14); main courses 110F–160F ($19.30–$28). AE, DC, MC, V.

Open: Lunch Mon–Sat noon–3pm; dinner Mon–Sat 7pm–12:30am.

A chic coterie of neighborhood residents regard this belle époque eating place as their favorite local restaurant, and ebullient owner Paul Benmussa makes a special point to welcome them during their frequent visits as if they were members of his extended family. Customers include such politicians as Giscard d'Estaing, members of the press, and such show-business personalities as Roman Polanski and Sydney Pollack. Conversation in this scarlet-and-black restaurant can be even noisier than in less expensive establishments.

Specialties include breast of duckling; red mullet with basil in puff pastry; and several terrines, including one made from scallops. There is also a range of well-prepared meat dishes. In winter, seafood and oysters are shipped in from Brittany. The ice-cream sundaes (listed with other desserts on a special menu) are particularly delectable. There's a small outdoor terrace, but most guests prefer to eat inside on one of the semiprivate banquettes.

Ⓕ FROMMER'S SMART TRAVELER: RESTAURANTS

1. Select the prix-fixe (fixed-price) menu. Most restaurants offer both fixed-price and à la carte menus. The latter is more adventurous but at least 30% more expensive.

2. If you have a big appetite but don't want to pay the prices for multicourse dinners in typical Paris restaurants, head for one of those all-you-can-eat places, such as La Taverne du Sergent Recruteur (see p. 144).

3. Look for the *plats du jour* (daily specials) on any à la carte menu. They're invariably fresh and often carry a lower price tag than regular à la carte listings.

4. Drink *vin ordinaire* (table wine served in a carafe). It costs only a fraction of the price of bottled wine.

5. Remember that anything consumed standing up at a counter in Paris or sitting on a stool at the bar is invariably cheaper than if consumed at a table.

6. To keep costs really low, patronize rue de la Huchette on the Left Bank (Métro: St-Michel). It has some of the cheapest restaurants in Paris, serving mainly Greek cuisine. Or turn onto rue Zavier-Privas, where couscous (the most famous dish of North Africa, made from semolina, stewed vegetables, and stewed meat) is found in many establishments.

LA FERMETTE MARBEUF 1900, 5 rue Marbeuf, 8e. Tel. 47-23-31-31.
Cuisine: FRENCH. **Reservations:** Recommended. **Métro:** F. D. Roosevelt or Alma.
$ Prices: Appetizers 42F–96F ($7.40–$16.80); main courses 100F–150F ($17.50–$26.30); fixed-price menu 175F ($30.60). AE, DC, MC, V.
Open: Lunch daily noon–3pm; dinner daily 7:30–11:30pm.

La Fermette has a turn-of-the-century decor, reasonable prices, fine cuisine, and a location just a short distance from the Champs-Elysées. The hand-painted tiles and stained-glass windows of the twin dining rooms contribute to the establishment's listing as a national historic monument. Guests come here for the fun of it all, as well as for the well-prepared and flavorful cuisine.

Specialties are likely to include sweetbreads with a ragoût of wild mushrooms, a basil-flavored fillet of sole with fresh noodles, a bavarois of salmon, and several beef dishes. For dessert, try the chocolate cake with a bittersweet icing.

LE 30 [CHEZ FAUCHON], 30 place de la Madeleine, 8e. Tel. 47-42-56-58.
Cuisine: FRENCH. **Reservations:** Recommended, especially at lunch. **Métro:** Madeleine.
$ Prices: Appetizers 70F–200F ($12.30–$35); main courses 140F–220F ($24.50–$38.50). AE, DC, MC, V.
Open: Lunch Mon–Sat 12:15–2:30pm; dinner Mon–Sat 7:30–10:30pm

In 1990 one of Europe's most legendary delicatessens (Fauchon) transformed one of its upper rooms into an airy and elegant pastel-colored showplace dotted with neo-Grecian columns and accessories. It caught on immediately as the preferred luncheon restaurant for many bankers, stockbrokers, and merchants in the area of place de la Madeleine. Menu selections are prepared with the freshest ingredients available from the display racks downstairs, and might include a cassoulet of lobster served with a basil-flavored shellfish sauce, a curried version of fried sweetbreads, suprême of sea bass with fennel, and a luscious assortment of cheeses and pastries.

If you're in the mood for Italian food, Fauchon also operates a somewhat less expensive restaurant, **La Trattoria,** next door at 26 place de la Madeleine (tel. 47-42-60-11), where main courses tend to run 70F to 100F ($12.30 to $17.50).

INEXPENSIVE

LA BOUTIQUE A SANDWICHS, 12 rue du Colisée, 8e. Tel. 43-59-56-69.
   Cuisine: ALSATIAN/SWISS. **Reservations:** Recommended. **Métro:** F. D. Roosevelt
$ Prices: Appetizers 24F–45F ($4.20–$7.90); main courses 36F–75F ($6.30–$13.10); sandwiches from 15F ($2.60). MC.
   Open: Lunch Mon–Sat 11:45am–1am. **Closed:** Aug 1–20.

 La Boutique à Sandwichs is run by two brothers from Alsace, Hubert and Claude Schick. If you're in the Champs-Elysées area, it's a good place to drop in for sandwiches in many types and shapes. You can dine downstairs at the counter, or crowd into the tiny upstairs room, which is extremely busy at lunch. Here they offer an unusual specialty, raclette valaisanne. To make this fondue dish, a wheel of cheese is used, part of it is melted, and scraped right onto your plate. It is served with pickles and boiled potatoes, the latter resting in a pot with a crocheted hat. The other house specialty is Pickelfleisch garni (Alsatian corned beef). Naturally, the apple strudel is the dessert most diners order.

MINIM'S, 76 Faubourg St.-Honoré, 8e. Tel. 42-66-10-09.
   Cuisine: FRENCH. **Reservations:** Recommended. **Métro:** Concorde.
$ Prices: Appetizers 45F–75F ($7.90–$13.10); main courses 80F–110F ($14–$19.30). AE, DC, MC, V.
   Open: Mon–Sat 10am–6:30pm.

This is Pierre Cardin's "alimentary boutique" on this fashionable street near the Elysée Palace. It's really an ideal luncheon restaurant for suburbanites who are spending their day shopping, and a good choice for afternoon tea or a quick, well-prepared snack. The name, of course, is a tongue-in-cheek adaptation of Cardin's acquisition, Maxim's, and like the decor of its counterpart, the teahouse is filled with art nouveau lighting fixtures and stained glass.

You dine at small tables near a collection of turn-of-the-century silver maidens that I was told came from the collection of Cardin himself. It's totally appropriate here to order only a plat du jour. These change daily but might include eggplant caviar, carpaccio with salad, and confit de canard (duck). You can also order sandwiches, as well as pastries prepared according to the recipes of Maxim's. A deluxe delicatessen fills an adjoining room, and an arts boutique is upstairs.

2. 16TH ARRONDISSEMENT

VERY EXPENSIVE

FAUGERON, 52 rue de Longchamp, 16e. Tel. 47-04-24-53.
Cuisine: FRENCH. **Reservations:** Required. **Métro:** Trocadéro.

$ Prices: Appetizers 140F–210F ($24.50–$36.80); main courses 180F–260F ($31.50–$45.50); fixed-price lunch 290F–650F ($50.80–$113.80); fixed-price dinner 350F–650F ($96.30–$113.80). AE, MC V.

Open: Lunch Mon–Fri 11:30am–2pm; dinner Mon–Fri 7:30–10pm (Apr–Sept only, dinner Sat 7:30–10pm). **Closed:** Aug.

Henri Faugeron is an inspired chef who many years ago established this restaurant as an elegant yet unobtrusive backdrop for his superb cuisine, which he calls "revolutionary." He is viewed as a culinary researcher, and his menu always includes one or two platters from the classic French table—perhaps a leg of lamb baked seven hours or rack of hare in the traditional French style. Much of his cookery depends on the season and on his shopping, selecting only the freshest ingredients in the market. Game dishes, frogs' legs, oysters, scallops—whatever—Monsieur Faugeron and his chefs prepare food with style. In this he is aided by Jean-Claude Jambon, one of the premier sommeliers of France—indeed, of the world.

JOEL ROBUCHON, 59 av. Raymond Poincaré, 16e. Tel. 47-27-12-27.
Cuisine: FRENCH. **Reservations:** Required, six to eight weeks in advance. **Métro:** Trocadéro.

$ Prices: Appetizers 250F–450F ($43.80–$78.80); main courses 250F–500F ($43.80–$87.50); fixed-price menus 890F–1,100F ($155.80–$192.50). AE, DC, MC, V.

Open: Lunch Mon–Fri 12:30–2:30pm; dinner Mon–Fri 7:30–10:30pm **Closed:** July.

⭐ This is where Joël Robuchon, chef and proprietor, basks in his reputation as the country's most innovative cook. Some critics say his restaurant is the finest in France. He is a master of the cuisine moderne, sometimes called *cuisine actuelle*. Foods produced here are light and delicate, with outstanding flavors. He even bakes his own bread fresh every day, and he is known to spend long hours in the kitchen testing (or inventing) new recipes. He has fish and shellfish shipped fresh from Brittany so it doesn't have to linger at the Rungis wholesale market.

Early in 1994, the restaurant moved into new premises: a 1920s-era town house where guests climb a monumental staircase to reach a trio of carefully decorated dining rooms one floor above street level. (The celebrated kitchens and an in-house bakery and pastry kitchen are located on the second and third floors, respectively.)

Among the delectable offerings have been such dishes as kidneys and sweetbreads diced and sautéed with mushrooms, canette rosée (duckling that has been roasted and braised, and flavored with spices such as ginger, nutmeg, cinnamon, and other Chinese-influenced touches), shellfish-filled ravioli steamed in cabbage leaves, and chicken for two, poached in a pig's bladder. His mashed potatoes, once labeled "the silliest dish in the world," are hailed here as a masterpiece—and they are. But the chef won't reveal his secret.

EXPENSIVE

LA GRANDE CASCADE, Bois de Boulogne, 16e. Tel. 45-27-33-51.
   Cuisine: FRENCH. **Reservations:** Required. **Transportation:** You must take a taxi or drive; there's no Métro stop nearby.
$ Prices: Appetizers 145F–310F ($25.40–$54.30); main courses 210F–390F ($36.80–$68.30); *menu d'affaires* 285F ($49.90). AE, DC, MC, V.
   Open: Mid-Apr to Oct lunch daily noon–3pm, dinner daily 7:30–10:30pm; Nov to mid-Dec and mid-Jan to mid-Apr lunch daily noon–3pm. **Closed:** Mid-Dec to mid-Jan.

This is a garden house—a belle époque shrine for lunch, afternoon tea, or dinner in the heart of Paris's fashionable park. Originally, this indoor-outdoor restaurant was built by Baron Haussmann and was used as a hunting lodge for Napoléon III. At the turn of the century it was converted into a restaurant and drew the chic of its day, including Colette.

Today's humbler guest can select a table, choosing the more formal interior with its gilt, crystal, and glass roof, or the more popular front terrace. At the latter, under either parasols or portico shelter, you can order a meal, a drink, or an old-fashioned afternoon tea with a generous helping of the chef's favorite cake. Soft lights at night from the tall frosted lamps and the sound of the nearby cascade enhance the romantic feeling of the place.

The restaurant features such à la carte selections as duckling foie gras, fish poached in seaweed and basil, and veal sweetbreads in truffle-flavored butter. A spectacular finish is provided by crêpes soufflés à l'orange.

LE VIVAROIS, 192 av. Victor-Hugo, 16e. Tel. 45-04-04-31.
   Cuisine: FRENCH. **Reservations:** Required. **Métro:** Pompe.
$ Prices: Appetizers 105F–300F ($18.40–$52.50); main courses 235F–490F ($41.10–$85.80); fixed-price lunch 360F ($63). AE, DC, MC, V.
   Open: Lunch Mon–Fri noon–2pm; dinner Mon–Fri 8–10pm. **Closed:** Aug and Sat–Sun

Le Vivarois has been called a revelation by food critics. This restaurant opened in 1966 with a modern decor (including chairs by Knoll), and it was, from the start, popular with the American crowd. The American magazine *Gourmet* once hailed it as "a restaurant of our time . . . the most exciting, audacious, and important restaurant in Paris today." It still maintains its standards.

Le Vivarois is the personal statement of its supremely talented owner-chef, Claude Peyrot. His menu is constantly changing. One food critic once said, and quite accurately, "the menu changes with the marketing and his genius." He does a most recommendable lobster ravioli and coquilles St-Jacques (scallops). To many his most winning dish is rognons de veau (veal kidneys).

Madame Peyrot is one of the finest maîtres d'hôtel in Paris. Shell guide you beautifully through wine selections so you'll end up with the perfect complement to her husband's superlative cuisine.

MODERATE

LE PETIT BEDON, 38 rue Pergolèse, 16E. Tel. 45-00-23-66.
   Cuisine: FRENCH. **Reservations:** Required. **Métro:** Argentine.
$ Prices: Appetizers 80F–100F ($14–$17.50); main courses 90F–150F ($15.80–$26.30); fixed-price menus 175F–240F ($30.60–$42). AE, DC, MC, V.
   Open: Lunch daily noon–1:30pm; dinner daily 8–11:30 pm.

Le Petit Bedon is traditional but also innovative. The dining room is simply decorated and warm and inviting with only 14 tables. The menu frequently changes. For an appetizer, you might try the thinly sliced salmon, which has been cured and smoked. A black pepper from South America brings out the right seasoning in the dish. If you visit in early spring, you can order milk-fed lamb from the Dordogne region of France. The lamb is delicate and tender and prepared to perfection. The kitchen is also known to do marvelous twists with Challons duckling. Other main dishes include mushroom ravioli, foie gras, and a Rösti of scallops. A masterpiece of desserts is a plate of mixed sorbets; not only is its presentation a work of art, but you are allowed to try to guess the flavors.

3. 17TH ARRONDISSEMENT

EXPENSIVE

GUY SAVOY, 18 rue Troyon, 17e. Tel. 43-80-40-61.
   Cuisine: FRENCH. **Reservations:** Required, one week in advance. **Métro:** Charles-de-Gaulle–Etoile.
$ Prices: Appetizers 185–240F ($32.40–$42); main courses 180F–300F ($31.50–$52.50); fixed-price lunch 380F ($66.50); fixed-price dinner 750F ($131.30). AE, MC, V.
   Open: Lunch Mon–Fri noon–2pm; dinner Mon–Fri 7:30–10:30pm.

⭐ Guy Savoy serves the kind of food that Monsieur Savoy himself likes to eat, and it is prepared with consummate skill. When the five or six "hottest" chefs in Europe are named today, he most often is mentioned, and deservedly so. Don't eat all day, then come here and order his menu dégustation. Although it runs to nine courses, the portions are small; you won't be satiated before the meal has run its course.

What will you get? The menu changes with the seasons, but might, at the time of your visit, include a light cream soup of lentils and crayfish; foie gras of duckling with aspic of duckling and gray salt; and red snapper with a liver and spinach sauce served with crusty potatoes. If you visit in the right season, you may have a chance to order such masterfully prepared game as mallard or venison, even game birds. He is fascinated with the *champignon* in all its many varieties, and has been known to serve as many as a dozen different types of mushrooms, especially in the autumn.

MICHEL ROSTANG, 20 rue Rennequin, 17e. Tel. 47-63-40-77.
   Cuisine: FRENCH. **Reservations:** Required. **Métro:** Ternes.
$ Prices: Appetizers 190F–300F ($33.30–$52.50); main courses 200F–300F ($35–$52.50); *menu dégustation* 495F–680F ($86.60–$119). AE, MC, V.

Open: Lunch Mon–Fri 12:30–2:30pm; dinner Mon–Sat 8–10:30pm
Closed: First two weeks in Aug.

⭐ Monsieur Rostang is one of the most creative chefs of Paris. He's the fifth generation of one of the most distinguished French "cooking families," who have been connected with the famed Bonne Auberge at Antibes on the French Riviera.

Small and intimate, the restaurant offers a menu of bourgeois cuisine that changes constantly, depending on Rostang's inspiration. His specialties are likely to include ravioli filled with goat cheese and coated with a sprinkling of chervil bought fresh that morning in the market. If the mood strikes him, he might prepare a young Bresse chicken, considered the finest in France, served with a delicate chervil sauce (as you may have guessed, Rostang is much enamored of fresh chervil). Another specialty is duckling cooked in its own blood.

From October to March he is likely to offer quail eggs with a coque of sea urchins. He also prepares on occasion a delicate fricassée of sole. Many interesting wines from the Rhône are available, including Châteauneuf du Pape and Hermitage.

MODERATE

GOLDENBERG'S, 69 av. de Wagram, 7e. Tel. 42-27-34-79.
   Cuisine: JEWISH/DELI. **Reservations:** Required. **Métro:** Ternes or Charles-de-Gaulle–Etoile.
$ **Prices:** 35F–140F ($6.10–$24.50); main courses 100F–160F ($17.50–$28); fixed-price menus 95F–100F ($16.60–$17.50). V.
   Open: Daily 9am–midnight.

This is a Jewish delicatessen-restaurant in the Champs-Elysées area. Its founder, Albert Goldenberg, was known as "the doyen of Jewish restaurateurs in Paris," and rightly so, since he opened his first delicatessen in Montmartre in 1936. The deli, like many of its New York counterparts, has the front half reserved as the specialty takeout section and the back half for in-house dining. The menu features such specialties as carpe farcie (stuffed carp), blini, cabbage borscht, and pastrami, one of the most popular items. Naturally, everything tastes better if accompanied by Jewish rye bread. For those who want to really get in the spirit, the menu offers Israeli as well as French wines.

INEXPENSIVE

L'ETOILE VERTE, 13 rue Brey, 17e. Tel. 43-80-69-34.
   Cuisine: FRENCH. **Reservations:** Recommended. **Métro:** Charles-de-Gaulle–Etoile.
$ **Prices:** Appetizers 18F–95F ($3.20–$16.60); main courses 52F–95F ($9.10–$16.60); fixed-price menus 69F–145F ($12.10–$25.40). AE, DC, MC, V.
   Open: Lunch daily 11am–3pm; dinner daily 6:30–11pm.

⭐ This "Green Star" is a sign for economy diners. The decor is so simple as to be forgettable, but a large array of well-prepared foods emerges from the kitchen in back, and the staff is helpful. The cookery is that of a typical French bistro menu of long ago: rabbit pâté, veal Marengo, fresh oysters, coq au vin in Cahors, sweetbreads with sautéed endive, mussels ravigote, châteaubriand béarnaise, and ris de veau (sweetbreads). Its least expensive menu, with drink included, is served from 11am to 9pm.

4. 1ST ARRONDISSEMENT

VERY EXPENSIVE

LE GRAND VEFOUR, 17 rue de Beaujolais, 1er. Tel. 42-96-56-27.

Cuisine: FRENCH. **Reservations:** Required. **Métro:** Louvre.

$ Prices: Appetizers 150F–320F ($26.30–$56); main courses 220F–380F ($38.50–$66.50); fixed-price lunch 305F–750F ($53.40–$131.30); fixed-price dinner 750F ($131.30). AE, DC, MC, V.

Open: Lunch Mon–Fri 12:30–2:15pm; dinner Mon–Fri 7:30–10:15pm.

⭐ Le Grand Véfour has been an eating place since the reign of Louis XV, and it has had its ups and downs. Although the exact date of its opening as the Café de Chartres is not precisely known, it is more than 200 years old and is classified as a historical treasure. It got its present name in 1812, when Jean Véfour, former chef to a member of the royal family, owned it. Since that time it has attracted such notables as Napoléon and Danton and a host of writers and artists, such as Victor Hugo, Colette, and Jean Cocteau (who designed the menu cover in 1953).

Located amid the arcades of the Palais-Royal, the restaurant had lost its earlier glamour by the early 20th century and was simply a little corner café. It had another "up" period after World War II, under Raymond Oliver, one of the most famous modern French chefs, but as he aged, it again fell into decline. Fortunately, Jean Taittinger of the Taittinger Champagne family, with the Concorde hotel group, purchased the restaurant, and it has now reached—perhaps even surpassed—its former glories. From Limoges china, you can feast at a table bearing a brass plaque with the name of a famous former occupant.

The chef, Guy Martin, a native of the Savoy region of France, would surely please the gastronome and former patron Brillat-Savarin, if he were alive today. Monsieur Martin brings originality to French classics. Try his foie gras ravioli in a light truffle cream sauce, or perhaps a delicate white-bean soup flavored with truffles. Some newer dishes are pigeon in the style of Rainier of Monaco, parmentier of oxtail with truffles, and sea scallops with flap mushrooms. Fresh roasted sole and sea scallops in a velvety pumpkin sauce are other specialties. He also brings in omble chevalier, or char, a troutlike fish from Lake Geneva, which he feels is so delectable that he prepares it simply, merely sautéeing it and serving it meunière.

EXPENSIVE

CARRE DES FEUILLANTS, 14 rue de Castiglione, 1er. Tel. 42-86-82-82.

Cuisine: FRENCH. **Reservations:** Required. **Métro:** Tuileries, Concorde, Opéra, or Madeleine.

$ Prices: Appetizers 128F–178F ($22.40–$31.20); main courses 198F–260F ($34.70–$45.50); fixed-price dinner 560F ($98). AE, DC, MC, V.

Open: Lunch Mon–Fri noon–2pm; dinner Mon–Sat 7:30–10:30pm.

⭐ Alain Dutournier established his reputation as a leading chef de cuisine at Au Trou Gascon, now run by his wife, Nicole. He moved his showcase to this restaurant, a beautifully restored 17th-century convent, and immediately became an over-night success. The interior is like a turn-of-the-century bourgeois house, with several small salons. These open onto an inviting skylit interior courtyard, across from which a glass-enclosed kitchen can be viewed (no secrets here).

Monsieur Dutournier likes to call his food *cuisine du moment.* He has a whole network of little farms that supply him with the fresh produce on which he casts his magic spell. He is especially known for his beef butchered from one of the oldest breeds of cattle in France, the *race Châlosse* from western France.

The sommelier has an exciting selection, including several little-known wines along with a fabulous collection of Armagnacs.

MODERATE

ESCARGOT-MONTORGUEIL, 38 rue Montorgueil, 1er. Tel. 42-36-83-51.

Cuisine: FRENCH. **Reservations:** Required. **Métro:** Les Halles.

$ **Prices:** Appetizers 60F–120F ($10.50–$21); main courses 100F–150F ($17.50–$26.30); fixed-price lunch 200F ($35); fixed-price dinner 190F–320F ($33.30–$56). AE, DC, MC, V.

Open: Lunch daily noon–2:30pm; dinner daily 7:30–11pm. **Closed:** Part of Aug.

The "golden snail" of Les Halles is as golden as ever. Even if the famous market has moved elsewhere, the Escargot-Montorgueil is firmly entrenched, the building supposedly dating from the days of Catherine de Médicis. The restaurant opened its doors in the 1830s, and inside it looks it. (The decor has been described as "authentic Louis Philippe.") The greats, such as Sarah Bernhardt, have paraded through here. The food—in the grand bistro tradition—remains consistently good. The restaurant is run by Madame Saladin-Terrail, known as Kouikette, sister of Claude Terrail, the guiding hand behind La Tour d'Argent.

Everybody but the regulars appears to order escargots, although this dish doesn't seem to get much attention from the chef. I recommend the pieds de porcs and the feather turbot soufflé.

JOE ALLEN, 30 rue Pierre-Lescot, 1er. Tel. 42-36-70-13.

Cuisine: AMERICAN. **Reservations:** Recommended for dinner. **Métro:** Les Halles.

$ **Prices:** Appetizers 30F–82F ($5.30–$14.40); main courses 68F–134F ($11.90–$23.50). MC, V.

Open: Daily noon–2am.

About the last place in the world you'd expect to find Joe Allen is Les Halles, that once-legendary Paris market. But the New York restaurateur long ago invaded Paris with the American hamburger. It easily wins as the finest burger in the city because Joe originally set out to match those served at P. J. Clarke's in New York.

Joe Allen's "little bit of New York"—complete with imported red-checked tablecloths, a green awning over the entrance, and waiters who speak English—was made possible by "grants" from such fans as Lauren Bacall, whose poster adorns one of the walls. The decor is in the New York saloon style, complete with brick walls, oak floors, movie stills, and a blackboard menu listing such items as black-bean soup, chili, and apple pie. A spinach salad makes a good beginning. The barbecued ribs are succulent as well.

Joe Allen's also claims that it is the only place in Paris where you can have real New York cheesecake or pecan pie. The pecans are imported from the United States. Thanks to French chocolate,

Joe claims, "we make better brownies than those made in the States." Giving the brownies tough competition is the California chocolate mousse pie, along with the strawberry Romanoff and the coconut cream pie.

Thanksgiving dinner at Joe Allen's in Paris is becoming a tradition (but you'll need a reservation way in advance).

PHARAMOND, 24 rue de la Grande-Truanderie, 1er. Tel. 42-33-06-72.
    Cuisine: FRENCH. **Reservations:** Required. **Métro:** Les Halles or Châtelet.
$ Prices: Appetizers 75F–145F ($13.10–$25.40); main courses 90F–145F ($15.80–$25.40). AE, DC, MC, V.
    Open: Lunch Tues–Sat 12:30–2:30pm; dinner Mon–Sat 7:30–10:45pm.

The restaurant, part of a neo-Norman structure built in 1832, sits on a street in Les Halles. For an appetizer (available between October and April) work your way through half a dozen of the Breton oysters. Next, the main dish to order here is tripes à la mode de Caen, served over a charcoal burner. Tripe is a delicacy, and if you're at all experimental you'll find no better introduction to it anywhere. Try the coquilles St-Jacques au cidre (scallops in cider) if you're not up to tripe. Other main dish specialties include grillade au feu de bois, as well as filets de sole normande.

LA ROSE DE FRANCE, 24 place Dauphine, 1er. Tel. 43-54-10-12.
    Cuisine: FRENCH. **Reservations:** Recommended. **Métro:** Cité or Pont-Neuf.
$ Prices: Appetizers 57F–91F ($10–$15.90); main courses 85F–120F ($14.90–$21); fixed-price menus 210F–350F ($36.80–$61.30). MC, V.
    Open: Lunch Mon–Fri noon–2pm; dinner Mon–Fri 7–10pm.

This restaurant is located in the old section of Ile de la Cité near Notre-Dame, just around the corner from the old Pont-Neuf. You'll dine with a crowd of young Parisians who know that they can expect a good meal at reasonable prices. In warm weather the sidewalk tables overlooking the Palais de Justice are the most popular.

Main dishes include sweetbreads, veal cutlet flambéed with calvados, fillet of beef en croûte, and lamb seasoned with the herbs of Provence. For dessert, try the fruit tart of the day, a sorbet, or iced melon (in summer only).

INEXPENSIVE

CHEZ PAUL, 15 place Dauphine, 1er. Tel. 43-54-21-48.
    Cuisine: FRENCH. **Reservations:** Required. **Métro:** Pont-Neuf.
$ Prices: Appetizers 46F–66F ($8.10–$11.60); main courses 82F–142F ($14.40–$24.90). MC, V.
    Open: Lunch Wed–Sun noon–2:30pm; dinner 7:30–10:15pm.
    Closed: Aug.

 This address used to be given out to first-time visitors by in-the-know Parisians who wanted to tell them about that out-of-the-way bistro where no foreigner ever sets foot. But Chez Paul, on this historic square on the Ile de la Cité, is too good a secret to keep. Nevertheless, the late food expert Waverly Root once wrote of Chez Paul's "resistance to degeneration," and so it remains an unexpected setting for fine food: The effect inside is much like a cold-water flat. The main-dish specialty is escalope papillote.

For dessert, try baba à la confiture flambé au rhum.

LESCURE, 7 rue de Mondovi, 1er. Tel. 42-60-18-91.

Cuisine: FRENCH. **Reservations:** Not accepted. **Métro:** Concorde.

 $ Prices: Appetizers 25F–45F ($4.65–$8.35); main courses 35F–100F ($6.50–17.50); four-course fixed-price menu 98F ($17.20). MC, V.

Open: Lunch Mon–Fri noon–2:15pm; dinner Mon–Fri 7–10pm.

Closed: Two weeks in Aug.

Lescure is a small, inexpensive restaurant in the high-priced place de la Concorde district. Right off rue de Rivoli, the restaurant has been serving good food since 1919. In fair weather, a few sidewalk tables are placed outside; inside, the decor is rustic with an exposed kitchen. Simple, hearty cooking is the rule. You might begin with a pâté en croûte. Main-course house specialties include confit de canard and salmon in a green sauce. My favorite dessert is one of the chef's fruit tarts.

LA MOISANDERIE, 52 rue de Richelieu, 1er. Tel. 42-96-92-93.

Cuisine: FRENCH. **Reservations:** Recommended. **Métro:** Louvre.

$ Prices: Appetizers 70F–135F ($12.30–$23.60); main courses 100F–195F ($17.50–$34.10); fixed-price menus 110F–225F ($19.30–$39.40). AE, DC, MC, V.

Open: Lunch daily noon–3pm; dinner Tues–Sat 7–10:30pm.

This conveniently located bistro, though relatively unknown, has good, reasonably priced food. Although La Moisanderie is small, with tables just big enough for sparrows, everything goes smoothly. It has a homey, rustic French decor: wood paneling covered with 16th-century tapestries, a brick fireplace, a basket of crusty bread, and a counter of mouth-watering homemade pastries. To begin, you are offered hors d'oeuvres, a soup, or marinated herring. Next comes a meat or fowl course—perhaps stuffed chicken, pork with mushrooms, grilled liver, or veal cutlet in a cream sauce with mushrooms. Fancier dishes include steak with cognac and orange duck. For dessert, help yourself from a large glass bowl of fresh fruit salad, unless you prefer a wedge of green-apple tart. It gets crowded, so go early.

5. 2ND & 9TH ARRONDISSEMENTS

EXPENSIVE

RESTAURANT OPERA, in Le Grand Hôtel Inter-Continental, place de l'Opéra, 2e. Tel. 40-07-32-32.

Cuisine: FRENCH. **Reservations:** Recommended. **Métro:** Opéra.

$ Prices: Appetizers 94F–196F ($16.50–$34.30); main courses 124F–198F ($21.70–$34.70); fixed-price menus 285F–450F ($49.90–$78.80). AE, DC, MC, V.

Open: Lunch Mon–Fri noon–2:30pm; dinner Mon–Fri 7–11pm.

This is the most elegant and prestigious restaurant within a hotel

whose history has been intricately linked to that of Paris itself since
its construction in 1860. If you opt for a meal here, your predecessors will have included Salvador Dalí, Harry Truman, Josephine
Baker, Marlene Dietrich, Maurice Chevalier, Maria Callas, and
Marc Chagall, who often came here while working on the famous
ceiling of the nearby Opéra. On August 25, 1944, Charles de
Gaulle placed this famous restaurant's first food order in a newly
freed Paris—a cold plate to go.

Today you can enjoy a predinner drink in a comfortable but
lavishly ornate bar before heading for a table in what some diners
compare to a gilded jewel box. Menu choices change with the seasons, but might include thinly sliced fillets of hare served with a
marmalade of red peppers, asparagus in puff pastry with a mousseline of watercress, consommé of seafood with a saffron cream
sauce, stuffed pig's foot braised with ginger and fresh herbs, and
fillet of lamb with rosemary, cooked in a salt crust. Your dessert
might be warm cherries with sorbet and white cheese.

MODERATE

BAR ROMAIN, 6 rue de Caumartin, 9e. Tel. 47-42-98-04.
  Cuisine: FRENCH. **Reservations:** Recommended for lunch and
  late-night suppers; otherwise, not required. **Métro:** Opéra or
  Madeleine.
$ Prices: Appetizers 40F–170F ($7–$29.80); main courses 98F–130F
  ($17.20–$22.80). AE, DC, MC, V.
  Open: Mon–Sat noon–1am.

Despite its unimaginative facade and the fact that several other establishments in the neighborhood have the same name, this is one
of the most unusual and distinguished outlets for food and drink in
town. It began in 1905 as a wine bar, where virtually everyone of
importance along the *grands boulevards* could mingle with the actors and comedians appearing in the 9th arrondissement's many
cabarets and music halls. In keeping with the turn of the century's
obsession with voluptuous art, the bar was richly fitted with
Carrara marble, mahogany paneling, and 13 murals by Surand,
winner of the coveted Grand Prix de Rome.

Although one of the original panels today hangs in the Louvre,
and five others were auctioned off 10 years ago by Sotheby's, seven
of the original panels remain, fixed in their turn-of-the-century
gloom above the long and narrow bar. Staring down from their
settings are mythical representations of everyone from Vesta with
her Virgins to Nero and Caligula entering Rome on gilded chariots.
The clientele that bustles around below includes a loyal group of
the neighborhood's bankers and merchants, a scattering of fashion
models, and many of the musical stars and agents involved at the
famous Théâtre de l'Olympia, just around the corner.

No one will mind if you just drop in for a drink, although during the lunch hour, most of the tables are filled with businesspeople.
After 5pm, the street level is reserved exclusively for drinking, and
diners move downstairs into a basement-level dining room richly outfitted like a dining car on a turn-of-the-century train. Lunches bustle
with workaday energy, while dinners are more leisurely and, perhaps, more romantic.

Run by the brother-sister team of Jacques and Monique
Bescond, the establishment serves virtually any kind of cocktail you
can think of, as well as a series of savory platters that emerge

miraculously from what's probably the smallest kitchen in Paris. Most dishes seem to be from time-honored recipes handed down by someone's grandfather, and include smoked salmon, châteaubriand, entrecôte, soup of the day, terrine maison, and a specialty version of steak tartare of which the establishment is especially proud.

CHEZ GEORGES, 1 rue du Mail, 2e. Tel. 42-60-07-11.
   Cuisine: FRENCH. **Reservations:** Required. **Métro:** Bourse.
$ Prices: Appetizers 40F–95F ($7–$16.60); main courses 100F–155F ($17.50–$27.10). AE, MC, V.
   Open: Lunch Mon–Sat 12:30–2pm; dinner Mon–Sat 7:30–10pm.

This bistro is something of a local landmark. At lunch it's heavily patronized by members of the Bourse (the stock exchange), which is about a block away. The owner serves what he calls *"la cuisine typiquement bourgeoise,"* or "food from our grandmother in the provinces." Waiters bring around bowls of appetizers, such as celery rémoulade, to get you started. Then you can follow with such favorites as fillet of duckling with flap mushrooms, sweetbreads with morels, veal kidneys in the style of Henri IV (with béarnaise sauce), pavé du Mail (fillet of beef with mustard, crème, and herb sauce), and fillet of fish with a crème fraîche sauce. You can also enjoy a classic cassoulet. Beaujolais goes well with this hearty food.

BUDGET

LE DROUOT, 103 rue Richelieu, 2e. Tel. 42-96-68-23.
   Cuisine: FRENCH. **Reservations:** Not accepted, except for groups of 20 or more. **Métro:** Richelieu-Drouot.
$ Prices: Appetizers 20F–35F ($3.50–$6.10); main courses 35F–60F ($6.10–$10.50). MC, V.
   Open: Lunch daily 11:45am–3pm; dinner daily 6:30–10pm.

One of the best budget restaurants in the 2nd arrondissement, Le Drouot is usually packed with economy-minded Parisians who know where to go for well-prepared, filling food. Similar to the tradition of the famous *bouillons* at the turn of the century, a breadman comes around to see that your plate is full. For an appetizer, you might choose ham from the Ardennes or perhaps artichoke bottoms in vinaigrette. Among the main courses offered, I'd recommend pepper steak with french fries or the fillet of turbot in hollandaise sauce. Chocolate mousse is the special dessert.

LE GRAND ZINC, 5 Faubourg Montmartre, 9e. Tel. 47-70-88-64.
   Cuisine: FRENCH. **Reservations:** Not required. **Métro:** Rue Montmartre.
$ Prices: Appetizers 38F–60F ($6.70–$10.50); main courses 85F–130F ($14.90–$22.80); fixed-price menu 160F ($28). AE, DC, MC, V.
   Open: Lunch Mon–Sat noon–3pm; dinner Mon–Sat 7pm–1am.

Le Grand Zinc may be in an unfashionable quarter, but Paris of the 1880s survives here, as exemplified by the spirit lamps hanging inside. You make your way into the restaurant past baskets of seafood in which you can inspect the *bélons*, or brown-fleshed oysters, from Brittany, a traditional favorite and available all year-round. The atmosphere is bustling in the tradition of a brasserie.

Specialties include steak au poivre, magret de canard with grilled peppers, côte de boeuf (prepared only for two diners), confit de canard (duck) prepared in the style of Toulouse and served with ratatouille, and grilled fillet of turbot with beurre blanc (white butter sauce).

HARD ROCK CAFE, 14 bd. Montmartre, 9e. Tel. 42-46-10-00.
   Cuisine: AMERICAN. **Reservations:** Not accepted. **Métro:** Rue Montmartre.
$ Prices: Appetizers 28F–62F ($4.90–$10.90); sandwiches, salads, and platters 62F–99F ($10.90–$17.30); fixed-price lunch 69F ($12.10). MC, V.
   Open: Daily 11:30am–2am.

Parisian Americaphiles soak up the ambience and nostalgia of the recent past at this French branch of what might be the most successful chain of restaurants ever to hit the world since the first café was established in London in 1971. Like its counterparts, which now stretch from London to Reykjavik, the Hard Rock Café offers one of Paris's largest collections of rock 'n' roll memorabilia as well as musical selections from 35 years of rock 'n' roll classics. These are pumped out at reasonable levels during lunchtime, and at slightly less reasonable levels every evening, much to the delight of the crowd, which appreciates both the music and the juicy steaks, hamburgers, veggie burgers, salads, and heaping platters of informal, French-inspired food. As you dine, scan the high-ceilinged room for such venerated objects as the stage tuxedo worn by Buddy Holly, Jim Morrison's leather jacket, Jimi Hendrix's psychedelic vest, or the black-and-gold bustier sported by Madonna during one of her concerts in Paris.

6. 10TH ARRONDISSEMENT

MODERATE

BRASSERIE FLO, 7 cour Petites-Ecuries, 10e. Tel. 47-70-13-59.
   Cuisine: FRENCH. **Reservations:** Recommended. **Métro:** Château-d'Eau or Strasbourg–St-Denis.
$ Prices: Appetizers 40F–110F ($7–$19.30); main courses 90F–200F ($15.80–$35); fixed-price menu 185F ($32.40). AE, DC, MC, V.
   Open: Lunch daily noon–3pm; dinner daily 7pm–1:30am.

Brasserie Flo is a remembrance of things past. You walk through an area of passageways, stumbling over garbage littering the streets, then come upon this sepia world of turn-of-the-century Paris: old mahogany, leather banquettes, and brass-studded chairs. Some of the choicest people come here (it's the principal rival of the more celebrated Lipp in St-Germain-des-Prés)—and it isn't even expensive.

The thing to order, of course, is "la formidable choucroute" (sauerkraut), but don't expect just a heap of sauerkraut: The mound is surrounded by ham, bacon, and sausages. It's bountiful in the best tradition of Alsace. The onion soup is always good, as is guinea hen with lentils. Look for the plats du jour, ranging from roast pigeon to fricassée of veal with sorrel.

JULIEN, 16 rue du Faubourg St-Denis, 10e. Tel. 47-70-12-06.

Cuisine: FRENCH. **Reservations:** Required. **Métro:** Strasbourg–St-Denis.

$ Prices: Appetizers 33F–99F ($5.80–$17.30); main courses 73F–169F ($12.80–$29.60); fixed-price lunch (and after 11pm) 109F ($19.10); fixed-price dinner 185F ($32.40). AE, DC, MC, V.

Open: Lunch daily noon–3pm; dinner daily 7pm–1:30am.

Julien offers an opportunity to dine in one of the most sumptuous belle époque interiors in Paris. Located in an area not far from Les Halles, it began life at the turn of the century as an elegant place but declined after World War II, becoming a cheap restaurant; however, the decor remained, albeit grimy and unappreciated. From a dingy working-class eating place, it has now been restored to its former elegance, the dirt cleaned off, and the magnificence of the fin-de-siècle dining area brought back to life.

The food served here is *cuisine bourgeoise*, but without the heavy sauces formerly used. Excellently prepared dishes include soups such as Billi-By (a creamy mussel soup as good as that served at Maxim's), fish soup, and onion soup. Among the main courses are grilled lobster with whiskey, fresh salmon with sorrel, and châteaubriand béarnaise. The wine list is good and reasonably priced.

7. 5TH & 6TH ARRONDISSEMENTS

VERY EXPENSIVE

JACQUES CAGNA, 14 rue des Grands-Augustins, 6e. Tel. 43-26-49-39.

Cuisine: FRENCH. **Reservations:** Required. **Métro:** St-Michel.

$ Prices: Appetizers 170F–330F ($29.80–$57.80); main courses 220F–400F ($38.50–$70); fixed-price lunch 270F ($47.30); fixed-price dinner 480F ($84). AE, DC, MC, V.

Open: Lunch Mon–Sat noon–2pm; dinner Mon–Sat 7:30–10:30pm.

Closed: Aug.

 Both the clientele and the food are considered among the most sophisticated and/or grandest in Paris. The establishment is located in a 17th-century town house decorated with massive timbers and a delectable color scheme of pinkish beige, plus a series of 17th-century Dutch paintings. The main dining room is located one flight above street level.

A specialty is the Aberdeen Angus beef, aged for a full three weeks, which chef Cagna imbues with a shallot-flavored sauce rich with herbs and seasonings.

The menu changes but typical dishes are likely to include lobster and bay scallops in puff pastry, lobster salad with baby vegetables, small snails baked with potatoes, fillet of barbue with hot oysters, scallops with truffle juice, and Challons duckling with burgundy sauce, or perhaps veal cutlets flavored with ginger and lime.

LA TOUR D'ARGENT, 15–17 quai de la Tournelle, 5e. Tel. 43-54-23-31.

Cuisine: FRENCH. **Reservations:** Required. **Métro:** Maubert-Mutualité or Pont-Marie.

$ Prices: Appetizers 240F–685F ($42–$119.90); main courses

290F–395F ($50.80–$69.10); fixed-price lunch 375F ($65.60). AE, DC, MC, V.

Open: Lunch Tues–Sun noon–2:30pm; dinner Tues–Sun 8–10:30pm.

La Tour d'Argent is a national institution. The view over the Seine and the apse of Notre-Dame from this penthouse restaurant is superb.

La Tour d'Argent traces its history back to 1582, when a restaurant of some sort stood on this site. The fame of the establishment spread during its ownership by Frédéric Delair, who bought the fabled wine cellar of Café Anglais. He was the one who started the practice of issuing certificates to diners who ordered the house specialty—pressed duckling (caneton). The birds, incidentally, are numbered.

Under the sharp eye of its current owner, Claude Terrail, the cooking is superb and the service impeccable. Dresden china adorns each table. Although a quarter of the menu is taken up with various ways you can order duck, I assure you that the kitchen *does* know how to prepare other dishes. Especially recommended are tournedos of salmon and fillet of beef Tour d'Argent. To begin your meal, I recommend the salad of scallops and truffles.

EXPENSIVE

CLOSERIE DES LILAS [Pleasure Garden of the Lilacs], 171 bd. du Montparnasse, 6e. Tel. 43-26-70-50.
Cuisine: FRENCH. **Reservations:** Required. **Métro:** Port-Royal or Vavin.

$ Prices: Appetizers 70F–200F ($12.30–$35); main courses 180F–230F ($31.50–$56). Brasserie, appetizers 55F–120F ($9.60–$21); main courses 120F–230F ($21–$40.30). AE, DC, V.

Open: Restaurant, lunch daily 12:30–2:30pm, dinner daily 7:30pm–12:30am. Brasserie, daily noon–1am.

The famous people who have sat in the Closerie watching the falling leaves blow along the streets of Montparnasse are almost countless: Gertrude Stein, Ingres, Henry James, Châteaubriand, Picasso, Apollinaire, Lenin and Trotsky at the chess board, and Whistler, who would expound the "gentle art" of making enemies.

To get a seat in what is called the "bateau" section of the restaurant is difficult. However, you can enjoy waiting for a seat at the bar and ordering the best champagne julep in the world. You can order such dishes as poached haddock, beef with a salad, or even steak tartare. The cooking is classic. Try the escargots façon de veau à la moutarde (veal kidneys with mustard) or ribs of veal in a cider sauce.

MODERATE

AUBERGE DES DEUX SIGNES, 46 rue Galande, 5e. Tel. 43-25-46-56.
Cuisine: FRENCH. **Reservations:** Required for dinner. **Métro:** Maubert-Mutualité or St-Michel.

$ Prices: Appetizers 70F–200F ($12.30–$35); main courses 130F–220F ($22.80–$38.50); fixed-price lunch 140F–230F ($24.50–$40.30); fixed-price dinner 230F ($40.30). AE, DC, MC, V.

Open: Lunch daily 12:30–2pm; dinner daily 7:30–10:30pm.

This restaurant was once the chapel of St-Blaise. Auvergne-born Georges Dhulster has this place well under control, and many visitors prefer to come here in the evening to enjoy the view of floodlit Notre-Dame (without having to pay the prices charged by Tour d'Argent) and the Church of St-Julien-le-Pauvre. Try to get a table upstairs with a view of the garden, but be prepared for a wait.

The inspiration for the dishes served here comes from the ancient French province of Auvergne. Menu selections include médaillons of veal with morels, confit of goose prepared in the traditional style, fillet of turbot with a julienne of eggplant and essence of thyme, gigot de lotte, and a *petite marmite des pêcheurs* flavored with saffron.

INEXPENSIVE

LE BISTRO DE LA GARE, 59 bd. du Montparnasse, 6e. Tel. 45-48-38-01.
  Cuisine: FRENCH. **Reservations:** Not accepted. **Métro:** Montparnasse-Bienvenue.
$ Prices: Appetizers 22F–75F ($3.90–$13.10); main courses 69F–110F ($12.10–$19.30); fixed-price menus 60F–76F ($10.50–$13.30). MC, V.
  Open: Daily 11:30–1am.

In addition to offering low-cost, well-prepared meals, this unusual establishment has an art nouveau decor that is classified as a national treasure by the government. The crowds who elbow into this place wait for an empty table at the stand-up bar, where an employee offers a free glass of kir to anyone obliged to wait for more than a few minutes. The menu listings are straightforward but flavorful, including several kinds of grilled steak, duck, and terrines. A wide assortment of desserts is available as well as house wine sold in carafes. You'll find other restaurants belonging to this popular chain at strategic locations throughout the city.

LA CAFETIERE, 21 rue Mazarine, 6e. Tel. 46-33-76-90.
  Cuisine: FRENCH. **Reservations:** Recommended. **Métro:** Odéon.
$ Prices: Appetizers 42F–60F ($7.40–$10.50); main courses 82F–155F ($14.40–$27.10). MC, V.
  Open: Lunch Mon–Sat 12:15–2:30pm; dinner daily Mon–Sat 7:15–11:30pm; Sun brunch 11:30am–5pm.

In the heart of the Odéon district is this tiny neighborhood bistro that serves good food at reasonable prices. Dining is on two levels, and the restaurant serves both lunch and dinner daily, including Sunday, when many other nearby bistros are closed. A coffeepot theme sets the decor, and the service is always laudable. Founder and owner Louis Diet, a former merchant seaman, sees to it that his kitchen turns out tenderloin of beef in mustard sauce, rack of lamb, duck fillet with baked apples, and filet meldoise.

AUX CHARPENTIERS, 10 rue Mabillon, 6e. Tel. 43-26-30-05.
  Cuisine: FRENCH. **Reservations:** Required. **Métro:** Mabillon.
$ Prices: Appetizers 35F–75F ($6.10–$13.10); main courses 85F–115F ($14.90–$20.10); fixed-price menu 135F ($23.60). AE, DC, MC, V.
  Open: Lunch Mon–Sat noon–3pm; dinner Mon–Sat 7:30–11:30pm.

Aux Charpentiers was once the rendezvous of the master carpenters, whose guild was next door. Nowadays it's where the young men of St-Germain-des-Prés take their dates for inexpensive meals in a pleasant atmosphere. Although not especially imaginative, the food is well prepared in the best tradition of

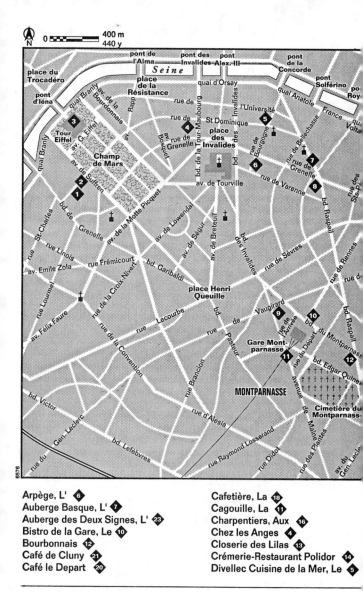

Arpège, L' ◆ **6**	Cafetière, La **18**
Auberge Basque, L' **7**	Cagouille, La **11**
Auberge des Deux Signes, L' **23**	Charpentiers, Aux **16**
Bistro de la Gare, Le **10**	Chez les Anges **4**
Bourbonnais **12**	Closerie des Lilas **13**
Café de Cluny **21**	Crémerie-Restaurant Polidor **14**
Café le Depart **20**	Divellec Cuisine de la Mer, Le ◆ **5**

cuisine bourgeoise. Appetizers include pâté of duck and rabbit terrine. Especially recommended as a main course is the roast duck with olives. Each day of the week a different plat du jour is offered, with time-tested French home-cooking: petit salé aux lentilles, pot-au-feu, and boeuf à la mode are among the main dishes on the menu. The chef suggests platters of fresh fish daily. There is a large choice of Bordeaux wines direct from the châteaus, including Château Gaussens.

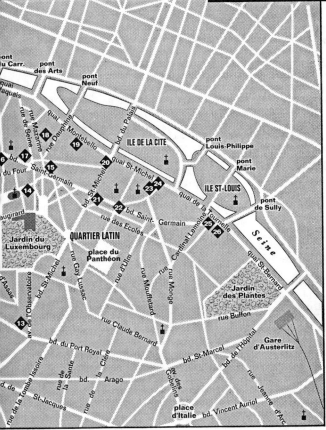

Drug Store, Le 🟤22
Gauloise, La ❶
Jacques Cagna 🟤19
Jules Verne, Le ❸
Maine-Montparnasse Tower
   (Le Ciel de Paris) ❾
Moissonier 🟤26

Petite Chaise, La ❽
Procope, Le 🟤15
Pub Saint-Germain-des-Prés 🟤17
Tea Caddy, The 🟤24
Tour d'Argent, La 🟤25
Western, Le ❷

CREMERIE-RESTAURANT POLIDOR, 41 rue Monsieur-le-Prince, 6e. Tel. 43-26-95-34.
  Cuisine: FRENCH. **Reservations:** Not accepted. **Métro:** Odéon.
$ Prices: Appetizers 15F–62F ($2.60–$10.90); main courses 50F–85F ($8.80–$14.90); fixed-price menu 100F ($17.50). No credit cards.

Open: Lunch daily noon–2:30pm; dinner Mon–Sat 7pm–12:30am, Sun 7–11pm.

Ⓢ Crèmerie Polidor is the most characteristic bistro in the Odéon area, serving the *cuisine familiale*. It still uses the word *crèmerie* in its title, a term dating back to the early part of this century when the restaurant specialized in frosted cream desserts, but its origin dates back to 1845.

In time it became one of the Left Bank's oldest and most established literary bistros. In fact, it was André Gide's favorite, and Hemingway, Valéry, Artaud, Charles Boyer, and Kerouac have also dined here.

The atmosphere is one of lace curtains, polished brass hat racks, and drawers in the back where repeat customers lock up their cloth napkins. It is frequented largely by students and artists, who always seem to head for the rear. Overworked but smiling waitresses serve such dishes as pumpkin soup, snails from Burgundy, rib of beef with onions, rabbit with mustard sauce, and veal in white sauce, followed by such desserts as a raspberry or lemon tart. The menu changes daily.

MOISSONNIER, 28 rue des Fosses St-Bernard, 5e. Tel. 43-29-87-65.

Cuisine: FRENCH. **Reservations:** Required for dinner. **Métro:** Jussieu or Cardinal-Lemoine.

$ Prices: Appetizers 40F–60F ($7–$10.50); main courses 80F–140F ($14–$24.50). MC, V.

Open: Lunch Tues–Sun noon–2:30pm; dinner Tues–Sat 7–9:15pm. **Closed:** Aug.

Come here for real French country cooking, the kind many discriminating palates visit Paris just to sample. Big portions of solid old-fashioned food are served, beginning with *saladiers*, large glass salad bowls filled with a selection of charcuterie. You might also select some excellent terrines, perhaps of Lyonnais sausages. The specialties, from Burgundy and Lyon, include such main dishes as duck with turnips and rack of herb-flavored lamb.

LE PROCOPE, 13 rue de l'Ancienne-Comédie, 6e. Tel. 43-26-99-20.

Cuisine: FRENCH. **Reservations:** Recommended. **Métro:** Odéon.

$ Prices: Appetizers 47.50F–122F ($8.30–$21.40); main courses 89.50F–152.50F ($15.70–$26.70). AE, DC, MC, V.

Open: Daily 8am–2am.

Le Procope, originally opened in 1686 by a Sicilian named Francesco Procopio dei Coltelli, is the oldest café in Paris. More of a restaurant than it was originally, it is sumptuously decorated with gilt-framed mirrors, antique portraits of former illustrious clients, crystal chandeliers, banquettes of Bordeaux-colored leather, and marble-top tables.

Former clients have included La Fontaine, Voltaire, Benjamin Franklin, Rousseau, Anatole France, Robespierre, Danton, Marat, Bonaparte (as a youth), Balzac (who drank endless cups of very strong coffee), and Verlaine (who preferred the now illegal absinthe). There are two levels for dining: the spacious upstairs section or the more intimate street-level room. Fresh oysters and shellfish are served from a refrigerated display. A well-chosen selection of classic French dishes is presented, including baby duckling with spices and "green coffee" or "drunken chicken."

8. 7TH ARRONDISSEMENT

VERY EXPENSIVE

L'ARPEGE, 84 rue de Varenne, 7e. Tel. 47-05-09-06.
  Cuisine: FRENCH. **Reservations:** Required. **Métro:** Varenne.
$ Prices: Appetizers 260F–380F ($45.50–$66.50); main courses 300F–400F ($52.50–$70); fixed-price lunch 390F–890F ($68.25–$155.75); fixed-price dinner 890F ($155.75). AE, DC, MC, V.
  Open: Lunch Mon–Fri noon–1:30pm; dinner Mon–Fri 7:30–9:45pm.
One of the most talked-about and superexpensive restaurants in Paris is L'Arpège, where chef Alain Passard prepares many of his youthful and charming culinary specialties. The restaurant is in a prosperous residential neighborhood, across from the Rodin Museum on the site of what for years was the world-famous l'Archestrate, where Passard once worked in the kitchens.

Amid an intensely cultivated modern decor of etched glass, burnished steel, monochromatic oil paintings, and pearwood paneling, you can enjoy specialties that have been heralded as among the most innovative in recent culinary history. These might include, for example, cabbage stuffed with crabmeat or gamecock with chicken livers and herb-flavored onions. Or try the sweetbreads prepared with exotic mushrooms and truffle juice, or the John Dory with celery juice and asparagus flavored with sage. For dessert, try the chocolate beignets or a sugared tomato with a vanilla stuffing. The wine list is something to write home about.

LE DIVELLEC CUISINE DE LA MER, 107 rue de l'Université, 7e. Tel. 45-51-91-96.
  Cuisine: FRENCH. **Reservations:** Required. **Métro:** Invalides.
$ Prices: Appetizers 60F–300F ($10.50–$52.50); main courses 200F–425F ($35–$74.40). AE, DC, MC, V.
  Open: Lunch Tues–Sat noon–2pm; dinner Tues–Sat 7–10pm.
  Closed: Aug 3–Sept 3.
This is one of the great seafood restaurants in all of France. In a long, narrow modern room, you can select some of the most unusual seafood combinations of cuisine moderne. Thanks to Brittany-born chef Jacques le Divellec, dining here is like dining at the captain's table on a private yacht.

Many sophisticated Parisian palates consider the simplest dishes here the best. The more experimental dishes include fillet of stingray with truffles, terrine of foie gras studded with crayfish, gratin of codfish, mousseline of shellfish with fillet of John Dory, and turbot with noodles tinted with squid ink. Other specialties include tournedos of tuna with goose liver and truffled toast and red mullet with black tagliatelle. Most diners prefer to begin with half a dozen oysters.

LE JULES VERNE, Tour Eiffel, Champ-de-Mars, 7e. Tel. 45-55-61-44.
  Cuisine: FRENCH. **Reservations:** Required. **Métro:** Trocadéro, Ecole-Militaire, or Bir-Hakeim.
$ Prices: Appetizers 160F–400F ($28–$70); main courses 200F–400F ($35–$70); fixed-price lunch 290F ($590.80); fixed-price dinner 660F ($115.50). AE, DC, MC, V.
  Open: Lunch daily noon–2:30pm; dinner daily 7:30–9:30pm.

Today the institution of drinking and dining inside the monument that symbolizes Paris is still alive and well. Many visitors view the elevator ride to the second platform of the Eiffel Tower as one of the highlights of their experience. After the ride, you are ushered into a decor as black as the Parisian night outside, with only strategically placed spotlights set on each of the minimalist tables. The end result seems to bring the twinkling Paris panorama into the restaurant itself.

All of this would be merely a fantasy for ex-aviators and the child in each of us were it not for the exquisite food prepared by a culinary team. The menu changes with the season, but might include ravioli of sweetbreads with lobster sauce, scallops with sweet-and-sour sauce, duck liver with aged vinegar sauce, fillet of turbot with seaweed and a butter flavored with sea urchins, or a cassolette of fresh hot oysters with cucumbers.

MODERATE

L'AUBERGE BASQUE, 51 rue de Verneuil, 7e. Tel. 45-48-51-98.
  Cuisine: FRENCH. **Reservations:** Recommended. **Métro:** Rue du Bac.
$ Prices: Appetizers 60F–100F ($10.50–$17.50); main courses 90F–130F ($15.80–$22.80); fixed-price menu 150F ($26.30). MC, V.
  Open: Lunch Mon–Sat noon–2:30pm; dinner Mon–Sat 7:30–10:30pm.

Owners Monsieur and Madame Rourre come from the Basque country near the Spanish border, and their excellent meals reflect the rich cookery of that area as well as their daily market selections. Among their satisfied diners are famous sportsmen and French TV stars. You might begin with their Basque pâté, then follow with a pipérade, the famous omelet of the region. They also prepare both magret and confit of canard (duck). Various fresh fish dishes are also served, along with a selection of cheese and fresh fruit tarts. Wines are well chosen.

CHEZ LES ANGES, 54 bd. de Latour-Maubourg, 7e. Tel. 47-05-89-86.
  Cuisine: FRENCH. **Reservations:** Required. **Métro:** Latour-Maubourg.
$ Prices: Appetizers 62F–145F ($10.90–$25.40); main courses 107F–161F ($18.70–$28.20); fixed-price lunch 230F ($40.30) without wine, 295F ($51.60) with wine. AE, DC, MC, V.
  Open: Lunch Mon–Sat noon–2pm; dinner Mon–Sat 7–11pm.

The encyclopedia *Larousse gastronomique* reported that "Burgundy is undoubtedly the region of France where the best food and the best wines are to be had." Whether or not that's true, the "Angels" does serve some of the finest Burgundian meals in Paris. The most classic main dish is sauté de boeuf bourguignon, as well as fricassée of veal kidneys. Other main dishes include suprême de barbue (brill) au beurre de poivrons rouges, cassolette of scallops with sea urchins, and tranche épaisse de foie de veau (thickly sliced calves' liver). The goat-cheese selection is varied. Desserts are rich, including a sorbet made with fresh strawberries and cassis.

INEXPENSIVE

LA PETITE CHAISE, 36–38 rue de Grenelle, 7e. Tel. 42-22-13-35.

Cuisine: FRENCH. **Reservations:** Required. **Métro:** Sèvres-Babylone.

$ Prices: Appetizers 55F–65F ($9.60–$11.40); main courses 110F–130F ($19.30–$22.80); fixed-price menu 170F ($29.80). MC, V.

Open: Lunch daily noon–2:15pm; dinner daily 7–11pm.

This is one of the oldest restaurants in Paris, dating from 1680. Very Parisian, it invites you into its world of terra-cotta walls, cramped but attractive tables, wood paneling, and ornate gilt wall sconces. Its special feature is its set meal, which is likely to include such specialties as chicken Pojarski (minced, breaded, and sautéed), noisettes of lamb with green beans, quenelles de brochet (made with pike), trout meunière, escalope de veau normand, and pavé steak with Roquefort sauce. The cheese tray, especially the Cantal and Brie, is always respectable, and the desserts are smooth and satisfying.

9. 15TH ARRONDISSEMENT

EXPENSIVE

LA GAULOISE, 59 av. de la Motte-Picquet, 15e. Tel. 47-34-11-64.

Cuisine: FRENCH. **Reservations:** Required. **Métro:** La Motte-Picquet–Grenelle.

$ Prices: Appetizers 60F–120F ($10.50–$21); main courses 100F–160F ($17.50–$28); fixed-price menu 180F ($31.50). AE, DC, MC, V.

Open: Lunch daily 12:30–2:30pm; dinner daily 7:30–11pm.

With its fire-engine-red canopy that may remind you of a Parisian bistro of the 1930s, La Gauloise has long been an outstanding favorite in the area. Politicians and athletes in particular love its tobacco-tinged walls—in fact, no one wants to see anything changed around here. A member of the staff goes to local markets every morning to seek only the freshest of ingredients, and from the collected bounty the chef prepares his *suggestions du marché* (market selections) to tempt hungry diners. The cuisine, which is traditional and French, might include such dishes as bouillabaisse, an aiguillette of tuna and marinated salmon served with a warm vinaigrette, veal kidneys with mustard sauce, a rack of lamb roasted with mustard and parsley, and fillet of beef béarnaise. During the summer, you can eat outdoors near a collection of potted conifers and parasols, below the roar of an elevated subway track.

MODERATE

LE WESTERN, in the Hilton Hotel, 18 av. de Suffren, 15e. Tel. 42-73-92-00.

Cuisine: STEAKS. **Reservations:** Required. **Métro:** Bir-Hakeim.

$ Prices: Appetizers 45F–85F ($7.90–$14.90); main courses 82F–155F ($14.40–$27.10); fixed-price lunch 150F ($26.30). AE, DC, MC, V.

Open: Lunch daily noon–3pm; dinner daily 7–11pm.

American meat and French wine are what it's all about at Hilton's re-creation of the Old West in Paris. The steaks served at this blend of cattle ranch and French elegance are imported from Kansas, and are as good as anything you'd find in Abilene. Each of the waiters is dressed cowboy-style; the maître d'hotel is in sheriff's garb.

Contrary to expectations, this has become one of those chic Parisian places where many of the French go to rubberneck at the unusual (for Europe) costumes and decor. You might begin your meal with a crab cocktail, jumbo shrimp, or a Caesar salad, to be followed by one of the array of grilled steaks, or if not that, a Roquefort-stuffed chopped sirloin or a saddle chop of salt-marsh lamb with mint jelly.

The portions are large, but if you are still hungry, there is a selection of French cheese and pastries. At trail's end (according to the menu), you might want a steaming cup of outlaw's coffee (made with Kentucky bourbon instead of Irish whiskey).

10. 14TH ARRONDISSEMENT

MODERATE

BOURBONNAIS, 29 rue Delambre, 14e. Tel. 43-20-61-73.
 Cuisine: FRENCH. **Reservations:** Required. **Métro:** Edgar-Quinet or Vavin.
 $ Prices: Appetizers 38F–100F ($6.70–$17.50); main courses 85F–130F ($14.90–$22.80); fixed-price menus 125F–160F ($21.90–$28). AE, DC, MC, V.
 Open: Lunch Mon–Fri 12:30–2pm; dinner Mon–Sat 7–11pm.
 Closed: Aug 1–15.

Bourbonnaise showcases the talents of Roger Le Meur in the heart of Montparnasse. Don't come here for the decor, because it's rather unappealing, with conspicuously heavy and overly rustic furniture. Instead, come for the food: Monsieur Le Meur is a grand chef, some of his culinary inspiration coming from the oldest of his grandmother's recipes. For example, you might enjoy codfish peasant-style or coq au vin with fresh noodles. Perhaps you'll try his foie gras maison or veal kidneys in a mustard sauce. A specialty is the fisherman's platter with sole, monkfish, and salmon served with a saffron-flavored cream sauce. There is also an array of *petits vins* at very reasonable prices.

LA CAGOUILLE, 10–12 place Constantin-Brancusi, 14e. Tel. 43-22-09-11.
 Cuisine: SEAFOOD. **Reservations:** Required. **Métro:** Montparnasse-Bienvenue.
 $ Prices: Appetizers 60F–140F ($10.50–$24.50); main courses 100F–200F ($17.50–$35); fixed-price two-course menu 150F ($26.30); fixed-price three-course menu 250F ($43.80). AE, DC, MC, V.
 Open: Lunch daily 12:30–2pm; dinner daily 7:30–10:30pm.
 Closed: May 1–10, Aug 8–30, and Dec 24–Jan 3.

This is the domain of the burly Gérard Allemandou, a native of the Cognac district. Here you can sample one of the most splendid selections of cognacs from smaller properties ever amassed in Paris.

But that's not why everyone comes here. It's because you get some of the freshest and most reasonably priced fish in Paris. Fresh from Rungis, the huge red mullet is grilled to perfection. Salmon steak is usually slightly underdone and served without a sauce (a dieter's dream come true). Ungarnished barnacles, grilled snapper, mussels sautéed in cast-iron pans—you get a Neptunian parade of natural and pure fish here. Peppered butter and sea salt are trademarks of the place; a "teardrop" of butter is the adornment for the accompanying perfectly steamed vegetables. The decor is ultraclean and minimalist; the "nonwelcome" is bistro-style, but no one seems to mind.

11. 3RD & 4TH ARRONDISSEMENTS

VERY EXPENSIVE

L'AMBROISIE, 9 place des Vosges, 4e. Tel. 42-78-51-45.
   Cuisine: FRENCH. **Reservations:** Required. **Métro:** St-Paul.
$ Prices: Appetizers 210F–520F ($36.80–$91); main courses 190F–380F ($33.30–$66.50). V.
   Open: Lunch Tues–Sat noon–1:45pm; dinner Tues–Sat 8–10:15pm.

⭐ Bernard Pacaud is one of the most talented chefs in Paris, and his cuisine has drawn world attention. He trained at the prestigious Vivarois before deciding to strike out on his own, first on the Left Bank and now at this ideal location in Le Marais on its square evoking memories of Victor Hugo. Try for a table in the garden. The restaurant lies within an early 17th-century town house originally built by the duc de Luynes, which served as the Paris home of the 19th-century actress whose stage name was Rachel.

Pacaud's tables are nearly always filled with satisfied diners, who visit to see where his imagination will take him next. His cooking has a certain simplicity and yet is the height of elegance.

The dishes change with the seasons, but might at the time of your visit include a rondelle of scallops and truffles served with an étuvée of leeks; a croustillant de bar acidulé with a confit of fennel and olives; Bresse chicken "demi-deuil," studded with truffles and served with a truffled cream sauce; and aiguillette of duckling with a coriander-gizzard sauce.

MODERATE

BOFINGER, 5–7 rue de la Bastille, 4e. Tel. 42-72-87-82.
   Cuisine: FRENCH/ALSATIAN. **Reservations:** Recommended.
   Métro: Bastille.
$ Prices: Appetizers 40F–106F ($7–$18.60); main courses 70F–182F ($12.30–$31.90); fixed-price three-course menu 140F–166F ($24.50–$29.10). AE, DC, MC, V.
   Open: Lunch daily noon–3pm; dinner daily 7:30pm–1am.
Bofinger was founded in the 1860s, and is the oldest Alsatian brasserie in town—and certainly one of the best. It's actually a dining palace, resplendent with shiny brass. Much restored, it looks better than ever. If you prefer, you can dine on an outdoor terrace, weather permitting.

The fashionable make their way at night through the Marais

district, right off the place de la Bastille, to this bustling, popular brasserie. In their floor-length white aprons, the waiters bring dish after dish of satisfying fare at reasonable prices. Choucroute (sauerkraut) is the preferred dish, accompanied by a vast array of bacon, sausages, and a pork chop. *Tip:* Look for the chef's specials. He features a different one every day, including a superb stew the French call "cassoulet."

INEXPENSIVE

L'AMBASSADE D'AUVERGNE, 22 rue de Grenier-St-Lazare, 3e. Tel. 42-72-31-22.
   Cuisine: FRENCH. **Reservations:** Recommended. **Métro:** Rambuteau.
$ **Prices:** Appetizers 46F–130F ($8.10–$22.80); main courses 76F–118F ($13.30–$20.70). MC, V.
   Open: Lunch daily noon—2pm; dinner daily 7:30–11pm.

In an obscure district of Paris, this rustic tavern serves the hearty cuisine bourgeoise of Auvergne, the heartland of France. You enter through a busy bar, with heavy oak beams, hanging hams, and ceramic plates. At the entrance is a display of the chef's specialties: jellied meats and fowl, pâtés, plus an assortment of regional cheeses and fresh fruits of the season. Rough wheat bread is stacked in baskets, and rush-seated ladderback chairs are placed at tables covered with bright cloths. Stem glassware, mills to grind your own salt and pepper, and a jug of mustard are on each table.

Specialties include cassoulet with lentils, pot-au-feu, confit de canard, codfish casserole, and stuffed cabbage. Some of these specials are featured on one day of the week only. For a side dish, I recommend aligot, a medley of fresh potatoes, garlic, and Cantal cheese.

LE BRISE-MICHE, 10 rue Brise-Miche, 4e. Tel. 42-78-44-11.
   Cuisine: FRENCH. **Reservations:** Recommended. **Métro:** Rambuteau, Hôtel-de-Ville, or Châtelet–Les Halles.
$ **Prices:** Appetizers 40F–83F ($7–$14.50); main courses 66F–100F ($11.60–$17.50); fixed-price menu 70F ($12.30). AE, DC, V.
   Open: Daily 8am–midnight (full menu available daily noon–midnight.)

Whimsical, sometimes chaotic, and firmly entrenched in the avant-garde aesthetic that surrounds its neighbor, the Centre-Pompidou, this is one of the most appealing low-cost restaurants in the district. Named after the bread rations (les brise-miches) that were issued from its premises during World War II, it occupies an enviable location next to the medieval church of St-Merri and the neighborhood's most charming fountain. In nice weather, tables and chairs overlook about a dozen spinning, spitting, and bobbing fountains, each designed like characters in a surrealistic play, which cavort in the waters of the Stravinsky fountain. (The sculptures are the work of Jean Tinguely and Niki de Saint-Phalle.) Each table is provided with a round loaf of bread, crayons, and paper place mats for doodlings that, if good enough, are framed and proudly displayed as part of the restaurant's permanent decor.

No one will mind if you order just a glass of wine, priced from 10F to 40F ($1.80 to $7), depending on the vintage. Menu choices include a range of "maxi salads," tagliatelle with smoked salmon, fillet of duckling with peaches, a half chicken roasted à l'ancienne, steaks in pepper sauce, and tarte Tatin with crème fraîche which (if you choose) can be flambéed in calvados.

CHEZ JO GOLDENBERG, 4 rue des Rosiers, 4e. Tel. 48-87-20-16.
  Cuisine: JEWISH/CENTRAL EUROPEAN. **Reservations:** Recommended. **Métro:** St-Paul.
$ **Prices:** Appetizers 20F–70F ($3.50–$12.30); main courses 70F–80F ($12.30–$14). AE, DC, MC, V.
  Open: Daily noon–1am.
On this "Street of the Rose Bushes" this is the best-known restaurant. Albert Goldenberg, the king of Jewish restaurateurs in Paris, long ago moved to another restaurant in choicer surroundings at 69 av. de Wagram, 17e. But his brother Joseph remained at the original establishment, which opened in 1936.
  Dining here is on two levels. Look for the collection of samovars and the white fantail pigeon in a wicker cage. Interesting paintings and strolling musicians add to the ambience. The carpe farcie (stuffed carp) is a preferred selection, but the beef goulash is also good. I also like the eggplant moussaka, and pastrami is one of the most popular items. The menu also offers Israeli wines, but Monsieur Goldenberg admits that they're not as good as French wines.

AU GOURMET DE L'ISLE, 42 rue St-Louis-en-l'Ile, 4e. Tel. 43-26-79-27.
  Cuisine: FRENCH. **Reservations:** Required. **Métro:** Pont-Marie.
$ **Prices:** Appetizers 32F–90F ($5.60–$15.80); main courses 65F–85F ($11.40–$14.90); fixed-price menu 125F ($21.90). MC, V.
  Open: Lunch Wed–Sun noon–2pm; dinner Wed–Sun 7–10pm.
This restaurant is savored by its loyal habitués. The setting is beautiful: a beamed ceiling and candlelit tables. Many Parisian restaurants approach this in decor, but where other establishments on this popular tourist island fall short (in the food department), this little "Gourmet Island" succeeds.
  In the window you'll see a sign A.A.A.A.A., which, roughly translated, stands for the Amiable Association of Amateurs of the Authentic Andouillette. These chitterling sausages are soul food to the French. Popular and tasty, too, is la charbonnée de l'Isle, a savory pork with onions. An excellent appetizer is the stuffed mussels in shallot butter. Your palate will fare as well as your wallet if you order the fixed-price menu.

BUDGET

AQUARIUS, 54 rue Ste-Croix-de-la-Bretonnerie, 4e. Tel. 48-87-48-71.
  Cuisine: VEGETARIAN. **Reservations:** Not required. **Métro:** Hôtel-de-Ville. **RER:** Châtelet–Les Halles.
$ **Prices:** Appetizers 18F–29F ($3.20–$5.10); main courses 35F–54F ($6.10–$9.50); fixed-price menu 52F ($9.10). No credit cards.
  Open: Mon–Sat noon–9:45pm. **Closed:** Aug.
Aquarius is one of the best-known vegetarian restaurants in Le Marais, which has many health-conscious residents who insist on no smoking. Neither wine nor spirits are sold, but you can enjoy a fruit-flavored beverage. Meals, regardless of what you order, seem to overflow with raw or steamed vegetables. Aquarius is open for lunch, tea, snacks, and dinner.

LA TAVERNE DU SERGENT RECRUTEUR, 41 rue St-Louis-en-l'Ile, 4e. Tel. 43-54-75-42.
  Cuisine: FRENCH. **Reservations:** Recommended. **Métro:** Pont-Marie.

$ Prices: All-you-can-eat menu 190F ($33.30). V.
Open: Dinner daily 7pm–2am.

⑤ La Taverne du Sergent Recruteur occupies a 17th-century setting on the historic Ile St-Louis. But many buildings on this island do that. What makes La Taverne so popular is that it offers an all-you-can-eat meal. You more or less make your own salad with the items placed before you, including black radishes, fennel, celery, cucumbers, green pepper, hard-boiled eggs, and carrots. After that, a huge basket of sausages is brought around, and you can slice as you wish, sampling one or all. The carafe of wine, either red, white, or rose, is bottomless. Plats du jour, ranging from beef to veal, change daily. You usually select from three different items. Next, a large cheese board makes the rounds, and, if you're still upright, you can select chocolate mousse or ice cream for dessert.

12. 18TH & 19TH ARRONDISSEMENTS

EXPENSIVE

BEAUVILLIERS, 52 rue Lamarck, 18e. Tel. 42-54-54-42.
Cuisine: FRENCH. **Reservations:** Required. **Métro:** Lamarck-Caulaincourt.
$ Prices: Appetizers 134F–192F ($23.50–$33.60); main courses 159F–209F ($27.80–$36.60); fixed-price lunch 185F ($32.40) without wine, 300F ($52.50) with wine; fixed-price dinner 320F ($56) without wine (wine may be ordered separately). AE, MC, V.
Open: Lunch Tues–Sat noon–2pm; dinner Mon–Sat 7:15–10:30pm.

This Montmartre hideaway is reputed to be the favorite Parisian restaurant of master chef Paul Bocuse, who drops in whenever he's visiting from Lyon. The decor is unabashedly romantic, dripping with art nouveau touches that the owners have accumulated since the restaurant was converted from a bakery years ago. Chef Edouard Carlier is the secret behind the success of this restaurant, whose tables are very much in demand.

Amid 19th-century statues, old engravings, and massive bouquets of flowers, you can enjoy subtle transformations of traditional French dishes. Specialties include a flan of mussels with zucchini, duckling en cocotte with a confit of lemons, and a succulent leg of lamb with tarragon. During the summer the restaurant moves outside near a wide stairway leading up to the famous Butte.

COCHON D'OR [Golden Pig], 192 av. Jean-Jaurès, 19e. Tel. 42-45-46-46.
Cuisine: FRENCH. **Reservations:** Required. **Métro:** Porte de Pantin.
$ Prices: Appetizers 45F–200F ($7.90–$35); main courses 78F–210F ($13.70–$36.80). AE, MC, V.
Open: Lunch daily noon–2:30pm; dinner daily 7:30–10:30pm.

The chic come here for some of the best food in the city, even though it means journeying out to the remote Porte de Pantin in the 19th arrondissement. The restaurant's history goes back to the turn of the century, when it was created as a bistro for butchers in skullcaps. Nowadays it's run by the Ayral family, who extend personal greetings. You are served large portions at high prices, but they represent good value due to the quality of the produce and the care that goes into the preparation.

One dish I'd recommend is the charcoal-grilled côte de boeuf with moelle (marrow) sauce, for two. It is usually accompanied by a potato soufflé. Known mainly by gastronomes, an especially satisfying choice is the onglet grillé, one of the best beef cuts I've ever sampled in Paris.

INEXPENSIVE

LE MAQUIS, 69 rue Caulaincourt, 18e. Tel. 42-59-76-07.
Cuisine: FRENCH. **Reservations:** Required. **Métro:** Lamarck-Caulaincourt.
$ Prices: Appetizers 32F–42F ($5.60–$7.40); main courses 70F–120F ($12.30–$21); fixed-price lunch 63F–110F ($11–$19.30). MC, V.
Open: Lunch Mon–Sat noon–2pm; dinner Mon–Sat 8–10pm.

 Montmartre, for all its local color and atmosphere, has never been a great place for dining—with three or four exceptions. However, if you don't mind leaving the place du Tertre and taking a 12-minute walk down the Butte, you'll be amply rewarded at this attractive restaurant, which has a tiny terrace open in the fair-weather months. The menu is limited, but select. Among the tasty courses are sauerkraut of fish, rabbit fricassée, curried mussels, coq au vin, a fillet of sole served with two butters, and pheasant with cabbage. The desserts are often elaborate concoctions.

BUDGET

LE GRAIN DE FOLIE, 24 rue de la Vieuville, 18e. Tel. 42-58-15-57.
Cuisine: VEGETARIAN. **Reservations:** Recommended. **Métro:** Abbesses.
$ Prices: Appetizers 18F–35F ($3.20–$6.10); main courses 60F–100F ($10.50–$17.50); fixed-price menus 60F–100F ($10.50–$17.50). No credit cards.
Open: Lunch Mon–Fri 11am–2:30pm; dinner Mon–Fri 6–11pm; Sat–Sun 11am–midnight.

Simple, wholesome, and unpretentious, this is an all-vegetarian restaurant whose cuisine has been inspired by France, Greece, California, and India. The menu includes an array of salads, cereal products, vegetarian tarts and terrines, and all-vegetable casseroles. Dessert selections might include an old-fashioned tarte aux pommes fines or a fruit salad. Either a simple array of wines or a frothy glass of vegetable juice might accompany your meal.

LA MAISON ROSE, 2 rue de l'Abreuvoir, 18e. Tel. 42-57-66-75.
Cuisine: FRENCH. **Reservations:** Not required. **Métro:** Blanche or Lamarck-Caulaincourt.
$ Prices: Appetizers 42F–92F ($7.40–$16.10); main courses 79F–92F ($13.80–$16.10); fixed-price menus 72F–105F ($12.60–$18.40). MC, V.
Open: Winter daily 11:30am–10pm; summer daily 11:30am–midnight.
Painted a rosy shade of pink, this building, classified as a historic monument, once housed the atelier of Utrillo. Legend has it that Utrillo's friends used to lock him in during his periods of greatest emotional distress and financial crisis so that he could produce

something to sell. Later, Aznavour sang here. In summer the terrace with the most desirable tables quickly fills up. Selected specialties include fish soup, confit or magret de canard (duck), foie gras, blanquette de veau (veal) à l'ancienne, boeuf bourguignon, and paupiettes of sole à la mousseline.

13. 12TH ARRONDISSEMENT

EXPENSIVE

AU TROU GASCON, 40 rue Taine, 12e. Tel. 43-44-34-26.
   Cuisine: FRENCH. **Reservations:** Required. **Métro:** Daumesnil.
$ **Prices:** Appetizers 88F–138F ($15.40–$24.20); main courses 158F–198F ($27.70–$34.70); fixed-price menus 200F–450F ($35–$78.80). AE, DC, MC, V.
   Open: Lunch Mon–Fri noon–2pm; dinner Mon–Fri 7:30–10pm.
   Closed: Aug.

One of the most acclaimed chefs in Paris today, Alain Dutournier, launched his cooking career in the Gascony region of southwest France. His parents mortgaged their own inn to allow Dutournier to open a turn-of-the-century bistro in an unchic part of the 12th arrondissement. At first he got little business, but word soon spread that this man was a true artist in the kitchen who knew and practiced authentic cuisine moderne. Today he has opened another restaurant in Paris, but he left his secret recipes with the kitchen staff. The owner's wife, Nicole, is still there to greet you, and the wine steward has distinguished himself for his exciting *cave* containing several little-known wines along with a fabulous collection of Armagnacs. It is estimated that the cellar has some 350 varieties of wine.

Here you can enjoy the true cookery of Gascony, which means cassoulet, wild salmon with smoked bacon, foie gras, and Gascon ham prepared in farmer's style.

MODERATE

LE TRAIN BLEU, in the Gare de Lyon, 12e. Tel. 43-43-09-06.
   Cuisine: FRENCH. **Reservations:** Recommended. **Métro:** Gare de Lyon.
$ **Prices:** Appetizers 70F–240F ($12.30–$42); main courses 110F–190F ($19.30–$33.30); fixed-price menus 195F–280F ($34.10–$49). AE, DC, MC, V.
   Open: Lunch daily noon–3pm; dinner daily 7–11:30pm.

This is one of the most interesting restaurants in Paris, with an almost overwhelming decor made all the more unusual because of its location within a railway station. To reach it, climb the ornate double staircase that faces the grimy platforms of the Gare de Lyon. Both the restaurant and the station were built simultaneously with the Grand Palais, the Pont Alexandre III, and the Petit Palais as part of the World Exhibition of 1900. As a fitting sequel for a train ride from anywhere in the south of France, the station's architects designed a restaurant whose decor is now classified as a national artistic treasure. Inaugurated by the French president in 1901, the restaurant displays an army of bronze statues, a soaring and lavishly frescoed ceiling, mosaics, mirrors, old-fashioned banquettes, and 41 belle époque murals. Each of these celebrates the distant corners of the French-speaking world, which are linked to Paris by its rail network. (The depictions of Marseilles, Algiers, and the North African port of Sousse are particularly appealing.)

Service is attentive and efficient in case you're about to catch a train to someplace. A formally dressed staff will bring steaming platters of soufflé of brill, escargots in chablis sauce, calves' head ravigote, steak tartare, loin of lamb provençal, veal kidneys in mustard sauce, rib of beef for two, and rum baba.

14. SPECIALTY DINING

HOTEL DINING

BICE, in the Hôtel Balzac, 6 rue Balzac, 8e. Tel. 45-61-97-22.

  Cuisine: ITALIAN. **Reservations:** Required. **Métro:** George-V.

$ **Prices:** Appetizers 65F–125F ($11.40–$21.90); main courses 130F–140F ($22.80–$24.50). AE, DC, MC, V.

  Open: Lunch Mon–Fri noon–4pm; dinner Mon–Sat 7pm–midnight.

  Closed: First three weeks of Aug.

This is the exclusive restaurant of one of the most elegant four-star hotels of Paris, lying just off the Champs-Elysées. From around the world the rich and famous flock to this classically refined establishment. It is an offshoot of the restaurant Bice, which opened in Milan in 1936—under the direction of "Mama Bice"—and has since gone international with branches in New York and Los Angeles, among other cities. The well-prepared (and well-received) cuisine features many specialties from Northern Italy, mainly pastas. Try tagliolini with shrimp and ossobuco of veal with risotto alla milanese. Begin with a caprese salad with mozzarella and tomato or a vegetable carpaccio with a vinaigrette sauce.

VENANTIUS, in the Hôtel Ambassador, 16 bd. Haussmann, 9e. Tel. 48-00-06-38.

  Cuisine: FRENCH. **Reservations:** Required. **Métro:** Richelieu-Drouot or Chaussée d'Antin.

$ **Prices:** Appetizers 95F–280F ($16.60–$49); main courses 155F–240F ($27.10–$42). AE, DC, MC, V.

  Open: Lunch Mon–Fri noon–2:30pm; dinner Mon–Fri 7–10:30pm.

  Closed: Aug and one week in Feb.

This is one of Paris's unusual new enclaves of culinary fashion, superbly decorated, and rapidly gaining a devoted clientele. Situated on the lobby level of a previously recommended hotel (see Chapter 4), its decor consists of an intricate series of floral murals patterned on models found in ancient Pompeii, and an autumnal color scheme of maize and gold designed by noted decorator Sybille de Margerie. Named after Venantius (medieval bishop of Poitiers, patron saint of French chefs), the restaurant has only 50 seats at tables spaced far enough apart to allow conversation that won't be overheard by fellow diners.

A well-trained staff under the direction of chef Gérard Fouché prepares a menu that changes with the seasons, but might include a civet of oysters flavored with truffled duckling, marinated salmon in a tartine of anchovies, a salad of mâche and hare served with a sweet-and-sour beet sauce, fillets of turbot in tomato shells with a mustard-vinaigrette sauce, fillet of lotte with parsley layered with Basque piperade, braised sweetbreads with a truffled risotto, veal kidneys with an escargot-butter sauce, and a pissaladière of eggplants served with oregano-flavored shank of lamb. Desserts include chocolate soufflé with pistachio ice cream and apple tart with vanilla sauce.

DINING WITH A VIEW
EXPENSIVE

BATEAUX-MOUCHES, pont de l'Alma, place de l'Alma, 8e. Tel. 42-25-96-10.
   Cuisine: FRENCH. **Reservations:** Required. **Métro:** Alma-Marceau.
$ Prices: Fixed-price cruise and lunch 320F ($56) Mon–Sat, 350F ($61.30) Sun; fixed-price cruise and dinner 520F ($91). AE, DC, MC, V.
   Open: Lunch cruise Tues–Sun 1–2:45pm; dinner cruise daily 8:30–10:45pm.

Nothing comes close to this combination of sightseeing and dining. For dinner, men are required to wear jackets and ties. During the dinner cruise, live music is featured.

LE CIEL DE PARIS [Maine-Montparnasse Tower], 33 av. du Maine, 15e. Tel. 45-38-52-35.
   Cuisine: FRENCH. **Reservations:** Required. **Métro:** Montparnasse-Bienvenue.
$ Prices: Fixed-price menu 275F ($48.10). AE, DC, MC, V.
   Open: Lunch daily noon–3pm; dinner daily 7pm–midnight.

Overshadowing the Left Bank quarter of Montparnasse, the tower, completed in 1973, covers an entire block and houses some 80 shops, including Galeries Lafayette and more than 200 offices. Its floors are served by rapid elevators that speed visitors from the lobby to the top floor in less than 40 seconds. The charge for the elevator is 35.50F ($6.20) for adults and 28F ($4.90) for children. From April to October it's open daily from 9:30am to 11pm. Off-season hours are 10am to 10pm. Sightseers go to Montparnasse 56, the covered, glassed-in observation deck on the 56th floor, where a panoramic view of Paris opens from every side. Your ticket includes an audiovisual presentation of the glamour of Paris, an exhibit showing how the tower was built, and highlights of the Paris skyline far above. The Belvédère bar/café, good for lunch, a quick snack, or a drink, is also in the Montparnasse 56 complex.

Le Ciel de Paris is the tallest restaurant in the city, where you can enjoy a full dinner—set menu only—at a reasonable price. When you have finished your meal, you may ask the waiter to give you a ticket for Montparnasse 56. There is no charge to take the elevator going directly to the restaurant from the lobby.

LE JULES VERNE, Tour Eiffel, Champ-de-Mars, 7e. Tel. 45-55-61-44.
   Cuisine: FRENCH. **Reservations:** Required. **Métro:** Trocadéro, Ecole-Militaire, or Bir-Hakeim.

Ⓕ FROMMERS COOL FOR KIDS: RESTAURANTS

La Samaritaine *(see p. 112).* Kids will love the sandwiches and fries served at this café with a view of Paris.

La Boutique à Sandwichs *(see p. 119).* If you're in the Champs-Elysées area, drop in for the sandwiches, which come in all shapes and types.

Le Western *(see p. 139).* Kids get a thrill out of seeing the servers dressed in western costumes at this unusual steak house.

Le Drug Store *(see p. 152).* This version of an American coffee shop/snack bar is sure to please the younger set.

Bertillion *(see p. 152).* When they're screaming for ice cream, Bertillion is the place to go.

$ Prices: Appetizers 160F–400F ($28–$70); main courses 200F–400F ($35–$70); fixed-price lunch 290F ($50.80); fixed-price dinner 660F ($115.50). AE, DC, MC, V.
  Open: Lunch daily noon–2:30pm; dinner daily 7:30–9:30pm.
This restaurant is reached by taking an elevator ride up to the second level. It's best at night, when you can dine and survey the City of Lights. For details, see Section 8, above.

LA TOUR D'ARGENT, 15–17 quai de la Tournelle, 5e. Tel. 43-54-23-31.
  Cuisine: FRENCH. **Reservations:** Required. **Métro:** Maubert-Mutualité or Pont-Marie.
$ Prices: Appetizers 240F–685F ($42–$119.90); main courses 290F–395F ($50.80–$69.10); fixed-price lunch 375F ($65.60). AE, DC, MC, V.
  Open: Lunch Tues–Sun 12:30–2:30pm; dinner Tues–Sun 8–10:30pm.
This is one of the most spectacular dining views in all of Paris, despite its lethal prices. Nothing equals its view of the illuminated flying buttresses of Notre-Dame at night. For details, see Section 7, above.

MODERATE

RESTAURANT DE LA MAISON FOURNAISE, Ile des Impressionistes/Ile du Golf Fleuri, Châtou. Tel. 30-71-41-91.
  Cuisine: FRENCH. **Reservations:** Required. **Directions:** From central Paris, take the RER line Al west to Reuil-Malmaison. When you get there, walk to the most westerly end of the train platform, then exit onto the street, and walk for 5 minutes along the right-hand side of the boulevard, heading toward the commercial center of Châtou. The boulevard will soon become a bridge that crosses the Seine. Midway across the bridge, signs will point you down a ramp and staircase toward the Ile du Golf Fleuri/Ile des Impressionistes and the Restaurant Maison Fournaise.
$ Prices: Appetizers 57F–80F ($10–$14); main courses 75F–125F ($13.10–$21.90). AE, MC, V.

Open: Lunch daily noon–2pm; dinner daily 7:30–10pm.

In 1825, a far-sighted boat-builder, Alphonse Fournaise, bought what had until then been a humble fisherman's cottage on an island in the Seine, about 12 miles west of Paris's center. In 1837 the first railway line in France was built between Paris and nearby St-Germain, suddenly placing the humble cottage on the touristic map in a very big way. Alphonse and his family rushed to capitalize on the phenomenon, establishing their hideaway as a luxurious restaurant/bordello where bedrooms and boats were rented by the hour and food and wine were always available for whoever felt rich enough to pay. The island site soon became the preferred playground of many of the French impressionists. There are at least 38 paintings in world-class museums today by such artists as Renoir, Vlaminck, Manet, Degas, and Seurat that all depict in one way or another the heady and majestic scenery at La Maison Fournaise during the late 19th century. (The boat-builder and his daughter, Alphonsine, were the subject of two of Renoir's most renowned portraits. Other group portraits painted on the island, including Renoir's *Le Déjeuner des Canotiers*, are now among the world's most famous paintings.)

In 1979 the suburban town of Châtou bought the dilapidated premises, declared it a civic monument, and installed a small museum. In the 1990s, a private subcontractor was allowed to open a restaurant on the premises. Today groups of Parisians once again travel west to savor the pleasures of La Maison Fournaise.

Some of the menu listings have been inspired by Madame Fournaise herself, while others are more modern. Your meal might include terrine of rabbit à la Mère Fournaise, fillet of haddock steamed in seaweed, roast lamb with a tartine of garlic, roasted hare with a basil-cream sauce, and médaillons of tuna with bacon and sesame sauce.

The premises accommodate a small museum, open Wednesday through Sunday from 11am to 5pm; it is best visited in conjunction with a meal at the restaurant.

FOR BREAKFAST

EXPENSIVE

HOTEL DE CRILLON, 10 place de la Concorde, 8e. Tel. 44-71-15-00.
   Cuisine: FRENCH. **Reservations:** Two or three days in advance for Mon–Fri breakfasts, one day in advance for Sat–Sun breakfasts. **Métro:** Concorde.
$ Prices: Breakfast 140F–200F ($24.50–$35). AE, DC, MC, V.
   Open: Breakfast daily 7–10:30am.

To experience a luxurious French breakfast, dress the part and head for the Hôtel de Crillon. Along with the international diplomatic and business elite, enjoy your breakfast in style amid the marble and crystal of the Restaurant des Ambassadeurs. The sausages are from England, but the several varieties of cheese are purely French. Fresh fruit is also served. This is a chic place for power breakfast *à la francaise*. A standard continental breakfast costs 140F ($24.50). The 160F ($28) breakfast is called *petit déjeuner des affaires* (business breakfast). The *buffet des gourmets* is an English-inspired breakfast buffet, costing 200F ($35).

BUDGET

CAFE DE CLUNY, 20 bd. St-Michel, or 102 bd. St-Germain, 5e. Tel. 43-26-68-24.

Cuisine: FRENCH. **Reservations:** Not required. **Métro:** St-Michel.

$ Prices: Continental breakfast 40F ($7); café au lait (coffee with milk) 20F ($3.50); plats du jour 50F–60F ($8.80–$10.50). MC, V.

Open: Daily 7am–1am.

Among the hundreds of Left Bank cafés, this one, located strategically at the intersection of these two famous avenues, overlooks the hub of the Left Bank and the Musée de Cluny. The long open hours will enable you to begin the day here with a morning omelet and come back at night for a brandy. Breakfast is served at any time, day or night. In the afternoon and until closing you can order various grillades and salads, including steak with pommes frites (french fries) and roast loin of pork.

FOR BRUNCH

EXPENSIVE

HOTEL MERIDIEN ETOILE, 81 bd. Gouvion-St.-Cyr, 17e. Tel. 40-68-34-34.

Cuisine: FRENCH. **Reservations:** Recommended. **Métro:** Porte Maillot.

$ Prices: Brunch 300F ($52.50) adults; 150F ($26.30) children under 12. AE, DC, MC, V.

Open: Oct–Jun Sun 12:30–4pm.

In my opinion, the greatest place for brunch in Paris is "Le Sunday Jazz Brunch," which takes place in the lobby of the Hôtel Méridien. Jazz artists entertain while you eat smoked salmon and enjoy excellent roasts and various hot and cold dishes. For details on the Jazz Club Lionel Hampton, see "The Club and Music Scene" in Chapter 9.

LIGHT MEALS & FAST FOOD

MODERATE

CHICAGO PIZZA FACTORY, 5 rue de Berri, 8e. Tel. 45-62-50-23.

Cuisine: AMERICAN. **Reservations:** Accepted only for 10 or more people. **Métro:** Champs-Elysées–Clemenceau.

$ Prices: Salads 23F–54F ($4–$9.50); pizza (for two) 83F–148F ($14.50–$25.90); fixed-price "express" lunches 48F–68F ($8.40–$11.90). MC, V.

Open: Daily 11:45am–1am.

Sometimes you may get a craving for pizza that nothing else will satisfy. If so, head for the Chicago Pizza Factory, right off the Champs-Elysées, in what was once a garage but is now a "Cheers"-style bar. While music or sports broadcasts are aired from the States, you can order deep-dish pizza and other hometown favorites, such as garlic bread, salad, pecan pie, and cheesecake—but no burgers.

CITY ROCK CAFE, 13 rue de Berri, 8e. Tel. 47-23-07-72.

Cuisine: AMERICAN. **Reservations:** Not required. **Métro:** George-V or F. D. Roosevelt.

$ Prices: Platters 50F–100F ($8.80–$17.50). AE, DC, V.
　Open: Daily noon–3am.

This is where young French people flock to enjoy plenty of good, hot American food. When you walk in you'll be greeted by one of Marilyn Monroe's old dresses hanging on the wall, vintage movie posters, and a nostalgic 1950s atmosphere. Rock 'n' roll is here to stay along with such down-home favorites as cheeseburgers, chili, and banana splits, as well as various Tex-Mex specialties, such as tacos and burritos.

FAUCHON, 26 place de la Madeleine, 8e. Tel 47-42-60-11.
　Cuisine: FRENCH. **Reservations:** Not required. **Métro:**
　Madeleine.
$ Prices: Plats du jour 40F–95F ($7–$16.60). AE, DC, MC, V.
　Open: Mon–Sat 9:40am–7pm.

For epicureans this has been the *haut* grocery store of Paris since 1886, a sort of Parisian version of Fortnum and Mason. In fact, it's such a symbol of the establishment that French Maoists once launched what the press called "a daring caviar and foie gras heist in broad daylight" at this exclusive store.

　What many people don't know about Fauchon is that it offers a reasonably priced cafeteria-style lunch. First, place your order at the counter, then pay at the cashier's desk and receive a ticket to give to the clerk behind this counter. The only hitch is that you have to stand at the fast-food counter while you eat. Try the Fauchon's club sandwich and a scoop of ice cream. In the afternoon, Fauchon's cakes and pastries make tea a delight.

LE DRUG STORE, 149 bd. St-Germain-des-Prés, 6e. Tel. 42-22-92-50.
　Cuisine: FRENCH. **Reservations:** Recommended. **Métro:** St-
　Germain-des-Prés.
$ Prices: Appetizers 20F–40F ($3.50–$7); main courses 60F–90F
　($10.50–$15.80). AE, DC, MC, V.
　Open: Restaurant daily 11am–2am; café daily 9am–2am.

This is the most popular of a chain of coffee shop/soda fountain/snack bar/newsstand/boutiques. When they were opened, these establishments were dismissed by many French as American vulgarisms but they are, in fact, very Parisian today. Le Drug Stores sell everything from mustache cups to hearts of palm. The most popular item to order is a hamburger on a toasted bun. Some of the desserts are smothered in enough whipped cream to make them immoral. The restaurant is located one floor above street level and serves typically French food throughout the day, whereas the street-level café is appropriate for morning coffee, afternoon pastries, and drinks and light meals throughout the evening.

　There's another Drug Store at Publicis Champs-Elysées, 133 av. des Champs-Elysées, 8e (tel. 47-23-54-34).

ICE CREAM

For some of the best ice cream in Paris, try **Bertillion,** 31 rue St-Louis-en-l'Ile, 4e (tel. 43-54-31-61; Métro: Pont-Marie), which is open Wednesday through Sunday from 10am to 1pm. In business some three dozen years, this store sells some of the most delectable ice-cream flavors ever concocted. Two scoops of ice cream cost 38F ($6.70).

TEAROOMS & PATISSERIES
BUDGET

LADUREE, 16 rue Royale, 8e. Tel. 42-60-21-79.
   Cuisine: FRENCH. **Reservations:** Recommended for lunch.
   Métro: Concorde.
$ Prices: Café au lait 20F ($3.50); pot of tea 30F ($5.30); plats du
   jour 110F–140F ($19.30–$24.50). MC, V.
   Open: Mon–Sat 8:30am–7pm; Sun 10am–7pm.

Here, more than at any other salon de thé in Paris, the clientele
look important and affluent. In turn-of-the-century grandeur, you
can sip tea or coffee at tables barely big enough to hold a napkin.
Diners order light lunches or just-baked pastries while talking quietly beneath the ceiling frescoes of the main salon. Visit for lunch
from noon to 2pm to order from a limited menu of traditional
French dishes, such as boeuf bourguignon.

THE TEA CADDY, 14 rue St-Julien-le-Pauvre, 5e. Tel. 43-
   54-15-56.
   Cuisine: FRENCH. **Reservations:** Not required. **Métro:** St-
   Michel.
$ Prices: Pot of tea 25F ($4.40); homemade pastries 30F–35F
   ($5.30–$6.10). No credit cards.
   Open: Thurs–Sat and Mon noon–7pm; Sun 11:30am–7pm.
   Closed: Aug.

This just might be the best spot in Paris for a pot of tea. You'll
recognize it by the stained-glass windows set into the oak door of
what was probably once a stable. Their "ensemble" of furniture,
fabrics, flowers, and darkened paneling would remind tea lovers of
a little corner of London except for a view of Notre-Dame, which
rises across the river. Situated next to the park of what might be
"the most famous lesser-known church of Paris" (St-Julien-le-
Pauvre), Tea Caddy is famous for its homemade marmalade, which
accompanies the scones; its homemade pastries; and its half-dozen
kinds of tea. These include Indian, Chinese, and Russian teas, plus
varieties infused with jasmine and mango.

LATE NIGHT/24-HOUR DINING
MODERATE

AU PIED DE COCHON, 6 rue Coquillière, 1er. Tel. 42-36-
   11-75.
   Cuisine: FRENCH. **Reservations:** Recommended for lunch but
   not accepted for dinner after 8:30pm. **Métro:** Les Halles.
$ Prices: Appetizers 50F–100F ($8.80–$17.50); main courses 80F–
   150F ($14–$26.30). AE, DC, MC, V.
   Open: 24 hours.

The onion soup of Les Halles still lures visitors. Although the great
market has moved to Rungis, near Orly Airport, traditions are long
in dying. Besides, where in Paris can you be assured of getting a
good meal at 3am if not at the famous "Pig's Foot"? The house
specialty is the namesake: pig's feet grilled and served with
béarnaise sauce, as well as the classic onion soup. Of course, you
can sample any of the other tempting fares as well. Try the suck-
ling pig St-Eustache or another well-known specialty, andouillette

or chitterling sausage with béarnaise sauce.

Outside on the street, you can buy some of the freshest oysters in town. The attendants will even give you slices of lemons to accompany them, and you can down them right on the spot.

INEXPENSIVE

CAFE LE DEPART, 1 place St-Michel, 5e. Tel. 43-54-24-55.
Cuisine: FRENCH. **Reservations:** Not accepted. **Métro:** St-Michel.
$ Prices: Platters 27F–67F ($4.70–$11.70); sandwiches 17F–41F ($3–$7.20); crêpes 17F–43F ($3–$7.50). AE, DC, MC, V.
Open: 24 hours.

One of the most popular cafés on the Left Bank is open 24 hours a day. On the banks of the Seine, within view of both the steeple of the Sainte-Chapelle and the dragon statue of place St-Michel, it is conveniently located for most visitors.

The decor is warmly modern, dominated by shades of brown, and with etched mirrors reflecting the faces of a diversified clientele. House cocktails include everything from a tequila sunrise to a Bloody Mary. If you're hungry, select from warm and cold snacks, including sandwiches. The most popular late-night order is a grilled entrecôte with french fries.

PUB SAINT-GERMAIN-DES-PRES, 17 rue de l'Ancienne-Comédie, 6e. Tel. 43-29-38-70.
Cuisine: FRENCH. **Reservations:** Not required. **Métro:** Odéon.
$ Prices: Bottle of beer 20F–80F ($3.50–$14); meals 125F–150F ($21.90–$26.30). AE, DC, MC, V.
Open: 24 hours.

For late-night drinking, this is one of the most popular spots on the Left Bank. In the evening, there's both rock and variety band entertainment. The pub is the only one in the country to offer 24 draft beers and 500 international beers. There are nine different rooms and 500 seats, making it the largest pub in France. Leather booths make for a great late-night quiet snack.

LOCAL FAVORITES

RUE DES ROSIERS If the idea of corned beef, pastrami, schmaltz herring, and dill pickles excites you, then head out for one of the most colorful old neighborhoods in Paris, the rue des Rosiers in the 4th arrondissement (Métro: St-Paul). There is something of the air of a little village about the place. The blue-and-white Star of David is prominently displayed. North African overtones, reflecting the arrival of Jews from Morocco, Tunisia, and especially Algeria, appeared long ago.

John Russell wrote that the rue des Rosiers is "the last sanctuary of certain ways of life; what you see there, in miniature, is Warsaw before the ghetto was razed."

The best time to go is Sunday morning, when many parts of Paris are sleeping. You can actually wander up and down the street, eating as you go—perhaps selecting an apple strudel, a slice of pastrami on Jewish rye bread, even pickled lemons, smoked salmon, and merguez, the typical smoked sausages of Algeria. If you want to have a proper sit-down meal, you'll find many spots.

PICNIC FARE & WHERE TO EAT IT

Paris is full of shops that sell picnic food; some can be found at most *charcuteries* (gourmet food shops), *pâtisseries (pastry shops)*, or *boulangeries* (bakeries). Prices are a bit high, but that's just Paris.

For the most elegant picnic makings in town, go to **Fauchon, 26** place de la Madeleine, 8e (tel. 47-42-60-11; Métro: Madeleine or Concorde), recommended in "Light Meals and Fast Food," above. Here you'll find a complete charcuterie and a famous pastry shop. It's the best-known food shop in town, said to offer 20,000 kinds of imported fruits, vegetables, and other exotic delicacies, snacks, salads, and canapés—all packed to take out.

Another gourmet supplier, **Peltier,** 66 rue de Sèvres (tel. 47-34-06-62; Métro: Sèvres-Babylone), was founded in 1961 and has since then been one of the city's leading pâtisseries (try its delectable tarte au chocolat). One section of the shop is devoted to take-out items, including salads, sandwiches, pastries, terrines, cheese, and quiches, and, of course, bottles of wine. It's closed on Monday.

These are just two of thousands of shops throughout Paris. You can pick up a variety of pâtés or terrines, which can be consumed cold, as well as quiches and salads (but don't buy anything likely to go bad on a hot day). Many of the salads are made with a vinaigrette dressing, which preserves them better. And don't forget the condiments, such as olives and pickles. Food critic Patricia Wells has called the Parisian charcuterie a "little touch of heaven." She likes to go from shop to shop sampling this and that. That way, she claims, you can make a picnic lunch a "true Parisian feast."

Armed with some sauterne or champagne, or whatever it is you like to drink, you're ready to head for your picnic in the park.

My favorite picnic spot is the **Bois de Boulogne,** but, depending on which part of town you're in, you may find the Right Bank **Jardin des Tuileries** (covered in one of our walking tours in Chapter 7) or the **Parc Monceau** equally enticing. At the **Bois de Boulogne,** you can, if you have a child with you, tie in a visit here with a trip to the Jardin d'Acclimation (read about it in "Cool for Kids" in Chapter 6).

Again, if you have children, you may want to take them to the **Bois de Vincennes** (Métro: Picpus), a big, popular patch of woodland with fine trees, two boating lakes, and a racecourse. This park, a favorite spot for family outings, adjoins the 14th-century Castle of Vincennes, open to visitors.

15. CAFÉS

Contrary to general belief, the coffeehouse is not a French invention. It began in 17th-century Vienna and flourished in London long before taking root in France. But when the Parisians adopted it, they infused it with such Gallic flair and local flavor that it became an accepted symbol of their inimitable brand of joie de vivre.

It would be extremely difficult to estimate how many cafés there are in Paris. A single block in the central arrondissements may have three or four. They thin out somewhat in the farther suburbs, but each still has customers.

It's also difficult to define their precise function. Cafés aren't restaurants, although the larger ones may serve complete and excellent meals. They aren't bars, although they offer an infinite variety of alcoholic potions. And they aren't coffee shops in the Anglo-American sense of the word, because they'll serve you a bottle of champagne just as readily as an iced chocolate.

Parisians use them as combination club/tavern/snack bars, almost as extensions of their living rooms. They are spots where you can read your newspaper or meet a friend, do your homework or write your memoirs, nibble at a hard-boiled egg or drink yourself into oblivion. At cafés you meet your dates to go on to a show or to stay and talk. Above all, cafés are for people-watching.

Perhaps their single common denominator is the encouragement of leisurely sitting. Regardless of whether you have one small coffee or the most expensive cognac in the house, nobody badgers, pressures, or hurries you. If you wish to sit there until the place closes, *eh bien,* that's your affair. For the café is one of the few truly democratic institutions—a solitary soda buys you the same view and sedentary pleasure as an oyster dinner.

All cafés sport an outdoor portion. Some have merely a few tables on the pavement, while others have immense terraces, glassed in and heated in winter. Both types, however, fulfill the same purpose. They offer a vantage point from which to view the passing parade.

Coffee, of course, is the chief drink. It comes black in a small cup, unless you specifically order it *au lait* (with milk). Tea (*thé,* pronounced "tay") is also fairly popular, but it is not of the same quality.

The famous apéritifs, French versions of the before-dinner drink, are the aniseed-flavored, mild-tasting Pernod, Ricard, and Pastis, all mixed with ice and water. There are also St. Raphaël and Byrrh, tasting rather like port wine, and the slightly less sweet Dubonnet. As an apéritif, a local favorite is the Italian Campari, drunk with soda and ice, very bitter and refreshing. Try it at least once.

If you prefer beer, I advise you to pay a bit more for the imported German, Dutch, or Danish brands, which are incomparably better than the local brew. If you insist on the French variety, at least order it *à pression* (draft), which is superior.

There is also a vast variety of fruit drinks, as well as Coca-Cola and the specifically French syrups, like Grenadine. They're very much like the stuff you get at home. But French chocolate drinks—either hot or iced—are absolutely superb and on a par with the finest Dutch brands. They're made from ground chocolate, not a chemical compound.

Cafés keep delightfully flexible hours, depending on the season, the traffic, and the part of town they're in. Nearly all of them stay open until 1 or 2am; a few are open all night.

Now just a few words on café etiquette. You don't pay when you get your order—only when you intend to leave. Payment indicates that you've had all you want. *Service compris* means the tip is included in your bill, so it really isn't necessary to tip extra; still, feel free to leave an extra franc or so if the service has been attentive.

You'll hear the locals call the *garçon*, but as a foreigner it would be more polite to say *monsieur. All* waitresses, on the other hand, are addressed as *mademoiselle*, regardless of age or marital status.

In the smaller establishments, you may have to share your table. In that case, even if you haven't exchanged a word with your table companion, when you leave it is customary to bid them good-bye with a perfunctory *messieurs et dames.*

BRASSERIE LIPP, 151 bd. St-Germain, 6e. Tel. 45-48-53-91.

On the day of Paris's liberation in 1944, former owner Roger Cazes (now deceased) spotted Hemingway, the first man to drop in for a drink. Then and now, famous people often drop by the Lipp for its beer, wine, and conversation. The food is secondary, yet quite good, providing you can get a seat (an hour and a half waiting time is customary if you're not a friend of the management). The specialty is sauerkraut garni. You can perch on a banquette, admiring your face reflected—along with that of, say, Françoise Sagan—in the "hall of mirrors." The Lipp was opened in 1870–71, following the Franco-Prussian War, when its founder, Monsieur Lipp, fled German-occupied territory for Paris. It's been a Parisian tradition ever since. Even if you don't go inside for a drink, you can sit at a sidewalk café table, enjoying a cognac and people-watching. **Open:** Daily 8am–2am, although restaurant service is only noon–12:30am. **Closed:** Eight days for Christmas and mid-July to mid-Aug. **Prices:** Plats du jour 85F–120F ($14.90–$21); café au lait 16F ($2.80). **Métro:** St-Germain-des-Prés.

CAFE BEAUBOURG, 100 rue St-Martin, 4e. Tel. 48-87-63-96.

Located across the all-pedestrian plaza from the Centre Pompidou, this is an avant-garde café with soaring concrete columns and a minimalist decor designed by the noted architect Christian de Portzamparc. Many visitors consider this establishment's decor as unusual as its clientele, many of whom are associated with the neighborhood's iconoclastic shops and galleries. In warm weather, tables are set up on the sprawling outdoor terrace, providing a panoramic vantage point of the neighborhood's goings-on for the young and the restless. **Open:** Mon–Fri 8am–1am, Sat–Sun 8am–2am. **Prices:** Glass of wine 22F–35F ($3.90–$6.10), beer 25F–40F ($4.40–$7), cocktails 57F ($10), American breakfast 100F ($17.50), sandwiches and platters 20F–110F ($3.50–$19.30), ice creams 30F–45F ($5.30–$7.90). **Métro:** Rambuteau or Hôtel-de-Ville.

CAFE COSTES, 4–6 rue Berger (place des Innocents), 1er. Tel. 45-08-54-39.

Proud of its minimalist and avant-garde decor (by noted architect Philippe Starck), this café has a polite and helpful staff, a splendid view over the elegant fountain in the place des Innocents (a subtly pleasing palette of earth tones and marble), and an undeniable sense of hip. Furniture, including the chairs, are of brushed aluminum and stainless steel. This is the favorite hangout of Paco Rabanne and many of his models. **Open:** Daily 8am–2am. **Prices:** Continental breakfast 50F ($8.80), brunch (continental breakfast with eggs and bacon) 80F ($14), sandwiches and platters 30F–70F ($5.30–$12.30). **Métro:** Les Halles.

CAFE DE FLORE, 172 bd. St-Germain, 6e. Tel. 45-48-55-26.

Sartre, the granddaddy of existentialism and a key figure in the

Resistance movement, often came here during World War II. Wearing a leather jacket and beret, he sat at his table and wrote his trilogy, *Les Chemins de la liberté* (The Roads to Freedom). In *A Memoir in the Form of a Novel (Two Sisters)*, Gore Vidal introduces his two main characters with "I first saw them at the Café de Flore in the summer of 1948. They were seated side by side at the center of the first row of sidewalk tables, quite outshining Sartre and de Beauvoir, who were holding court nearby." Camus, Picasso, and Apollinaire also frequented the Flore. The café is still going strong, although the famous folks have moved on. **Open:** Daily 7am–1:30am. **Closed:** July. **Prices:** Café espresso 21F ($3.70), glass of beer 40F ($7). **Métro:** St-Germain-des-Prés.

CAFE DE LA PAIX, place de l'Opéra, 8e. Tel. 40-07-30-10.

This hub of the tourist world virtually commands the place de l'Opéra, and the legend goes that if you sit there long enough, you'll see someone you know passing by. Huge, grandiose, and frighteningly fashionable, it harbors not only Parisians, but, at one time or another, nearly every visiting American—a tradition that dates from the end of World War I. Once Emile Zola and Oscar Wilde sat on the terrace; later, Hemingway and F. Scott Fitzgerald frequented it. **Open:** Daily 10am–1:30am. **Prices** (including service): Café espresso 15F ($2.60); fixed-price menu 129F ($22.60); daily specials 88F ($15.40); beer 28F ($4.90). **Métro:** Opéra.

LA COUPOLE, 102 bd. du Montparnasse, 14e. Tel. 43-20-14-20.

Once a leading center of Parisian artist life, La Coupole is now a bastion of traditionalism in Montparnasse in the grand Paris brasserie style. This big, attractive café has, however, grown more fashionable with the years, attracting fewer locals—such as Sartre and de Beauvoir in the old days—and rarely a struggling artist. But some of the city's most interesting foreigners show up. Former patrons included Josephine Baker, Henry Miller, Dalí, Calder, Hemingway, Dos Passos, Fitzgerald, and Picasso. Today you might see Gerard Depardieu.

The sweeping outdoor terrace is among the finest in Paris. At one of its sidewalk tables, you can sit and watch the passing scene, ordering a coffee or a cognac VSOP. The food is quite good, despite the fact that the dining room resembles a railway station. Try, for example, such main dishes as sole meunière, curry d'agneau (lamb), or cassoulet. The fresh oysters and shellfish are especially popular. A breakfast buffet is served from 7:30 to 10:30am Monday through Friday. **Open:** Daily noon–2am. **Prices:** Breakfast buffet 78F ($13.70); coffee 21F ($3.70); complete meal from 250F ($43.80). **Métro:** Vavin.

DEUX-MAGOTS, 170 bd. St-Germain, 6e. Tel. 45-48-55-25.

This legendary café is still the hangout for the sophisticated residents of St-Germain-des-Prés and a tourist favorite in summer. Visitors, in fact, virtually monopolize the limited number of sidewalk tables. Waiters rush about, seemingly oblivious to your needs. Off-season, it's not a lonesome café, since the regulars quickly learn who's who.

The Deux-Magots was once a gathering place of the intellectual elite, including Sartre, Simone de Beauvoir, and Jean Giraudoux. Inside are two large Asian statues that give the café its name. The crystal chandeliers are too brightly lit, but the regulars seem to be accustomed to the glare. After all, some of them even read newspapers there. **Open:** Daily 7:30am–1:30am. **Prices:** Café espresso 21F ($3.70), beer 25F–40F ($4.40–$7). **Métro:** St-Germain-des-Prés.

FOUQUET'S, 99 av. des Champs-Elysées, 8e. Tel. 47-23-70-60.

Fouquet's has been collecting anecdotes and a patina since it was founded at the turn of the century. A celebrity favorite, it has attracted Chaplin, Chevalier, Dietrich, Mistinguett, even Churchill and Roosevelt. The premier café on the Champs-Elysées, it sits behind a barricade of potted flowers at the edge of the sidewalk. You can choose a table outdoors in the sunshine or retreat to the glassed-in elegance of the leather banquettes and the rattan furniture of the street-level grill room. Although Fouquet's is a full-fledged restaurant, with an additional dining room on the second floor, most visitors come by just for a glass of wine, coffee, or a sandwich. **Open:** Café daily 9am–2am. In restaurant, lunch daily noon–3pm, dinner daily 7:30pm–12:30pm. **Prices:** Glass of wine from 50F ($8.80); sandwiches 70F ($12.30), full meals from 250F ($43.80). **Métro:** George-V.

LE MANDARIN, 148 bd. St-Germain, 6e. Tel. 46-33-98-35.

This elegantly decorated corner café is thronged with young people of the Left Bank or visitors soaking up the atmosphere of St-Germain-des-Prés. At the brass bar you can order fine wines, certainly a coffee. Decorated with lace-covered hanging lamps, brass trim, and lots of exposed wood, the establishment serves good food, including crêpes or onion soup. **Open:** Sun–Thurs 8am–2am; Fri–Sat 8am–4am. **Prices:** Café au lait 27F ($4.70), crêpes 22F–44F ($3.90–$7.70), whiskey-soda 62F ($10.90). **Métro:** Odéon or Mabillon.

LA ROTONDE, 105 bd. du Montparnasse, 6e. Tel. 43-26-68-84.

Once patronized by Hemingway, the original Rotonde faded into history but it is still a memory, drawn from the pages of *The Sun Also Rises.* Papa wrote, "No matter what café in Montparnasse you ask a taxi driver to bring you to from the right bank of the river, they always take you to the Rotonde." Lavishly upgraded, the reincarnation of La Rotonde has an art deco paneled elegance, sharing the once-hallowed site with a motion-picture theater. If you stand at the bar, prices are lower. **Open:** Daily 7am–2am. **Prices:** Complete meal 200F ($35); fixed-price lunch or dinner 139F ($24.30), glass of wine 23F–46F ($4–$8.10). **Métro:** Vavin.

LE SELECT, 99 bd. du Montparnasse, 6e. Tel. 45-48-38-24.

Le Select may be a notch down the social ladder from the other glittering cafés of Montparnasse, but I find it the liveliest and friendliest. It opened in 1923 and really hasn't changed very much. At one time it was the favorite hangout of Cocteau. They serve 40 different whiskeys and 20 different cocktails, some rather exotic. **Open:** Sun–Thurs 8am–2:30am, Fri–Sat 8am–3:30am. **Prices:** Coffee 22F ($3.90), hard drinks from 60F ($10.50). **Métro:** Vavin.

WHAT TO SEE & DO IN PARIS

The main attraction of Paris is . . . Paris. You'll make that discovery yourself the moment you start sightseeing. For, unless you're taking an organized tour, you are likely to become so enthralled by the vistas you find en route to a particular sight that you run the risk of never getting there.

No single palace, museum, church, or monument is as captivating as any of the hundreds of streets of this city. They work like sirens' songs on a visitor's senses, luring you into hours of aimless rambling when you should be steering resolutely toward some three-star edifice.

I know—it has happened to me more times than I want to remember. And knowing this, I've divided the sightseeing discussion into easy-to-use sections to help you match your interests with all the attractions Paris has to offer.

SUGGESTED ITINERARIES

IF YOU HAVE 1 DAY The most practical way to see Paris in a day is to take a **guided tour,** since you can't possibly master the city on your own in such a short period of time. Start the day by ordering a café au lait or a café crème and croissants at a sidewalk café. The Cityrama tour, mentioned in "Organized Tours," below, begins at 9:30am. A double-decker bus will take you for a fast two-hour ride through the city, past Notre-Dame and the Eiffel Tower. After the tour, have lunch and go to the **Louvre** for a guided tour, in English, of its most important artworks. If you'd rather explore the museum on your own, pick up an Audioguide in English at the rental counter located in the Hall Napoléon on the mezzanine level and set out. With what's left of the afternoon, stroll along the banks of the **Seine,** ending up at **Notre-Dame** as the sun sets over Paris. If you have an early dinner at a nearby bistro, you may still have the time and energy to attend the Lido or Folies Bergère (see "The Club and Music Scene" in Chapter 9).

IF YOU HAVE 2 DAYS Start your second day by taking a **Bateaux-Mouches cruise** on the Seine (see "Organized Tours," below), with departures from Pont de l'Alma at place de l'Alma on the Right Bank (Métro: Alma-Marceau). Then go the **Eiffel Tower** for lunch with a spectacular view (see my recommendation of

- The world's oldest "grocery store," Les Halles, moved in 1969—its first relocation in eight centuries.

- Rising 981 feet, the Eiffel Tower was the tallest building in the world in 1889.

- Place Denfert-Rochereau was once called place d'Enfer, or the "Square of Hell"—it was stacked with millions of bones from old charnel houses in 1785.

- On the narrow Seine island Allée des Cygnes stands a smaller version of the Statue of Liberty.

- The place de Charles de Gaulle–Etoile was the world's first organized traffic circle.

- Pont-Neuf (New Bridge) isn't new at all. It is the oldest (1607) and most famous bridge in Paris.

- The Sorbonne began in 1253 as modest lodgings for 16 theology students.

- In 1938 workmen discovered 3,350 22-karat gold coins weighing 1.3 grams each at 51 rue Mouffetard. A note said they belonged to Louis Nivelle, royal counselor to Louis XV, who mysteriously disappeared in 1757.

Jules Verne in "Dining with a View" in Chapter 5).

Next, head the for **Arc de Triomphe,** a perfect place to begin a stroll down the **Champs-Elysées,** the main boulevard of Paris, until you reach the Egyptian obelisk at **place de la Concorde.** This grand promenade, one of the most famous long walks in the world, is included in one of my walking tours (see Chapter 7).

IF YOU HAVE 3 DAYS Spend your first and second days as above. Spend your third morning exploring **Sainte-Chapelle** and the **Conciergerie.** Have lunch, perhaps on the Ile St-Louis, and then take a walking tour. Afterward, spend two or three hours at the Musée d'Orsay.

IF YOU HAVE 5 DAYS On your fourth day, take an organized tour or go on your own to visit **Versailles,** 13 miles south of Paris. After viewing the palace and gardens, head back to the city for an evening stroll through the **Latin Quarter,** perhaps dining in a Left Bank bistro. With a good map, try walking along some of the livelier streets, such as rue de la Huchette and rue Monsieur-le-Prince.

On your fifth day, spend the morning roaming around **Le Marais.** By all means, pay a visit to the **Musée Picasso** and have lunch near the historic **place des Vosges.** Afterward, you might want to head toward **Montmartre** (again, see the walking tour in Chapter 7 for specific sightseeing suggestions). Try to time your visit so you'll be at the **Basilica of Sacré-Coeur** at sunset.

1. THE TOP ATTRACTIONS

THE TOP MUSEUMS

There are people—and you might agree with them—who find visiting museums in Paris redundant. Why sacrifice the sunshine to pursue art and culture through dim museum corridors when every Seine-side stroll brings you vistas the masters have

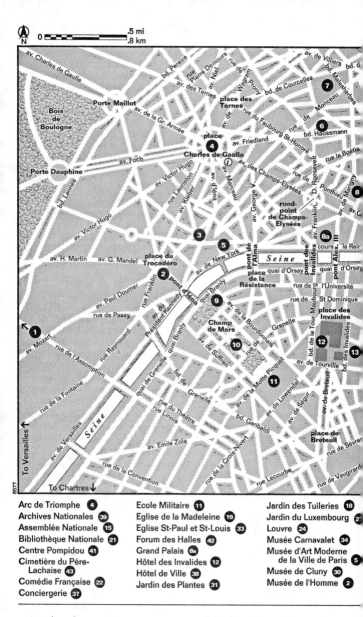

painted and every city square is a model of architectural excellence?

If that's your view, stick with it. Of the almost 100 highly worthy Paris museums, only one is a requirement for the world traveler: the Louvre. Some say that the Musée d'Orsay should also be singled out for that honor. But all the rest can be guiltlessly left to people with serious and specific interests, or saved up for that proverbial (and inevitable) rainy day or for your next visit.

Paris museums fit into three categories: city museums, national museums, and those run by private organizations. The municipal

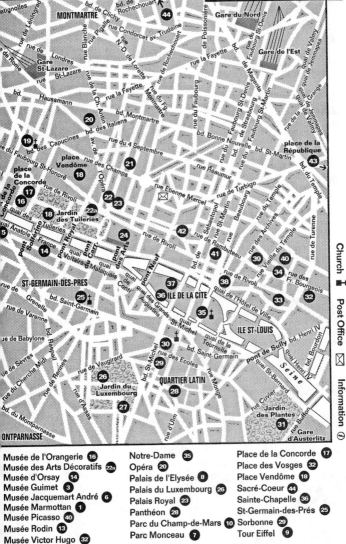

Musée de l'Orangerie **16**	Notre-Dame **35**	Place de la Concorde **17**
Musée des Arts Décoratifs **22a**	Opéra **20**	Place des Vosges **32**
Musée d'Orsay **14**	Palais de l'Elysée **8**	Place Vendôme **18**
Musée Guimet **3**	Palais du Luxembourg **26**	Sacré-Coeur **44**
Musée Jacquemart André **6**	Palais Royal **23**	Sainte-Chapelle **36**
Musée Marmottan **1**	Panthéon **28**	St-Germain-des-Prés **25**
Musée Picasso **40**	Parc du Champ-de-Mars **10**	Sorbonne **29**
Musée Rodin **13**	Parc Monceau **7**	Tour Eiffel **9**
Musée Victor Hugo **32**		

and national museums have fairly standard hours. They are often closed on Tuesday and national holidays. Fees vary, but half-price tickets are usually provided to students, children ages 3 to 7, and extra-large families or groups. If you want to museum-hop in earnest, pick a Sunday, when most museums let you in for half price.

Whatever time of the year you come, Paris seems to be deeply involved with one or another outstanding exhibition—touted madly from the lampposts by huge and colorful posters. In the halls and museum rooms across the city, there are at least 15 special shows on during any given week—a Chagall retrospective, Giacometti sculptures, Art of the Workers' Movement, the public life of Napoléon. . . . The fees charged depend on the exhibit.

I've discussed what I consider the top five museums in Section 1. For information on other Paris museums, see Section 2, "More Attractions," below.

To find out what's showing while you're in town, stop at the Welcome Office, 127 av. des Champs-Elysées (tel. 49-52-53-54; Métro: Charles-de-Gaulle–Etoile). Here you can pick up a free copy of the English-language booklet *Paris Weekly Information,* published by the Paris Convention and Visitors' Bureau; open daily from 9am to 8pm in summer, daily from 9am to 6pm in winter.

MUSEE DU LOUVRE, quai du Louvre, Ier. Tel. 40-20-50-50.

The largest palace in the world, housing a collection of up to 300,000 works of art, the Musée du Louvre is both impressive and exhausting. There's so much to see, so many endless hallways to get lost in that—regardless of how much you may enjoy exploring a museum on your own—here I suggest you start with the guided tour. At least do so until you get the lay of the land. You can always go back to see what you missed.

The entrance to the museum is through I. M. Pei's 71-foot-high glass pyramid in the Louvre's courtyard. First announced in 1983 by President Mitterrand, the modern structure opened in 1990 to acclaim by some, denunciation by others. The pyramid shelters an underground complex of shops and restaurants and, most importantly, increases the gallery space of the Louvre by an astonishing 80%. It also provides garages for all those tour buses that previously created havoc on rue de Rivoli. In addition, automatic ticket machines here help relieve those long, long lines of former days.

The museum buildings are immensely interesting in themselves. French kings have lived on this site by the Seine since the 13th century, but much of the present grand residence was built by Napoléon I and his nephew, Napoléon III. The palace was converted to a museum after the Revolution; the royal arts collections provided the first exhibits. The palace rooms don't function perfectly as skillfully lit museum rooms (for which the Louvre apologizes), but they provide sumptuous settings, which at times even compete with the displays.

Be sure to see at least the highlights of the collection. To the left of the main entrance, at the crest of a graceful flight of stairs, stands the *Winged Victory,* cloak rippling in a wind that blew two centuries before the birth of Christ. In the Department of Greek Antiquities, on the ground floor, stands the supple statue of *Venus de Milo,* the warm marble subtly tinted by sunlight. Upstairs, in the Salle des Etats, covered with bulletproof glass and surrounded by art students, photographers, and awe-struck tourists, hangs the gently chiding portrait *Mona Lisa.*

Among the various museum departments are Egyptian Antiquities, Oriental Antiquities (the world's most complete collection), Greek and Roman Antiquities, Objets d'Art and Furniture, Paintings, and Sculpture.

There are so mant other things to see as well: six more da Vincis (near the *Mona Lisa*), voluptuous Titians, Frans Hals's *The Gypsy,* the enormously lifelike Egyptian *Seated Scribe.* But one can't even start to list the items in this museum. Nor could you see them all if you took three days and brought your lunch. The only blessing is that there is a cutoff point—the collection doesn't go beyound the 19th century.

The Richelieu wing, inaugurated in 1993, houses the museum's collection of northern European and French paintings, along with decorative arts, French sculpture, Oriental antiquities (a rich collection of Islamic art), and the salons of Nepoléon III. Works include artists such as Bosch, Dürer, Rubens, and Vermeer. Constructed from 1852 to 1857, the Richelieu wing was virtually rebuilt, adding some 230,000 square feet of exhibition space. In 165 rooms, plus three covered courtyards, some 12,000 works of art alone are displayed in this newly created section.

Tours: 90-minute English tours daily at 9am, 10am, 10:30am, 11:30am, 2:30pm, and 3:30pm (subject to change—so please call to confirm). The cost is 30F ($5.30).

Admission: 35F ($6.10) adults; children under 18 free.

Open: Mon and Thurs–Sun 9am–5:30pm, Wed 9am–9:30pm.

Métro: Palais-Royal or Musée-du-Louvre.

MUSEE DE L'ORANGERIE DES TUILERIES, Jardin des Tuileries, place de la Concorde, 1er. Tel. 42-97-48-16.

After the Louvre, walk to the river's edge, to the place de la Concorde. Often set aside for special exhibits, this museum, a gem among galleries, has an outstanding collection of art and one celebrated display: Claude Monet's exquisite *Nymphéas* (executed between 1915 and 1927), a light-filtered tangle of lily pads and water, paneling the two oval ground-floor rooms, the construction of which was supervised by the artist himself.

The renovated building also shelters the Walter-Guillaume collection, which includes more than 24 Renoirs, including *Young Girl at a Piano.* Cézanne is represented by 14 works, notably *The Red Rock,* and Matisse by 11 paintings. Rousseau's 9 works are highlighted by *The Wedding,* and the dozen paintings by Picasso reach their brilliance in *The Female Bathers.* Other outstanding paintings are by Utrillo (10 works in all), Soutine (22), and Derain (28).

Admission: 26F ($4.60) adults, 14F ($2.50) ages 18-24, half price on Sun. Children under 18 free.

Open: Wed–Mon 9:45am–5:15pm. **Métro:** Concorde.

MUSEE D'ORSAY, 1 rue de Bellechasse, 7e. Tel. 40-49-48-14.

⭐ Standing across the Seine from the Louvre, the defunct but handsome neoclassical rail station, the Gare d'Orsay, has been transformed into one of the greatest art museums in the world. The museum houses thousands of pieces of sculpture and painting in 80 different galleries. It also displays belle époque furniture, photographs, objets d'art, architectural models, even a cinema. A detailed, wide-ranging panorama of international art is presented from the period between 1848 and 1914, from the birth of the Second French Republic to the dawn of World War I. It is a repository of art and civilization of the century just past.

A monument to the Industrial Revolution, the Orsay station, once called "the elephant," is covered by an arching glass roof, flooding the museum with light. The museum displays works ranging from the creations of academic and historic painters such as Ingres to romanticists such as Delacroix, to neorealists such as Courbet and

Daumier. In a setting once used by Orson Welles to film a nightmarish scene in *The Trial*, based on a Kafka work, are displayed the impressionists and postimpressionists, including Cézanne, van Gogh, and the Fauves, along with Matisse, the cubists, expressionists, and the abstract painters. You get the sunny wheatfields by Millet, works from the Barbizon School, the misty landscapes of Corot, and brilliant-hued Gauguins.

But it is mainly the impressionists that keep the crowds lining up. The impressionists, unified in opposition to the dictatorial Académie des Beaux-Arts, chose for their subject matter the world around them, ignoring ecclesiastical or mythological scenes, and insisted on bathing their canvases in light. They painted the Seine, Parisians strolling in the Tuileries, even railway stations such as the Gare St-Lazare (some critics considered Monet's choice of the latter unforgivable vulgarity). The impressionists were the first to paint the most characteristic feature of Parisian life: the sidewalk café, especially in what was then the artists' quarter of Montmartre.

Perhaps the most famous painting displayed from this era is Manet's *The Picnic on the Grass*, which, when it was first exhibited, was decried as *au grand scandale des gens de bien*. Painted in 1863, it depicts a forest setting with a nude woman and two fully clothed men. Two years later, his *Olympia* created another scandal, showing a woman lounging on her bed and wearing nothing but a flower in her hair and high-heeled shoes. Attending her is an African maid. Zola called Manet "a man among eunuchs."

One of Renoir's brightest, most joyous paintings is here—the *Moulin de la Galette*, painted in 1876. Degas is represented by his paintings of racehorses and dancers; his 1876 café scene *Absinthe* remains one of his most reproduced works. Paris-born Claude Monet was fascinated by the changing light effects on Rouen Cathedral, and in a series of five paintings he makes the old landmark live as never before.

One of the most celebrated works is by an American—Whistler's *Arrangement in Gray and Black: Portrait of the Painter's Mother* perhaps better known as *Whistler's Mother*. It is said that this painting heralded the advent of modern art, although many critics denounced it at the time as "Whistler's Dead Mother" because of its funereal overtones. Today the painting has been hailed as a "veritable icon of our consciousness." As far as Whistler was concerned, he claimed he made "Mummy just as nice as possible."

Admission: 32F ($5.60) adults, 17F ($3) ages 18–24 and over 60; children 17 and under free.

Open: Tues–Wed and Fri–Sat 10am–6pm, Sun 9am–6pm, Thurs 10am–9:45pm. June 20–Sept 20, museum opens at 9am. **Métro:** Solférino. **RER:** Musée d'Orsay.

CENTRE GEORGES POMPIDOU, on the plateau Beaubourg, east of bd. de Sébastopol, 4e. Tel. 42-77-12-33.

It was Georges Pompidou's dream to create a large cultural center in Paris that would include every form of 20th-century art. As President of France (in 1969), he launched the project for a "temple devoted to art." That center was finally inaugurated in 1977 by yet another French president, Valéry Giscard d'Estaing.

The building housing the center was called "the most avant-garde building in the world" because of its radical exoskeletal design, but Parisians are more likely to refer to it as "the refinery." The colorfully painted pipes and ducts that crisscross the transparent facade

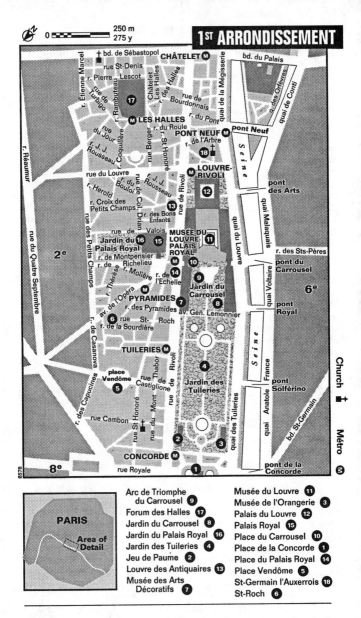

Arc de Triomphe du Carrousel 9		Musée du Louvre 11
Forum des Halles 17		Musée de l'Orangerie 3
Jardin du Carrousel 8		Palais du Louvre 12
Jardin du Palais Royal 16		Palais Royal 15
Jardin des Tuileries 4		Place du Carrousel 10
Jeu de Paume 2		Place de la Concorde 1
Louvre des Antiquaires 13		Place du Palais Royal 14
Musée des Arts Décoratifs 7		Place Vendôme 5
		St-Germain l'Auxerrois 18
		St-Roch 6

are actually the practical housings for the intricate electrical, heating, and telephone systems that service the center. Even the escalators are housed in tubes on the outside of the building. Thus the vast interior has no need for walls, and a grand feeling of open space is created. When walls are needed for exhibits, moving partitions are rolled into place.

All this uniqueness has made the Pompidou Center Paris's favorite sightseeing attraction, surpassing even the Eiffel Tower in the number of tourists who visit.

The **Musée National d'Art Moderne** can be entered on the fourth floor. It offers a large collection of 20th-century art, including French and American masterpieces from the Fauves up to expressionist and abstract works. All the trends of modern art are displayed on two floors in well-lit rooms of varying sizes.

Featured are works by such artists as Ernst (a sculpture, *The Imbecile),* Kandinsky, Vuillard, Bonnard, Utrillo, Chagall, Dufy, Gris, Léger, and Pollock, as well as sketches by Le Corbusier and stained glass by Rouault. Modern sculpture includes works by Calder, Moore, and Epstein. Galeries Contemporaines, on the ground floor, demonstrates the trends in artistic activity today. Special exhibitions and demonstrations are constantly being staged in the Grande Galerie. Guided tours are available.

In addition to the modern art museum, the center contains the largest consulting library in Paris, with more than a million volumes and documents. Its Center of Industrial Design contains exhibits and research facilities in the field of architecture, space planning, publishing, and visual communications. A cinémathèque offers visitors a historical tour of filmmaking. The top-floor restaurant and cafeteria offer a panoramic view of Paris.

Admission: All-day pass 60F ($10.50) adults, 55F ($9.60) ages 18–24 and over 60; children under 18 free. Museum of Modern Art only, 30F ($5.30). Free admission Sun morning.

Open: Mon and Wed–Fri noon–10pm, Sat–Sun 10am–10pm.
Métro: Rambuteau, Hôtel-de-Ville, or Châtelet.

MUSEE PICASSO, 5 rue de Thorigny, 3e. Tel. 42-71-25-21.

⭐ When it opened at the beautifully restored Hôtel Sale (salt mansion), the press hailed it as a "museum for Picasso's Picassos." And that's what it is. Almost overnight it became one of the most popular attractions in Paris. The greatest Picasso collection in the world, acquired by the state in payment of inheritance taxes totaling around $50 million, consists of 203 paintings, 158 sculptures, 16 collages, 19 bas-reliefs, 88 ceramics, and more than 1,500 sketches and 1,600 engravings, along with 30 notebooks.

The paintings include a remarkable 1901 self-portrait and such masterpieces as *Le Baiser* (The Kiss), painted at Mougins on the Riviera in 1969, and the 1970 *Reclining Nude and the Man with a Guitar.* It's easy to stroll through the handsome museum seeking your own favorite work (mine is a delightfully wicked one, *Young Man with a Lobster,* painted in Paris in 1941). The museum owns several intriguing studies for *Les Demoiselles d'Avignon,* the painting that initiated cubism.

Many of the major masterpieces such as *The Crucifixion* and *Nude in a Red Armchair* should remain on permanent view. However, because the collection is so vast, temporary exhibitions, such as one featuring the studies of the *Minotaur,* are opened to the public at the rate of two a year. In addition to Picasso's own art, works by other masters from his private collection are displayed, including the contributions of such world-class artists as Cézanne, Rousseau, Braque, Matisse, Derain, and Miró. Picasso was fascinated with African masks, and many of these are on view as well.

The mansion was constructed in 1656 by Aubert de Fontenay, who collected the dreaded salt tax in Paris.

Admission: 26F ($4.60) adults, 17F ($3) children ages 18–25; children under 18 free.

Open: Apr–Sept Wed–Mon 9:30 am–5:30 pm; off-season Wed–Mon 9:30am–1pm. **Métro:** St-Paul, Filles-du-Calvaire, or Chemin-Vert.

Basilique Notre-Dame
  des Victoires ③
Bibliothèque
  Nationale ⑥
Hôtel Colbert ⑤
La Bourse ②
Musée
  Cognacq-Jay ⑧
Notre-Dame de
  Bonne Nouvelle ①
Place de l'Opéra ⑦
Place des Victoires ④

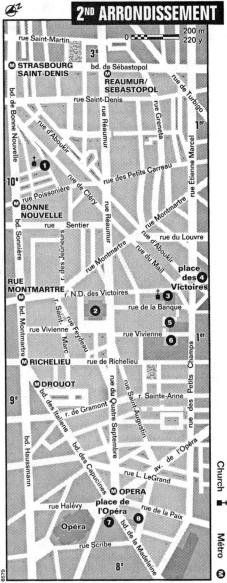

THE SEINE ISLANDS

The "egg from which Paris was hatched," **Ile de la Cité,** lies quietly in the shadow of Notre-Dame. The home of French kings until the 14th century, the island still has a curiously medieval air, with massive gray walls rising up all around you, relieved by tiny patches of parkland.

NOTRE-DAME, 6 place du parvis Notre-Dame, 4e. Tel. 43-26-07-39.

★ The Cathedral of Paris and one of civilization's greatest edifices, this is more than a building—it's like a book written in stone and wood and glass. It can be read line by line, the Virgin's Portal alone telling four different picture stories. The doors of Notre-Dame did, in fact, take the place of religious texts during the ages when few of the faithful were literate.

The cathedral replaced two Romanesque churches (Ste-Marie and St-Etienne), which stood on the spot until 1160. Then Bishop Maurice de Sully, following the example of Suger, the abbot of St-Denis, undertook the new structure, and building continued for more than 150 years. The final result was a piece of Gothic perfection, not merely in overall design but in every detail. The rose window above the main portal, for instance, forms a halo 31 feet in diameter around the head of the statue of the Virgin.

More than any other building, Notre-Dame is the history of a nation. Here, the boy-monarch Henry VI of England was crowned king of France in 1422, during the Hundred Years' War when—but for Joan of Arc—France would have become an English dominion. Of course, that is how history is viewed in the English world. A French historian, on the other hand, might point out that the Plantagenets were French, not English, and that England would have become a French/Anjou dominion.

Here, Napoléon took the crown out of the hands of Pope Pius VII, and crowned himself emperor.

Here, General de Gaulle knelt before the altar on August 26, 1944, to give thanks for the liberation of Paris—imperturbably praying while sniper bullets screeched around the choir galleries.

Because of the beauty of its ornaments and of its symbolic meaning of redemption of all evil, Notre-Dame is a joyous church. However, those devils and gargoyles grinning from its ledges add a genuinely macabre touch. You can almost see Victor Hugo's hunchback peering from behind them.

There are many cathedrals larger than Notre-Dame, but the interior has a transcending loftiness that makes it seem immense. The flat-topped twin towers flanking the entrance rise to 225 feet. You can climb the 387 steps, leading to a magnificent view. Incidentally, on national holidays and feast days, you can hear the thunder of the "Bourdon", the 13-ton bell that hangs in the South Tower.

Approached through a garden behind Notre-Dame is the **Le Memorial de la Déportation,** jutting out on the very tip of the Ile de la Cité. Birds chirp nowadays, the Seine flows gently by—but the memories are far from pleasant. It is a memorial to French martyrs of World War II, who were deported to such camps as Auschwitz and Buchenwald. In blood-red are the words, "Forgive, but don't forget." The memorial can be visited daily from 10am to noon and 2 to 7pm. Admission is free.

Admission: Treasury 15F ($2.60) adults, 5F (90¢) children under 18; tower 23F ($4) adults, 12F ($2.10) children.

Open: Cathedral daily 8am–7pm, but tourists are asked to refrain from visiting on Sun. Free organ concerts Sun at 5:30pm. Treasury Mon–Sat 10am–6pm, tower Wed–Mon 10am–4:30pm.

Métro: Cité, Hôtel-de-Ville, or Maubert.

CONCIERGERIE, 1 quai de l'Horloge, 1er. Tel. 43-54-30-06.

★ The most sinister building in France squats on the north bank of the Ile de la Cité (near the Pont au Change) and forms part of the huge Palais de Justice. Its name is derived

⭐ FROMMER'S FAVORITE PARIS EXPERIENCES

A Stroll Along the Faubourg St-Honoré   In the 1700s it was home to the wealthiest of Parisians, but today it's home to the stores that cater to the wealthy. Even if you don't purchase anything, it's great window-shopping with all the big names: Hermès, Larouche, Courrèges, Cardin, Saint-Laurent.

A Languid Afternoon of Café Sitting   The Parisian café is an integral part of life. Whether you have one small coffee or the most expensive cognac in the house, nobody will hurry you.

Afternoon Tea at Muscade   Drinking tea in London has its charm, but the Parisian salon de thé is unique. Skip those cucumber-and-watercress sandwiches and get down to the business of rich, luscious desserts, like golden pains au chocolat. Muscade, 36 rue de Monpensier, 1er (tel. 42-97-51-36; Métro: Louvre), is open daily noon to 8:30pm.

A Night at the Ballet   Renoir may have hated the building, but a night at the Opéra is still one of the highlights of any trip to Paris. The Opéra, at place de l'Opéra, is now the major center for ballet in Paris, and an evening here takes you back to the Second Empire world of marble and gilt and grand staircases, all sheltered under a controversial ceiling by Chagall. Dress with pomp and circumstance.

A Day at the Races   Paris has eight racing tracks. The most famous (and the classiest) is Longchamp, in the Bois de Boulogne, 16e, the site of the Prix de l'Arc de Triomphe and Grand Prix. If it's a major social event, you'll have to dress up, of course. Take the Métro to Porte d'Auteuil, then a special bus from there to the track. *Paris-Turf*, the racing paper, has details about racing times.

from the title concierge (constable), once borne by a high official of the Royal Court. But its reputation stems from the Revolution.

Even on warm days, a chill wind seems to blow around its two bleak towers, and the gray, massive walls feel eternally dank. Here, as nowhere else in Paris, you can see the tall, square shadow of the guillotine.

The Conciergerie was the country's chief prison after the fall of the Bastille. When the Reign of Terror got under way, the Conciergerie turned into a kind of stopover depot en route to the "National Razor."

You forget everything else as you enter those courtyards and passages. There are the splendid remnants of a medieval royal palace in there, complete with refectory and giant kitchen. But the only features that imprint themselves on the mind are the rows of cells and the doghouse hovel in which prisoners—shorn and bound—sat waiting for the dung cart that was to carry them to the blade.

First came the "aristos"—led by Marie Antoinette, the duc d'Orléans, brother of the king, and the notorious Madame du Barry. Then came the moderate liberals known as "Girondins." Then followed the radicals with their leader Danton. At their heels were the ultraradicals along with their chief, the frozen-faced Robespierre. Finally, as the wheel turned full circle, it was the turn of the relentless public prosecutor Fouquier-Tinville, together with the judges and jury of the Revolutionary Court.

They all had their brief stay in those cells, followed by the even briefer ride to the guillotine. Among the few who stayed there but lived to write about it was America's Thomas Paine, who remembered chatting in English with Danton.

Admission: 25F ($4.40) adults, 17F ($3) ages 18–24, 6F ($1.10) children under 17.

Open: Apr–Sept daily 9:30am–6:30pm; Oct–Mar daily 10am–5pm. **Métro:** Cité, Châtelet, or St-Michel. **RER:** St-Michel.

LA SAINTE-CHAPELLE, Palais de Justice, 4 bd. du Palais, 4e. Tel. 43-54-30-09.

⭐ Within the same building complex as the Conciergerie, but spiritually a thousand miles away, is La Sainte-Chapelle. One of the oldest, most beautiful, and most unusual churches in the world, it was built in 1246 for the express purpose of housing the relics of the Crucifixion, which had been sent from Constantinople at tremendous expense. But the relics were later transferred to Notre-Dame, leaving La Sainte-Chapelle an empty showcase, albeit a magnificent one.

Actually, it consists of two separate churches, one humble, the other superb. The lower chapel was for servants, the upper for the gentry—and one glance will tell you the difference. The gentry, in fact, were the royal household, and you can still see the small grated window from which Louis XI could participate in the service without being noticed.

The outstanding feature of the chapel, though, is the stained glass. Fifteen windows flood the interior with colored light—deep blue, ruby red, and dark green—and depict more than a thousand scenes from the Bible.

Admission: 26F ($4.60) adults, 17F ($3) ages 18–24, 6F ($1.10) ages 7–17; ages 6 and under free.

Open: Apr–Sept daily 9:30am–6pm; Oct–Mar daily 10am–5pm. **Métro:** Cité or St-Michel. **RER:** St-Michel.

ILE ST-LOUIS, 4e.

⭐ As you walk across the little iron footbridge from the rear of Notre-Dame toward the Ile St-Louis, you'll enter a world of tree-shaded quays, aristocratic town houses and courtyards, restaurants, and antique shops. The twin island of the Ile de la Cité is primarily residential, and plaques on the houses' facades make it easy to identify the former residences of the famous who have lived here—such as Marie Curie, who lived at 36 quai de Béthune, near Pont de la Tournelle.

The most exciting mansion is the **Hôtel de Lauzun**, at 17 quai d'Anjou; note that you need special permission to visit. It was the home of the duc de Lauzun, a favorite of Louis XIV, until his secret marriage angered the king and the duc was sent to the Bastille. Baudelaire lived here in the 19th century, squandering his family fortune and penning poetry that would be banned in France until 1949.

Voltaire lived at 2 quai d'Anjou, in the **Hôtel Lambert,** with his mistress, and their quarrels here were legendary. The mansion also housed the Polish royal family for over a century.

Farther along, at no. 9, stands the house where Honoré Daumier, the painter, sculptor, and lithographer, lived between 1846 and 1863. Here he produced hundreds of lithographs satirizing the bourgeoisie and attacking government corruption—his caricature of Louis-Philippe landed him in jail for six months.

Métro: Sully-Morland or Pont-Marie.

THE GRAND PROMENADE & NEARBY ATTRACTIONS

I get a bit tired of repeating "the most in the world," but, of course, the Champs-Elysées is the world's most famous promenade. Extending from the place de la Concorde like a broad, straight arrow to the Arc de Triomphe at the far end, it presents its grandest spectacle at night.

For a complete description of this walk, refer to the walking tour of the Grand Promenade in Chapter 7.

PLACE DE LA CONCORDE, 1er.

Regarded by many as the most beautiful urban square in the world, this immense 85,000-square-yard expanse is so vast that your eye can't take it in at one glance. The center of the oval is swarming with cars, a motorist's nightmare, but the hugeness of the place seems to swallow them up.

In the middle, looking pencil-small, rises a 33-century-old obelisk from Egypt, flanked by cascading fountains. Grouped around the outer edges are eight statues representing eight French cities. Near the statue of Brest was the spot where the guillotine stood during the Revolution. On Sunday morning of January 21, 1793, King Louis XVI lost his royal head there, to be followed by 1,343 other victims, including Marie Antoinette and, subsequently, Danton and Robespierre, the very men who had launched the Terror.

The place de la Concorde borders the Tuileries on the east, and on the west the second great showpiece of Paris, the Champs-Elysées.

Métro: Concorde

JARDIN DES TUILERIES, place de la Concorde, 1er. Tel. 42-60-38-01.

Stretching along the right bank of the Seine, from the place de la Concorde to the court of the Louvre, this exquisitely formal garden was laid out as a royal pleasure park in 1564, but thrown open to the public by the French Revolution. Filled with statues and fountains and precisely trimmed hedges, it's just a bit too artificial for comfort. The nicest features are the round ponds on which pleasantly disorderly kids sail armadas of model boats.

Métro: Tuileries.

ARC DE TRIOMPHE, place Charles de Gaulle–Etoile, 16e. Tel. 43-80-31-31.

This is one of the great Paris symbols, the largest triumphal arch in the world and the centerpiece of the entire Right Bank. It stands as the focus of 12 radiating avenues on the place Charles de Gaulle–Etoile, giving it an unequaled position and making it pretty difficult to reach for the uninitiated. The best—in fact, the only— way to get there through the traffic is to use the underground passage leading from the Champs-Elysées.

The arch was begun on Napoléon's orders in 1806 to com- memorate the victories of his Grande Armée. But it was not completed for another 10 years, when the Grande Armée had long been shattered. Ever since then, the arch has born witness to France's defeats as well as its triumphs.

Twice—in 1871 and 1940—German troops tramped through it in their moments of victory. And twice—in 1919 and 1945— Allied armies staged victory parades through those buttresses.

The arch is 162 feet high and 147 feet wide—a stone fanfare of military glory—and its price. It's ornamented with martial scenes and engraved with the names of the 128 victories of Napoléon and the 600 generals who participated in them.

But underneath burns the Flame of Remembrance that marks the tomb of France's Unknown Soldier. The effect at night is magi- cal—if only that light weren't burning for millions of young men who lost their lives in war.

Admission: 30F ($5.30) adults, 16F ($2.80) ages 18–24; 17 and under free.

Open: Apr–Sept daily 10am–5:30pm; Oct–Mar daily 10am– 4:15pm. **Métro:** Charles-de-Gaulle–Etoile.

PALAIS ROYAL, place du Palais-Royal on rue St-Honoré, 1er.

Facing the Louvre, the gardens of the Palais Royal have long been associated with France's most prominent historical figures. The gardens were planted in 1634 for Cardinal Richelieu, who pre- sented them to Louis XIII. As a child, the future Louis XIV played around the fountain, nearly drowning once.

Perhaps its most auspicious event occurred at the long-ago demol- ished Café Foy in the Palais Royal, where Camille Desmoulins jumped up on a table and shouted for the mob "to fight to the death," thus marking the first words of the French Revolution. From here an armed mob set off for the Bastille on July 14, 1789.

An 18-year-old lieutenant named Napoléon Bonaparte met his first prostitute in the Palais Royal, and Robespierre and Danton dined here. And during the Directoire, gambling dens flourished.

In time the property became the residence of the ducs d'Orléans. Philippe-Egalité, a cousin of Louis XVI, built his apartments on the grounds, and subsequently rented them to prostitutes. By the 20th century those same apartments were rented by such artists as Colette and Cocteau.

Today it's hard to imagine its former life. From place Colette, you enter the Court of Honor, colonnaded on three sides. The palace is the headquarters of the Councils of State, and the Court of Honor is a parking lot during the day. In the center of the Palais Royal is the Galerie d'Orléans, with two fountains and colonnades. Stroll through the gardens or down the Galerie Montpensier, filled with little shops.

Métro: Louvre.

PLACE VENDOME, 8e.

This is the textbook example of classical French architecture,

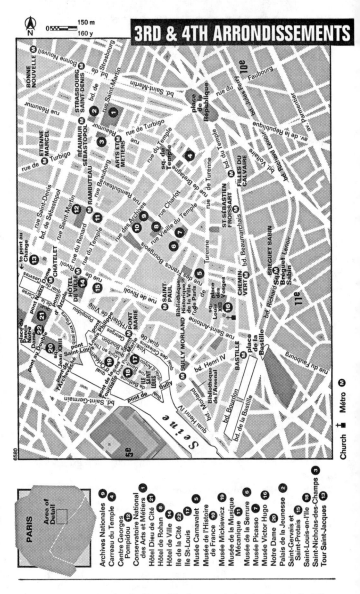

a pure gem set in the fashionable heart of the Right Bank. The pillared palaces encircling the square include the Ritz Hotel as well as the Ministry of Justice. The center is crowned by a 144-foot-high column, erected to commemorate Napoléon's greatest victory—Austerlitz. The actual column is stone, but the enclosing spiral band of bronze was cast from the 1,200 cannons (a fantastic number) captured by the emperor in the battle. The statue on top of the pillar is, of course, Napoléon, restored there after being pulled down twice: once by Royalist reactionaries, the second time by Communard revolutionaries—an odd combination.

Métro: Opéra.

LA GRANDE ARCHE DE LA DEFENSE, place du parvis de la Défense. Tel. 49-07-27-57.

Designed as the architectural centerpiece of the sprawling and futuristic satellite suburb of La Défense, this massive steel-and-masonry arch rises 35 stories from the pavement. Built with the blessing of President François Mitterrand, and ringed with soaring office buildings and a circular avenue (*périphérique*), the design of which imitates that which surrounds the more famous Arc de Triomphe, the deliberately overscaled archway is the latest major landmark to dot the Paris skyline. High enough to shelter the cathedral of Notre-Dame below its heavily trussed canopy, the monument was designed as an extension of the panorama that interconnects the Louvre, the Arc du Carroussel, the Champs-Elysées, the Arc de Triomphe, the avenue de la Grande Armée, and the place du Porte Maillot into one magnificently engineered straight line. An elevator carries visitors to an observation platform, from which visitors get an idea of the carefully conceived geometry of the surrounding street plan.

Admission: 35F ($6.10) adults, 25F ($4.40) ages 4–18; 3 and under free.

Open: Mon–Fri 9am–5pm, Sat–Sun 10am–7pm. **RER:** La Défense.

AROUND THE EIFFEL TOWER

From the place du Trocadéro, you can step between the two curved wings of the **Palais de Chaillot** and gaze out on a view that is nothing short of breathtaking. At your feet lie the **Jardins du Trocadéro,** centered by fountains. Directly in front, the Pont d'Iéna spans the Seine. Then, on the opposite bank, rises the iron immensity of the **Tour Eiffel.** And beyond, stretching as far as your eye can see, the **Champ-de-Mars,** once a military parade ground but now a garden landscape with arches and grottoes, lakes and cascades.

TOUR EIFFEL, Champ-de-Mars, 7e. Tel. 45-50-34-56.

Strangely enough, this symbol of Paris wasn't meant to be a permanent structure at all. Erected specifically for the Universal Exhibition of 1889, it was destined to be pulled down a few years later. But by then, wireless telegraphy had appeared on the scene and the 985-foot tower—the tallest on earth—presented a handy signaling station. Radio confirmed its role. During the German advance on Paris in 1914, the powerful beam from the top effectively jammed the enemy's field radios.

You could write a page with nothing but figures about the tower. The plans for it covered 6,000 square yards of paper, it weighs 7,000 tons, and contains 2½ million rivets. But enough of that. Just stand underneath the tower and look straight up. It's like a rocket of steel lacework shooting into the sky. If nothing else, it is a fantastic engineering achievement.

Gustave Eiffel, "the universal engineer," who had previously constructed hundreds of bridges and even the inner structure of the Statue of Liberty, had the overall responsibility for the project of

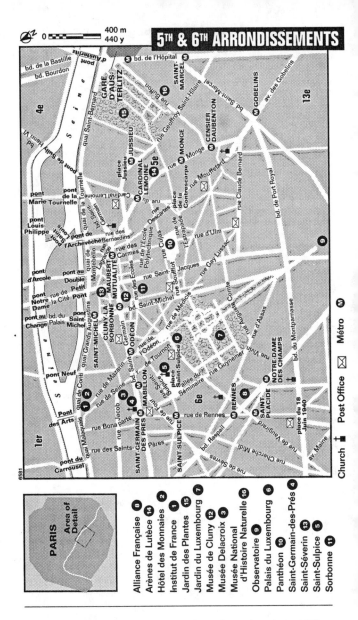

5TH & 6TH ARRONDISSEMENTS

0 ⌖ 400 m / 440 y

Alliance Française ❽
Arènes de Lutèce ⓮
Hôtel des Monnaies ❷
Institut de France ❶
Jardin des Plantes ⓯
Jardin du Luxembourg ❼
Musée de Cluny ⓬
Musée Delacroix ❸
Musée National d'Histoire Naturelle ⓰
Observatoire ❾
Palais du Luxembourg ❻
Panthéon ❿
Saint-Germain-des-Prés ❹
Saint-Séverin ⓭
Saint-Sulpice ❺
Sorbonne ⓫

Church ✝   Post Office ⊠   Métro Ⓜ

building the tower. Architects and aesthetes hated it. ("That damned lamppost ruins the skyline.") The Parisians loved it. Almost overnight it became a part of local legend. A dozen poems were written about it and at least as many ghastly pieces of music, including an *Eiffel Tower Waltz*. By 1910 its permanence had been confirmed—the "lamppost" was there to stay.

You can visit the tower in three stages. Taking the elevator to the first landing, you'll have a view over the rooftops of Paris.

The second landing provides a panoramic view of the city. The third and final stage gives the most spectacular view, allowing you to identify many monuments and buildings.

The tower is well equipped with restaurants—two dining rooms (one deluxe), a snack bar, and a drinking bar at various levels await your decision. On the ground level, the 1899 lift machinery is open to visitors in the eastern and western pillars. On the first level, a ciné-museum showing films on the tower is open when the tower is. Eiffel's office has been re-created on the fourth level, with wax figures of the engineer receiving Thomas Edison.

But it's the view that most people desire, and this extends for 42 miles, theoretically. In practice, weather conditions tend to limit it. Nevertheless, it's fabulous, and the best time for visibility is about an hour before sunset.

Admission: First landing 20F ($3.50), second landing 36F ($6.30), third landing 53F ($9.30).

Open: Sun–Thurs 10am–11pm, Fri–Sat 10am–midnight. **Métro:** Trocadéro, Ecole-Militaire, or Bir-Hakeim. **RER:** Champ de Mars–Tour Eiffel.

CHAMP-DE-MARS AND ECOLE MILITAIRE, 7e.

Leave some time to explore the Champ-de-Mars, the gardens between the Eiffel Tower and the Military School. Designed in 1170, the gardens are the world's fair grounds of Paris and the scene of many military parades.

The **Ecole Militaire** was founded in 1751 with the help of one of France's best-known mistresses, Madame de Pompadour. The classical design is by A.J. Gabriel. The school prepared young men for military careers, including Napoléon, who entered in 1784 and graduated a year later as a 16-year-old lieutenant. According to accounts, he wasn't popular with his classmates, many of whom openly made fun of him—one wrote, "All boots, no man." Another French general, Charles de Gaulle, also studied here. You'll need special permission to go inside.

Métro: Trocadéro, Ecole-Militaire, or Bir-Hakeim.

HOTEL DES INVALIDES, place des Invalides, 7e. Tel. 44-42-37-72.

This is not a "hôtel," but a palace and a church combined, which today houses a great museum, dozens of military administration offices, and the **tomb of Napoléon.**

The monumental ensemble was originally built by Louis XIV as a stately home for invalid soldiers (hence the name). There are still a few living there, but most of the enormous space is taken up by the Musée de l'Armée, various army bureaus, and the crypt beneath the dome in the rear that makes it one of Paris's greatest showpieces.

The **Musée de l'Armée** is the finest military museum in the world—outdistancing even Britain's Imperial War Museum in amassed martial relics. Its collection of arms dates back so far it seems to include the first rock thrown by Neolithic man. The museum sets out the war paraphernalia of every age—bronze spearheads and medieval crossbows, intricately engraved armor and doughboy drabs—leading up with a flourish and the recorded strains of "Tipperary" to the bugle that sounded the cease-fire on November 7, 1918, before the general cease-fire on November 11, 1918. The shrinelike aura is distressing. The detail is fascinating.

The west wing, on your right as you enter the courtyard, houses suits of armor, especially in the new so-called Arsenal—arms belonging to the kings and dignitaries of France. The Salle Orientale in the west wing shows arms from the Far East and from Muslim countries of the Middle East, from the 16th to the 19th centuries. Turkish armor (see Bajazet's helmet) and weapons, as well as Chinese and Japanese armor and swords, are on exhibit. Moreover, the west wing houses exhibits from World Wars I and II.

You can gain access to the **Musée des Plans-Reliefs** through the west wing. It is a unique collection in scale model of French towns and monuments.

The east wing, on your left, shows objects dating from the 17th century to 1914. Off the entrance hall in the hushed Salle Turenne (a plaque at the door cues you to proper respect) fly the battleflags of France, including those of Bonaparte's regiments and some shredded remnants of standards from 1940. Opposite, in the Salle Vauban, 18 mounted figures illustrate the showy uniforms of the French cavalry. Go upstairs to view souvenirs of the Napoleonic campaigns, next to the bed in which the great Corsican died, as well as the personal effects from his island exile.

The gloss of the show tends to veil the truth that war is a matter of death and heartbreak. But occasionally it comes through, simply and effectively, as in the display of a silvery cuirass, pierced by a jagged wound the size and shape of a softball—the breastplate of a Carabinier downed by a cannon at Waterloo.

Invalides is a shrine, and like most shrines, impersonal. Napoléon rests in a sarcophagus of red granite on a pedestal of green granite. Surrounding the tomb are 12 figures of victories. The pavement of the crypt consists of a mosaic of laurel leaves.

It took 19 years for the British to release the body of their most illustrious prisoner, who had originally been buried near his house of banishment. Finally, on December 15, 1840, Napoléon's second funeral took place in Paris. The golden hearse was taken through crowds of mourners who had braved a snowstorm to pay their last respects to the nation's hero.

The same golden dome also covers the tombs of Napoléon's brothers, Joseph and Jérôme, his son (who was never crowned), and Marshal Foch, who led the Allied armies to victory in 1918.

Admission: 32F ($5.60) adults, 22F ($3.90) children 7–18; children 6 and under free. The ticket, valid for two consecutive days, covers admission to the Musée de l'Armée, Napoléon's Tomb, and the Musée des Plans-Reliefs.

Open: Apr–Sept daily 10am–6pm; Oct–Mar daily 10am–5pm. **Métro:** Latour-Maubourg, Varenne, or St-François-Xavier.

MONTMARTRE

This name has spread chaos and confusion in many an unwary tourist's agenda. So just to make things clear—there are three of them.

The first is boulevard Montmartre, a busy commercial street nowhere near the mountain. The second is the tawdry, expensive, would-be-naughty, and utterly phony amusement belt along boulevard de Clichy, culminating at place Pigalle (the "Pig Alley" of World War II GIs). The third—the Montmartre I'm talking about—lies on top, and on the slopes, of the actual *mont*.

The best way to get there is to take the Métro to Anvers, then walk to the nearby rue de Steinkerque, and ride the curious little funicular to the top. It operates daily between 6am and 11pm.

Montmartre used to be the artists' village, glorified by such masters as Utrillo, and painted, sketched, sculpted, and photographed by ten thousand lesser lights. The tourists, building speculators, and nightclub entrepreneurs came and most of the artists went. But a few still linger. And so does some of the village charm that once drew them. Just enough to give you a few delightful hours, and leave you nostalgic for a past you wish you'd known.

The center point, the **place du Tertre,** looks like an almost-real village square, particularly when the local band is blowing and puffing oompah music. All around the square run terrace restaurants with dance floors and colored lights. Gleaming through the trees is the Basilica of Sacré-Coeur.

Behind the church and clinging to the hillside below are steep and crooked little streets that seem—almost—to have survived the relentless march of progress. **Rue des Saules** still has Montmartre's last vineyard, plus a cabaret. **Rue Lepic** still looks—almost—the way Renoir and the melancholy van Gogh and the unfortunate genius Toulouse-Lautrec saw it. This—almost—makes up for the blitz of portraitists and souvenir stores and postcard vendors up on top.

The traditional way to explore Montmartre is on foot, although many visitors who are not in tip-top physical shape find the uphill climb to Paris's highest elevation arduous. Those who prefer can take a white-sided, diesel-powered "train," which rolls on rubber tires along the steep streets on a 35-minute guided tour. **Le Petit Train de Montmartre** carries 55 passengers who can listen to an English commentary as they pass by the district's major landmarks. Boarding is at either the place du Tertre (beside the Church of St-Pierre) or near the Moulin Rouge in the place Blanche. Trains run throughout the year, beginning at 9:30am and continuing until midnight between June and September, and until 7pm the rest of the year. Depending on the season, departures are scheduled every 30 to 45 minutes. The cost is 30F ($5.30) for adults, half price for children. For information, call Promotrain, 131 rue de Clignancourt, 18e (tel. 42-62-24-00).

For a more detailed look at Montmartre, see the walking tour in Chapter 7.

BASILICA OF SACRE-COEUR, place St-Pierre, 18e. Tel. 42-51-17-02.

After the Eiffel Tower, Sacré-Coeur is the most outstanding landmark of Paris. Its five domes and campanile, all gleaming white, make it look like a 12th-century Byzantine church. In fact, the basilica was planned as a votive offering after France's defeat by the Prussians in 1870. Rich and poor alike contributed money to build it. Construction was approved in 1873, but the church wasn't consecrated until 1919.

Like the Eiffel Tower, the design of Sacré-Coeur stirred up controversy. One Parisian called it "a lunatic's confectionery dream." Zola dubbed it "the basilica of the ridiculous." Supporters of Sacré-Coeur included poet Max Jacob and artist Maurice Utrillo. Utrillo never tired of drawing and painting it, and he and Jacob came here regularly to pray.

Try to visit Sacré-Coeur at dusk; from the top steps, there's a spectacular view as the city lights come on. The view from the dome extends 35 miles on a clear day. You can also walk around the inner dome to get a bird's-eye view of the church interior.

Admission: Church free; dome 15F ($2.60); crypt 10F ($1.80).

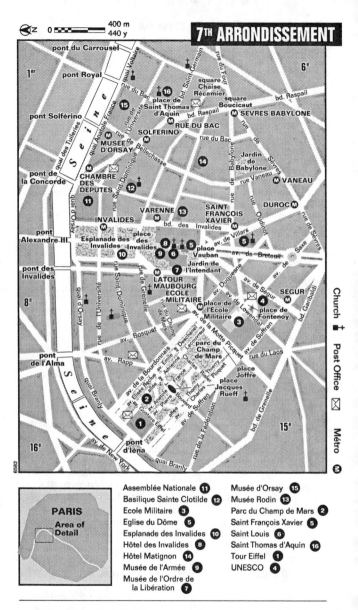

7TH ARRONDISSEMENT

Church **†**

Post Office ⊠

Métro **Ⓜ**

Assemblée Nationale ⑪	Musée d'Orsay ⑮
Basilique Sainte Clotilde ⑫	Musée Rodin ⑬
Ecole Militaire ③	Parc du Champ de Mars ②
Eglise du Dôme ⑤	Saint François Xavier ⑤
Esplanade des Invalides ⑩	Saint Louis ⑥
Hôtel des Invalides ⑧	Saint Thomas d'Aquin ⑯
Hôtel Matignon ⑭	Tour Eiffel ①
Musée de l'Armée ⑨	UNESCO ④
Musée de l'Ordre de la Libération ⑦	

Open: Church daily 7am–11pm; dome and crypt daily 9am–6pm. **Métro:** Abbesses or Anvers.

LE MARAIS

Very few cities on earth boast an entire district that can be labeled a sight. Paris has several. One of them—Le Marais, or the marsh-land—is the vaguely defined maze of streets north of the place de la Bastille.

During the 17th century this was a region of aristocratic mansions, which lost their elegance when the fashionable set moved elsewhere. The houses lost status, but they remained standing. Le Marais is becoming increasingly fashionable by today's standards and many artists and craftspeople are moving in. The government is restoring many of the mansions.

You can take the Métro to the **place de la Bastille** to begin a stroll around the district. The actual Bastille, of course, is gone now. But as the history books tell us, the mob attacked this fortress on July 14, 1789, sparking the French Revolution. To commemorate the storming, Bastille Day on July 14 is a major French holiday. Once the prison contained eight towers, housing such illustrious tenants as "The Man in the Iron Mask" and the marquis de Sade.

Be careful of the speeding cars when you cross the square to look at the Colonne de Juillet. Surprisingly, it honors the victims of the July Revolution of 1830 that marked the fall of Charles X, not the victims of the Bastille.

France honored the bicentennial of the French Revolution in 1989 by building the 3,000-seat Opéra Bastille on the south side of the square. The Opéra opened in 1990, with five moving stages. The launching of this cultural center, along with major restoration of the area, has turned the formerly dreary Bastille section into a chic neighborhood, rivaling the Marais, which garnered so much publicity in the 1970s and 1980s.

From the place de la Bastille, head up rue St-Antoine, cutting right on rue des Tournelles, with its statue honoring Beaumarchais (author of *The Barber of Seville*). Take a left again onto the Pas-de-la-Mule, "the footsteps of the mule," which will carry you to the place des Vosges.

See Section 4, "Special-Interest Sightseeing," for information on the Maison de Victor Hugo, also in Le Marais.

PLACE DES VOSGES, 3e.

An enchanted island rather than a city square, this silent, serenely lovely oasis is the oldest square in Paris and—in my opinion—the most entrancing.

Laid out in 1605 by order of Henri IV, it was once called the Palais Royal and was the scene of innumerable cavaliers' duels. The Revolutionary government changed its name but—luckily—left its structure intact. In the middle is a tiny park, and on three sides an encircling arcaded walk, supported by arches and paved with ancient, worn flagstones.

That's all, but the total effect is so harmonious, so delicately balanced between mellow stone and green trees, that it works like a soothing balm on the nerves.

Métro: St-Paul or Chemin-Vert.

MUSEE CARNAVALET, 23 rue de Sévigné, 3e. Tel. 42-72 21-13.

This museum covers the history of the city from the prehistoric period to the present time. One room is crammed with signposts from the 17th and 18th centuries, designed to let the unlettered know that here at the sign of the tree worked a carpenter, and here where a pig was portrayed you could buy your cold cuts. The striking collection of memorabilia from the French Revolution includes the chessmen with which Louis XVI passed time while imprisoned in the Temple, as well as the boyish diary of the dauphin and some effects of Marie Antoinette. You can see the model of the Bastille, of which there is now not a trace.

There is more, such as antique furniture of various periods, including a jewelry shop designed by Mucha in 1900. The mansion that houses the exhibits, built in 1545, is considered a prime example of Renaissance architecture. The tour continues across the courtyard at the Hôtel le Peletier de St-Fargeau. There, exhibits cover the time of the Revolution up to the present, with many paintings and even the bedroom of Marcel Proust.

Admission: 26F ($4.60) adults, 14F ($2.50) students under age 25; under 18 and over 60 free.

Open: Tues–Sun 10am–5:40pm. **Métro:** St-Paul or Chemin-Vert.

2. MORE ATTRACTIONS

QUARTIER LATIN

The Latin Quarter lies on the Left Bank in the 5th arrondissement and consists of the streets winding around the University of Paris, of which the Sorbonne is only a part.

The logical starting point is the place St-Michel, right on the river, decorated by an impressive fountain. This was the scene of some of the most savage fighting during the uprising of the French Resistance in August 1944. Here—as in many, many other spots—you'll see the sombre name tablets, marking the place where a Resistance fighter fell: "Ici est Tombé—le 19 Août 1944. Pour la Libération de Paris."

Running straight south is the main thoroughfare of the quarter, the wide, pulsating boulevard St-Michel (called boul' Mich' by the locals). But we'll turn left and dive into the warren of dogleg alleys adjoining the river—rue de la Huchette, rue de la Harpe, ru St-Séverin. Thronged with students; tingling with the spice smells of Arabian, African, and Vietnamese cooking; narrow, twisting, and noisy—the alleys resemble an Asian bazaar more than a European city. This impression is aided by the incredibly garish posters advertising horror movies, belly dancers, and sticky Algerian sweets, the crush of humanity, and the honking of cars bullying a path through the swarming crowds.

We emerge at the Church of St-Séverin and are back in Paris again. Dating from the 13th century, this flamboyant Gothic edifice acts like a sanctuary of serenity.

Head down rue St-Jacques and Paris reasserts itself completely. The next crossing is boulevard St-Germain, lined with sophisticated cafés and some of the most avant-garde fashion shops in town.

MUSEE DE CLUNY, 6 place Paul-Painlevé, 5e. Tel. 43-25-62-00.

An enchanting museum, with some of the most beautiful medieval art extant, the Musée de Cluny stands back from the intersection of boulevards St-Michel and St-Germain in a walled courtyard—one of two Gothic private residences of the 15th century left in Paris.

Dark, rough-walled, and evocative, the Cluny is devoted to the church art and castle crafts of the Middle Ages, jewelry (votive crowns of the Visigothic kings and a golden altar from Basel), sculpture, stained glass, and tapestries—among them the world-famous series of *The Lady and the Unicorn* gracefully displayed in a circular room on the second floor. The painstakingly depicted *Life of St. Stephen* hangs in the shadowy chapel, while a third series is concerned with the colorful life at court. The building also includes the remains of an A.D. 200 Roman bathhouse with a well-preserved frigidarium.

Admission: 26F ($4.60) adults, 17F ($3) ages 18–24; 17 and under free.

Open: Wed–Mon 9:45am–5:15pm. **Métro:** Cluny–La Sorbonne.

PANTHEON, place du Panthéon, 5e. Tel. 43-54-34-51.

This strangely splendid cross between a Roman temple and a church has at some time been both and is now neither. But it towers impressively on the Left Bank as one of the city's most illustrious landmarks.

Originally the site of a Roman temple, which grew into a medieval abbey, it was constructed as the Church of Ste-Geneviève in the 18th century, finishing up with the capitollike dome, as well as noble Roman pillars.

Then the Revolutionary government decided to convert it into a purely patriotic shrine for the nation's greats. Under Napoléon it again became a church. Since 1885, however, it has reverted to being a nonreligious temple—a worthy receptacle for those the nation wished to honor.

The interior is stark and bare, with an austere grandeur all its own. It houses the tombs of Rousseau and Voltaire, of Victor Hugo and Emile Zola, of Louis Braille, and of the African Felix Eboué, who rallied his equatorial colony to the colors of de Gaulle at a time when no other French administrator dared to do so.

Admission: 26F ($4.60) adults, 17F ($3) ages 18–24, 6F ($1) ages 7–17, 6 and under free.

Open: June–Sept daily 10am–5:15pm; Oct–May daily 10am–4:45pm. **Métro:** St-Michel or Monge.

CHURCH OF ST-SEVERIN, rue des Prêtres, 5e. Tel. 43-25-96-63.

This flamboyant Gothic building, named for the 6th-century recluse St. Séverin, lies just a short walk from the Seine. Given to Paris in the 11th century by Henri I, it slowly began to adopt some of the architectural features of Notre-Dame, located across the river.

The present church was built from 1210 to 1230, then reconstructed in 1458. The tower was completed in 1487, the chapels between 1498 and 1520. Hardouin-Mansart designed the Chapel of the Communion in 1673 when he was 27 years old.

Before entering, walk around the church to examine its gargoyles, birds of prey, and reptilian monsters projecting from the top. To the right, facing the church, is the "garden of ossuaries" of the 15th century. Inside, the stained glass is a stunning adornment.

Admission: Free.

Open: Daily 8am–7pm. **Métro:** St-Michel or Maubert-Mutualité.

LES HALLES DISTRICT

The area around the Church of St-Eustace has always had a bad reputation. Centuries ago a Parisian described it as "ideal for assassinations," and it was in front of 11 rue de la Ferronnerie that Henri IV ("Vert Galant") was assassinated by Ravaillac. Nearby is the banking center of Paris, rue des Lombards.

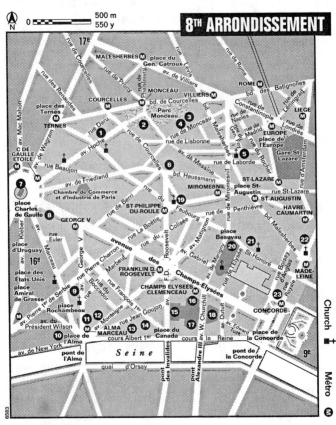

8TH ARRONDISSEMENT

0 ⎯⎯⎯ 500 m
⎯⎯⎯ 550 y

Area of Detail

PARIS

American Cathedral in Paris ❾
Arc de Triomphe ❼
Crazy Horse Saloon ⓫

Eglise de la Madeleine ㉒
Grand Palais ⓰
Hôtel Crillon ㉓
Musée Cernuschi ❸
Musée d'Art Moderne ❿
Musée Jacquemart André ❻
Musée Nissim de Camondo ❹
Notre Dame de la Consolation ⓭
Office de Tourisme ❽
Palais de la Découverte ⓯

Palais de l'Elysée ⓴
Parc Monceau ❷
Petit Palais ⓲
St-Alexandre-Nevsky ❶
St-Augustin ❺
St-Jean-Baptiste ⓮
St. Michael's English Church ㉑
St-Philippe-du-Roule ⓳
Théâtres des Champs Elysées ⓬
Université Paris IV ⓱

LES FORUM DES HALLES, 1er.

This large complex, much of it underground, contains dozens of shops, several restaurants and movie theaters, and a wax museum. Les Forum des Halles opened in 1979 on the site of the major wholesale fruit, vegetable, and meat market in Paris. The zinc-roofed Second Empire building was torn down after wholesalers moved to the contemporary steel-and-glass structure at Rungis, a suburb near Orly Airport. Replacing the old "umbrellas of iron" is the French version of a modern mall, popular with tourists and residents alike.

Elegantly dressed Parisians drinking cognac with bloody butchers at Les Halles were once a typical early-morning Parisian scene; today, although the old market has moved, it's still a tradition after a night on the town to have a bowl of onion soup at Les Halles, usually at Au Pied de Cochon ("Pig's Foot") or at Au Chien Qui Fume ("Smoking Dog"). Les Halles is one of the few places where you can eat at any hour of the night. Some writers have suggested that eccentric 19th-century poet Gérard de Nerval was the original night owl here.

Métro: Les Halles. **RER:** Châtelet–Les Halles.

CHURCH OF ST-EUSTACHE, 2 rue du Jour, 1er. Tel. 42-36-31-05.

In my opinion, this mixed Gothic and Renaissance church completed in 1637 is rivaled only by Notre-Dame. It took nearly a century to build. Many famous Parisians have passed through the doors of St-Eustache. Madame de Pompadour and Richelieu were baptized here, and Molière's funeral was held here in 1673. The church has been known for its organ recitals ever since Liszt played here in 1866. Inside is the black-marble tomb of Jean-Baptiste Colbert, the minister of state under Louis XIV. On top of his tomb is a marble statue of the statesman flanked by statues of *Abundance* by Coysevox and *Fidelity* by J. B. Tuby. There's a side entrance to the church on rue Rambuteau.

Open: Daily 7:30am–7:30pm. **Métro:** Les Halles.

ST-GERMAIN-DES-PRES

This was the postwar home of existentialism, associated with Jean-Paul Sartre, Simone de Beauvoir, Albert Camus, and an intellectual, bohemian crowd who gathered at the Café de Flore, the Brasserie Lipp, and Deux-Magots. Among them, the black-clad poet Juliette Greco was known as "la muse de St-Germain-des-Prés," and to Sartre she was the woman who had "millions of poems in her throat." Her long hair, black slacks, black sweater, and black sandals launched a fashion trend adopted by young women from Paris to California.

In the 1950s new names appeared, like Françoise Sagan, Gore Vidal, and James Baldwin, but by the 1960s the tourists were just as firmly entrenched at the Café de Flore and Deux-Magots. Today St-Germain-des-Prés remains a bohemian and intellectually stimulating street life, full of many interesting bookshops, art galleries, *cave* nightclubs, and bistros and coffeehouses.

ST-GERMAIN-DES-PRES CHURCH, 3 place St-Germain-des-Prés, 6e. Tel. 43-25-41-71.

This church's Romanesque tower, topped by an 11th-century spire, is the most enduring landmark in the village of St-Germain-des-Prés, dating from the 6th century, when Childebert, the son of Clovis, the "creator of France," founded a Benedictine abbey on the site. Unfortunately, the marble columns in the triforium are all that remain from that period. The abbey was a pantheon for Merovingian kings, and their tombs are found in the St-Symphorien Chapel at the entrance to the church. During the restoration of these tombs in 1981, Romanesque paintings were discovered on the triumphal arch of the chapel.

The present building, the work of four centuries, has a Romanesque nave and a Gothic choir with fine capitals. Among the people interested in the church were Descartes and Jean-Casimir, the king of Poland who abdicated his throne.

Across from St-Germain-des-Prés church is the Deux-Magots, the former cafe retreat of the existentialists. As you leave the church, turn right on the rue de l'Abbaye and have a look at the pink 17th century Palais Abbatial.

Open: Daily 8am–7:30pm. **Métro:** St-Germain-des-Prés.

CHURCH OF ST-SULPICE, rue St-Sulpice, 6e. Tel. 46-33-21-78.

The square on which the church stands has been much celebrated, and it's worth stopping for a moment in this 18th-century square with its fountain by Visconti, portraying four 18th-century bishops: Fénelon, Massillon, Bossuet, and Fléchier.

Work began on the church in 1646; the facade, "bastardized classic," was completed in 1745. Many architects, including Le Van, worked on the building. Some were summarily fired; others, such as the Florentine Servandoni, were discredited. One of the two towers was never completed.

The main reason to visit St-Sulpice is to see the Delacroix frescoes in the Chapel of the Angels (first on your right as you enter). Seek out his muscular Jacob wrestling with an angel. On the ceiling St. Michael is struggling with the Devil, and yet another mural depicts Heliodorus being driven from the temple. Painted in the final years of his life, the frescoes are a high point in Delacroix's career.

One of the most notable treasures inside the 360-foot-long church is Servandoni's rococo Chapel of the Madonna, with a marble statue of the Virgin, by Pigalle. The church contains one of the world's largest organs, with more than 6,500 pipes, and an 18th-century case depicted by Chalgrin. The Sunday mass concerts—made famous by Charles Widor—draw many visitors.

One of the largest and most prestigious churches in Paris, St-Sulpice was sacked during the Revolution and converted into the Temple of Victory. Camille Desmoulins, the revolutionary who instigated the raid on the Bastille, was married here.

Open: Daily 7:30am–7:30pm. **Métro:** St-Sulpice.

RUE VISCONTI, 6e.

This narrow street was originally designed for pushcarts. Balzac established his printing press in 1825 at no. 17. Balzac's venture ended in bankruptcy—which forced the author back to his writing desk. In the 17th century the French dramatist Racine lived across the street. Such celebrated actresses as Champmeslé and Clairon were also in residence. Nearby is the Musée Eugène Delacroix (see below).

MUSEE EUGENE DELACROIX, 6 place de Furstenberg. Tel. 43-54-04-87.

From 1857 through 1863 the great Romantic painter Delacroix had his last studio here, in one of the most bewitching small squares in all Paris. The artist's apartment and rear-garden atelier have been transformed into a museum of his work. This is no poor artist's shabby studio, but the very tasteful creation of a solidly established man. Sketches, lithographs, watercolors, and oils are hung throughout, and a few personal mementos remain, including a lovely mahogany paint box.

Note: To see the work that earned Delacroix his sure niche in art history, go to the Louvre for such passionate paintings as his *Liberty Leading the People on the Barricades*, or to the Church of

St-Sulpice, also in St-Germain-des-Prés (Métro: Mabillon), for the famed fresco, *Jacob Wrestling with the Angel*, among others.

Admission: 12F ($2.10) adults, 8F ($1.40) ages 18–25 and over 60, 17 and under free.

Open: Wed–Mon 9:45am–5:15pm. **Closed:** Holidays. **Métro:** St-Germain-des-Prés.

MONTPARNASSE

For the "lost generation," life centered around the literary cafés of Montparnasse. Artists, especially American expatriates, frequented the famous brasserie cafés: Le Dôme, La Coupole, La Rotonde, and Le Select. Most were seeking refuge from the tourists that had overrun Montmartre. Picasso, Modigliani, and Man Ray came this way, as did Hemingway and Fitzgerald when he was poor (when he wasn't you'd find him at the Ritz). William Faulkner, Archibald MacLeish, Isadora Duncan, Miró, James Joyce, Ford Madox Ford, even Trotsky—all were here, except Gertrude Stein, who would not frequent the cafés. To see her, you needed an invitation to her salon at 27 rue de Fleurus. She bestowed the privilege of her presence on Sherwood Anderson, Elliot Paul, and, briefly, Hemingway. When not receiving, she was busy buying the paintings of Cézanne, Renoir, Matisse, and Picasso. One writer said that her salon was engaged in an international conspiracy to promote modern art.

The life of Montparnasse still centers on its cafés and exotic nightclubs, many of them only a shadow of what they used to be. Its heart is at the crossroads of boulevard Raspail and boulevard du Montparnasse, one of the settings of *The Sun Also Rises*.

CEMETERY

PERE-LACHAISE CEMETERY, 16 rue du Repos. 20e. Tel. 43-70-70-33.

This graveyard, the largest in Paris, contains more illustrious dead than any other place on earth.

A map costing 10F ($1.80), available at the main entrance, will help you find the tombs, and they read like a roll call of international renown. There are Napoléon's marshals Ney and Masséna, and the British admiral Sir Sidney Smith who, by holding the fortress of Acre, made the Corsican taste his first defeat.

There are the poets, playwrights, and novelists Beaumarchais, Balzac, Wilde, Colette, La Fontaine, Molière, Apollinaire, and Daudet, the composers Chopin and Rossini, the painter Corot, the singer Piaf, and a legion more. The tomb of rock star Jim Morrison (1971) has been one of the most visited graves.

But the most somber note in Père-Lachaise is a piece of wall called **Mur des Fédéres.** It was among the graves of this cemetery that the last-ditch fighters of the Paris Commune—the world's first anarchist republic—made their final desperate stand against the troops of the regular French government in May 1871. They were overwhelmed, stood up against this wall, and shot in batches. All died except a handful who had hidden in vaults and lived for years in the cemetery like wild animals, venturing into Paris at night to forage for food.

Open: Mar 15–Nov 5, Mon–Fri 7:30am–6pm, Sat 8:30am–6pm, Sun 9am–6pm; Nov 6–Mar 14 Mon–Fri 8am–5:30pm, Sat 8:30am–5:30pm, Sun 9am–5:30pm. **Métro:** Père-Lachaise.

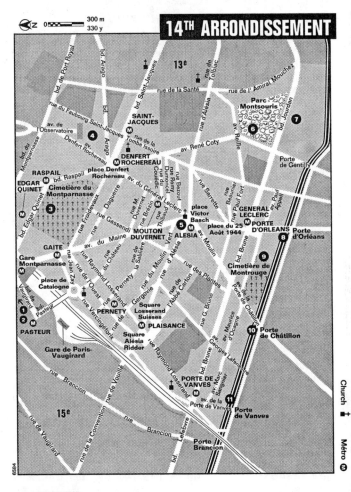

14ᵀᴴ ARRONDISSEMENT

300 m
330 y

Church ■ †   Métro Ⓜ

PARIS

Area of Detail

Cimetière du Montparnasse ❸
Cimetière de Montrouge ❾
Cité Internationale Universitaire de Paris ❼
Galeries Lafayette ❶
Observatoire de Paris ❹
Parc Montsouris ❻

Porte de Châtillon ❿
Porte d'Orléans ❽
Porte de Vanves ⓫
Saint-Pierre de Montrouge ❺
Tour Montparnasse ❷

MORE MUSEUMS

Below is a partial listing of the balance of the city's museums. Be sure to refer back to Section 1, "The Top Attractions," for details on where to get information.

CITE DES SCIENCES ET DE L'INDUSTRIE, La Villette, 30 av. Corentine-Cariou. 19e. Tel. 40-05-80-00.

A city of science and industry has emerged here. When its core was originally built in the 1960s, it was touted as the most modern slaughterhouse in the world. But when the site was abandoned as a failure in 1974, its echoing vastness and unlikely location on the northern edge of the city presented the French government with a problem. In 1986 the converted premises opened as the world's most expensive ($642 million) science complex designed to "modernize mentalities" as a first step in the process of modernizing society.

The place is so vast, with so many exhibits that a single visit gives only an idea of the scope of the Cité. What you'll see is something akin to a futuristic airplane hangar. Busts of Plato, Hippocrates, and a double-faced Janus gaze silently at a tube-filled, space-aged riot of high tech girders, glass, and lights—something akin to what a layman might think of the interior of an atomic generator.

The sheer dimensions of the place are awesome, a challenge to the arrangers of the constantly changing exhibits. Some of the exhibits are couched in an overlay of Gallic humor, including seismographic activity as presented in the comic-strip adventures of a jungle explorer. There is the silver-skinned geodesic dome (called the Géode) that shows the closest thing to a 3-D cinema in Europe on the inner surfaces of its curved walls; it is a 112-foot-high sphere with a 370-seat theater.

Explora, a permanent exhibit, is housed on the three upper levels of the building; its displays focus on four themes: the universe, life, matter, and communication. The Cité also has a multimedia library and a planetarium. An "inventorium" is designed for children.

The Cité is in La Villette park, the city's largest, with 136 acres of greenery—twice the size of the Tuileries. Here you'll find a belvedere, a video workshop for children, and information about exhibitions and events, along with a café and restaurant.

Admission: Cité Pass (entrance to all exhibits), 45F ($7.90) adults, 35F ($6.10) ages 7–25, free for children under 7; Géode 55F ($9.60) adults, 37F ($6.50) children 17 and under.

Open: Tues 10am–6pm, Wed noon–9pm, Thurs–Fri 10am–6pm, Sat–Sun and holidays noon–8pm. Show times at Géode, Tues–Sun on the hour 10am–9pm. **Métro:** Line 7 to Porte de la Villette station.

MANUFACTURE DES GOBELINS, 42 av. des Gobelins, 13e. Tel. 43-37-12-60.

If you enjoyed seeing the tapestries at the Musée de Cluny (see above), you might also enjoy watching how they are made. Tapestry work is still being done at Les Gobelins in the same way and on looms like those used at the founding of the factory in 1662. You can tour the workshops where weavers sit behind huge screens of thread, patiently thrusting stitch after stitch into work that may take up to three years to complete.

Tours: Given in French Tues–Thurs 2–2:45pm for 33F ($5.80) adults, 24F ($4.20) children under 17. **Métro:** Gobelins.

MANUFACTURE NATIONALE DE SEVRES, place de la Manufacture, Sèvres, 7e.

Madame de Pompadour loved Sèvres porcelain. She urged Louis XV to order more of it, thus ensuring its standing among the fashionable people of the 18th century. Two centuries later, it's still chic.

The Sèvres factory has been owned by the state for over two centuries. It was founded originally in Vincennes, and moved to Sèvres, a riverside suburb of Paris, in 1756. The factory's commercial service sells porcelain to the public Monday through Saturday (closed holidays).

Next door, the **Musée National de Céramique de Sèvres** (tel. 45-34-99-05) shelters one of the finest collections of faience and porcelain in the world, some of which belonged to Madame du Barry, Pompadour's hand-picked successor. On view, for example, is the "Pompadour rose" (which the English insisted on calling the "rose du Barry"), a style much in vogue in the 1750s and 1760s. The painter Boucher made some of the designs used by the factory, as did the sculptor Pajou (he did the bas-reliefs for the Opéra at Versailles). The factory pioneered what became known in porcelain as the Louis XVI style—it's all here, plus lots more, including works from Meissen (archrival of Sèvres). Admission is 18F ($3.20) for adults, 12F ($2.10) for seniors and ages 19 to 25; free for children under 18. It's open Wednesday through Monday 10am to 5pm.

Métro: Pont-de-Sèvres, then walk across the Seine to the Left Bank.

MUSEE D'ART MODERNE DE LA VILLE DE PARIS, 11–13 av. du Président Wilson, 16e. Tel. 47-23-61-27.

Along the Seine, next door to the Palais de Tokyo, visitors will find a permanent collection of paintings and sculpture as well as temporary exhibitions on contemporary movements and individual artists. On display are works by Chagall, Matisse, Léger, Braque, Picasso, Dufy, Utrillo, Delaunay, Rouault, and Modigliani. See, in particular, Pierre Tal Coat's *Portrait of Gertrude Stein*. The Musée des Enfants has exhibitions and shows for children.

Admission: 35F ($6.10) adults, 14F ($2.50) ages 18–24; 17 and under free.

Open: Tues–Fri noon–7pm, Sat–Sun 10am–7pm. **Métro:** Iéna or Alma-Marceau.

MUSEE MARMOTTAN, 2 rue Louis-Boilly, 16e. Tel. 42-24-07-02.

Time was when nobody but a stray art scholar ever visited the museum on the edge of the Bois de Boulogne. Nowadays it is quite popular. The rescue from obscurity actually occurred on February 5, 1966, when the museum fell heir to more than 130 paintings, watercolors, pastels, and drawings of Claude Monet, the painter considered the father of impressionism. A gift of Monet's son, Michel, an octogenarian safari-lover who died in a car crash, the bequest was valued at $10 million at the time. Of the surprise acquisition, one critic wrote, "Had an old widow in Brooklyn suddenly inherited the fortune of J. P. Morgan, the event would not have been more startling."

The owner of the museum, the Académie des Beaux-Arts, was immediately embarrassed with a lack of space. The Marmottan was just a small town house, adorned with First Empire furniture and objets d'art (although it did own Monet's *Impression: Sunrise*, which named the movement). The house had once been owned by a dilettante, Paul Marmottan, who had donated it, along with his treasures, to the academy. The solution was to go underground.

Now you can trace the evolution of Monet's art, especially his eternal obsession with waterlilies. Presented are about 30-odd pictures of his house at Giverny that so inspired him. Exceptional paintings include his celebrated 1918 *The Willow*, his 1905 *Houses of Parliament*, his undated *African Lilies*, as well as paintings by Monet's masters, Boudin and Delacroix, and by his fellow impressionists (see especially a portrait of the 32-year-old Monet by Renoir). You can also see the extensive collection of miniatures donated by Daniel Waldenstein.

Admission: 35F ($6.10) adults, 15F ($2.60) children ages 12–18; children 11 and under free.

Open: Tues–Sun 10am–5:30pm. **Métro:** La Muette.

MUSEE NATIONAL AUGUSTE RODIN, 77 rue de Varenne, 7e. Tel. 44-18-61-10.

Auguste Rodin, the man credited with freeing French sculpture of classicism, once lived and had his studio in the charming 18th-century mansion Hôtel Biron, across the boulevard from Napoléon's Tomb in the Hôtel des Invalides. Today the house and garden are filled with his works, a soul-satisfying feast for the Rodin enthusiast.

In the cobbled Court of Honor, within the walls as you enter, you'll see *The Thinker* crouched on his pedestal to the right of you; *The Burghers of Calais* grouped off to the left of you; and to the far left, the writhing *Gates of Hell*, atop which *The Thinker* once more meditates. There's a third *Thinker* inside the museum before a second-floor window. In the almost too-packed rooms, men and angels emerge from blocks of marble, hands twisted in supplication, and the nude torso of Balzac rises up from a tree. Wander back from the house through the long wooded garden where more sculptures await you under the trees.

Admission: Tues–Sat 26F ($4.60) adults, 17F ($3) ages 18–25; 17 and under free.

Open: Apr–Sept Tues–Sun 10am–5:45pm; Oct–Mar Tues–Sun 10am–5pm. **Métro:** Varenne.

MORE CHURCHES

VAL-DE-GRACE, 1 place Alphonse-Lavern, 5e. Tel. 43-29-12-31.

According to an old proverb, to understand the French you must like Camembert cheese, the Pont Neuf, and the dome of Val-de-Grâce.

The church was built by Louis XIII in gratitude for being granted an heir—his wife, Anne of Austria, gave birth to the future Sun King after 23 years of childless marriage. In 1645, seven years after his birth, Louis XIV laid the first stone for the church, which replaced a run-down Benedictine monastery. Mansart designed the facade in the Jesuit style. Le Duc designed the dome, and the painter Mignard decorated it with frescoes. Other architects included Le Mercier and Le Muet. In 1793 the church was converted into a military hospital, and in 1850 it became an army medical school.

Admission: Free.

Open: Mon–Sat 9am–noon and 2–5pm. Touring prohibited during services. **Métro:** Port-Royal. **Bus:** 38.

BASILICA OF ST-DENIS, place de l'Hôtel de Ville à St-Denis. Tel. 48-09-83-54.

The first Gothic building in France that can be dated precisely, St-Denis was named for the first bishop of Paris, who became the patron saint of the French monarchy. In 1429 Joan of Arc surrendered here, and three centuries later Napoléon married Marie-Louise here. This is also considered "the birthplace of the Crusades."

Area of Detail

PARIS

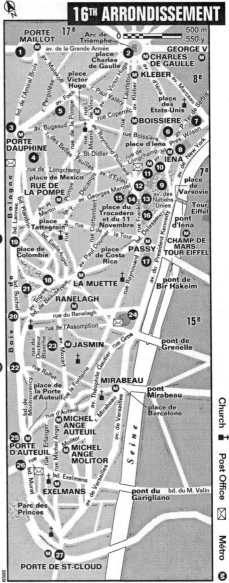

16TH ARRONDISSEMENT

500 m
550 y

Arc de Triomphe **2**
Cimetière de Passy **15**
Hippodrome d'Auteuil **22**
Jardin Ranelagh **18**
Jardins du Trocadéro **9**
Maison de
Radio-France **24**
Musée Armenian &
Musée d'Ennery **5**
Musée de l'Art Modern **8**
Musée du Cinéma **10**
Musée Clemenceau **16**
Musée de la
Contrefaçon **4**
Musée Guimet **6**
Musée Henri
Bouchard **23**
Musée de l'Homme **13**
Musée de la Marine **14**
Musée Marmottan **21**
Musée des
Monuments Français **12**
Musée du Vin **17**
Palais de Chaillot **12**
Palais Galliera **7**
Porte d'Auteuil **25**
Porte Dauphine **3**
Porte Maillot **1**
Porte Molitor **26**
Porte de la Muette **19**
Porte de Passy **20**
Porte de St-Cloud **27**

Church ■ †

Post Office ☒

Métro Ⓜ

You are conducted through the crypt on a guided tour (in French only). Royal burials began here in the 6th century and continued until the Revolution—it's the burial place of five royal dynasties. François I, Louis XII, Anne of Brittany, Henri II, and Catherine de Médicis are all entombed here. However, the revolutionaries stormed through, smashing many marble faces and dumping royal remains in a lime-filled ditch in the garden. The royal remains were reburied under the main altar during the 19th century.

In the 12th century Abbot Suger placed an inscription on the bronze doors of St-Denis: "Marvel not at the gold and expense, but at the craftsmanship of the work." The massive facade, with its crenelated parapet on the top similar to the fortifications of a castle, has a rose window. The stained glass windows, in stunning colors— mauve, purple, blue, and rose—were restored in the 19th century. In the Middle Ages it was believed that Suger had ground up sapphires, emeralds, and rubies to create the rich colors. The sculpture designed for the tombs—some two stories high—spans the country's artistic development from the Middle Ages to the Renaissance.

Admission: 26F ($4.60) adults; 17F ($3) students and over 60; 6F ($1.10) under 18.

Open: May–Sept daily 10am–7pm; off-season daily 10am–5pm. **Métro:** St-Denis.

ST-ETIENNE-DU-MONT, place Ste-Geneviève, 5e. Tel. 43-54-11-79.

St-Etienne-du-Mont is dedicated to Ste-Geneviève, the patron saint of Paris. Her tomb was destroyed during the Revolution, but the stone on which her coffin rested has now been given a place of honor. Pascal and Racine are also interred here.

The church took more than a century to build, beginning in 1492. The Gothic interior contains a remarkable rood screen across the nave. The carved-wood pulpit is supported by a seminude Samson who clutches a bone in one hand, having slain the lion at his feet. The fourth chapel on the right as you enter contains an impressive example of 16th-century stained glass.

The church replaced a small abbey founded by Clovis and dedicated to Ste-Geneviève. All that remains of the former abbey is the Tower of Clovis, now part of the Lycée Henri IV. It's visible from rue Clovis.

Open: Daily 7:30am–noon and 2:30–7pm. **Closed:** Mon in July–Aug. **Métro:** Cardinal-Lemoine.

ST-GERMAIN L'AUXERROIS, 2 place du Louvre, 1er. Tel. 42-60-13-96.

Once this was the church for the Palace of the Louvre, attended by royalty, courtesans, and artists. The majestic church shares place du Louvre with Perrault's colonnade and has 260 feet of stained glass, including Renaissance rose windows. Around the chancel is an intricate 18th-century grille. The churchwarden's pews are skillfully carved, based on the 17th-century designs by Le Brun. Behind the pews is a 15th-century triptych and a poorly lit Flemish retable. The organ was originally ordered by Louis XVI for Sainte-Chapelle.

Built on the site of a primitive chapel, the church contains the foundation stones of its original 11th-century belfry. The crypt contains the tombs of sculptor Coysevox and architect Le Vau.

The darkest day in its history was August 24, 1572. The ringing of its bells unintentionally signaled the St. Bartholomew's Day Massacre, in which many Protestants died.

Open: Daily 8am–7:30pm. **Métro:** Louvre.

PARKS & GARDENS

The most famous garden, the Tuileries, is covered on one of my walking tours of Paris in Chapter 7, and in "The Top Attractions" section, above. In this section, I explore some of the other outstanding gardens and parks of Paris.

JARDIN DU LUXEMBOURG, 6e. Tel. 43-29-12-78.

These classic French gardens, formally laid out and well groomed, are the best on the Left Bank. Even the trees are planted in designs. A large water basin in the center is encircled with urns and statuary on pedestals. The statue of Ste-Geneviève, the patron saint of Paris, has pigtails reaching to her thighs, and another memorial is dedicated to Stendhal.

In the past the gardens were frequented by artists. Watteau came this way, as did Verlaine. Gertrude Stein would cross the gardens to catch the bus to meet Picasso in his studio at Montmartre. In the 1920s the gardens were a feeding ground for poverty-stricken Montparnasse artists. Hemingway told a friend that the Luxembourg Gardens "kept us from starvation." He used to wheel a baby carriage and child through the gardens until the gendarme went across the street for a glass of wine. Then the writer would lure a pigeon with corn, kill it, and hide it under a blanket.

Today the park is a favorite of students from the Sorbonne and of children. On May Day, crowds carrying lilies of the valley throng the park to welcome spring.

The Italianate Luxembourg Palace, overlooking the gardens, was built in 1612 for Marie de Médicis, the much-neglected wife and later widow of the roving Henri IV. She planned to live there with her "witch" friend, Leonora Galigai.

The queen stayed at the palace only briefly before she was exiled by her son, Louis XIII, for plotting to overthrow him. She reportedly died impoverished in Germany. The 21 paintings she commissioned from Rubens, now in the Louvre, were actually intended for her palace.

Admission: Special permission required in advance to visit the palace.

Métro: Odéon. **RER:** Luxembourg.

BOIS DE BOULOGNE, Porte Dauphine, 16e. Tel. 40-67-97-02.

One of the most spectacular parks in Europe, the bois is often referred to as the main lung of Paris. It would take more than a week to see everything here: lakes, islands, an artificial waterfall, deluxe restaurants, a theater, and two racetracks. You can travel through the park by car or horse-drawn carriage, but many of its hidden pathways are accessible only on foot. Porte Dauphine is the main entrance.

The park, located in western Paris, was once a royal hunting ground. Baron Haussmann designed the park after Emperor Napoléon III made the land public in 1852. In the late 19th century, elegantly attired couples rode along avenue Foch in carriages, but today you're more likely to see middle-class picnickers. (Beware of prostitutes and muggers at night.)

Separating Lac Inférieur from Lac Supérieur is the Carrefour des Cascades (Grand Cascade); you can stroll under this artificial waterfall. The Lower Lake contains two islands connected by a footbridge, accessible by boat from the east bank. There's a café/restaurant on one of them. Restaurants in the bois are numerous, elegant, and expensive. The Pré-Catelan contains a deluxe restaurant and a Shakespearean theater in a garden, reputedly planted with trees mentioned in the bard's plays.

Longchamp and Auteuil are the park's two racetracks. The annual Grand Prix is run in June at Longchamp, the site of a medieval abbey, and the event attracts the most fashionable and best-dressed people of Paris. Directly south of Longchamp is the Grand Cascade.

The 60-acre Bagatelle Park is the site of a small palace built by the comte d'Artois (later Charles X), who won a bet with his sister-in-law, Marie Antoinette, that he could build the palace in three months. Visit the Bagatelle in late May to see one of the finest and best-known rose gardens in Europe.

Métro: Les Sablons, Porte Maillot, or Porte Dauphine.

PARC MONCEAU, 8e. Tel. 42-27-39-56.

This park was built in 1778 for the duc d'Orléans, the richest man in Paris at the time. Philippe-Egalité, as he was commonly known, was fond of pleasure and debauchery. No ordinary park would do. Designed by Carmontelle, the park originally included an Egyptian-style obelisk, a medieval dungeon, a thatched alpine farmhouse, a Chinese pagoda, a Roman temple, an enchanted grotto, various chinoiseries, and a waterfall. The park was opened to the public by Napoléon III.

Today all that remains of the fanciful features are a pyramid and an oval naumachie fringed by a colonnade. Newer statuary and monuments were added, one honoring Chopin. Baby carriages are a common sight, and in spring the park blooms with a spectacular display of red tulips and magnolias.

Métro: Monceau or Villiers.

NEARBY ATTRACTIONS

MUSEE NATIONAL DE LA RENAISSANCE, Le Château d'Ecouen, Ecouen. Tel. 39-90-04-04.

A visit to this museum, just outside Paris on the northern route to Chantilly, can easily be tied in with a visit to St-Denis. Called Le Château d'Ecouen, the castle was constructed between 1538 and 1555 for the high constable, Anne de Montmorency. In 1805 Napoléon used the building as a school for daughters of the Legion d'Honneur.

Valéry Giscard d'Estaing, the former French president, converted the space into a Renaissance museum. Set in a park, the château contains an exceptional collection of tapestries and paintings. Be sure to see the best-known tapestry, the 245-foot-long *David and Bathsheba*.

Admission: 20F ($3.60) Mon–Sat, 13F ($2.30) Sun.

Open: Wed–Mon 9:45am–12:30pm and 2–5:15pm. **Métro:** St-Denis/Porte de Paris; then bus 268C to Ezanville, which stops near the museum.

VINCENNES

CHATEAU DE VINCENNES, av. de Paris, 12e. Tel. 43-28-15-48.

About 5 miles east of Notre-Dame, encircled by the Bois de Vincennes, this château, like Versailles, was originally a hunting lodge. At the south of the town of Vincennes, the castle was built by Louis VII ("The Young") in 1164. Inspired by the Sainte-Chapelle in Paris, Charles V added a chapel in 1379. Louis XIV, however, wasn't especially fond of Vincennes; he, of course, had another home in mind.

The château has been rebuilt several times since, and the present

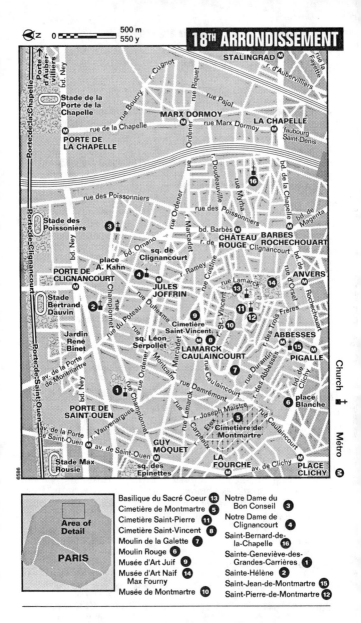

18TH ARRONDISSEMENT

500 m
550 y

STALINGRAD

r. d'Aubervilliers
rue de la Fayette
rue Cugnot
rue Riquet
rue Pajol

Porte
d'Aubervilliers
bd. Ney

Stade de la
Porte de la
Chapelle

MARX DORMOY

rue de la Chapelle
rue Marx Dormoy

LA CHAPELLE

faubourg
Saint-Denis

PORTE DE
LA CHAPELLE

rue Ordener

rue des Poissonniers

rue des Poissonniers

rue Doudeauville

rue Myha

bd. de la Chapelle

Saint-Bernard-de-
la-Chapelle ❶❻

Stade des
Poissoniers

❸†

rue Ordener

rue Marcadet

bd. Barbès
rue des Poissonniers

bd. de
Magenta

CHÂTEAU
ROUGE

BARBÈS
ROCHECHOUART

bd. Ney

Porte-de-Clignancourt

bd. Ornano

sq. de
Clignancourt
place
A. Kahn

❸
r. de Clignancourt

ANVERS

PORTE DE
CLIGNANCOURT

❹

r. Ramey
r. Custine

rue Lamarck

❶❸

rue d'Orsel

rue Rochechouart

Stade
Bertrand
Dauvin

❷

JULES
JOFFRIN

rue Duhesme

St.-Vincent

❶❹

rue du Poteau

❾

❶❶†
❶❷

rue des Trois Frères

Jardin
René
Binet

rue du Poteau

Cimetière
Saint-Vincent

❶⓪

ABBESSES

Porte-de-Saint-Ouen

sq. Léon
Serpollet

Montcalm

LAMARCK
CAULAINCOURT

rue Durantin
rue des Abbesses

❶❺■

PIGALLE

bd. Ney

rue Championnet

rue Ordener

rue Marcadet

❼

rue Caulaincourt

rue Damrémont

rue Lamarck

place
Blanche
❻

bd. de Clichy

PORTE DE
SAINT-OUEN

rue Championnet

r. Vauvenargues

r. Joseph Maistre

rue Capelet

Étex

❺
Cimetière de
Montmartre
†††

rue Caulaincourt

av. de la Porte
de Saint-Ouen

av. de Saint-Ouen

GUY
MÔQUET

sq. des
Épinettes

LA
FOURCHE

av. de Clichy

PLACE
CLICHY

Stade Max
Rousie

Church ■ †

Métro Ⓜ

Basilique du Sacré Coeur ❶❸
Cimetière de Montmartre ❺
Cimetière Saint-Pierre ❶❶
Cimetière Saint-Vincent ❽
Moulin de la Galette ❼
Moulin Rouge ❻
Musée d'Art Juif ❾
Musée d'Art Naïf ❶❹
Max Fourny
Musée de Montmartre ❶⓪

Notre Dame du
Bon Conseil ❸
Notre Dame de
Clignancourt ❹
Saint-Bernard-de-
la-Chapelle ❶❻
Sainte-Geneviève-des-
Grandes-Carrières ❶
Sainte-Hélène ❷
Saint-Jean-de-Montmartre ❶❺
Saint-Pierre-de-Montmartre ❶❷

Area of
Detail

PARIS

---

structure is merely a shell of its former self, which was once
known as the "Versailles of the Middle Ages." In time the château
was to become a porcelain factory, an arsenal under Napoléon,
and a supply depot for the Nazis. Now it's being restored by the
government. Its most memorable role was that of a prison, whose
most famous prisoner was Mirabeau, the revolutionary and
statesman.

Admission: 25F ($4.40); students under 26 and those over 60,
14F ($2.50).

Open: May–Sept daily 9:30am–7:pm; Oct–Apr daily 10am–5pm.
Métro: Château de Vincennes. **RER:** Château de Vincennes.

ST-GERMAIN-EN-LAYE

Gourmet cooks know that béarnaise sauce was invented here, although it is generally better known for its greater distinctions. Only 13 miles northwest of Paris, St-Germain-en-Laye traditionally drew Parisians escaping the summer heat.

CHATEAU VIEUX, place de la Gare. Tel. 34-51-53-65.

The château, next to the train station, itself has served as a royal getaway since it was built in the 12th century by François I. Louis XIV stayed here at the palace, although he eventually abandoned it for Versailles, and James II died here. Napoléon III ordered that the château—built on a hill on the left bank of the Seine—be turned into a museum tracing the history of France from the cave dwellers until the Carolingian era. And so it is today: the Musée des Antiquités Nationales, with displays of tools, stones, arms, and jewelry used or worn by the early settlers of Gaul.

Sainte-Chapelle, the oldest section of the Château Vieux, is of special interest. Built by St. Louis in the 1230s, this chapel can be visited only with the custodian's permission. At the end of the tour of the château, stroll through **Le Nôtre's gardens,** open daily 7am to 9:30pm.

Admission: 20F ($3.50); students, children, and those over 60, 13F ($2.30).

Open: Wed–Mon 9am–5:15pm. **Transportation:** A-1 to St-Germain-en-Laye.

MUSEE DEPARTMENTAL DU PRIEURE, 2 bis, rue Maurice Denis. Tel. 39-73-77-87.

This museum, installed in the oldest building in St-Germain-en-Laye, was built in 1678 by the marquise de Montespan, a paramour of Louis XIV. From World War I to World War II it was inhabited by Maurice Denis, a painter who lived here until his death in 1943. Here he befriended a group of artists, known as "Nabis," including Paul Sérusier. Nabis masters such as Bonnard and Vuillard are represented in the exhibition, along with members of the Pont-Aven group, including Gauguin and Emile Bernard. Works by other artists, including Toulouse-Lautrec, are also exhibited. You can visit a chapel decorated by Denis, as well as his atelier.

Admission: 25F ($4.40) adults; children under 12 free.

Open: Wed–Fri 10am–5:30pm, Sat–Sun 10am–6:30pm. **Transportation:** A-1 to St-Germain-en-Laye.

WHERE TO STAY AND DINE

PAVILLON HENRI IV, 21 rue Thiers, 78100 St-Germain-en-Laye. Tel. 39-10-15-15. Fax 39-73-93-73. 39 rms (all with bath), 3 suites. TV TEL **Transportation**: A-1 to St-Germain-en-Laye, then a five-minute walk.

$ Rates: 490F–750F ($85.75–$131.25) single; 1,000F–1,300F ($175–$227.50) double; from 1,900F ($332.50) suite. Breakfast 50F ($8.75) extra. AE, DC, MC, V.

In the 1500s Henri IV built the Château Neuf on this terrace as a hideaway for his illegitimate children. The castle was later bequeathed to the comte d'Artois, the brother of Louis XVI, who planned to demolish it until the Revolution aborted his plans.

The château was partly rebuilt in 1836, and today the remains comprise the illustrious Pavillon Henri IV hotel, where Dumas wrote *The Three Musketeers*. Standing at the edge of the belvedere gardens of the old château, it is still elegantly old-fashioned. A corner room has been set aside as a museum, in remembrance of where the Sun King romped with Madame de Montespan. The fortunate visitors who get to spend a night here will find handsomely furnished bedrooms and a good restaurant. You can always order the classic dishes here—carré d'agneau rôti (roast lamb); rognon de veau (veal kidney) dijonnaise; and, of course, pommes soufflés, which were invented here, along with sauce béarnaise, which is just the thing to top your chateaubriand. A fixed-price lunch is offered Monday through Friday only, costing 24F ($4.20); otherwise, à la carte lunches or dinners average 350F ($61.30).

3. COOL FOR KIDS

There are fewer special spots for children in Paris than there are, say, in Amsterdam or Copenhagen. But there are some, plus others that will charm both sides of the generation. When you're weary of dragging the kids on your rounds, forcibly inculcating culture, try refreshing the family spirit with a few of these.

MUSEUMS

The only problem for parents in Paris museums is that all the exhibits are identified in French and unless you managed to struggle past that silly aunt's plume in high school or are an expert on the subject under study, you aren't going to distinguish yourself with explanations.

CITE DES SCIENCES ET DE L'INDUSTRIE, La Villette, 30 av. Corentin-Cariou, 19e. Tel. 40-05-80-70.

Perhaps no museum in Paris is more geared to receive and delight children than Cité des Sciences et de l'Industrie. It has entire areas set aside just for them. Of course, many of its exhibits will enthrall both adult and child equally.

For admission prices and opening hours, see "More Museums," above.

MUSEE DE LA MARINE, in the Palais de Chaillot, place du Trocadéro, 16e. Tel. 45-53-31-70.

If your kids have seawater in their veins, take them to this Navy Museum, which features a kaleidoscopic collection of models, maps, figureheads, and whole craft, tracing the development of shipping. The most magnificent item on show is the actual "Boat of the Emperor," a gilt-crowned, oar-driven longboat built in 1811 for Napoléon's trip to Antwerp.

Admission: 31F ($5.40) adults, 16F ($2.80) ages 5–12 and over 60; children 4 and under free.

Open: Wed–Mon 10am–6pm. **Métro:** Trocadéro.

MUSEE GREVIN, 10 bd. Montmartre, 9e. Tel. 42-46-13-26.

The desire to compare the Musée Grévin to Madame Tussaud's of London is almost irresistible. Grévin is the number one waxworks of Paris, having opened in 1882. From Charlemagne to the mistress-collecting Napoléon III, it shows memorable moments from French history in a series of tableaux.

Depicted are the consecration of Charles VII in 1429 in the Cathedral of Reims (Joan of Arc, dressed in armor and carrying her standard, stands behind the king); Marguerite de Valois, first wife of Henri IV, meeting on a secret stairway with La Molle who was soon to be decapitated; Catherine de Médicis with the Florentine alchemist Ruggieri; Louis XV and Mozart at the home of the marquise de Pompadour; and Napoléon on a rock at St. Helena, reviewing his victories and defeats.

Two shows are staged frequently throughout the day. The first, called the "Palais des Mirages," starts off as a sort of Temple of Brahma, and through magically distorting mirrors, changes into an enchanted forest, then a fête at the Alhambra at Granada. A magician is the star of the second show, "Le Cabinet Fantastique"; he entertains children of all ages.

The museum also presents contemporary personalities in the sports world as well as the leaders of many countries. One display presents 50 of the world's greatest film actors.

Admission: 48F ($8.40) adults, 34F ($6) children under 13.

Open: Daily 1–7pm; during French school holidays daily 10am–7pm. Ticket office closes at 6pm. **Métro:** Montmartre or Richelieu-Drouot.

MUSEE NATIONAL D'HISTOIRE NATURELLE, 57 rue Cuvier, 5e. Tel. 40-79-35-86.

Among the other museums frequented by the children of Paris is the Musée National d'Histoire Naturelle, in the Jardin des Plantes. Its history dates back to 1635, when it was founded as a scientific research center by Guy de la Brosse, physician to Louis XIII, but that period is a fleeting moment compared to the eons of history covered inside the huge museum complex. In the galleries of paleontology, anatomy, and mineralogy, your little genius can trace the history and evolution of life on earth, wondering at the massive skeletons of dinosaurs and mastodons, and staring fascinated at the two-headed animal embryos floating forlornly in their pickling jars. Within the museum grounds are tropical hothouses containing thousands of species of unusual plant life along with small animal life in simulated natural habitats.

Admission: 25F ($4.40) adults, 15F ($2.60) ages 18–24, 6F ($1.10) ages 17 and under.

Open: Wed–Mon 10am–5pm. **Métro:** Jussieu or Austerlitz.

PARKS & ZOOS

The large inner-city parks all have playgrounds with tiny merry-go-rounds and gondola-style swings. If you're staying on the Right Bank, take the children for a stroll through the **Tuileries,** where there are donkey rides, ice-cream stands, and a marionette show. At the circular pond, you can rent a toy sailboat. On the Left Bank, equivalent delights exist in the **Luxembourg Gardens.** If you take in the gardens of the **Champ-de-Mars,** you can combine a donkey ride for the children with a visit to the nearby Eiffel Tower for the entire family.

JARDIN D'ACCLIMATION, on the northern edge of the Bois de Boulogne, 16e. Tel. 40-67-90-82.

The definitive children's park in Paris is the Jardin d'Acclimation. This is the kind of place that satisfies tykes and adults alike—but would be regarded in horror by anyone in his or her teens. The visit starts with a ride from Porte Maillot to the Jardin entrance, through a stretch of wooded park, on a jaunty, green-and-yellow narrow-gauge train. Inside the gate is an easy-to-follow layout map. The park is circular, and if you follow the road in either direction it will take you all the way around and bring you back to the train at the end.

En route you will discover a house of mirrors, an archery range, miniature golf, zoo animals, an American-style bowling alley, a puppet theater (only on Thursday, Saturday, Sunday, and holidays), a playground, a hurdle-racing course, and a whole conglomerate of junior-scale rides, shooting galleries, and waffle stalls. You can trot the kids off on a pony or join them in a boat on a mill-stirred lagoon. Fun to watch (and a superb idea for American cities to copy) is "La Prévention Routière," a miniature roadway operated by the Paris police. The youngsters drive through it in small cars equipped to start and stop and are required by two genuine Parisian gendarmes to obey all street signs and light changes.

Admission: 10F ($1.75) adults, 5F (88¢) ages 3–10; under 3 free.

Open: Daily 10am–6pm. **Métro:** Sablons.

PARC ZOOLOGIQUE DE PARIS, Bois de Vincennes, 53 av. de St-Maurice, 12e. Tel. 44-75-20-10.

Without a doubt, the best zoo this city has to offer is in the Bois de Vincennes—on the outskirts, but quickly reached by Métro. This modern zoo displays its animals in settings as close as possible to their natural habitats. Here you never get that hunched-up feeling about the shoulders from empathizing with a leopard in a cage too small for stalking. The lion has an entire veldt to himself, and you can view each other comfortably across a deep protective moat. On a cement mountain reminiscent of Disneyland's Matterhorn, lovely Barbary sheep leap from ledge to ledge or pose gracefully for hours watching the penguins in their pools at the mountain's foot. The animals seem happy here and are consequently playful. Keep well back from the bear pools or your drip-dries may be dripping wet.

Admission: 35F ($6.10) adults; 20F ($3.50) ages 6–16, students 16–25, and over 60; 5 and under free.

Open: May–Sept Mon–Sat 9am–6:30pm; off-season Mon–Sat 9am–5:30pm. **Métro:** Porte Dorée or Château de Vincennes.

PUPPET SHOWS

You can take in a puppet show while visiting the above-mentioned parks—but, once again, all the words are French. Still, they're a great Paris tradition and worth seeing, if only for the joy of sharing a French child's typical experience. The shows are given at the **Tuileries** at 3:15pm on Wednesday, Saturday, and Sunday, all summer long. At the **Luxembourg Gardens,** you'll see puppet productions of sinister plots set in Gothic castles and Asian palaces. Prices vary depending on the extravagance of the production. Some young critics think the best puppet shows are held in the **Champ-de-Mars.** Performance times in both the Luxembourg Gardens and the Champ-de-Mars vary with the day of the week and the production being staged. But all are colorfully and enthusiastically produced—and received. You may have to whisper the story line to your monolingual offspring as you go along, but when Red Riding Hood pummels the Wolf over the head with an umbrella, they'll be contorted in glee like the rest of the half-pint audience. That's international kid-talk.

MONTMARTRE

On Sunday afternoon entire French families crowd up to the top of the Butte Montmartre to join in the fiesta atmosphere. Start by taking the Métro to Anvers and walking to the Funiculaire de Montmartre.

The funiculaire is a small, silvery cable car that slides you gently up the steep, grassy hillside to Sacré-Coeur on the hillcrest. Once on top, follow the crowds to the place du Tertre, where a Sergeant Pepper–style band will usually be blasting off-key and where you can have the kids' pictures sketched by local artists.

4. SPECIAL-INTEREST SIGHTSEEING

FOR THE LITERARY ENTHUSIAST

MAISON DE VICTOR HUGO, 6 place des Vosges. Tel. 42-72-10-16.

The house where Victor Hugo lived and worked from 1832 to 1848 has been turned into a museum devoted to the novelist. You probably know Hugo as a literary giant, but here you'll also see the drawings, carvings, and pieces of furniture he made. The windows of the museum overlook the square.

Admission: 17F ($3) adults, 9F ($1.60) children 7–17; children 6 and under free.

Open: Tues–Sun 10am–5:40pm. **Closed:** National holidays. **Métro:** St-Paul, Bastille, or Chemin-Vert.

MAISON DE BALZAC, 47 rue Raynouard, 16e. Tel. 42-24-56-38.

This unpretentious house on the slope of a hill in Passy, a residential district of Paris, was the home—or more accurately, the hideaway—of the great French novelist Honoré de Balzac from 1840 to 1847. The Balzac museum is almost completely unfurnished, but it does contain mementos, documents, manuscripts, and other items associated with the writer. Throughout the house are scattered caricature drawings of Balzac, whose amusing appearance and eccentric dress lent themselves to ridicule. Among the better-known mementos is the famed Limoges coffeepot that Balzac's "screeching owl" kept hot during the long nights while he wrote *La Comédie humaine*. Also enshrined here are Balzac's writing desk and chair.

The house contains a library of special interest to scholars, as well as a small courtyard and garden. While the main entrance is on rue Raynouard, the back door leads to rue Berton—a fortunate situation for Balzac, who often had to make hasty retreats from his many creditors.

Admission: 18F ($3.20); 19F ($3.30) Sun; children under 18 free.

Open: Tues–Sun 10am–5:45pm. **Métro:** Passy or La Muette.

FOR THE "UNDERGROUND" ENTHUSIAST

LES CATACOMBS, 1 place Denfert-Rochereau, 14e. Tel. 43-22-47-63.

In the Middle Ages the Catacombs were quarries, but in 1785 city officials decided to use them as a burial ground, since the existing cemeteries were considered a health hazard. First opened to the public in 1810, the Catacombs consist of 1,000 yards of tunnel containing 6 million skeletons arranged in skull-and-crossbones fashion. In 1830 the prefect of Paris closed the Catacombs to the viewing public as obscene and indecent. Later, during World War II, the Catacombs were the headquarters of the French Underground. Today they are illuminated with overhead electric lights over their entire length.

Admission: 27F ($4.70) adults, 15F ($2.60) students; under 6 free.

Open: Tues–Fri 2–4pm, Sat–Sun 9–11am and 2–4pm. **Métro:** Denfert-Rochereau.

THE SEWERS OF PARIS [LES EGOUTS], Pont de l'Alma. 7e. Tel. 47-05-10-29.

Some say Baron Haussmann will be remembered mainly for the vast, complicated network of sewers he erected. The *égouts* of the city, as well as telephone and telegraph pneumatic tubes, are constructed around a quartet of principal tunnels, one of them 18 feet wide and 15 feet high. It's like an underground city, with the street names clearly labeled. Further, each branch pipe bears the number of the building to which it is connected (guides are fond of pointing out Maxim's). These underground passages are truly mammoth, containing pipes bringing in drinking water and compressed air as well as telephone and telegraph lines.

That these sewers have remained such a popular attraction is something of a curiosity in itself. They were made famous by Victor Hugo's *Les Misérables.* "All dripping with slime, his soul filled with a strange light," Jean Valjean in his desperate flight through the sewers of Paris is one of the heroes of narrative drama.

A documentary movie on the sewer system is offered, as well as a museum.

Tours: Tours begin on the Left Bank at Pont de l'Alma, where a stairway leads into the bowels of the city. Admission is 25F ($4.30) adults, 20F ($3.50) students; under 10 and over 60 free.

Open: May–Oct Sat–Wed 11am–6pm; winter Sat–Wed 11am–5pm. **Closed:** Three weeks in Jan for maintenance. **Métro:** Alma-Marceau. **RER:** Pont de l'Alma.

FOR VISITING AMERICANS

Many Left Bank streets hold memories for Americans, and none more so than **rue Monsieur-le-Prince,** 6e, in the Odéon section (Métro: Odéon). During a famous visit in 1959, Martin Luther King, Jr., came to call on Richard Wright, Mississippi-born African-American novelist famous for *Native Son.* King climbed to the third-floor apartment at no. 14, only to find that Wright's opinions on the Civil Rights Movement conflicted with his own. Whistler rented a studio at no. 22, and at no. 49 Longfellow lived for a short time in 1826. Oliver Wendell Holmes, Sr., lived at no. 55.

After strolling along this street, you can dine at the former haunt of such figures as Kerouac and Hemingway. See my recommendation of Crèmerie-Restaurant Polidor (41 rue Monsieur-le-Prince, 6e) under "5th & 6th Arrondissements" in Chapter 5.

HARRY'S NEW YORK BAR, 5 rue Daunou, 2e. Tel. 42-61-71-14.

F. Scott Fitzgerald and Ernest Hemingway drank a lot here, Gloria Swanson talked about her affair with Joseph Kennedy, and even Gertrude Stein showed up. And the place is still going strong. See also "Specialty Bars and Clubs" in Chapter 9.

Métro: Odéon or Pyramides.

LA ROTONDE, 105 bd. Montparnasse, 6e. Tel. 43-26-68-84.

Americans tended to drink on the Right Bank, notably in the Ritz Bar, when they had money. When they didn't, they headed for one of the cafés of Montparnasse, which, according to Hemingway, usually meant La Rotonde.

Métro: Raspail.

DEUX-MAGOTS, 170 bd. St-Germain, 6e. Tel. 45-48-55-25.

This long established watering hole of St-Germain-des-Prés is where Jake Barnes meets Lady Brett in Hemingway's *The Sun Also Rises.*

Métro: St-Germain-des-Prés.

HOTEL ST-GERMAIN-DES-PRES, 36 rue Bonaparte, 6e. Tel. 43-26-00-19.

Another legendary woman of letters, Janet Flanner, correspondent for *The New Yorker*, lived here in the 1920s until she had enough money to stay at the Crillon (see "Paris Accommodations," Chapter 4).

Métro: St-Germain-des-Prés.

HOTEL SELECT, 1 place de la Sorbonne, 5e. Tel. 46-34-14-80.

Right in the heart of the Latin Quarter, this previously recommended hotel once housed news commentator Eric Sevareid for about 60¢ a night when he was a struggling reporter for the *Paris-Herald* in 1937. One of his major accomplishments at the time was getting a rare interview with Gertrude Stein.

Métro: St-Michel.

SHAKESPEARE AND COMPANY, 37 rue de la Bûcherie, 5e. No phone.

The most famous bookstore on the Left Bank was Shakespeare and Company, on rue de l'Odéon, home to the legendary Sylvia Beach, the "mother confessor to the Lost Generation." Hemingway, Fitzgerald, and Gertrude Stein were all frequent patrons. In recent decades, visitors would be likely to find Anaïs Nin, the diarist noted for her description of struggling American artists in 1930s Paris, in the store. At one point she helped her companion, Henry Miller, publish *Tropic of Cancer*, a book so notorious in its day that returning Americans trying to slip a copy through Customs often had it confiscated as pornography. When times were hard, Ms. Nin herself wrote pornography for a dollar a page.

Today the shop is located on rue de la Bûcherie, where expatriates still come to swap books and the latest literary gossip.

Open: Daily 11am–midnight. **Métro:** St-Michel.

5 RUE ST-LOUIS-EN-L'ILE, Ile St-Louis, 4e.

This was the address of William Aspenwell Bradley, literary

agent to the Lost Generation, who drew up the contract for *The Autobiography of Alice B. Toklas* by Gertrude Stein. In addition to Stein, he represented Edith Wharton, author of *House of Mirth* and *The Age of Innocence* (awarded the Pulitzer Prize in 1921). Other illustrious clients included Thornton Wilder, who himself won the Pulitzer Prize for *The Bridge of San Luis Rey* and *Our Town*. Back from driving ambulances with Hemingway on the Italian front in 1918, John Dos Passos also became one of Bradley's clients. His famous books include *Three Soldiers* (1921), *U.S.A.* (1937), and *Adventures of a Young Man* (1939).

Métro: Pont-Marie.

19 RUE TOURNON, 6e.

This was the home of John Paul Jones, the American revolutionary hero credited with the famous line, "I have not yet begun to fight." After having captured the 50-gun British frigate HMS *Serapis*, he was honored by Louis XVI. Upon meeting Jones, Abigail Adams noted, "I should sooner think of wrapping him up in cotton wool and putting him in my pocket, than sending him to contend with cannon balls." She noted that he seemed aware of "how often the ladies use baths, what color best suits a lady's complexion, what cosmetics are most favorable to the skin." But on July 18, 1792, he died destitute. Even though he'd been penniless, he was honored with a lavish state funeral.

Métro: Odéon.

2 RUE DE L'UNIVERSITE, 7e.

When Benjamin Franklin arrived in Paris in December 1776, he stayed here. In short time, he moved to 52 rue Jacob, 6e (Métro: St-Germain-des-Prés), and later, as minister to the court at Versailles, he moved into the Hôtel de Valentinois, 62 rue Raynouard, 16e (Métro: Passy), about half a mile from the center of Paris. Beloved by the French, Franklin left Passy on July 11, 1785, at the age of 79.

Métro: Rue du Bac or St-Germain.

LE PROCOPE, 13 rue l'Ancienne-Comédie, 6e. Tel. 43-26-99-20.

Dating from 1686, this is the oldest café in Paris and the restaurant of choice for such historical figures as Franklin and Jefferson (see "5th and 6th Arrondissements" in Chapter 5).

Métro: Odéon.

HOTEL DE PONTALBA, 41 rue du Faubourg St-Honoré, 8e.

Did you ever wonder where Lindbergh slept after his solo flight across the Atlantic? He stayed at the American ambassador's residence, the Hôtel de Pontalba, dating from 1720, and once owned by financier Baron Edmond de Rothschild. It's still the American ambassador's residence and not open to the public.

Métro: Concorde or Champs-Elysées.

5. ORGANIZED TOURS

The most popular way to get acquainted with Paris is on a two-hour double-decker bus tour that takes you past the major attractions. There isn't time to stop at each point of interest, but you'll get a nice view out the numerous large windows. Seats are comfortable, and individual earphones are distributed with a recorded commentary in 10 different languages. Contact **Cityrama,** 4 place des Pyramides, 1er (tel. 44-55-61-00). Tours depart daily between 9:30am and 2:30pm, for 145F ($25.40). **Métro:** Palais-Royal.

A separate tour of the nighttime illuminations leaves daily at 10pm in summer and 9pm in winter. The cost is 145F ($25.40).

Bateaux-Mouches cruises on the Seine depart frequently from the Pont de l'Alma on the Right Bank. Boat facilities vary; some include open sun decks, bars, and restaurants. All provide commentaries in six languages, including English. Tours depart daily every 30 minutes from 10am to 11:30pm; in good weather, boats leave every 15 minutes. Dinner cruises depart at 8:30pm; ties and jackets are required for men. Fares are 40F ($7) for adults and 20F ($3.50) for children for a ride lasting about 1½ hours; luncheon cruises cost 320F ($56) Monday through Saturday or 350F ($61.30) on Sunday; a deluxe dinner cruise costs 520F ($91). Call 42-25-96-10 for information and reservations. **Métro:** Alma-Marceau.

6. SPECIAL & FREE EVENTS

FREE CONCERTS & OTHER EVENTS

Many cultural events in Paris are free. Concerts, films, and lectures are sponsored by foreign nations, such as the United States and Great Britain. Inquire at the **Centre Culturel Britannique,** 9–11 rue de Constantine, 7e (tel. 49-55-73-00). **Métro:** Invalides.

For the best free concert in Paris, hear organ music played in one of the old churches. Most concerts are held on Sunday afternoon, and are usually listed in *Pariscope*, the guide to entertainment events.

At the **Institut Néerlandais,** 121 rue de Lille, 7e (tel. 47-05-85-99), free concerts feature jazz, classical, and contemporary music from the Netherlands. **Métro:** Assemblée Nationale.

Free chamber-music concerts are presented at the **American Church,** 65 quai d'Orsay, 7e (tel. 47-05-07-99). **Métro:** Invalides.

STREET ENTERTAINMENT

The spacious forecourt of the **Centre Georges Pompidou,** plateau Beaubourg, is a free "entertainment center" featuring mimes, fire-eaters, would-be circus performers, and sometimes first-rate musicians. **Métro:** Rambuteau or Hôtel-de-Ville.

Classical-music students, often from the Conservatoire National, give free concerts in the corridors of the **Métro.** A hat (or violin case) is passed to collect donations.

If you're in Paris during one of **the major festivals,** you can join in the fun for free. On summer solstice (June 21) clowns, fire-eaters, and other performers roam the streets. On July 14 (Bastille Day) the French traditionally drink wine and dance in the streets. There are also fireworks displays, free concerts, and a parade of tanks down the Champs-Elysées.

A DAY AT THE RACES

Paris boasts an army of avid horse-racing fans who disperse whenever possible to any of the city's eight racetracks. Information on any of the races being held in Paris during your visit is available in such newspapers and magazines as *Tierce, Paris-Turf, France-Soir,* or *L'Equipe.* These are sold at kiosks throughout the city.

The premier bastion of the French horse-racing world is the **Hippodrome de Longchamp,** Bois de Boulogne (tel. 44-30-75-00). Established in 1855, during the autocratic but pleasure-loving reign of Napoléon III, it carries the most prestige, the greatest number of promising Thoroughbreds, and the largest purse in France. The most important racing months at Longchamp are late June *(Le Grand Prix de Paris)* and early October *(Prix de l'Arc de Triomphe).* **Métro:** Auteuil, then one of the shuttle buses that operate on race days.

Another venue for horse racing is the **Hippodrome d'Auteuil,** also in the Bois de Boulogne (tel. 45-27-12-24). Known for its steeplechases and obstacle courses, it sometimes attracts more than 50,000 Parisians at a time who appreciate the park's open-air promenades as much as they do the equestrian events. Established in 1870, the event is scattered over a sprawling 30 acres of parkland, each of which is designed to show to maximum advantage the skill and agility of both horses and riders. **Métro:** Auteuil.

Also popular, a bit rougher, and the most frequented by blue-collar gambling enthusiasts, is the **Hippodrome de Vincennes,** Bois de Vincennes (tel. 47-42-07-70). Less prestigious than either of its competitors, it holds most of its racing events under floodlights during evening hours in midwinter. **Métro:** Château de Vincennes.

CHAPTER 7

STROLLING AROUND PARIS

1. **THE GRAND PROMENADE**
2. **MONTMARTRE**
3. **THE LATIN QUARTER**
4. **LES GRANDS BOULEVARDS**
5. **ILE ST-LOUIS**

The best way to discover Paris is on foot, using your own shoe leather. This chapter is organized into a series of walking tours of the major attractions and districts of the City of Lights.

Try to spend one day walking the Grand Promenade—the Champs-Elysées—which takes you from the Arc de Triomphe to the Tuileries.

WALKING TOUR 1 — The Grand Promenade

Start: Arc de Triomphe.
Finish: Jardin des Tuileries.
Time: Three leisurely hours; the distance is 2 miles.
Best Time: Sunday morning.
Worst Time: Rush hour.

This is a lengthy walking tour, but it's the most popular walk in Paris. Start at the:

1. **Arc de Triomphe** (see Chapter 6 for details) at place Charles-de-Gaulle–Etoile from which 12 grand avenues radiate. Stand there for a moment (somewhere safe from traffic) and gaze down the long:

2. **Champs-Elysées,** which has been called "the highway of French grandeur." This street has witnessed some of the greatest moments in French history and some of its worst, such as when Hitler's armies paraded down the street in 1940. Louis XIV ordered the construction of the 1.1-mile avenue in 1667. Originally called the Grand-Cour, and designed by Le Nôtre, it was renamed avenue des Champs-Elysées after the Elysian Fields (the home of the virtuous dead) in 1709.

   Stroll along this street. On one side it's a chestnut-lined park; on the other, a commercial avenue of sidewalk cafés, automobile showrooms, airline offices, cinemas, lingerie boutiques, even hamburger shops. The Champs-Elysées has obviously lost the fin-de-siècle elegance described by Proust in *Remembrance of Things Past*. Head down the avenue toward place de la Concorde, staying on the left-hand side. When you reach the:

3. **Rue de Berri,** turn left to no. 20, site of Thomas Jefferson's residence from 1785 to 1789. In its place today is a large modern apartment building. Back on the avenue again, continue to Rond-Point des Champs-Elysées. Close by is a philatelist's delight, the best-known open-air stamp market in Europe, held on Thursday and Sunday.

REFUELING STOP Make it **Fouquet's,** 99 av. des Champs-Elysées (see Chapter 5 for a complete description). Founded in 1901 and still serving coffee and food, this is an institution. In summer you can enjoy the flowers, and in winter the glass screens will shelter you from the winds. Take plenty of money.

Continue down the avenue until you reach avenue Winston-Churchill on your right (from here there's a good panorama, looking toward the Invalides). Ducking traffic and pausing for a view, cross to the other side of the avenue and go along avenue de Marigny. On your right will be the:

4. **Palais de l'Elysée,** the "French White House," whose main entrance is along fashionable Faubourg St-Honoré. Napoléon abdicated here. Now occupied by the president of France, it can't be visited without an invitation.

Back at Rond-Point and avenue Winston-Churchill, you come to the:

5. **Grand Palais,** which was constructed for the World Exhibition of 1900, as was the:

6. **Petit Palais** (whose entrance is on avenue Winston-Churchill), which now houses the Musée d'Art Moderne de la Ville de Paris (see Chapter 6 for details). Postponing a visit for the moment, continue along this avenue—now the garden-district section—until you come to the landmark:

7. **Place de la Concorde,** an octagonal traffic hub built in 1757 to honor Louis XV. The statue of the king was torn down in 1792 and the name of the square was changed to place de la Revolution (following the Reign of Terror in 1795, it was named place de la Concorde). Floodlit at night, the square is dominated by an Egyptian obelisk from Luxor, considered the oldest human-made object in Paris. It was carved around 1200 B.C. and presented to France in 1829 by the viceroy of Egypt. During the Reign of Terror, the dreaded guillotine was erected on this spot and claimed the lives of thousands of people.

On each side of the obelisk are two fountains with bronze-tailed mermaids and bare-breasted sea nymphs. Gray-beige statues ring the square, honoring the cities of France. To symbolize France's loss of Alsace and Lorraine to Germany in 1871, the statue of Strasbourg was covered with a black drapery that wasn't lifted until the end of World War I (when the territory was restored). Two of the palaces on place de la Concorde are today the Ministry of the Navy and the deluxe Hôtel Crillon. They were designed in the 1760s by Ange-Jacques Gabriel. For a spectacular sight, look down the Champs-Elysées. The gateway to the Tuileries is flanked by the *Winged Horses* of Coysevox.

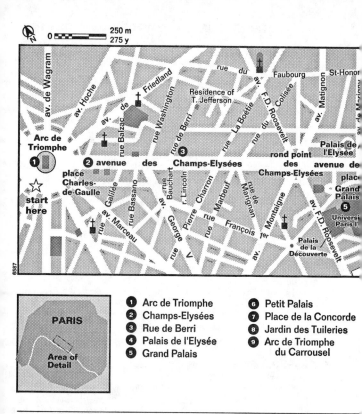

- ❶ Arc de Triomphe
- ❷ Champs-Elysées
- ❸ Rue de Berri
- ❹ Palais de l'Elysée
- ❺ Grand Palais
- ❻ Petit Palais
- ❼ Place de la Concorde
- ❽ Jardin des Tuileries
- ❾ Arc de Triomphe du Carrousel

REFUELING STOP The **Bar of the Hôtel Crillon,** 10 place de la Concorde, is one of the best places in the world to have a drink. Fashion designer Sonia Rykiel has given it new luster, and the drinks, the setting, the ambience, and the atmosphere of "Paree" remain undiminished over the decades.

From Place de la Concorde, you can enter the:
8. **Jardin des Tuileries,** as much a part of Paris as the Seine. These statue-studded gardens were designed by Le Nôtre, the gardener to Louis XIV. About 100 years before that, a palace was ordered built here by Catherine de Médicis, which was occupied by Louis XVI after he left Versailles. Napoléon I called it home. Twice attacked by the people of Paris, it was finally burned to the ground in 1871 and never rebuilt. The gardens, however, remain, the trees arranged geometrically in orderly designs. Even the paths are straight, instead of winding as in English gardens. The fountains, though, soften the sense of order and formality.

The neoclassical statuary is often insipid and is occasionally desecrated by rebellious "art critics." Seemingly half of Paris is found in the Tuileries on a warm spring day, listening to the chirping birds and watching the daffodils and red tulips bloom.

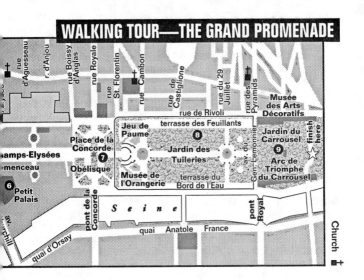

Fountains bubble, and parents push baby carriages around the grounds where 18th-century revolutionaries killed the king's Swiss guards.

At the end of your walking tour of the Tuileries—2 miles from place Charles-de-Gaulle–Etoile—you'll be at the:

9. Arc de Triomphe du Carrousel, at the cour du Carrousel. Accommodating three walkways and supported by marble columns, the monument honors the Grande Armée, celebrating Napoléon's victory at Austerlitz on December 5, 1805. The arch is surmounted by statuary, a chariot, and four bronze horses. At this point, you'll be at the doorstep of the Louvre.

WALKING TOUR 2 — Montmartre

Start: Place Pigalle.
Finish: Place Pigalle.
Time: Five hours—more if you break for lunch. It's a 3-mile trek.
Best Time: Any day that it isn't raining. Set out by 10am at the latest.
Worst Time: After dark.

The traditional way to explore Montmartre is on foot. It's the highest point in the city, and visitors who find it too much of a climb will want to take the miniature train along the steep streets (35 min). **Le Petit Train de Montmartre,** which passes all the major landmarks, seats 55 passengers who can listen to the English commentary. Board at either place du Tertre (the Church of St-Pierre) or place Blanche (near the Moulin Rouge). Trains run daily from 10am to 7pm. For information contact Promotrain, 131 rue de Clignancourt, 18e (tel. 42-62-24-00).

The simplest way to reach Montmartre is to take the Métro to Anvers, then walk up rue du Steinkerque toward the funicular. Funiculars run to the precincts of Sacré-Coeur every day from 6am to 11pm.

FROM PLACE PIGALLE TO MONT CENIS Those who prefer to walk can take the Métro to place Pigalle. Turn right after leaving the station and proceed down boulevard de Clichy, turn left at the Cirque Medrano, and begin the climb up rue des Martyrs. Upon reaching rue des Abbesses, turn left and walk along this street, crossing the place des Abbesses. Walk uphill along rue Ravignan, which leads directly to place Emile-Goudeau, a tree-studded square in the middle of rue Ravignan. At no. 13, across from the Timhotel, stood:

1. **Bateau-Lavoir (Boat Washhouse),** called the cradle of cubism. Although gutted by fire in 1970, it has been reconstructed by the city of Paris. Picasso once lived here and, in the winter of 1905–1906, painted one of the world's most famous portraits, *The Third Rose* (Gertrude Stein). Other residents have included Kees van Dongen and Juan Gris. Modigliani had his studio nearby, as did Rousseau and Braque.

   Rue Ravignan ends at place Jean-Baptiste-Clément. Go to the end of the street and cross it onto rue Norvins (which will be on your right). This intersection, one of the most famous street scenes of Montmartre (and painted by Utrillo), is the meeting point of rues Norvins, St-Rustique, and des Saules. Turn right and head down rue Poulbot. At no. 11 you'll come to the:

2. **Espace Montmartre Dalí.** This phantasmagorical world of Dalí features 300 original works by the artist, including his famous 1956 lithograph of *Don Quixote*.

REFUELING STOPS Chances are, you'll be in Montmartre for lunch. Many restaurants, especially those around place du Tertre, are unabashed tourist traps. You'll be asked eight times if you want your portrait sketched in charcoal. However, **La Maison-Rose,** 2 rue de l'Abreuvoir (see Chapter 5 for a complete description), is a good bargain. This was once the atelier of Utrillo, and the famous French singer Charles Aznavour used to perform here. The little pink house is about 300 yards from place du Tertre. But if you want better food, then leave the place du Tertre area and take a 12-minute walk down the Butte to **Le Maquis,** 69 rue Caulaincourt (see Chapter 5 for details). The food is reasonable, and in sunny weather you can try for a seat on the tiny terrace. The restaurant is open Tuesday through Saturday.

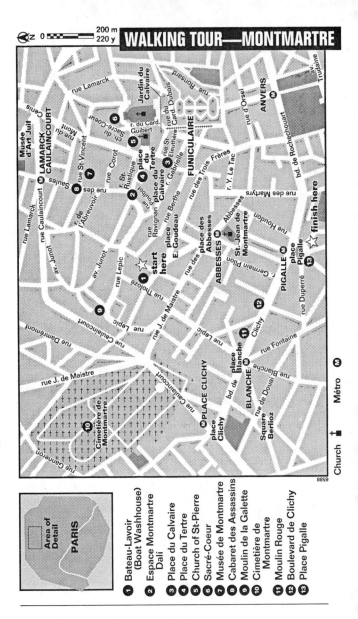

200 m
220 y

N ... 0

Area of Detail

PARIS

Bateau-Lavoir (Boat Washhouse)

Espace Montmartre Dali

Place du Calvaire

Place du Tertre

Church of St-Pierre

Sacré-Coeur

Musée de Montmartre

Cabaret des Assassins

Moulin de la Galette

Cimetière de Montmartre

Moulin Rouge

Boulevard de Clichy

Place Pigalle

Church **†■**   Métro **M**

The rue Poulbot crosses the tiny:

3. Place du Calvaire, which offers a panoramic view of Paris.
On this square (a plaque marks the house) lived artist,
painter, and lithographer Maurice Neumont (1868–1930).
From here, follow the sounds of an oompah band to:

4. Place du Tertre, the old town square of Montmartre. Its
cafés are overflowing, its art galleries (in and out of doors)
always overcrowded. Some of the artists still wear berets, and
the cafés bear such names as La Bohème—you get the point.

Everything is so loaded with local color—applied as heavily as on a Seurat canvas—it gets a little redundant.

Right off the square fronting rue du Mont-Cenis is the:

5. Church of St-Pierre. Originally a Benedictine abbey, it has played many roles—Temple of Reason during the French Revolution, food depot, clothing store, even a munitions factory. Nowadays it's back to being a church. In 1147 the present church was consecrated; it's one of the oldest in Paris. Two of the columns in the choir stall are the remains of a Roman temple. Note among the sculptured works a nun with the head of a pig, a symbol of sensual vice. At the entrance of the church are three bronze doors sculpted by Gismondi in 1980. The middle door depicts the life of St. Peter. The left door is dedicated to St. Denis, first bishop of Paris, and the right door to the Holy Virgin.

Facing St-Pierre, turn right and follow rue Azaïs to Sacré-Coeur.

6. Sacré-Coeur, overlooking square Willette. See Chapter 6 for a complete description. Facing the basilica, take the street on the left (rue du Cardinal Guibert), then turn left onto rue du Chevalier-de-la-Barre and go to rue du Mont-Cenis, taking a right.

FROM MONT CENIS TO PLACE PIGALLE Continue on this street to rue Corot, at which point turn left. At no. 12 is the:

7. Musée de Montmartre (tel. 46-06-61-11), with a wide collection of mementos of *vieux Montmartre*. This famous 17th-century house was formerly occupied by Dufy, van Gogh, and Renoir. Suzanne Valadon and her son, Utrillo, also lived here. It's open Tuesday through Sunday from 11am to 6pm. Admission is 25F ($4.40) for adults, 15F ($2.60) for children.

From the museum, turn right heading up rue des Saules past a winery, a reminder of the days when Montmartre was a farming village on the outskirts of Paris. A grape-harvesting festival is held here every October.

The intersection of rue des Saules and rue St-Vincent is one of the most visited and photographed corners of the Butte. Here, on one corner, sits the famous old:

8. Cabaret des Assassins, long ago renamed Au Lapin Agile (see Chapter 9 for details).

Continue along rue St-Vincent, passing the Cimetière St-Vincent on your right. Utrillo is just one of the many famous artists buried here. Take a left turn onto rue Girardon and climb the stairs. In a minute or two, you'll spot on your right two of the windmills *(moulins)* that used to dot the Butte. One of these:

9. Moulin de la Galette (entrance at 1 av. Junot), was immortalized by Renoir.

Turn right onto rue Lepic and walk past no. 54. In 1886, van Gogh lived here with Guillaumin. Take a right turn onto rue Joseph-de-Maistre, then left again on rue Caulaincourt until you reach the:

10. Cimetière de Montmartre, second in fame only to Père-Lachaise. The burial ground (Métro: Clichy) lies west of the Butte, north of boulevard de Clichy. Opened in 1795, the cemetery is the final resting place of such well-known composers, artists, and writers as: Berlioz (d. 1869), Offenbach

(d. 1880), Heinrich Heine, Stendhal, the Goncourt brothers, Alfred de Vigny, and Théophile Gautier. I like to pay my respects at the tomb of Alphonsine Plessis, the heroine of *La Dame aux camélias*, and Madame Récamier, who taught the world how to lounge.

From the cemetery, take avenue Rachel, turn left onto boulevard de Clichy, and go to place Blanche, where an even better-known windmill than the one in Renoir's painting stands, the:

11. Moulin Rouge, one of the most talked-about nightclubs in the world. It was immortalized by Toulouse-Lautrec.

From place Blanche, you can begin a descent down:

12. Boulevard de Clichy, fighting off the pornographers and hustlers trying to lure you into tawdry sex joints. With some rare exceptions—notably the citadels of the *chansonniers*—boulevard de Clichy is one gigantic tourist trap. Still, as Times Square is to New York, boulevard de Clichy is to Paris: Everyone who comes to Paris invariably winds up here. The boulevard strips and peels its way down to:

13. Place Pigalle, center of nudity in Paris. The square is named after a French sculptor, Pigalle, whose closest association with nudity was a depiction of Voltaire in the buff. Place Pigalle, of course, was the notorious "Pig Alley" of World War II. Toulouse-Lautrec had his studio right off Pigalle at 5 av. Frochot. When she was lonely and hungry, Edith Piaf sang in the alleyways, hoping to earn a few francs for the night.

WALKING TOUR 3 — The Latin Quarter

Start: Place St-Michel.
Finish: The Panthéon.
Time: Three hours, not counting stops.
Best Time: Any school day, Monday through Friday, from 9am to 4pm.
Worst Time: Sunday morning, when everybody is asleep.

This is the precinct of the Université de Paris (known for its most famous constituent, the Sorbonne), where students meet and fall in love over coffee and croissants. Rabelais named it the *quartier latin* after the students and the professors who spoke Latin in the classroom and on the streets. The sector teems with belly dancers, exotic restaurants, sidewalk cafés, bookstalls, *caveaux*, and *clochards* and *chiffonniers* (bums and ragpickers).

A good starting point for your tour is:

1. Place St-Michel (Métro: Pont St-Michel), where Balzac used to get water from the fountain when he was a youth. This center was the scene of much Resistance fighting in the summer of 1944. The quarter centers around:

2. Boulevard St-Michel to the south, which the students call "boul Mich." From place St-Michel, with your back to the Seine, turn left down:

3. Rue de la Huchette, the setting of Elliot Paul's *The Last Time I Saw Paris*. Paul first wandered into this typical street

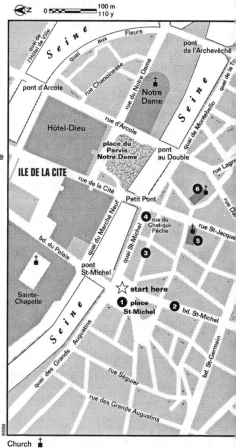

PARIS

Area of Detail

❶ Place St-Michel
❷ Boulevard St-Michel
❸ Rue de la Huchette
❹ Rue du Chat-qui-Pêche
❺ Church of St-Séverin
❻ Church of St-Julien-le-Pauvre
❼ Musée de Cluny
❽ Sorbonne
❾ Church of the Sorbonne
❿ Panthéon

Church ✝

"on a soft summer evening, and entirely by chance," in 1923. Although much has changed since his time, some of the buildings are so old that they have to be propped up by timbers. Paul captured the spirit of the street more evocatively than anyone, writing of "the delivery wagons, makeshift vehicles propelled by pedaling boys, pushcarts of itinerant vendors, knife-grinders, umbrella menders, a herd of milk goats, and the neighborhood pedestrians." Branching off from this street to your left is:

4. Rue du Chat-qui-Pêche (Street of the Cat Who Fishes), said to be the shortest, narrowest street in the world, containing not one door and only a handful of windows. It's usually filled with garbage or lovers—or both.

Now, retrace your steps toward place St-Michel and turn left at the intersection with rue de la Harpe, which leads to rue St-Séverin. At the intersection, take a left to see the:

5. Church of St-Séverin (see Chapter 6 for details). After a visit to this flamboyant Gothic church, go back to rue St-Séverin

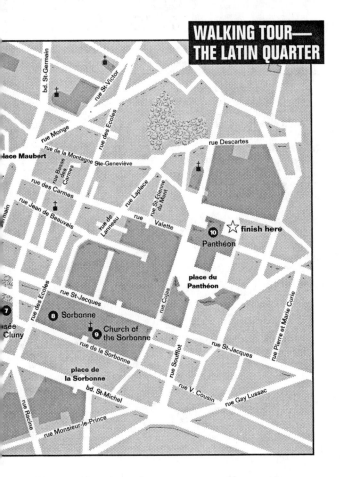

and follow it to rue Galande. Stay on rue Galande until you reach the:

6. Church of St-Julien-le-Pauvre. First stand at the gateway and look at the beginning of rue Galande, especially the old houses with the steeples of St-Séverin rising across the way—one of the most characteristic and most painted scenes on the Left Bank. Enter the courtyard and you'll be in medieval Paris. The garden to the left of the entrance offers the best view of Notre-Dame.

Everyone from Rabelais to Thomas Aquinas has passed through the doors of this church. Prior to the 6th century a chapel stood on this spot. The present structure goes back to the Longpont monks, who began work on it in 1170 (making it the oldest existing church in Paris). In 1655 it was given to the Hôtel Dieu, and in time it became a small warehouse for salt. In 1889 it was given to the followers of the Melchite Greek rite, a branch of the Byzantine church.

REFUELING STOP At 14 rue St-Julien-le-Pauvre, **The Tea Caddy** (tel. 43-54-15-56) is perhaps one of the most charming tea salons in Paris (see Chapter 5 for details). It serves light lunches, salads, omelets, quiches, and, of course, tea.

Return to rue Galande. Turn left at the intersection with rue St-Séverin. Continue on until you reach rue St-Jacques, then turn left and follow it to boulevard St-Germain. Turn right onto this boulevard and follow it until you reach rue de Cluny. Turn left and follow the street to the entrance to the:

7. Musée de Cluny (see Chapter 6 for details). Even if you're rushed, take time out to see the *The Lady and the Unicorn* tapestry. After your visit to the Cluny Museum, exit onto boulevard St-Michel, but instead of heading back to place St-Michel, turn left, and walk down to place de la Sorbonne and the:

8. Sorbonne, a constituent of the Université de Paris, one of the most famous academic institutions in the world. Founded in the 13th century, it had become the most prestigious university in the West by the 14th century, attracting such professors as Thomas Aquinas; subsequently, it was reorganized by Napoléon in 1806.

At first glance from place de la Sorbonne, the Sorbonne seems architecturally undistinguished. In truth, it was rather indiscriminately reconstructed at the turn of the century. The same cannot be said for the:

9. Church of the Sorbonne (Métro: St-Michel), built in 1635 by Le Mercier, which contains the marble tomb of Cardinal Richelieu, a work by Girardon based on a design by Le Brun. At his feet is the remarkable statue *Learning in Tears.*

From the church take rue Victor Cousin south to the intersection with rue Soufflot. Turn left. At the end of this street lies the place du Panthéon and the:

10. Panthéon (see Chapter 6). Sitting atop Mont Ste-Geneviève, this nonreligious temple is the final resting place of such distinguished figures as Hugo, Zola, Rousseau, and Voltaire.

WALKING TOUR 4 — Les Grands Boulevards

Start: Place de la Madeleine.
Finish: Place Vendôme.
Time: Two hours, not counting stops; it's a 2-mile trek.
Best Time: Monday through Friday from 10am to 5pm, when the shops are open.
Worst Time: Rush hours.

Once there was nothing more fashionable than dining at a restaurant along one of the *grands boulevards.* They became chic in the mid-18th century, reached a pinnacle with the carriage trade, but were later abandoned in favor of the Champs-Elysées. Stretching from the Church of the Madeleine to Baron Haussmann's place de la République, the boulevards are lined with many fine department stores and shops.

The promenade begins at the Madeleine, one of the most imposing Grecian-inspired temples in the world.

1. **La Madeleine church** stands right in the heart of the Right Bank on the landmark place de la Madeleine. Actually, "La Madeleine" is a nickname—the church is dedicated to St. Mary Magdalene. An old, small parish church of the area was torn down, and construction of a new one began in 1764 but was stopped by the French Revolution. During Napoléon's reign, several projects by different architects were proposed—one architect hoped to build "The Temple of Glory," honoring the "Grande Armée." Finally a new church was built on this site, using the frame of the former church. It opened in 1842. The building resembles a huge Greek temple ringed with a Corinthian colonnade, its columns holding up an encircling frieze (one of the pediments depicts the Last Judgment). Bas-reliefs on the bronze door represent the Ten Commandments, and in niches along the facade are statues of saints. From the portal you have a panoramic vista down rue Royale to the Egyptian obelisk and through place de la Concorde up to the palace of the Assemblée Nationale. Inside the church, a trio of skylit domes illuminates the central nave, the gilded globe lanterns, and the inlaid marble floors. Take a look at the chapel, left of the entrance, where you will find the *Baptism of Jesus*, by Rude (who sculpted the famous *Marseillaise* on the Arc de Triomphe). Concerts are staged here at least once a month (tel. 42-65-52-17 for information).

   Boulevard de la Madeleine turns into boulevard des Capucines, where, at the:
2. **Hôtel Scribe,** at no. 14, a plaque honors those pioneers of the cinema, the Lumière brothers, who launched their films on December 28, 1895.

REFUELING STOP If you're ready for a snack, stop at **Café de la Paix,** 12 boulevard des Capucines. During the liberation of Paris, the Yanks practically established a beachhead at this world-famous "watering hole" across from American Express, and they've been firmly entrenched ever since. The long parade has included everybody from Harry Truman to the chanteuse Josephine Baker. Teas, breakfasts, and apéritifs are your best choices at what has been called the "factory of *la vie parisienne.*"

The tour now leads to place de l'Opéra, and its:
3. **Opéra,** which is no longer the musical center of Paris (the Opéra Bastille now has that honor), but it is still a showcase for ballet and concerts. Walk around the entire building to enjoy its magnificence. Inside you'll find memorabilia of such great dancers as Pavlova and Nijinsky. Designed by the young architect Charles Garnier during the Second Empire, its facade is adorned with marble and sculptures, including *The Dance* by Carpeaux. (This version is a copy; the original is in the Louvre.) At one time or another, most of the great, glittering

personages of Europe, including Henry James and "the divine Sarah" (Bernhardt), have descended the wide marble steps of the Grand Staircase. The auditorium's dome was decorated by Chagall in 1964.

To walk around the Opéra, take rue Halévy to rue Gluck, which leads into place Diaghilev, opening onto boulevard Haussmann. To head back, take rue Scribe, bypassing the offices of American Express on your right, then rue Auber. Then head down rue de la Paix, which intersects with rue Daunou.

REFUELING STOP Ready to rest your feet? **Harry's Bar,** 5 rue Daunou (see Chapter 9), has always been the place where Americans, along with a parade of world celebrities, have gone to drink. It is said that the 1920s roared louder here than anywhere else. Eisenhower made it his "second headquarters," and Gershwin worked on *An American in Paris* here. Have a drink and soak up some of the atmosphere.

Rue de la Paix honored Napoléon before its name was changed. Dating from 1806, the boulevard today is one of the most gilded shopping streets of the world. Each jewelry store, notably Cartier at no. 11, seems to offer a king's ransom of gems. Continue along rue de la Paix and eventually reach your final stop:

4. **Place Vendôme** (Metro: Opéra). Always aristocratic, sometimes royal, place Vendôme enjoyed its golden age during the Second Empire. Dress designers—the great ones, such as Worth—introduced the crinoline there. Louis Napoléon lived here, wooing his future empress at the Hôtel du Rhin. In its halcyon days the waltzes of Strauss echoed across the plaza.

Today banks and offices abound, but the most prestigious tenant on the plaza is the Ritz. Place Vendôme is one of the most harmonious squares in France, evoking the Paris of *le grand siècle*—that is, the age of Louis XIV. Originally planned by Mansart to honor Louis XIV, the square had a statue of the Sun King until the Revolution, when it was replaced briefly by *Liberty*. Today it's dominated by a column crowned by Napoléon, erected to celebrate his victory at Austerlitz. It was made of bronze melted from captured Russian and Austrian cannons. After Napoléon's downfall the statue was replaced by one of Henri IV, everybody's favorite king and every woman's favorite man. Later Napoléon surmounted it once again, this time in uniform and without the pose of a Caesar.

The Communards of 1871, who detested royalty and the false promises of emperors, pulled down the statue. They were allegedly led by the artist Courbet, who was jailed and fined the cost of restoring the statue. He couldn't pay it, of course, and was forced into exile in Switzerland. Eventually, the statue of Napoléon, wrapped in a Roman toga, won out. The plaza is one of the best known in Paris. It has attracted such tenants as Chopin, who lived at no. 12 until his death in 1849.

But who was Vendôme, you ask? He was the son (delicate writers refer to him as "the natural son") of the roving Henri IV and his best-known mistress, Gabrielle d'Estrées.

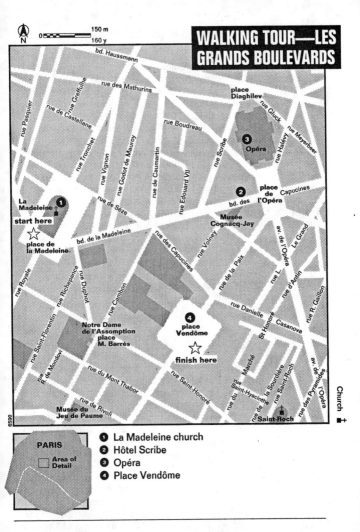

❶ La Madeleine church
❷ Hôtel Scribe
❸ Opéra
❹ Place Vendôme

PARIS
☐ Area of Detail

WALKING TOUR 5 — Ile St-Louis

Start: Pont St-Louis.
Finish: Pont St-Louis.
Time: 2½ hours.
Best Times: 9am to noon and 2 to 5pm any day.

As you walk across the little iron footbridge, pont St-Louis, with Notre-Dame behind you, you'll be entering Ile St-Louis—a world of tree-shaded quays, aristocratic town houses, courtyards, restaurants, and antique shops.

Sibling island of Ile de la Cité, Ile St-Louis is primarily residential; its denizens fiercely guard their heritage, privileges, and special position. When asked where they live, residents don't answer "Paris"; they say instead "Ile St-Louis," or sometimes just "Ile."

St-Louis, once two "islets," was originally named "Island of the Heifers." The two islands were joined during the reign of Louis XIII. Many famous people have occupied these patrician mansions, and they are identified by plaques on the facades.

On reaching the island, turn left and walk around the:

1. **Quai de Bourbon.** Two of the most splendid mansions on the island (no. 15 and no. 19) are the former homes of parliamentarians and display considerable architectural adornment. At pont Marie, the quay changes its name to quai d'Anjou.
   It is generally agreed that the most elegant mansion is the:

2. **Hôtel de Lauzun,** located at 17 quai d'Anjou. It is owned by the city and can be visited only with permission. Built in 1657, it is named after the 17th-century rogue duc de Lauzun, famous lover and sometime favorite of Louis XIV. At the hôtel, the French courtier was secretly married to "La Grande Mademoiselle" (the duchesse de Montpensier), much to the displeasure of Louis XIV, who dealt with the matter by hustling him off to the Bastille.
   That "flower of evil," Charles Baudelaire, the 19th-century French poet, lived at Lauzun with his "Black Venus," Jeanne Duval. While he was squandering the family fortune, Baudelaire was writing poems that celebrated the erotic. Although he had high hopes for them, they were dismissed by many as "obscene, vulgar, perverse, and decadent." (It was not until 1949 that the French court lifted the ban on all his works.) Baudelaire attracted such artists as Delacroix and Courbet to his apartment, which was often filled with the aroma of hashish. Occupying another apartment was the 19th-century novelist Théophile Gautier ("art for art's sake"), who is remembered today chiefly for his *Mademoiselle de Maupin.*
   Voltaire lived at 2 quai d'Anjou, in the:

3. **Hôtel Lambert** with his mistress Emilie de Breteuil, the marquise du Châteley, who had an "understanding" husband. The couple's quarrels at the Hôtel Lambert were known all over Europe (Emilie did not believe in confining her charms, once described as "nutmeg-grater skin" and "bad teeth," to her husband or her lover). But not even Frederick, king of Prussia, could permanently break up her liaison with Voltaire. The mansion was built by Louis Le Vau in 1645 for Nicolas Lambert de Thorigny, the president of the Chambre des Comptes. For a century the hôtel was the home of the royal family of Poland, the Czartoryskis, who entertained Chopin, among others.
   Continuing along quai d'Anjou, you'll reach the tip of the island, called:

4. **Square Barye,** all that remains from the terraced gardens that were built by the financier Bretonvilliers. With your back to the square you can now proceed along:

5. **Quai de Béthune.** The duc de Richelieu (great-nephew of Cardinal Richelieu) lived at no. 16, and Madame Curie resided at no. 36, near pont de la Tournelle, from 1912 until her death in 1934.

start here

finish here

pont St-Louis

pont Louis Philippe

voie G. Pompidou

quai de Bourbon

quai des Célestins

pont Marie

ILE SAINT-LOUIS

rue J. du Bellay

rue Boutarel

rue Le Regratier

r. St-Louis en l'Ile

quai d'Anjou

quai d'Orléans

rue Budé

rue des Deux Ponts

St-Louis en l'Ile

rue Poulletier

① Hôtel de Lauzun

Hôtel Lambert

quai de la Tournelle

pont de la Tournelle

Musée A. Mickiewicz

quai de Béthune

rue de Bretonvilliers

pont de Sully

Square Barye

Seine

Church

150 m
160 y

PARIS

Seine

Area of Detail

① Quai de Bourbon
② Hôtel de Lauzun
③ Hôtel Lambert
④ Square Barye
⑤ Quai de Béthune
⑥ Saint-Louis-en-l'Ile Church
⑦ Quai d'Orléans
⑧ Adam Mickiewicz Museum

Turn right onto rue de Bretonvilliers, which comes to an arcade. Turn left onto the principal street of the island, rue St-Louis-en-l'Ile, and pause at:

6. St-Louis-en-l'Ile Church, dating from 1726. It was built according to plans devised by the architect Le Vau, who also designed portions of the Louvre and Versailles. Inside look for a plaque presented by the city of St. Louis, Missouri, honoring its namesake. Badly attacked and damaged during the Revolution, the interior is elegantly decorated with gilt, marble, and woodwork, all 17th-century *grand siècle* style. It is open Tuesday through Saturday 9:30am to noon and 3 to 7pm, Sunday 9:30am to noon.

REFUELING STOP Try **Berthillon,** 31 rue St-Louis-en-l'Ile (tel. 43-54-31-61), famous for the best ice cream and sorbet in Paris. Some 50 flavors are served to "invasions" of tourists in summer (except in August). Open Wednesday through Sunday 10am to 8pm, they dispense their black-currant ice cream and their kumquat sorbet—you name it, they've got it, no matter how exotic. There's always a line.

Continue your stroll up rue St-Louis-en-l'Ile. Notable mansions include Hôtel Chenizot, 51 rue St-Louis-en-l'Ile, the archbishop's residence. Another resident of this mansion was the notorious noblewoman Térèsia Cabarrus, nicknamed "Notre-Dame de Thermidor" after sexual favors she offered to hordes of revolutionaries. Turn left down rue Bude until you come to:

7. **Quai d'Orléans,** which overlooks the Cité and enjoys many famous associations. The main attraction of the quay is the:

8. **Polish Library/Adam Mickiewicz Museum,** 6 quai d' Orléans (tel. 46-34-05-44), dedicated to Poland's greatest romantic poet (1798–1855), who spent 20 years in exile in Paris. The Chopin Room contains mementos of the composer. Other collections display 19th-century and contemporary Polish art and 18th- and 19th-century paintings and objets d'art mainly of the French and Italian schools. The library has 100,000 books, chiefly on Polish history and literature, archives on 19th-century Polish national insurrections, and the history of the Polish emigration to France as well as a cartographic section (old maps of Poland). The museum and art collections are open Thursday 3 to 6pm. The library reading room is open Tuesday through Friday 2 to 6pm and Saturday 10am to 1pm; closed from mid-July to mid-September. Admission is free.

Many expatriate Americans have lived on this quay, including the columnist Walter Lippmann (no. 18–20) in 1938. The novelist, James Jones, author of *From Here to Eternity*, lived at no. 10 from 1958 to 1975; many literary greats, including Henry Miller and William Styron, came to visit him here.

Having traversed the island, you have now returned to where you started, with a glorious view of Notre-Dame.

SAVVY
SHOPPING

Should you buy anything in Paris? Are there any good buys? Is there any item here that you can't find back home? Yes, there are items unique to France that are not easily found in America, and there is also the joy of bringing "something back from Paris," a reminder of your stay—memories of strolling along one of the chic boulevards of Paris, browsing in the smart boutiques, and finally, purchasing a scarf or handbag.

1. THE SHOPPING SCENE

BEST BUYS

Perfumes in Paris are almost always cheaper than in the States. That means all the famous brands—Guerlain, Chanel, Schiaparelli, Jean Patou. Cosmetics bearing French names, such as Dior and Lancôme, also cost less. Gloves, too, are a fine value.

Paris, with the possible exception of London, is stocked with more antiques and "curios" than any city of Europe. Of course, many visitors come to Paris just to shop for fashion. From Chanel to Yves Saint-Laurent, from Nina Ricci to Sonia Rykiel, the city literally overflows with fashion boutiques ranging from haute couture to daringly modern dress. Likewise, going hand in glove, fashion accessories in Paris are among the finest and best designed in the world. If you don't believe me, then ask Louis Vuitton or perhaps Céline. French lingerie may be every woman's dream. The top lingerie designers sell in Paris. Galeries Lafayette and Printemps have large sections.

AIRPORT TAX-FREE BOUTIQUES

You are better off buying certain products in the airport. In the duty-free shops at Orly and Charles de Gaulle airports, you will get a minimum discount of 20% on all items, and up to 50% on liquor, cigarettes, and watches. Among the items on sale are crystal, cutlery, chocolates, luggage, wine, whiskey, pipes and lighters, lingerie, silk scarves, perfume, knitwear, jewelry, cameras and equipment, cheeses, and antiques.

The drawbacks of airport shopping are that the selections are limited, and of course, you must carry your purchase with you onto the plane.

BUSINESS HOURS, TAXES & CUSTOMS

BUSINESS HOURS Shops are *usually* open Tuesday through Saturday from 9am to 7pm, but the hours can vary greatly. Small shops sometimes take a two-hour lunch break. The flea market and some other street markets are open on Saturday, Sunday, and Monday. That intriguing sign on shop doors reading ENTREE LIBRE means you may browse at will. SOLDES means "sale." SOLDES EXCEPTIONELLES means they're pushing it a bit.

TAX REFUNDS If you've been in the country less than six months, you are entitled to a refund on the value-added tax (VAT) on purchases made in France to take home—under certain conditions.

These export discounts range from 20% to 30%, but it depends on the item purchased, of course. The *détaxe*, or refund, is allowed on purchases of goods costing more than 2,000F ($350) in a single store, but it's not automatic. Food, wine, and tobacco don't count, and the refund is only granted on purchases you carry with you out of the country, not on merchandise you have shipped back home.

Here's what you must do:

Show the clerk your passport to prove you're eligible for the refund. You will then be given an export sales document in triplicate (two pink sheets and a green one), which you must sign. You'll also be given an envelope addressed to the store. Go early to your departure point, as there are sometimes queues waiting at the booth marked DÉTAXE at French Customs. If you're traveling by train, go to the détaxe area in the station before boarding. You can't get your refund documents processed on the train. The refund booths are outside the passport checkpoints, so you must take care of that business before you proceed with the passport check.

Only the person who signed the documents at the store can present them for the refund. Give the three sheets to the Customs official, who will countersign and hand you back the green copy. Save this in case problems arise about the refund. Give the official the envelope addressed to the store (be sure to put a stamp on the envelope). One of the processed pink copies will be mailed to the store for you. Usually you will be reimbursed by check in convertible French francs sent by mail to your home; sometimes the payment is made to a credit-card account. In some cases, you may get your refund immediately, paid at an airport bank window. If you don't receive your tax refund in four months, write to the store, giving the date of purchase and the location where the sheets were given to Customs officials. Include a photocopy of your green refund sheet.

U.S. CUSTOMS You're allowed to bring back into the United States overseas purchases with a retail value of $400, providing you have been out of the country at least 48 hours and you must have claimed no similar exemptions within 30 days. After your duty-free $400 is exceeded, a tax of 10% is levied on the next $1,000 worth of items purchased abroad.

You pay no duty on antiques or art, if such items are 100 years old or more, even if they cost $4 million or more. In addition, you're allowed to send one gift a day to family or friends back home, providing its value does not exceed $50. Perfumes costing more than $5, liquor, cigarettes, and cigars can't be sent duty-free.

SHIPPING IT HOME   There are restrictions on what merchandise can be shipped. Customs regulations change, so when in doubt it's best to check before you buy so that your purchase doesn't show up on a "prohibited" list.

If you buy something at a Parisian department store or an upscale boutique, ask the clerk about reliable shippers. Most major hotel desks in Paris also maintain up-to-date lists of shipping companies. Many shoppers even talk to their local shipping companies before they go. Remember, however, that there is always some degree of risk involved in shipping goods.

Check with the shipper in Paris to make sure you understand the arrangement that you've made, and ask about insurance. Don't forget to ask about duties and clearance fees in your home country, what kind of packing will be used, and whether there will be any warehouse penalties if you can't pick up the item right away.

2. SHOPPING A TO Z

ANTIQUES

LA COUR AUX ANTIQUAIRES, 54 rue du Faubourg St-Honoré, 8e. Tel. 42-66-58-77.

Near the Elysée Palace is an elegant Right Bank arcade frequented by the most discerning Parisians and international designers. At some 18 shops you can browse the offerings, including antiques, paintings, doll furniture, glass, porcelain, and objets d'art (usually from the 16th to the 20th century). **Open:** Mon 2–6:30pm, Tues–Sat 10:30am–6:30pm. **Métro:** Place de la Concorde or Madeleine.

LE LOUVRE DES ANTIQUAIRES, 2 place du Palais-Royal, 1er. Tel. 42-97-27-00.

The largest antique center in Europe attracts collectors, browsers, and those interested in everything from Russian icons to 19th-century furniture to art deco. The center stands across from a giant parking lot beside the Louvre. Housing some 240 dealers, the showrooms are spread across 2½ acres of well-lit modern salons. The building, a former department store, was erected in 1852, according to Napoléon's plans for the rue de Rivoli. Down an enormous flight of skylit stairs, past a café and reception area, you enter the inner sanctum where you find the dealers operating. **Open:** Tues–Sun 11am–7pm. **Métro:** Louvre.

THE VILLAGE SUISSE, 78 av. de Suffren, 15e, and 54 av. de la Motte-Picquet, 15e. Tel. 43-06-69-90.

This is a vast Left Bank complex of 200 antique shops and boutiques. Parisian interior decorators frequent the gallery for their wealthy clients, looking for oil paintings, silver, copper, pewter, or antique furniture from all major periods and styles. Bargain hunters should look elsewhere. **Métro:** La Motte-Picquet–Grenelle.

ART

**CARNAVALETTE, 2 rue des Francs-Bourgeois, 3e.
Tel. 42-72-91-92.**

Carnavelette is just off place des Vosges in the Marais. It sells unusual, one-of-a-kind engravings, plus a large collection of satirical 19th-century magazines and newspapers. **Open:** Daily 10:30am–6:30pm. **Métro:** St-Paul.

**GALERIE DOCUMENTS, 53 rue de Seine, 6e.
Tel. 43-54-50-68.**

Galerie Documents has one of the most original collections of old posters (1870–1930) in Paris. Many are inexpensive, although you could easily pay dearly for an original. The store will mail your poster home. **Open:** Tues–Sat 10:30am–12:30pm and 2:30–7pm. **Métro:** Odéon.

GALERIE MAEGHT, 12 rue St-Merri, 6e. Tel. 42-78-43-44.

In the heart of the Marais section of Paris, just a few steps from the Centre Pompidou, this gallery sells some of the best contemporary artwork in Paris, not only paintings and sculptures but photographs as well. **Open:** Tues–Sat 10am–1pm and 2–7pm. **Métro:** Rambuteau or Hôtel-de-Ville.

GALERIE 27, 27 rue de Seine, 6e. Tel. 43-54-78-54.

Galerie 27 sells lithographs by some of the most famous artists of the early 20th century, including Picasso. The inventory ranges from art posters selling for 50F ($8.80) each to original paintings by Chagall, Miró, Picasso, and Léger. **Open:** Mon–Sat 10am–1pm and 2:30–7pm. **Métro:** St-Germain-des-Prés.

MAEGHT EDITEUR & ADRIEN MAEGHT GALLERY, 42 rue du Bac, 7e. Tel. 45-48-31-01.

This gallery has an interesting collection of posters and pictorial books by important artists, such as Matisse. Exhibits include modern sculpture and engravings by established and unknown artists. **Open:** Tues–Sat 10am–1pm and 2–7pm. **Métro:** Rue du Bac.

ART NOUVEAU & ART DECO ACCESSORIES

SCHMOCK BROC, 15 rue Racine, 6e. Tel. 46-33-79-98.

Mlle Clément Nadine, one of the city's leading collectors of the increasingly fashionable art nouveau and art deco accessories, runs this specialty shop. Her boutique is on the Left Bank near the Théâtre de l'Odéon. The glorious, more flamboyant world of yesterday comes alive here, as you explore the collection of jewelry, lighting fixtures, whatever the owner herself has discovered on her frequent shopping expeditions. **Open:** Tues 10:30am–1:30pm, Sat 2:45–7:30pm. **Métro:** Odéon.

BOOKS

**THE ABBEY BOOKSHOP, 29 rue de la Parcheminerie, 5e.
Tel. 46-33-16-24.**

More than any other establishment in France, this offshoot of a distinguished bookshop in Toronto acts as a magnet for Canada's literary community in Paris. Occupying two floors of a shop near the Sorbonne, it sells an ample inventory of mostly paperback books dealing with philosophy, history, cooking, travel, and the history of film. There are also recent editions of most major Canadian newspapers and magazines. Most books are in English except for those published by Québecois publishers in Montréal. The establishment features poetry readings by Canadian poets, and serves complimentary coffee, tea, and (sometimes) cider to anyone browsing through its ample stacks. **Open:** Mon–Sat 11am–8pm. **Métro:** Cluny–La Sorbonne.

BRENTANO'S, 37 av. de l'Opéra, 2e. Tel. 42-61-52-50.

Brentano's is one of the leading English-language bookstores in Paris, offering guides, maps, novels, and nonfiction. **Open:** Mon–Sat 10am–7pm. **Métro:** Opéra.

W. H. SMITH & SON, 248 rue de Rivoli, 1er. Tel. 42-60-37-97.

Books, magazines, and newspapers published in the English-speaking world are widely available. You can get the *Times* of London, of course, and the Sunday *New York Times* is available every Monday. You'll find many American magazines, too. There's a fine selection of maps if you plan to do much touring. Across from the Tuileries, W. H. Smith also has excellent reference books, language books, and a special children's section. **Open:** Mon–Sat 9:30am–7:30pm. **Métro:** Concorde.

CHINA, SILVER, GLASSWARE & CRYSTAL

BACCARAT, 30 bis, rue de Paradis, 10e. Tel. 47-70-64-30.

Purveyor to kings and presidents of France since 1764, Baccarat produces world-renowned full-lead crystal requested by and created for perfectionists. A visit here is worth the time, even for visitors not intending to purchase. There is a museum of the company's most historic models on premises. **Open:** Mon–Fri 9am–6pm, Sat 10am–noon and 2–5pm. **Métro:** Château d'Eau, Poissonnière, or Gare de l'Est.

GALERIE D'AMON, 28 rue St-Sulpice, 6e. Tel. 43-26-96-60.

In St-Germain-des-Prés close to the Church of St-Sulpice, the Amon Gallery has a permanent exhibition of glasswork with a wide range of items from both France and abroad. Madeleine and Jean-Pierre Maffre display items in blown glass, blown engraved glass, sculptures, and paperweights by top glass workers. **Open:** Tues–Sat 11am–7pm. **Métro:** Odéon, St-Sulpice, or Mabillon.

LALIQUE, 11 rue Royale, 8e. Tel. 42-65-33-70.

Directed today by the granddaughter of the original founder, René Lalique, a silversmith who launched the shop during the belle époque, Lalique is known around the world for its glass sculpture and decorative lead crystal. The shop sells a wide range of merchandise at prices slightly lower than the celestial prices charged abroad. **Open:** Mon–Sat 9:30am–6:30pm, Tues–Fri 9:30am–6:30pm. **Métro:** Concorde.

LIMOGES-UNIC, 12 and 58 rue de Paradis, 10e. Tel. 47-70-54-49 or 47-70-61-49.

There's a wide stock of Limoges china such as Céralène, Haviland, and Bernardaud, as well as Villeroy & Boch, Hermès,

Baccarat, Lalique, Daum, St. Louis, and Sèvres crystal, Christofle & Ercuis silverware, and many other items for table decoration. **Open:** Mon–Sat 10am–6:30pm. **Métro:** Gare de l'Est or Poissonnière.

CHOCOLATE

DALLOYAU, 99–101 rue du Faubourg St-Honoré, 8e. Tel. 43-59-18-10.

When it was established in 1802, the newly rich bourgeoisie of Paris rushed to its doorstep to enjoy the luscious chocolate suddenly flooding the market from France's colonial plantations. Today, still very much in business, the shop can ship its chocolates, elegantly packaged, anywhere you specify. In addition to a variety of chocolates in a bewildering array of sweetnesses, it sells pastries, petits-fours, and cakes. The shop is located near some of the most fashionable clothing stores in Europe, provoking endless calorie-induced guilt from the appearance-conscious women browsing through the shops nearby. **Open:** Daily 9am–9pm. **Métro:** Champs-Elysées–Clemenceau.

LA MAISON DU CHOCOLAT, 225 rue du Faubourg St-Honoré, 8e. Tel. 42-27-39-44.

Racks and racks of chocolates are priced individually or by the kilo. Each is made from a blend of as many as six different kinds of South American and African chocolate, and flavorings include just about everything imaginable. Chocolate pastries are also sold. Everything here is made in the supermodern facilities in the establishment's cellars before being sent up on an old-fashioned dumbwaiter. **Open:** Mon–Sat 9:30am–7pm. **Closed:** Aug. **Métro:** Ternes.

CRAFTS

BOUTIQUE DU MUSEE DES ARTS DECORATIFS, 107 rue de Rivoli, 1er. Tel. 42-61-04-02.

This boutique connected with the Musée des Arts Décoratifs offers a variety of handsome household goods, some of them exact copies of items displayed in the museum. Craftspeople have copied faïence, molded crystal, art nouveau jewelry, porcelain boxes, scarves, and other items of fine workmanship and great beauty. There is no charge for admission, and you can find interesting items in low to expensive price ranges. **Open:** Daily 10:30am–6:30pm. **Métro:** Palais-Royal or Tuileries.

LE PRINTEMPS, 64 bd. Haussmann, 9e. Tel. 42-82-50-00.

In addition to its other merchandise, Le Printemps (see "Department Stores," below) offers one of the largest selections of handcrafts in Paris. **Métro:** Havre-Caumartin.

TROUSSELIER, 73 bd. Haussmann, 8e. Tel. 42-66-97-95.

Trousselier is a century old. At first you'll think it's simply a florist shop, with some artfully arranged sprays. But look again or touch and you'll see that every flower is artificial, shaped in silk and hand-painted by people who pursue this famous French craft. And what exquisite work! Everything is lifelike in the extreme. One cluster will bear a bud, a full-blown flower, and then one just past its prime and fading at the edges.

Founded in 1877, the establishment charges from 240F ($42) for a single silk flower handmade in their studios, and from 1,500F ($262.50) for a bouquet. Full-size trees, using natural trunks and artfully twisted limbs are also commissionable. Polyester flowers, imported from China, begin at 50F ($8.80) each. The prices reflect the high quality. **Open:** Mon–Fri 9:30am–6:30pm, Sat 10am–6pm. **Métro:** Havre-Caumartin.

DEPARTMENT STORES

GALERIES LAFAYETTE, 40 bd. Haussmann, 9e. Tel. 42-82-34-56.

A landmark in the Parisian fashion world and a beautiful example of the city's belle époque architecture, Galeries Lafayette is one of the leading department stores of the world. A special entrance marked WELCOME brings you to English-speaking hosts available to assist you with your shopping needs. The department store includes the Galfa Club men's store, Lafayette Sports, and the main store, featuring the latest in international fashion designs, unusual gifts, perfumes, and quality housewares. Finish your shopping day with an exceptional view of Paris on the Galeries Lafayette rooftop terrace. **Open:** Mon–Sat 9:30am–6:45pm. **Métro:** Chaussee d'Antin or Opéra. **RER:** Auber.

LE PRINTEMPS, 64 bd. Haussmann, 9e. Tel. 42-82-50-00.

The city's largest department store actually consists of three stores connected by bridges on the second and third floors. Go to Brummell for clothing for men, both sports and dress. Printemps de la Maison is mainly for records and books, furniture, and housewares, while Printemps de la Mode sells clothes for women, young people, and children. The ground floor is mainly for perfume, cosmetics, gifts, and Paris handcrafts. The perfumery at Printemps is one of the largest in Paris, maybe the largest.

Interpreters stationed at the Welcome Service in the basement will help you claim your discounts, find departments, and make purchases. International customers are also invited to one of the store's fashion shows held under the historic 1923 glass dome every Tuesday at 10am throughout the year, every Tuesday and Friday at 10am from March through October. **Open:** Mon–Sat 9:30am–7pm. **Métro:** Havre-Caumartin. **RER:** Auber.

LA SAMARITAINE, 19 rue de la Monnaie, 1er. Tel. 40-41-20-20.

A much more economical and family-oriented department store is La Samaritaine. It has a little bit of everything—and some good clothing buys. A restaurant on the premises serves meals Monday through Saturday from 11:30am to 3pm. **Open:** Mon–Sat 9:30am–7pm (till 10pm on Thurs). **Métro:** Pont-Neuf.

DISCOUNT SHOPPING

Paris no longer caters to just the well-heeled in its boutiques. Many formerly high-priced items are often on sale at tabs cut from 20% to 40% of their original price when displayed in a store along the Champs-Elysées. Several shops have opened that offer leftover merchandise from some of the better-known fashion houses. Of course, the famous labels have been cut out, but it's still the same clothing.

Discount houses tend to be crowded, often bustling, and a bit rushed. At each of the following stores, however, at least one of the employees speaks English.

ANNA LOWE, 35 av. Matignon, 8e. Tel. 43-59-96-61.

This is considered the premier boutique in Paris for the discriminating woman who wishes to purchase high-quality clothing—but at discount prices. The boutique lies only half a block from rue du Faubourg St-Honoré, where haute couture is much more expensively priced. All items sold by Anna Lowe (a former model herself) have the designer's label still attached, including Chanel, Valentino, Givenchy, and Guy Laroche. Prices are often half the normal selling price of a garment. The merchandise does not contain factory rejects or seconds. Some of the clothing is models' samples. Alterations are done for a nominal price, often within two or three days. **Open:** Mon–Sat 10:30am–7pm. **Métro:** Miromesnil.

MENDES (SAINT-LAURENT/CHRISTIAN LACROIX), 65 rue Montmartre, 2e. Tel 42-36-83-32.

This is where many of the fashion-conscious, but also budget-conscious, women of Paris come to buy ready-to-wear lines of Saint-Laurent called "sportswear." Sometimes discounts of "last season's" clothing average as much as 50%. There are no dressing rooms, no alterations, and no exchanges or refunds, but that doesn't prevent a battalion of determined women from buying clothes from the summer and winter collections six months after they appear in retail stores, but at reduced prices. (Clothes from the designers' winter collections arrive at Mendès in January; clothes from the summer collections arrive in mid-July.) All of the activity takes place on two floors of a building at the edges of the garment district. **Open:** Mon–Thurs 10am–6pm, Fri–Sat 10am–5pm. **Métro:** Les Halles.

FASHION

FOR CHILDREN

BONPOINT, 15 rue Royale, 8e. Tel. 47-42-52-63.

Located near Maxim's, Bonpoint is part of a well-known haute couture chain for children. Clothing is well tailored—and very expensive. The shop sells clothes for boys and girls ages 1 day to 16 years. Its strongest inventories are in formal dresses, confirmation dresses, and the long and elegant baptism robes, embroidered in France and edged in lace. **Open:** Mon–Sat 10am–7pm. **Métro:** Concorde.

FOR WOMEN

CELINE, 24 rue Francois, 1er, 8e. Tel. 47-20-22-83.

This is one of the best choices for ultraconservative, well-made clothes that Parisian women say almost never wear out. There's also a selection of elegant shoes and handbags. The store is especially famous for its heavyweight silk scarves, patterned in equestrian themes, and priced at around 1,000F ($175) each. Sales, where the price of these is reduced by around 40%, occur every year for three weeks in June and three weeks in January. **Open:** Mon–Sat 10am–6:30pm. **Métro:** F. D. Roosevelt.

CHANEL, 31 rue Cambon, 1er. Tel. 42-86-28-00.

The spirit of Chanel lives on, and her shop across from the Ritz is more than ever in business with haute couture, a landmark design showcase of classical French fashion. Prices, of course, are celestial. The shop also sells accessories, perfumes, cosmetic lines, and watches. **Open:** Mon–Sat 10am–7pm. **Métro:** Concorde or Tuileries.

CHANEL, 42 av. Montaigne, 8e. Tel. 47-23-74-12.

For Chanel's ready-to-wear, which is more reasonably priced but still very expensive, try this shop. It is said that every woman—at least those who can afford it—should own a "basic Chanel," and that it will never go out of style. Accessories are also sold here. **Open:** Mon–Sat 9:30am–6:30pm. **Métro:** F. D. Roosevelt.

CHRISTIAN DIOR, 26–32 av. Montaigne, 8e. Tel. 40-73-54-44.

World-famous for its custom-made haute couture, Christian Dior has a wide selection of both women's and men's ready-to-wear, sportswear, and accessories, including separate salons for shoes and leather goods, furs, children's clothing, and a variety of gift items, genuine and costume jewelry, lighters, and pens, among other offerings. **Open:** Mon–Sat 10am–6pm, Tues–Fri 9:30am–6:30pm. **Métro:** F. D. Roosevelt.

HERMES, 24 rue du Faubourg St-Honoré, 8e. Tel. 40-17-47-17.

Hermès is a legend, of course. The shop is especially noted for its scarves, made of silk squares that are printed with antique motifs. The establishment's famous silk scarves, among the most easily recognized in Europe, sell for 1,200F ($210) each, except during the annual January and June sales, when they're half price.

Three well-known Hermès fragrances, two for women and one for men, make excellent gift choices.

The gloves sold here are without peer, especially those for men in reindeer hide, doeskin, or supple kid. The leather-goods store at Hermès is the best known in Europe. The craftspeople working on the premises turn out the Hermès handbag, an institution that needs no sales pitch on these pages. **Open:** Mon–Sat 10am–6:30pm. **Métro:** Concorde.

LANVIN, 22 rue du Faubourg St-Honoré, 8e. Tel. 44-71-33-33.

Lanvin is the oldest existing fashion house in France. It was founded a hundred years ago by Jeanne Lanvin, who, at the age of 22, opened a milliner's shop a few yards from the Faubourg St-Honoré. Then, in 1909, she started in fashion through a chic clientele of young women and their mothers. In 1925, she diversified her activities, opening shops in many countries around the world and developing the men's and sport's departments as well as the perfume activity.

On the second floor of one of Lanvin's major shops, marvelous haute couture dresses are presented in the house's salon. On the first floor, chic and contemporary *prêt-à-porter* (ready to wear) day and evening dresses and ensembles are to be found together with beautiful Lanvin shawls. **Open:** Tues–Fri 9:30am–6:30pm. **Métro:** Concorde.

AUX MUSES D'EUROPE, 64 rue de Seine, 6e. Tel. 43-26-89-63.

Aux Muses d'Europe offers antique lace dresses of rare beauty, as well as contemporary clothing (1900–1950) and accessories. With items collected from all over France by the mother-daughter team of Marguerite and Katia Belleville, who consider themselves *antiquaires de mode*, the shop has appeared in nationwide television broadcasts in Japan and frequently welcomes actresses who need to dress in period costume. The shop is not large, but the clothing accessories, costume jewelry, bags, and gloves (1940–1950) are displayed on racks that reach the ceiling. Ask to see the lace-trimmed baby dresses as well.   **Open:** Mon 2–7pm, Tues–Sat 11am–7pm. **Métro:** Odéon or St-Germain-des-Prés.

PIERRE CARDIN COUTURE, 27 av. Marigny, 8e. Tel. 42-66-92-25.

Pierre Cardin boutiques seem to pop up on every corner. The ready-to-wear styles for women range from conservative to ultra-modern. All the clothing, no matter what style, is extremely well made. The most expensive and original Cardin designs are displayed at Pierre Cardin Couture, 14 place François-1er, 8e (tel. 45-63-29-13). **Open:** Mon–Sat 10am–7pm. **Métro:** Champs-Elysées–Clemenceau.

FOR MEN

ALAIN FIGARET, 21 rue de la Paix, 2e. Tel. 42-65-04-99.

Alain Figaret is one of France's foremost designers for men's shirts (sizes 14½ to 17½) and women's blouses (sizes 6 to 14). Although there is a broad range of fabrics, each shirt has the same classic appeal. The store prides itself on selling 100% cotton shirts and pure-silk neckties. They also sell men's underwear and elegant pajamas. **Open:** Mon–Sat 10am–7pm. **Métro:** Opéra.

LANVIN, 15 rue du Faubourg St-Honoré, 8e. Tel. 44-71-33-33.

This shop, one of the most elegant in Paris, is just one of many Lanvin boutiques throughout the city. Specializing in "the latest" conservative but stylish fashion, Lanvin also sells a handsome collection of shirts and ties and will custom-make shirts and suits. **Open:** Mon–Sat 10am–7pm. **Métro:** Concorde.

PIERRE CARDIN BOUTIQUE HOMMES, 59 rue du Faubourg St-Honoré, 8e. Tel. 42-66-92-25.

Pierre Cardin carries a large assortment of sophisticated men's clothing and some of the finest accessories available, including an unusual selection of men's shoes. As you'd expect, everything is expensive. **Open:** Mon–Sat 10am–7pm. **Métro:** Champs-Elysées–Clemenceau.

FOOD

FAUCHON, place de la Madeleine, 8e. Tel. 47-42-60-11.

At the place de la Madeleine stands one of the most popular sights in the city—not the church, but Fauchon, a vast shop crammed with gastronomical goodies. Never have I seen faces so rapt—not even before the *Mona Lisa*—as those of Parisians gazing at the Fauchon window display. Plump chickens coated in a glazing of sliced almonds, a thigh of lamb opening out like a cornucopia, filled with bright, fresh vegetables made to look like fruits. It's the French version of the Garden of Eden.

English-speaking hosts will assist you, if needed. In the fruit-and-vegetable department you'll find such items as rare mushrooms and fraises des bois (wild strawberries). The pastry and confectionery store features different types of pastry, candies, and a self-service stand-up bar. The candies, incidentally, are divine, including glazed tropical fruits, whiskey truffles, stuffed dates, and chocolate-dipped ginger. After seeing the self-service bar, you'll probably decide to stay for lunch. Go first to the display case, make your decision, then tell the cashier what you want. She'll give you a check for each item, which you in turn surrender to the serving woman. You may order an omelet, a shrimp salad, or even a club sandwich. A cup of ice cream makes a soothing dessert. Also on the premises are a cocktail department, a gifts department, a selection of porcelain and table settings, and an impressive collection of very drinkable wines. **Open:** Mon–Sat 9:40am–7pm. A "Mini-Fauchon," selling mainly food products, is open Mon–Sat 7–9pm. **Métro:** Madeleine.

HATS

E. MOTSCH, 42 av. George V, 8e. Tel. 47-23-79-22.
One of the most distinguished outlets for classic handmade hats for both men and women is E. Motsch, right off the Champs-Elysées. This sedate corner store, in business since 1887, offers almost every type of headgear, ranging from berets to Scottish tam-o'-shanters. The section for women contains some of the most stylish, if conservative, hats in Paris. **Open:** Tues–Fri 10am–6:30pm, Mon and Sat 10am–1pm and 2:15–6:30pm. **Métro:** George-V.

JEWELRY

VAN CLEEF & ARPELS, 22 place Vendôme, 1er. Tel. 42-61-58-58.
This is the headquarters of a store that was established around the turn of the century. A premier jewelry store of world renown (and numerous branches), its motto is, "There is nothing a man in love can refuse to the woman who makes him happy." This exclusive shop is known for its special settings and also carries a range of deluxe watches. **Open:** Mon–Fri 10am–6:30pm. **Métro:** Opéra or Tuileries.

LEATHER GOODS

GUCCI, 2 rue du Faubourg St-Honoré, 8e. Tel. 42-96-83-27.
This is one of the world's largest showcases for this fabled Italian designer, with his trademark red-and-green trim in leather goods. Gucci makes fine shoes and handbags, as well as other items, including wallets, gloves, and clothing. This outlet has an excellent selection of scarves and two-piece ensembles. Its sweaters are especially outstanding.

Gucci also maintains another outlet on the same street, at 350 rue du Faubourg St-Honoré, 8e (same phone), near the place

Vendôme (Métro: Tuileries), with more or less the same merchandise as that at the address above. **Open:** Both outlets Mon–Sat 9:30am–6:30pm. **Métro:** Concorde.

LINGERIE & BATHING SUITS

CADOLLE, 14 rue Cambon, 1er. Tel. 42-60-94-94.
All of Paris nostalgically remembers the founding mother of this store, Hermine Cadolle, as the person who in 1889 invented the brassiere. Today the store is managed by Hermine's great-great-and great-great-great-granddaughters, Alice and Poupie Cadolle. This is the place to go for a made-to-order or a ready-to-wear fit. For custom-made fit, it is best to make an appointment long in advance, preferably before leaving for France or at least as soon as you arrive.

Custom-made whalebone corsets are still available, and the nightgowns range from the demure to the scandalous. There is also a fashionable collection of bathing suits. This is the home of Cadolle's fine perfume, Le No. 9. **Open:** Mon–Sat 9:30am–1pm and 2–6:30pm. **Métro:** Concorde or Madeleine.

MALLS

FORUM DES HALLES, 1–7 rue Pierre-Lescot, 1er. Tel. 42-96-68-74.
Once the great old vegetable markets, Les Halles is now a vast crater in the middle of Paris, selling, among other things, clothing, accessories, food, and gifts. **Métro:** Etienne-Marcel.

LE CARROUSEL DU LOUVRE, 99 rue de Rivoli, 1er. Tel. 46-53-04-95.
This prestigious shopping complex in the center of historical Paris, next to the new entry hall of the Louvre, opened in 1993. All sorts of shops and services tempt you, and many branches are open on Sunday. Among these is the Virgin Megastore with recorded music, books, and videos. You can also purchase show and theater tickets here. Other outlets include the Body Shop, Via Oro (fashion accessories), Diane Claire (a range of mass-produced art objects), L'Herbier de Provence (health and beauty products), and Lalique (a branch of the famous boutique along the rue Royale). Esprit sells American sportswear, and L'Art du Parfum offers quality perfumes, beauty products, and cosmetics. In all, there are 60 boutiques and four halls dedicated to fashion shops, exhibitions, congresses, and seminars. **Métro:** Palais-Royal/Musée du Louvre.

MONTPARNASSE SHOPPING CENTRE, between rue de l'Arrivée and 22 rue de Départ, 14e. Tel. 45-38-52-87.
Boutiques in this shopping center offer men's and women's fashions, jewelry, perfume, cosmetics, gifts, shoes, art, wool, records, glasses, and children's wear. Shoppers will also find a branch of Galeries Lafayette, restaurants, a travel agent, and even a swimming pool inside. **Métro:** Montparnasse-Bienvenue.

PALAIS DES CONGRES DE PARIS BOUTIQUES, 2 place de la Porte-Maillot, 17 e. Tel. 40-68-26-24.
Palais des Congrès de Paris Boutiques, located inside the convention building, offers art, fine food, fashion, jewelry, toys, books, records, and children's wear. You'll also find a Japanese department store and hairdresser. **Métro:** Porte Maillot.

MARKETS

MARCHE AUX PUCES, av. de la Porte de Clignancourt.

⭐ A landmark, the Flea Market is both adored and abused. Even if you don't purchase one item (an unlikely possibility), it's an experience to be savored. This is a complex of 2,500 to 3,000 open stalls and shops on the fringe of Paris, selling everything from antiques to junk, from new to second-hand clothing. Occupying a vast triangular area, it is spread over half a mile and is almost impossible to cover entirely in just one visit.

The first clues showing you're there will be the stalls of cheap clothing along avenue de la Porte de Clignancourt. As you proceed, various streets will tempt you. Some of these streets are narrow, lined with little shops that start pulling out their offerings around 9am and start bringing them in around 6pm. Monday is the traditional day for bargain seekers, as there is smaller attendance at the market and a greater desire to cover on the part of the merchants to sell.

Naturally, you are supposed to bargain. Nobody pays the first price quoted. Many don't even pay the second or third price. Of course, a little basic French helps, too. The sound of an English-speaking voice is known to drive the price up right away. In addition to the permanent stalls, there are "dropcloth" peddlers as well. They spread out their wares on canvas or sheets (and are predictably viewed with scorn by the permanently installed vendors).

The big question everybody asks is, "Do you get any real bargains at the Flea Market?" Or, conversely, "Will you get fleeced?" Actually, it's all comparative. Obviously, the best buys have been skimmed by dealers (who often have a prearrangement to have items held for them). It's true, the same merchandise in the provinces of France will sell for less. But from the point of view of the visitor who has only a few days to spend in Paris—and only half a day for shopping—the Flea Market is worth the experience. **Open:** Sat–Mon 9am–6pm. **Métro:** Porte de Clignancourt. From there, turn left and cross bd. Ney, then walk north on av. de la Porte de Clignancourt. **Bus:** 56.

MARCHE AUX TIMBRES, off the Champs-Elysées.

The Marché aux Timbres draws the avid stamp collectors. Nearly two dozen stalls are set up on a permanent basis under shady trees on the eastern edge of the Rond-Point. The variety of stamps is almost unlimited—some common, some quite rare. **Open:** Generally Thurs and Sat–Sun 10am–7pm. **Métro:** Champs-Elysées–Clemenceau.

MARCHE AUX FLEURS, place Louis-Lépine, Ile de la Cité, 4e.

⭐ Artists love to paint the Flower Market; photographers love to click away. But for the most part, travelers go there to refresh their souls, enjoying a feast of fragrance. The stalls are ablaze with color, each a showcase of flowers, usually from the French Riviera (those that escaped a fate of being hauled to the perfume factories of Grasse). The Flower Market is along the Seine, behind the Tribunal de Commerce. **Open:** Daily 8am–4pm. **Métro:** Cité.

MARCHE AUX OISEAUX, place Louis-Lépine, Ile de la Cité, 4e.

The Bird Market comes alive with feathered creatures. Even if you don't plan to buy a rare parrot, you'll want to go for a look. From the Louvre to the Hôtel de Ville, you can visit the small stalls with vendors along the Seine. **Open:** Sun 9am–7pm. **Métro:** Cité.

MUSIC

VIRGIN MEGASTORE, 52–60 av. des Champs-Elysées, 8e. Tel. 40-74-06-48.
This is the largest music store in Paris, a virtual mecca for music lovers from throughout the world.

The Parisian outlet was opened in October 1988 and quickly became a social phenomena: 15,000 to 20,000 people visit the Megastore on the Champs-Elysées every day. Its size and design have helped make it a meeting place between artists and their audiences. A number of events have taken place in the Megastore—dedications, exhibitions, and musical performances (with Jessye Norman, Sting, Jim Jarmush, Jean-Paul Goude, Plácido Domingo, Tina Turner, Ray Bradbury, Robert Doisneau, Claudio Abbado, Metallica, and others). **Open:** Mon–Thurs 10am–midnight; Fri–Sat 10am–1am. **Métro:** F. D. Roosevelt.

PERFUME

FREDDY OF PARIS, 10 rue Auber, 9e. Tel. 47-42-63-41.
Freddy, near the American Express office and the Opéra, offers discounts of up to 40% on all name-brand perfumes, creams, novelties, gifts, handbags, scarves, ties, and costume jewelry. It also operates a mail-order service. **Open:** Mon–Fri 9am–6:30pm. **Métro:** Opéra. **RER:** Auber.

MICHEL SWISS, 16 rue de la Paix, 2e. Tel. 42-61-61-11.
The outside of Michel Swiss looks like many of the ultra-chic facades near the place Vendôme. But once you get inside (there's no storefront window), you'll see the major brands of luxury perfumes, cosmetics, leather bags, pens, neckties, fashion accessories, and gifts. All items are discounted by up to 32%, plus an additional tax discount for non-EC residents amounting up to 18.6%. The store is two flights above ground level, and is reached by a small elevator. **Open:** Mon–Sat 9am–6:30pm. **Métro:** Opéra.

PARFUMERIE FRAGONARD, 9 rue Scribe, 9e. Tel. 47-42-93-40.
In a Napoléon III town house, near the Paris Opéra, this perfume house contains a more edited version of the museum of perfume in Grasse (established in 1782 on the French Riviera). This Parisian shop is an outlet for the scent factories in Eze and Grasse. The aluminum containers in which it sells its scents are said to keep the perfume fresh for up to 10 years. **Open:** Mon–Sat 9am–6pm. **Métro:** Opéra.

SOUVENIRS & GIFTS

EIFFEL SHOPPING, 9 av. de Suffren, 7e. Tel. 45-66-55-30.
Have a free glass of cognac while you browse through the designer collections (Céline, Cerruti, Lanvin, Moschino, Saint-Laurent, to name just a few) of handbags, ties, scarves, watches, sunglasses, jewelry, perfumes, Lalique crystals, and much more. The tax-free

shopping center, only one block from the Eiffel Tower, offers good merchandise at discounted prices. The staff speak English. **Open:** Mon–Sat 9:15am–8pm; Sun 11am–8pm. **Métro:** Bir-Hakeim. **RER:** Champ de Mars.

STATIONERY

CASSEGRAIN, 422 rue St-Honoré, 8e. Tel. 42-60-20-08.

Cassegrain opened right after World War I, and it's been attracting letter writers ever since. It is considered by many the premier stationery shop in the city. Beautifully engraved stationery, most often in traditional patterns, is offered, although businesspeople can also get their business cards engraved to order. Several other items for the desk—many suitable for gifts—are for sale as well.

Cassegrain also has a shop at 81 rue des Sts-Pères, 6e. (tel. 42-22-04-76); Métro: Sèvres-Babylone). **Open:** Both stores Mon–Sat 10am–7pm. **Métro:** Concorde.

TABLEWARE & BED LINEN

AU BAIN MARIE, 10 rue Boissy d'Anglas, 8e. Tel. 42-66-59-74.

Between Hermès at Faubourg St-Honoré and the Hôtel Crillon is one of Paris's best choices for new and antique table and bedroom linen, some of it painstakingly embroidered. The two floors of merchandise include virtually everything that might touch a dining table, including tableware of many different styles, inspired by many different eras. There's also a collection of books relating to food and wine, and a good selection of bathroom towels. **Open:** Mon–Sat 10am–7pm. **Métro:** Concorde.

TOYS & KIDS' STUFF

AU NAIN BLEU, 406 rue St-Honoré, 8e. Tel. 42-60-39-01.

Any child you love is expecting a present from Paris, and at the "Blue Dwarf" you'll be bedazzled by the choice. Browse through this paradise of playthings that has been in business for a century and a half. It's a world of toy soldiers, stuffed animals, games, model airplanes, technical toys, model cars, even a "Flower Drum Kit." Puppets come in all shapes, sizes, and costumes. **Open:** Mon–Sat 9am–6:15 pm. **Métro:** Concorde.

RIGODON, 13 rue Racine, 6e. Tel. 43-29-98-66.

On a street branching off from place de l'Odéon is a puppet-and-doll world for every child, even for those who are children only at heart—but they're dolls to look at, not to play with. Hanging from the ceiling is one of the most varied collections of puppets in Paris. They come in all characters, sizes, and prices, and include everything from angels to witches on broomsticks to bat women with feather wings. Rigodon also makes porcelain dolls. The painting on the faces and the costumes are unique for each model, be it a queen with all her power or the amazon of the hunt. There are marionettes (with strings) from French artisans. **Open:** Mon 2–7pm, Tues–Sat 10:30am–7pm. **Métro:** Odéon.

PARIS NIGHTS

With five national theaters, including a new opera house and 55 theaters of lesser renown, Paris is both the hub of French culture and host to all the best on the international circuit. Whatever the season, the choice is fantastic: top pop stars, French classics, chamber concerts, lavish music-hall spectaculars. In one cavernous hall, an American singer might be belting out a standard to a packed crowd of Parisians, while in a shabby Left Bank lane, a young playwright anxiously watches his first work performed on the same small stage that launched Ionesco or Beckett.

Contemporary Paris has less nudity than London, less vice than Hamburg, and less drunkenness than San Francisco. Nevertheless, the quantity and the variety of Paris's nocturnal pleasures still beat those of any metropolis on earth. Nowhere else will you find such a huge and mixed array of clubs, bars, discos, cabarets, jazz dives, music halls, and honky-tonks, ranging—in the subtlest of gradations—from the corniest tourist traps to the most sophisticated connoisseurs' fare.

Of course, the cafés are an important part of Paris nightlife, but since most of them are open all day serving coffee, tea, alcoholic beverages, fruit and chocolate drinks—not to mention sandwiches, snacks, and full meals—they are discussed in Chapter 5, "Paris Dining."

1. THE PERFORMING ARTS

The only limitation to your enjoyment of French theater is language. Those of you with modest French can still delight in a lively, sparkling Molière at the Comédie-Française. But those with no French at all might prefer an evening that is longer on melody and shorter on speech.

Announcements of shows, concerts, even the opera programs are plastered all around town on kiosks. A better way to find out what's playing is to consult the English-language *Paris Passion* or *Pariscope*, *Une semaine de Paris*, a weekly entertainment guide that includes a section of arts, with full listings of theaters, concerts, and more.

Although ticket agents are scattered all over Paris, they are heavily concentrated near the Right Bank hotels. Avoid them if possible, because you can get less expensive tickets at the theater box offices. Remember to tip the usher who shows you to your seat. This holds true in movie houses as well as theaters. Performances start later in Paris than in London or New York—anywhere from

8 to 9:30pm—and Parisians tend to dine after the theater. You don't have to follow suit, since many of the modest, less expensive restaurants close as early as 9pm.

DISCOUNT TICKETS

Several agencies sell tickets for cultural events and plays at discounts of up to 50%.

One outlet for discount tickets is the **Kiosque Théâtre** at 15 place de la Madeleine, 8e (no phone; Métro: Madeleine), offering leftover tickets for about half price on the day of the performance. Tickets for evening performances are sold Tuesday through Friday from 12:30 to 8pm and on Saturday from 2 to 8pm. If you'd like to attend a matinee, buy your ticket on Saturday from 12:30 to 2pm or on Sunday from 12:30 to 4pm.

For discounts of 20% to 40% on tickets for festivals, concerts, and theater performances, try two locations of the **FNAC** department store chain: 136 rue de Rennes, 6e (tel. 44-09-18-00; Métro: Montparnasse-Bienvenue); or in the Forum des Halles, 1–7 rue Pierre-Lescot, 1er (tel. 42-61-81-18; Métro: Châtelet–Les Halles).

To qualify for these discounts, you must first purchase a *carte alpha* for 80F ($14), which is good for one year. These agencies are usually open Tuesday through Saturday from 10am to 7pm.

THEATER

COMEDIE-FRANÇAISE, 2 rue de Richelieu, 1er. Tel. 40-15-00-15.

If you've a taste for fine theater, don't let the language barrier scare you off—spend at least one night of your Paris stay at the Comédie-Française. Nowhere else will you see the French classics—Moliére, Racine—so beautifully staged in the original language. A national theater, it was established to keep the classics in the cultural mainstream and to promote the most important contemporary authors. **Prices:** Tickets 45F–165F ($7.90–$28.90). **Closed:** Aug 1–Sept 15. **Métro:** Palais-Royal.

OPERA

L'OPERA BASTILLE, place de la Bastille, 120 rue de Lyon 4e. Tel. 44-73-13-00.

The controversial building was designed by Canadian architect Carlos Orr, with curtains created by Issey Miyake, the Japanese fashion designer. The giant showplace was inaugurated in July 1989, and on March 17, 1990, the curtain rose on Hector Berlioz's opera *Les Troyens*. The main hall is the largest of any opera house in France, with 2,700 seats. The building also houses three additional concert halls, including an intimate room with only 250 seats. Both operas and symphony concerts are presented here.

Several concerts are presented free, in honor of certain French holidays. Write ahead for tickets to the Opéra de Paris Bastille, 120 rue de Lyon, 75012 Paris. **Prices:** Tickets 45F–570F ($7.90–$99.80). **Métro:** Bastille.

OPERA-COMIQUE, place Boildieu, 2e. Tel. 42-60-04-99.

For light-opera productions, try the Opéra-Comique. If possible, make arrangements two weeks before the performance. **Open:** Box office Mon–Sat 11am–7pm. **Closed:** July–Aug. **Prices:** 40F–490F ($7–$85.80). **Métro:** Richelieu-Drouot.

THEATRE MUSICAL DE PARIS, 1 place du Châtelet, 1er. Tel. 40-28-28-40.

The Théâtre Musical de Paris, presenting less expensive opera and ballet performances than l'Opéra or l'Opéra Bastille, is known for its good acoustics. **Prices:** Opera 70F–495F ($12.30–$86.60); concerts 70F–300F ($12.30–$52.50); ballets 70F–200F ($12.30–$35). **Closed:** July–Aug. **Métro:** Châtelet.

BALLET

L'OPERA PARIS GARNIER, place de l'Opéra, 9e. Tel. 40-01-17-89.

⭐ L'Opéra is the premier stage for ballet and musical productions. Because of the competition from the Opéra at the Bastille, the original opera has made great efforts to present more up-to-date works, including choreography by Jerome Robbins, Twyla Tharp, Agnes de Mille, and George Balanchine. This architectural wonder was designed as a contest entry by a young architect in the heyday of empire. The facade is adorned with marble and sculpture, including *The Dance* by Carpeaux. The great orchestral, operatic, and ballet companies of the world have performed here. **Prices:** Tickets 30F–370F ($5.30–$64.80). **Métro:** Opéra.

MAJOR CONCERT HALLS & ALL-PURPOSE AUDITORIUMS

The concert-going public is kept busy year-round in Paris, with daily offerings taking up full newspaper columns. Organ recitals are featured in the churches (the largest organ is in St-Sulpice); jazz shatters the peace of the city's modern art museum.

RADIO FRANCE SALLE OLIVIER MESSIAEN, 116 av. Président-Kennedy, 16e. Tel. 42-30-15-16.

The best orchestra in France belongs to Radio France, and top-flight concerts with guest conductors are presented in this auditorium. **Prices:** Tickets for Orchestre National de France 50F–190F ($8.80–$33.30), for the Orchestre Philharmonique 120F ($21). **Métro:** Passy-Ranelagh.

SALLE PLEYEL, 252 rue du Faubourg St-Honoré, 8e. Tel. 45-61-06-30.

Host to the Orchestre de Paris, the Salle Pleyel, a few blocks northeast of the Arc de Triomphe, has its season from September to Easter. **Prices:** Tickets 80F–250F ($14–$43.80). **Métro:** Ternes.

THEATRE DES CHAMPS-ELYSEES, 15 av. Montaigne, 8e. Tel. 49-52-50-00.

Opera, ballet, and concerts are performed at the Théâtre des Champs-Elysées, with both national and international orchestras. **Open:** Box office Mon–Sat 11am–7pm. **Closed:** Aug. **Prices:** Tickets 60F–450F ($10.50–$78.80). **Métro:** Alma-Marceau.

THEATRE NATIONAL DE CHAILLOT, place du Trocadéro, 16e. Tel. 47-27-81-15.

One of the largest halls is the Théâtre National de Chaillot; its programs are announced on billboards out front. **Prices:** Tickets 40F–400F ($7–$70). **Métro:** Trocadéro.

THE MAJOR CONCERT & PERFORMANCE HALLS

Comédie-Française, 2 rue de Richelieu, 1er (tel. 40-15-00-15). French and contemporary theater. Métro: Palais-Royal.

Opéra-Comique, place Boieldieu, 2e (tel. 42-60-04-99). Light-opera productions. Métro: Richelieu-Drouot.

L'Opéra Bastille, place de la Bastille, 120 rue de Lyon, 4e (tel. 44-73-13-00). Metro: Bastille.

L'Opéra Paris Garnier, place de l'Opéra, 9e (tel. 40-01-17-89). Ballet and musical performances. Métro: Opéra.

Radio France Salle Olivier Messiaen, 116 av. Président-Kennedy, 16e (tel. 42-30-15-16). The best orchestra concerts in Paris. Métro: Passy-Ranelagh.

Salle Pleyel, 252 rue du Faubourg St-Honoré, 8e (tel. 45-61-06-30). Home of the Orchestre de Paris. Métro: Ternes.

Théâtre des Champs-Elysées, 15 av. Montaigne, 8e (tel. 49-52-50-00). Operas, concerts, and ballets. Métro: Alma-Marceau.

Théâtre Musical de Paris, 1 place du Châtelet, 1er (tel. 40-28-28-40). Opera and ballet. Métro: Châtelet.

Théâtre National de Chaillot, place du Trocadéro, 16e (tel. 47-27-81-15). One of the largest concert halls in Paris. Métro: Trocadéro.

2. THE CLUB & MUSIC SCENE

Paris today is still a nirvana for night owls, even though some of its once-unique attractions have become common. The fame of Parisian nights was established in those distant days of innocence when Anglo-Americans still gasped at the sight of a bare bosom in a chorus line, and free love was something you only whispered about in polite transatlantic circles.

Some of the best and most genuinely Parisian attractions are the so-called *boîtes* in which chansonniers sing ballads and ditties intended only for local consumption. A few performers, like Edith Piaf and Juliette Greco, graduated to international fame from these places. But the lyrics that delight the patrons there are so slangy, so topically witty, so heavily laced with verbal innuendos and double-entendres that they're incomprehensible to foreigners. Your French would have to be more than good; it would have to be Pigalle-perfect.

Luckily, there are hundreds of other establishments where lingual ignorance is of no consequence. Sometimes it can even be an advantage, because the verses uttered by, say, a French rock group are every ounce as inane as their Stateside brethren's.

Many of the Right Bank—and a few of the Left Bank—hostelries are lavishly sprinkled with mademoiselles whose job it is to push a man's tab up to astronomical heights. They're incomparably skillful at it, and you could be in for a staggering bill including champagne, cigarettes, candy, teddy bear, and what-have-you. Under their gentle touch, an evening that might have cost you the equivalent of $25 can rapidly mount up to $300 and more—much more. Don't be afraid to respond with a firmly polite no to an unsolicited approach. The reaction is usually a regretful Gallic shrug, and she'll probably not try again. That way you'll retain control of your night's expenditures.

The other general rule to remember is that the Right Bank, by and large, is plusher, slicker, and more expensive than the Left, which has more of avant-garde entertainment, a younger clientele, and a minimum of professional "companions."

Before starting the round of establishments, let me repeat that this is a town for genuine night owls. Few spots begin swinging before 11pm and most acquire their full heads of steam around midnight—or later. Since the Métro stops running at 1am, be prepared to use taxis and to sleep in the next morning.

BOITES & MUSIC HALLS

The *chansonniers* (literally "song writers") provide bombastic musical satire of the day's events. This combination of parody and burlesque is a time-honored Gallic amusement and a Parisian institution. The wit and ridicule these performers shower upon prostitutes and presidents alike make for an extravagant revue. Songs are often created on the spot, depending for their inspiration on "the disaster of the day." The best boîtes of the chansonniers are on the tawdry boulevard de Clichy.

AU LAPIN AGILE, 22 rue des Saules, 18e. Tel. 46-06-85-87.

Picasso and Utrillo once patronized this little cottage near the top of Montmartre, formerly known as the Café des Assassins. It has been painted by artists, known and unknown, including Utrillo. For many decades it has been the heartbeat of French folk music, featuring folk songs, sing-alongs, and poetry readings. You'll sit at carved wooden tables in a low, dimly lit room with walls covered with bohemian memorabilia.

Songs include old French folk tunes, love ballads, army songs, sea chanteys, and music-hall ditties. You're encouraged to sing along, even if it's only the "oui, oui, oui—non, non, non" refrain of "Les Chevaliers de la Table Ronde." You can always hum along with "Larilette" and "Madelon." The best sing-alongs are on weeknights after tourist season ends. **Open:** Tues–Sun 9pm–2am. **Admission:** 110F ($19.30), including first drink. **Prices:** Drinks 30F ($5.30). **Métro:** Lamarck.

AU CAVEAU DE LA BOLEE, 25 rue de l'Hirondelle, 6e. Tel. 43-54-62-20.

You descend into the catacombs of the early-14th-century Abbey of St-André once a famous literary café that attracted such personages as Verlaine and Oscar Wilde, who downed (or drowned in) glass after glass of absinthe here. The French songs are good and bawdy and just what young students, who form a large part of the audience, like. Occasionally the audience sings along.

A fixed-price dinner, which is served Monday through Saturday at 8:30pm, is followed by a cabaret show. However, you won't understand the jokes and references made in the show unless your French is extremely good. The cabaret starts at 10:30pm and if you've already had dinner, you can order just a drink. In lieu of paying admission, you can order either dinner or a drink, or both.

You'll find this establishment, which seats only 24, on a tiny street leading into the western edge of the place St-Michel. The beginning of the street is down a short flight of steps under a giant archway beneath one of the square's grandiose buildings. **Admission:** Fixed-price dinner 230F ($40.30); entrance 100F ($17.50) if you don't order dinner. **Métro:** St-Michel.

CAVEAU DES OUBLIETTES, 11 rue St-Julien-le-Pauvre, 5e. Tel. 43-54-94-97.

It's hard to say which is more interesting in this place—the program or the environment. Located in the Latin Quarter and just across the river from Notre-Dame, this nightspot is housed in a genuine 12th-century prison—complete with dungeons, spine-crawling passages, and scattered skulls. The word *oubliette* means a dungeon with a trap door at the top as its only opening, but some victims were pushed through portholes into the Seine to drown. The caveau is beneath the subterranean vaults that communicated many centuries ago with the fortress prison of the Petit Châtelet.

Performers in medieval costumes sing French folk songs and tavern choruses—sentimental, comic, and bawdy—to exclusively tourist audiences. It's rather artificial and stagey, but with charm. There's nothing artificial, however, about the adjoining museum, which displays a working guillotine, chastity belts, and instruments of torture. **Open:** Mon–Sat 9pm–2am. **Admission** (including first drink): 140F ($24.50). **Métro:** St-Michel.

THEATRE DES DEUX ANES, 100 bd. de Clichy, 18e. Tel. 46-06-10-26.

If you speak colloquial French, you'll enjoy this revue of song and satire, down the street from the Moulin Rouge. A sign, LEAVE YOUR CHEWING GUM AT THE DOOR, sets the tone. **Open:** Performances Tues–Sun 9pm; box office Tues–Sun 11am–7pm. **Prices:** Tickets 180F ($31.50). **Métro:** Blanche.

MUSIC HALLS

That old music-hall format of sing a little, dance a little, juggle a few balls, and sprinkle generously with jokes, is very much alive and doing well in Paris today. The combination, slickly carried off, adds up to a top value in entertainment for the visitor.

OLYMPIA, 28 bd. des Capucines, 9e. Tel. 47-42-82-45.

The first-rank city music hall offering packed programs of professional talent and international stars is the Olympia, the cavernous hall where the likes of Charles Aznavour make frequent appearances. On one occasion the late Yves Montand appeared, but you had to reserve a seat four months in advance. A typical lineup would include an English rock duo singing its latest record hit, a showy group of Italian acrobats, a well-known French crooner, a talented dance troupe, a triple-jointed American juggling act/comedy team (doing much of their work in English), plus the featured "Big Name," all laced together neatly by a witty emcee and backed by an onstage band. **Open:** Shows presented Tues–Sun at 8:30pm, matinees at 2:30 or 5pm. **Prices:** Tickets 150F–250F ($26.30–$43.80). **Métro:** Opéra.

NIGHTCLUBS/CABARET

Leading off is an array without which no Paris roll call would be complete. While decidedly expensive, they give you your money's worth by providing some of the most lavishly spectacular floor shows to be seen anywhere.

FOLIES BERGERE, 32 rue Richer, 9e. Tel. 44-79-98-98.

⭐ According to legend, the first GI to reach Paris during the liberation of 1944 asked for directions to the Folies Bergère. His son and grandson do the same today. Even the old man comes back for a second look.

A roving-eyed Frenchman would have to be in his second century to remember when the Folies began. Opened in 1886, since the turn of the century the Folies Bergère has stood as the symbol of unadorned female anatomy. Fresh off the boat, Victorians and Edwardians—starved for a glimpse of even an ankle—flocked to the Folies to get a look at much more. The show palace, after a multi-million dollar refurbishment, opened again in 1993, and in some ways its new acts satirize its past extravagances. Bizarre physical types, sexual ambiguity, and even Felliniesque characters inhabit the stage today. The show's new producers hope that a more updated revue will attract Parisians and not just jetlagged foreign tourists. Of course, the elaborate costumes are still there—but there are a lot of new acts, perhaps Marie Antoinette in white wig on roller skates learning the Charleston from Josephine Baker wearing a costume of pineapples and singing "Don't Touch My Tomatoes." **Open:** Revue Tues–Sun 9:30pm, box office daily 11am–6pm. **Admission:** 129F–379F ($22.60–$66.30), with seats ranging from the gallery to a loge in the orchestra or balcony. A scale model at the box office shows locations of the various seats. **Métro:** Rue Montmartre or Cadet.

LIDO CABARET NORMANDIE, 116 bis, av. des Champs-Elysées, 8e. Tel. 45-76-56-10.

⭐ In a panoramic room with 1,200 seats, having excellent visibility, this palatial nightspot puts on an avalanche of glamour and talent, combined with enough showmanship to make the late Mr. Barnum look like an amateur. The permanent attraction is the Bluebell Girls, a fabulous precision ensemble of long-legged international beauties. The rest of the program changes. Go at least once in a lifetime. **Admission:** Dinner dance at 8:30pm 640F–810F ($112–$141.80), including half a bottle of champagne. La Revue at 10:15pm or 12:30am 465F ($81.40) minimum, including half a bottle of wine. Service and taxes included. **Métro:** George-V.

MOULIN-ROUGE, place Blanche, Montmartre, 18e. Tel. 46-06-00-19.

⭐ Toulouse-Lautrec, who put this establishment on the map about a century ago, probably wouldn't recognize it today. The windmill is still there and so is the cancan. But the rest has become a superslick, gimmick-loaded variety show with the accent heavy on the undraped female form. You'll see underwater ballets in an immense glass tank, a magnificent cascade, young women in swings and on trick stairs, all interspersed with animal acts, comic jugglers, and song trios. These are just a smattering of the acts usually found on the daily bill of fare. This multicolored candy-floss stuff is expertly staged, but any connection with the old Moulin-Rouge is purely coincidental. **Open:** Nightly, dinner 8pm, revue 10pm. **Prices:** Dinner and revue 670F–810F ($117.30–$141.80); revue only 465F ($81.40), including champagne. No minimum if you sit at the bar (where the view is not as good). Drinks around 90F ($15.80). **Métro:** Blanche.

LE PARADIS LATIN, 28 rue Cardinal-Lemoine, 5e. Tel. 43-25-28-28.

The building was Gustave Eiffel's only venture into theater architecture, using the same metallic skeleton format he used for the Eiffel Tower. This theater takes credit for formalizing the introduction of vaudeville and musical theater to Paris. This monument's darkest days came in 1903, when the premises became a warehouse. In the 1970s, it was transformed, glossier than ever, into one of the most successful cabarets in Paris. The patter of the master of ceremonies is in both French and English. The revue ends at midnight. **Open:** Wed–Mon, dinner revue 8pm; revue only 10pm. **Admission:** Dinner revue 670F ($117.30); revue only 465F ($81.40), including half a bottle of champagne. Drinks from 95F ($16.60). **Métro:** Jussieu or Cardinal-Lemoine.

MILLIARDAIRE, 68 rue Pierre-Charron, 8e. Tel. 42-25-25-17.

The stylish, elegant Milliardaire is just off the Champs-Elysées, reached through a backyard that is not nearly as plush as the interior. The program includes comics, jugglers, and first-rate dance interludes. The place maintains a popular and discreet piano bar open every night after the last show (1:30 to 4am). In the piano bar, drinks cost 130F ($22.80) each. **Open:** Two different shows staged nightly at 10pm and midnight. During July and Aug no shows are presented on Sun, and in Jan and Aug only one show is presented (at 11pm). **Prices:** Show and two drinks 340F ($59.50); show and half a bottle of champagne, 390F ($68.30). **Métro:** F.D. Roosevelt.

CRAZY HORSE SALOON, 12 av. George-V, 8e. Tel. 47-23-32-32.

⭐ Texans in ten-gallon hats are fond of "le Crazy," which is considered by many to be the leading nude dancing joint in the world. Alain Bernardin parodies the American West in the decor, but only purists claim that Cheyenne was never like this.

Two dozen performers do their acts entirely nude. Sandwiched between the more sultry scenes are three international variety acts. **Open:** Daily, first show (less than two hours) 8:45pm, second show 11:15pm. **Prices:** Drinks 350F–530 ($61.30–$92.80), including the cover charge and two drinks; third drink from 50F ($8.80). **Métro:** George-V or Alma-Marceau.

VILLA D'ESTE, 4 rue Arsène-Houssaye, 8e. Tel. 42-56-14-65.

Its owners book top singing talent from Europe and America. A short stroll from the Champs-Elysées, the Villa d'Este has been around for a long time, and the quality of its offerings remains high. The place is a *dinner-dansant* club more than a pure cabaret. The fixed-price menus include wine that becomes increasingly better as the price rises. It's also possible to attend and order only a drink. The doors open at 8pm, and an orchestra plays from 8:30pm. A comedy/cabaret/magic act lasts until around midnight, with dancing until 2am. Reservations are necessary. Every Sunday afternoon a tea dance with a live orchestra is presented from 3:30 to 8pm. **Prices:**

Fixed-price menus 380F–720F ($66.50–$126); drinks 150F ($26.30) each; tea-dance admission 80F–110F ($14–$19.30), including first drink. **Métro:** Charles-de-Gaulle–Etoile.

JAZZ & ROCK

You can probably listen and dance to more jazz in Paris than in any U.S. city, with the possible exception of San Francisco. The great jazz revival that long ago swept America is still going full swing in Paris, with Dixieland or Chicago rhythms being pounded out in dozens of jazz cellars, mostly called *caveaux*.

This is one city where you don't have to worry about being a self-conscious dancer. The locals, even young people, are not particularly good. The best dancers on any floor are usually American. And although Parisians take to rock with enthusiasm, their skill does not match their zest.

The majority of the jazz/rock establishments are crowded into the Left Bank near the Seine between rue Bonaparte and rue St-Jacques, which makes things easy for syncopation-seekers.

LE BILBOQUET, 13 rue St-Benoît, 6e. Tel. 45-48-81-84.

This restaurant, jazz club, and piano bar offers some of the best music in Paris. In the heart of St-Germain-des-Prés, the site was famous during the heyday of existentialism. The film *Paris Blues* was shot here. Jazz is played on the upper level in Le Bilboquet restaurant. The wood-paneled room has a copper ceiling, a sunken bar with brass trim, and a Victorian candelabrum. The tables are on a raised tier and elevated balcony. The menu is limited but classic French, specializing in carré d'agneau, fish, and beef. Appetizers include smoked salmon and terrines. **Open:** Le Bilboquet, nightly 8pm–2:45am, live music presented 10:45–2:45am. Club St-Germain disco (downstairs), Mon–Sat 11pm–5am. **Admission:** Free, but drinks cost 90F ($15.80). Clients can walk from one club to the other, but they have to buy a new drink each time they change venues. **Prices:** Dinner at Le Bilboquet 185F–325F ($32.40–$56.90); admission (without dinner) 120F ($21), including first drink. **Métro:** St-Germain-des-Prés.

TROIS MAILLETZ, 58 rue Galande, 5e. Tel. 43-54-42-94.

This medieval cellar once housed the masons who built Notre-Dame, many of whom carved their initials into the walls. Today it attracts jazz aficionados from all over the world. It's one of the few places in the district where students don't predominate. Musical celebrities appearing here have included Memphis Slim, Bill Coleman, and Nina Simone. Traditional French meals, such as salmon tartare and grills, are served in a restaurant adjacent to the piano bar during its entire opening time. Reservations are recommended on weekends. The restaurant and piano bar are on the main level, and the jazz is in the cellar. **Open:** Daily 10:30pm–"whenever"; piano bar, daily 6pm–5am. **Admission:** Cellar 60F–70F ($10.50–$12.30); restaurant and piano bar free. **Prices:** Meals from 150F ($26.30), drinks 65F ($11.40). **Métro:** Maubert-Mutualité.

CAVEAU DE LA HUCHETTE, 5 rue de la Huchette, 5e. Tel. 43-26-65-05.

This celebrated jazz cave draws a young crowd, mostly students, who dance to the music of well-known jazz combos. This caveau is reached by a winding staircase. In prejazz days, it was frequented by

Robespierre and Marat. **Open:** Sun–Fri 9:30pm–3am, Sat and holidays 9:30pm–4am. **Admission:** Sun–Thurs 55F ($9.60), Fri–Sat 70F ($12.30). Student Sun–Thurs 50F ($8.80), Fri–Sat 60F ($10.50). **Prices:** Drinks 18F ($3.20). **Métro:** St-Michel.

SLOW CLUB, 130 rue de Rivoli, 1er. Tel. 42-33-84-30.

One of the most famous jazz cellars in Europe, the Slow Club features the well-known French jazz band of Claude Luter, who played for 10 years with the late Sidney Bechet. **Open:** Tues–Thurs 10pm–3am, Fri–Sat and holidays 10pm–4am. **Admission:** Tues–Thurs 60F ($10.50), Fri–Sat and holidays 75F ($13.10). **Prices:** Drinks 18F ($3.20). **Métro:** Châtelet.

NEW MORNING, 7–9 rue des Petites-Ecuries, 10e. Tel. 45-23-51-41.

New Morning was named for Bob Dylan's 1969 album. The premises were once occupied by a daily newspaper and designed in 1981 to become a jazz club. The high-ceilinged loft allows jazz maniacs to dance, talk, flirt, and drink elbow-to-elbow at the stand-up bar. The appropriate dress code is jeans or whatever, and concerts and musical soirées might include a range of practically everything except disco. The only rule here seems to be that there are few rules. It might be open at 8:30pm or closed just any night, but when it's in business, closing (except on salsa nights) is at 1:30 or 2am. If a well-known performer can be booked on a Sunday, the place is open on Sunday. A phone call will let you know what's going on the night of your visit. No food is served. **Admission:** 120F–180F ($21–$31.50). **Métro:** Château d'Eau.

JAZZ CLUB LIONEL HAMPTON, in the Hotel Méridien, 81 bd. Gouvion-St-Cyr, 17e. Tel. 40-68-34-34.

This club prides itself on such guest stars as Lionel Hampton (after whom it was named), Fats Domino, and Nita Whitheker. **Open:** Mon–Sat 10:30pm–2am, Sun 10pm–2am. **Admission** (including first drink): 135F ($23.60). **Métro:** Porte Maillot.

DANCE HALLS & DISCOS

Although Paris is supposedly the birthplace of the discothèque, nobody here seems to know anymore what, precisely, constitutes one. Originally the discos were small, intimate dives where patrons danced to records—hence the term. Now, however, the tag is applied to anything from playground-size ballrooms with full orchestras to tiny bars with taped tunes—where they don't let you dance at all.

The entire region opposite and around the church of St-Germain-des-Prés is so honeycombed with dance dives of one sort or another, and they are so ephemeral (some have the life spans of sickly butterflies), that it's almost impossible to keep track of their coming and closing. What's hopping at the time of this writing might be a hardware store by the time you get there. But chances are there'll be two new joints in the same block.

The samples below are a few of the hundreds of spots where people go chiefly to dance—as distinct from others where the main attraction is the music.

LES BAINS, 7 rue du Bourg l'Abbé, 3e. Tel. 48-87-01-80.

This chic enclave has been pronounced "in" and "out" of fashion, but lately it's very in again, attracting some of the better-looking people of Paris, especially models of both sexes. Sometimes the dress the customer wears is more for show than for comfort. The name, Les Bains, comes from its old function when the place was a Turkish bath, attracting homosexual clients, none more notable than Marcel Proust. Sometimes it may be hard to get in if the bouncer doesn't like your looks. **Open:** Tues–Sun 11:30pm–6am. **Admission:** 140F ($24.50), including your first drink. Each drink thereafter 100F ($17.50). **Métro:** Réaumur-Sébastopol.

LE PALACE, 8 rue du Faubourg-Montmartre, 9e. Tel. 42-46-10-87.

One of the leading nightclubs of Paris, La Palace re-creates 1940s Hollywood glamour. It's designed in the spirit and allure of a Roman or Greek amphitheater, with four different bars scattered over three different levels. Music is recorded, and there's plenty of room to dance. Management does not allow sneakers or jeans with holes pierced in indiscreet places. **Open:** Tues–Sat 11:30pm–6am, Sun 5–11pm and 11:30pm–6am. **Admission:** Tues–Thurs 100F ($17.50), Fri–Sat 130F ($22.80), Sun 130F ($22.80) men, free for women. **Métro:** Rue Montmartre.

LA COUPOLE, 102 bd. du Montparnasse, 14e. Tel. 43-20-14-21.

La Coupole is reviewed separately as a historical landmark café. One of the big Montparnasse cafés and a former stronghold of bohemia, it is a throwback to the days when locals waltzed and tangoed to the strains of a live orchestra. If you caught *Last Tango in Paris* on the late show, it would help as a prelude to a visit here. In addition to its upstairs café, La Coupole has a large basement ballroom reserved for dancing. **Open:** Fri 9:30pm–4am, Sat–Sun 3–7pm and 9:30pm–4am. **Admission:** Café free. Ballroom, Sat matinee 90F ($15.80), Sun matinee 60F ($10.50); Fri–Sat nights 90F ($15.80). **Métro:** Vavin.

CLUB ZED, 2 rue des Anglais, 5e. Tel. 43-54-93-78.

One of the most frequented after-dark haunts in Paris offers . . . well, you name it. Just show up and be surprised by, say samba music straight out of Rio, nostalgic tunes from the 1960s, a jazz beat, and le rock on Sunday afternoon or Wednesday night. **Open:** Wed–Thurs 10:30pm–3:30am, Fri 10:30pm–4:30pm, Sun 4–8pm. **Closed:** Aug. **Admission:** First drink 50F–100F ($8.80–$17.50). **Métro:** Maubert-Mutualité.

LE BALAJO, 9 rue de Lappe, 11e. Tel. 47-00-07-87.

Remember the "little sparrow," Edith Piaf? This famous French chanteuse is still dearly remembered by the people of Paris, even the young ones who never saw her live but still listen to her recorded music. Le Balajo is the club—practically a national shrine—where Piaf used to appear frequently during her tortured lifetime. The place is still popular, a kind of "retro-hip" enclave where a nostalgic "Oh, to be young again" crowd dances side by side with increasing numbers of 20-year-olds who seem to be discovering the old favorites for the first time. Music varies from swing to bee-bop to music-hall favorites of the World War II era. Reggae, salsa, rock 'n' roll, and rap are also featured. **Open:** Afternoon dances Fri–Sat and Mon 2–6:30pm, Sun 3–7pm. Evening dances Thurs–Mon 10pm–5am. **Admission** (including first drink): 100F ($17.50) evenings, 50F (8.80) afternoons. **Métro:** Bastille.

RIVERSIDE CLUB, 7 rue Grégoire-de-Tours, 6e. Tel. 43-54-46-33.

There is sometimes a line at the door to this typical Left Bank cellar disco with an interesting, international crowd. Some dance *comme des foux* (like lunatics) to the music, which ranges from reggae to punk. **Open:** Daily 11pm–6am or 7am. **Admission** (including first drink): Sun–Thurs 80F ($14); Fri–Sat 90F ($15.80). **Prices:** Drinks 40F ($7). **Métro:** St-Michel or Odéon.

3. THE BAR SCENE

WINE BARS

Many Parisians now prefer to patronize wine bars instead of the traditional café or bistro. The food is often better and the ambiance more inviting. Wine bars come in a wide range of styles, from old traditional places to modern gathering centers.

WILLI'S WINE BAR, 13 rue des Petits-Champs, 1er. Tel. 42-61-05-09.

Journalists and stockbrokers alike are attracted to this popular wine bar in the center of the financial district, close to the Bourse. Surprisingly, it is run by two Englishmen, Mark Williamson and Tim Johnston. They offer about 250 different kinds of wine, and each week about a dozen "specials" are featured.

Very crowded at lunchtime, it often settles down to a lower decibel level in the evening, when you can better admire the 16th-century beams and the warm ambience. A blackboard menu lists the daily specials, which are likely to include brochette of lamb flavored with cumin or lyonnaise sausage in a truffled vinaigrette with pistachios, and a spectacular dessert—the chocolate terrine. You can enjoy wines by the glass. **Open:** Mon–Sat noon–2:30pm and 7–11pm. **Prices:** Fixed-price menu 155F ($27.10), wine by the glass 20F ($3.50). **Métro:** Bourse, Louvre, or Palais-Royal.

AU SAUVIGNON, 80 rue des Sts-Pères, 7e. Tel. 45-48-49-02.

Perhaps the best-known wine bar in Paris, Au Sauvignon is minuscule, although it overflows onto a covered terrace. Still, it has a very chic reputation. The owner is from Auvergne, and when he's not polishing his zinc countertop or preparing a plate of charcuterie, he will sell you wines by the glass. Beaujolais is the cheapest, and Puligny Montrachet the most expensive. Auvergne specialties, including goat cheese and terrines, are served if you'd like to have a snack with your wine. The fresh Poilane bread is ideal with the Auvergne ham, the country pâté, or the Crottin de Chavignol goat cheese. The place has a decor of old ceramic tiles and frescoes done by Left Bank artists. **Open:** Mon–Sat 8:30am–10:30pm. **Closed:** Major religious holidays; three weeks in Aug. **Prices:** Glass of wine 19F–39F ($3.30–$6.80); all wines cost an additional 2F (40¢) if consumed at a table. **Métro:** Sèvres-Babylone.

MA BOURGOGNE, 19 place des Vosges, 4e. Tel. 42-78-44-64.

This fine brasserie with a good selection of wines is situated in an area that has had a facelift and is lit up both day and night. You can come here to sit and contemplate this dreamy square, following in the footsteps of Victor Hugo. Under the arcades you can enjoy coffee or a glass of Beaujolais. Monsieur Aimé, the owner, selects all the wines himself. There are rattan sidewalk tables for summer sitting and a cozy room within with a beamed ceiling. Madame Aimé offers a wide choice of country dishes. Customers come from all over the city to eat her famous steak tartare. **Open:** Daily 8am–1am. **Closed:** Feb. **Prices:** Coffee 12F–20F ($2.10–$3.50), glass of wine from 20F ($3.50), plats du jour 80F–140F ($14–$24.50). **Métro:** St-Paul or Bastille.

LA TARTINE, 24 rue de Rivoli, 4e. Tel. 42-72-76-85.

Resembling a movie set, La Tartine is Old Paris. Inset mirrors, decorative brass details, a zinc bar, and frosted globe chandeliers frame the door. At any moment you expect to see Tito, Trotsky, or Lenin walk in the door (each was a former patron). At least 50 wines are offered at reasonable prices, and all categories of wine are served by the glass. A plate of charcuterie, pâté, or terrines is available; or you can order sandwiches. At least seven kinds of Beaujolais are offered, along with a large selection of Bordeaux. The light wine Sancerre is more favored than ever. With your wine, why not taste some young goat cheese from the Loire Valley? **Open:** Thurs–Mon 8am–10pm, Wed noon–10pm. **Closed:** Two weeks in Aug. **Prices:** Glass of wine 8.50F–15F ($1.50–$2.60), sandwiches 14F–40F ($2.50–$7), plate of food 14F ($2.50). **Métro:** St-Paul.

BARS & PUBS

These are Anglo-American imports to France and—with a few notable exceptions—strike an alien chord. They're about equally divided between those trying to imitate Stateside cocktail bars and those pretending to be British pubs. Some go to amazing lengths in the process.

Bar-hopping is fashionable with Paris's smart set, as distinct from café-sitting, which is practiced by the entire populace. Bar prices, therefore, are generally a fraction higher; this can be a big fraction if the place boasts a well-known bartender.

LE BAR, 10 rue de l'Odéon, 6e. Tel. 43-26-66-83.

Le Bar is the actual name of this small and intimate hangout right off the place de l'Odéon on the Left Bank. This place is permanently thronged with swarms of noisy, amorous, and argumentative university students and is an ideal spot to make contact with them—if that's what you would like. Plastered with posters, both antique and pop, it reverberates to the strains of an overworked jukebox. **Open:** Daily 5:30pm–2am. **Prices:** Beer from 20F ($3.50), drinks from 36F ($6.30). **Métro:** Odéon.

THE CHINA CLUB, 59 rue de Charenton, 12e. Tel. 43-43-82-02.

Situated close enough to the Opéra Bastille to attract an after-opera crowd, this is a night bar that appeals to Paris's night denizens of the fashion and arts communities. Decorated in a mostly red palette with overtones of the French colonial empire in Asia, it features a Chinese restaurant on the street level, a calm and quiet bar upstairs (with a scattering of chess boards), and a more animated (and occasionally raucous) bar in the cellar. No one dances, but everyone seems to talk. **Open:** Restaurant nightly

7pm–12:30am, bar nightly 7pm–1:30am. **Admission:** Free. Drinks from 60F ($10.50) each, meals from 200F ($35). **Métro:** Bastille.

PUB SAINT-GERMAIN-DES-PRÉS, 17 rue de l'Ancienne-Comédie, 6e. Tel. 43-29-38-70.

This is the only pub in the country to offer 24 draft beers and 500 international beers. Leather niches render drinking discreet. The decor consists of gilded mirrors on the walls, hanging gas lamps, and a stuffed parrot in a gilded cage. Leather-cushioned handrails are also provided for some mysterious purpose—guidance perhaps? You'll need it. There are nine different rooms and 500 seats, which makes the pub the largest in France. The atmosphere is quiet, relaxed, and rather posh, and it's open day and night. Genuine Whitbread beer is sold, and Pimm's No. 1 is featured. You can also order snacks or complete meals here. In the evening, there is band entertainment, both rock and variety. **Open:** Daily 24 hours. **Prices:** Beer 20F–80F ($3.50–$14), menus 125F–150F ($21.90–$26.30). **Métro:** Odéon.

RENAULT, 53 av. des Champs-Elysées, 8e. Tel. 42-25-28-17.

If you like to combine your hamburgers with shopping for a Renault, you'll be at the right place if you drop in at the Renault. At first you'll think you've come to an automobile showroom . . . and you have. But proceed to the rear, where a bar of "horseless carriages" is waiting. Here you can order either a fixed-price menu, an à la carte meal, or just a drink. **Open:** Daily 11am–1:30am. **Prices:** Fixed-price menu 78F–90F ($13.70–$15.80), à la carte meal 180F ($31.50), whiskey from 42F ($7.40) at the bar. **Métro:** F. D. Roosevelt.

GRAND HOTEL BARS

If you want to re-create the elegance of the salons of 18th-century France, try one of the bars of the grand hotels of Paris. Dress up, speak softly, and be prepared to spend a lot for a drink. You're not paying for the drink but for an ambience unmatched in most other places.

GEORGE V BAR, 31 av. George V, 8e. Tel. 47-23-54-00.

A visit to the monochromatic elegance of this bar affords an opportunity to see firsthand the carryings-on within one of Paris's most expensive and stridently international hotels. Further, if there's someone you're trying to avoid amid the tapestries and Regency antiques of the main lobby, this very *laissez-faire* watering hole provides a convenient hideaway. **Open:** Daily 11am–1:30pm. **Prices:** Mixed drinks from 75F ($13.10). **Métro:** George-V.

BAR OBELISQUE, in the Hôtel de Crillon, 10 place de la Concorde, 8e. Tel. 44-71-15-00.

Although some visitors consider the Bar Obélisque too stiff and self-consciously elegant to ever allow anyone to have a good time, the social and literary history of this bar is remarkable. Hemingway's fictional heroine Brett Ashley broke her promise to rendezvous there with Jake Barnes in *The Sun Also Rises*. Over the years it has attracted practically every upper-level staff member of the nearby American embassy, as well as a gaggle of visiting heiresses, stars, starlets, and wannabes. The decor of this place no longer basks in the 1950s glow so favored by past clients such as Janet Flanner (legendary Paris correspondent of *The New Yorker*), but it has been majestically upgraded by Sonia Rykiel under its new owner, the Concorde Group. Drinks are also served in the Crillon's *salon de thé*—the Jardin d'Hiver. **Open:** Daily noon–2am. **Prices:** Drinks from 80F ($14). **Métro:** Concorde.

BAR ANGLAIS, in the Hôtel Plaza Athénée, 25 av. Montaigne, 8e. Tel. 47-23-78-33.

On your way through this deluxe citadel, you'll pass a chattering telex machine, which carries recent quotes from the world's leading stock exchanges, in case you want to check on your investment portfolio. In the rarefied atmosphere of this elegant bar, it seems appropriate to do so. As its name would imply, the bar, located on the lower level of the hotel, has a decor that is vintage Anglo-Saxon, although the service is definitely French and the drinks are international. Every evening, during the permissive and oh-so-sophisticated hours between 11pm and 1:30am, a pianist and singer entertain an adult clientele in a medley of languages. **Open:** Daily 11am–1:30am. **Prices:** Drinks from 65F ($11.40) before 11pm, from 100F ($17.50) after 11pm. **Métro:** Alma-Marceau.

4. SPECIALTY BARS & CLUBS

GAY PARIS

Gay life is centered mostly around Les Halles and Le Marais, with the greatest concentration of gay clubs, restaurants, bars, and shops located between the Hôtel-de-Ville and Rambuteau Métro stops. Gay discos come and go so fast that even a magazine devoted somewhat to their pursuit, *Gai Pied*, has a hard time keeping up. That magazine is sold at many news kiosks, as is *Lesbia*, a monthly national lesbian magazine.

LE PALACE GAY TEA DANCE, 8 rue du Faubourg-Montmartre, 9e. Tel. 42-46-10-87.

If you're gay, lesbian, or bisexual, this is *the* gathering place in Paris on a Sunday afternoon. Both women and men are welcomed into this chatty, gossipy, fun environment whether you've come to dance or not. It's an international crowd, and if you don't want to drink beer or liquor, you can always sip coffee. For more details about Le Palace, see "Dance Halls and Discos," above, and Le Privilège, below. **Open:** Sun 5–11pm. **Admission:** 40F ($7) before 6pm, 60F ($10.50) after 6pm. **Métro:** Rue Montmartre.

LE PRIVILEGE, in the basement of Le Palace, 8 rue du Faubourg-Montmartre, 9e. Tel. 47-70-75-02.

In the basement of Le Palace (see above), this bar is one of the most popular watering holes for Parisian "lipstick lesbians," among others. Although attracting mainly women in the early evening hours, later on it draws a large number of gay men. You may be "screened" at the door before being allowed in. **Open:** Tues–Sun 11:30pm–6am. **Admission:** Included in the cover charge of 100F–130F ($17.50–$22.80) to Le Palace. **Prices:** Drinks 100F ($17.50). **Métro:** Rue Montmartre.

LA CHAMPMESLE, 4 rue Chabanais, 2e. Tel. 42-96-85-20.

With dim lighting, background music, and comfortable banquettes, La Champmeslé offers a cozy meeting place for women. It is, in fact, the leading women's bar of Paris. The club is housed within a 300-year-old building, decorated with exposed stone and heavy ceiling beams, with "retro"-style furnishings evocative of the 1950s. Every Thursday night one of the premier lesbian events of Paris—a cabaret—begins here at 10pm. The entrance price and drinks cost the same on Thursday as any other day. Josy is the charming entrepreneur who established this place in the mid-1970s. **Open:** Daily 6pm–2am. **Admission:** Free. **Prices:** Drinks 35F ($6.10). **Métro:** Pyramides.

MADAME ARTHUR, 75 bis, rue des Martyrs, 18e. Tel. 42-54-40-21.

Madame Arthur is one of the leading female-impersonator cabarets of Europe. This place Pigalle showplace, which attracts both straights and gays, is directed by Madame Arthur, who is no lady. The joke is that this place has been around so long it welcomed the invading armies of Julius Caesar—and it's still going strong. You can visit just to drink, or you can dine from a fixed-price menu, the most expensive one offering caviar. Reservations are a good idea. **Open:** Daily; show 10:30pm–12:30am. **Admission:** 165F ($28.90), including first drink. **Prices:** Drinks 80F ($14); fixed-price menus 295F–695F ($51.60–$121.60). **Métro:** Abbesses.

LE NEW MONOCLE, 60 bd. Edgar-Quinet, 14e. Tel. 43-20-81-12.

Although traditionally this has been a lesbians-only hangout since the old Montparnasse days of Gertrude Stein and Alice, it recently relaxed its entrance policy and now admits well-behaved men. Inside is a bar, dim lighting, and a dance floor ringed with chairs, banquettes, and comfortably battered 1950s-inspired accessories. No self-respecting lesbian with a sense of literary history would dream of going to Paris without stopping by just once for a drink. **Open:** Mon–Sat 3pm–4am, Sun 5pm–4am. **Admission:** 150F ($26.30), which includes one drink. Additional drinks 100F ($17.50) each. **Métro:** Edgar-Quinet.

LE BAR CENTRAL, 33 rue Vieille-du-Temple, 4e. Tel. 48-87-99-33.

Le Bar Central is one of the leading bars for men in the Hôtel de Ville area. In fact, it is probably the most famous gay men's bar in Paris today. The club has established a small hotel upstairs with a few facilities and only seven bedrooms. Singles cost 400F ($70) daily and doubles go for 480F ($84), including breakfast. Both the bar and its little hotel are within a 300-year-old building in the heart of Le Marais. The hotel caters especially to gay men, less frequently to lesbians. **Open:** Daily 4pm–2am. **Admission:** Free. **Prices:** Beer 15F ($2.60). **Métro:** Hôtel-de-Ville.

LE PIANO ZINC, 49 rue des Blancs-Manteaux, 4e. Tel. 42-74-32-42.

This ever popular place was founded by a German-born Francophile named Jürgen about 12 years ago; it is both a piano bar and a cabaret, filled with singing patrons who belt out old French *chansons* with humor and gusto, or do their version of Madonna, Piaf, Liza, and the inevitable Judy Garland. It defines itself as a gay bar, "but you can happily bring your grand-mère, as some of our clients do," management assures us. Le Piano Zinc occupies three floors of a building, and the cabaret is presented in the basement nightly at 10pm for no charge. **Open:** Daily 6pm–2am. **Admission:** One-drink ticket charge on Fri–Sat; otherwise free. **Prices:** Mixed drinks 42F ($7.40), beer 20F ($3.50). **Métro:** Rambuteau or Hôtel-de-Ville.

LITERARY HAUNTS

LA CLOSERIE DES LILAS, 171 bd. du Montparnasse, 6e. Tel. 43-26-70-50.

Hemingway, Picasso, Gershwin, and Modigliani all loved the Closerie, and it has once again become one of the hottest bars in Paris. Look for the brass nameplate of your favorite Lost Generation artist along the banquettes or at the well-oiled bar. **Open:** Daily 11am–2am. **Prices:** Scotch and soda 75F ($13.10), beer 32F ($5.60). **Métro:** Port-Royal.

HARRY'S NEW YORK BAR, 5 rue Daunou, 5e. Tel. 42-61-71-14.

⭐ *"Sank roo doe Noo,"* as the ads tell you to instruct your cab driver, is the most famous bar in Europe—quite possibly in the world. Opened on Thanksgiving Day in 1911, it's sacred to Hemingway disciples as the spot where Ernest did most of his Parisian imbibing. To others it's hallowed as the site where white lady and sidecar cocktails were invented in 1919 and 1931, respectively. Also, it is the birthplace of the Bloody Mary and French '75, as well as headquarters of the International Bar Flies (IBF).

The upstairs bar might sometimes be excessively hearty, a kind of catharsis for expatriates eager to unwind amid their fellow anglophones and their Gallic admirers. The ambience is more lighthearted in the cellar, where a freewheeling cabaret is performed every night from 10pm to 3am, with whatever singer, actor, or comedian the management can arrange on any given evening. Prices in the cellar are 10F ($1.80) higher, per drink, than those in the historic street-level bar. **Open:** Daily 10:30am–4am. **Closed:** Dec 24–25. **Prices** (in street-level bar): Dry martini 46F ($8.10), whiskey from 50F ($8.80). **Métro:** Opéra or Pyramides.

ROSEBUD, 11 bis, rue Delambre, 14e. Tel. 43-35-38-54.

The name is taken from Orson Welles's greatest film, *Citizen Kane.* Rosebud is just around the corner from the famous cafés of Montparnasse. It once attracted such devotees as the late Jean-Paul Sartre and Simone de Beauvoir, Eugene Ionesco, and Marguerite Duras. Drop in at night for a glass of wine or perhaps something to eat, maybe a hamburger or chili con carne. **Open:** Daily 7pm–2am. **Prices:** Light meals from 150F ($26.30), drinks 60F ($10.50). **Métro:** Vavin.

HISTORIC TAVERNS

AU FRANC PINOT, 1 quai de Bourbon, 4e. Tel. 43-29-46-98.

At the foot of Pont Marie, on the Ile St-Louis, is the severely paneled facade of the oldest wine bistro in Paris. It sits above a surprisingly deep cellar that plunges more than 30 feet below street level. Although the cellar was originally dug in 1637, local stone masons added a mezzanine just before World War I, creating the double tier of vaulted basements that today comprise Au Franc Pinot.

The establishment offers about two dozen vintages of French wine, which are sold by the glass. These are consumed at the large wooden bar on the street level, or at one of the small tables close by.

If you go down into the cellars, you'll find a cozy restaurant offering such specialties as lamb with crayfish in a tarragon cream sauce, or terrine of foie gras with fresh duckling from western France, and a limited selection of food that goes well with the large inventory of wines. Naturally, dozens of vintages are available in bottles as well. **Open:** Street-level wine bar Tues–Sat noon–11:30pm. In cellars, lunch Tues–Sat noon–3:30pm, dinner Tues–Sat 6–11:30pm. **Prices:** Glass of wine 20F–75F ($3.50–$13.10). Fixed-price lunch 150F ($26.30), fixed-price dinner 190F ($33.30); à la carte menu from 225F ($39.40). **Métro:** Pont-Marie.

TAVERNE HENRI-IV, 13 place du Pont-Neuf, 1er. Tel. 43-54-27-90.

Quite different from my other recommendations, this is called both a *taverne* and *bistro à vin*. The location couldn't be more magnificent—in a 17th-century building at the Pont Neuf, on the Ile de la Cité. The host, Monsieur Cointepas, does his own bottling, or at least some of it. His prize wines are listed on a blackboard menu. You might order a special Beaujolais or perhaps a glass of Chinon, the latter "tasting more of the earth"; all drinks are cheaper at the bar. Snacks include wild-boar pâté, and as the owner puts it, the price depends on what you spread on your slice of bread. Eight farmer's lunches are offered. **Open:** Mon–Sat 11:30am–9:30pm. **Closed:** Aug. **Prices** (including service): Glass of wine 20F–30F ($3.50–$5.30), snacks 20F–25F ($3.50–$4.40), farmer's lunch 60F ($10.50). **Métro:** Pont-Neuf.

EASY EXCURSIONS FROM PARIS

1. **VERSAILLES**
2. **FONTAINEBLEAU**
3. **EURO DISNEY RESORT**

Paris—the city that began on an island—is itself the center of a curious landlocked island known as the Ile de France.

Shaped roughly like a saucer, it lies encircled by a thin ribbon of rivers: the Epte, Aisne, Marne, and Yonne. Fringing these rivers are mighty forests with famous names—Rambouillet, St-Germain, Compiègne, and Fontainebleau. These forests are said to be responsible for Paris's clear, gentle air, and the unusual length of its spring and fall. This may be a debatable point, but there's no argument that they provide the capital with a series of excursion spots, all within easy reach.

The forests were once the possessions of kings and the ruling aristocracy, and they're still sprinkled with the magnificent châteaux, or palaces, of their former masters. Together with ancient hamlets, glorious cathedrals, and little country inns, they turn the Ile de France into a traveler's paradise. On a more modern note, Euro Disney attracts visitors from all over the world. Because of Paris's comparatively small size, it's almost at your doorstep.

The difficult question is deciding where to go. What I'm offering in this chapter is merely a handful of the dozens of possibilities for one-day jaunts.

1. VERSAILLES

13 miles SW of Paris, 44 miles NE of Chartres

GETTING THERE   By Train   Take the RER line (C5), which leaves every 15 minutes from Paris, to Versailles–Rive Gauche. Turn right when you exit. Eurailpass holders travel free.

By Métro   Get off at Pont de Sèvres and transfer to Bus 171. The trip takes 15 minutes. To get there from Paris, it's cheaper to pay with three Métro tickets from a *carnet* packet. You'll be let off near the gates of the palace.

By Car   Take the N10 highway. Park on place d'Armes in front of the palace.

ESSENTIALS   The town is dominated by the palace. Three main avenues radiate from place d'Armes in front of the palace. The tourist office is at 7 rue des Réservoirs (tel. 39-50-36-22).

The kings of France built a glittering private world for themselves, far from the grime and noise and bustle of Paris: the **Château de Versailles,** place d'Armes (tel. 30-84-74-00). Seeing all of the palace's rooms would take up an entire morning and leave you pretty exhausted, so you should probably skip some of them and save your energy for the park, which is the ultimate in French landscaping—every tree, shrub, flower, and hedge disciplined into a frozen ballet pattern and blended with soaring fountains, sparkling little lakes, grandiose stairways, and hundreds of marble statues. More like a colossal stage setting than a park—even the view of the blue horizon seems embroidered on—it's a Garden of Eden for puppet people, a place where you expect the birds to sing coloratura soprano.

Inside, the **Grand Apartments,** the **Royal Chapel,** and the **Hall of Mirrors** (where the Treaty of Versailles was signed) can be visited without a guide Tuesday through Sunday between 9:45am and 5pm (closed holidays). Admission is 40F ($7) for adults and 26F ($4.60) for those 25 and under and those over 60. Other sections of the château may be visited only at specific hours or on special days. Some of the sections are temporarily closed as they undergo restoration.

Try to save time to visit the **Grand Trianon,** which is a good walk across the park. In pink-and-white marble, it was designed by Hardouin-Mansart for Louis XIV in 1687. The Trianon is mostly furnished with Empire pieces. You can also visit the **Petit Trianon,** built by Gabriel in 1768. This was the favorite residence of Marie Antoinette, who could escape the rigors of court here. Once it was a retreat for Louis XV and his mistress, Madame du Barry. The Grand Trianon is open Tuesday through Sunday from 9:45am to noon and 2 to 5pm. Admission is 20F ($3.50). The Petit Trianon is open the same days from 2 to 5pm; admission is 12F ($2.10).

On Sunday, reduced rates are available to all visitors: 26F ($4.60) for the chateau, 13F ($2.30) for the Grand Trianon, 8F ($1.40) for the Petit Trianon. There is a combination ticket for the château and the Trianons, costing 60F ($10.50), but reduced to 45F ($7.90) on Sunday.

EVENING SPECTACLES The tourist office in Versailles (see above) offers a program of evening fireworks and illuminated fountains on several occasions throughout the summer. These spectacles are announced a full season in advance. The dates usually fall on Saturday night, although the schedules change from year to year. Spectators sit on bleachers clustered at the boulevard de la Reine entrance to the Basin of Neptune. The most desirable front-view seats cost 185F ($32.40), and standing room on the promenoir sells for 60F ($10.50); free for children under 10. Gates that admit you to the Grande Fête de Nuit de Versailles open 1½ hours before show time.

Tickets can be purchased in advance at the tourist office in Versailles, or in Paris at Agence Perroissier, 6 place de la Madeleine, 8e (tel. 42-60-58-31), and Agence des Théâtres, 78 av. des Champs-Elysées, 8e (tel. 43-59-24-60). If you've just arrived in Versailles from Paris, you can always take your chances and purchase tickets an hour ahead of showtime at boulevard de la Reine. The show lasts for 1½ hours.

From the beginning of May until the end of September, a less elaborate spectacle is staged each Sunday. Called Grandes Eaux

Musicales, it is a display of fountains in the park and costs only 20F ($3.50). Classical music is also played.

WHERE TO DINE

LES TROIS MARCHES, Hôtel Trianon Palace, 1 bd. de la Reine. Tel. 30-84-38-00.

Cuisine: FRENCH. **Reservations:** Required.

$ Prices: Appetizers 175F–250F ($30.60–$43.80); main courses 150F–300F ($26.30–$52.50); fixed-price lunch 260F ($45.50); fixed-price dinner 395F–750F ($69.10–$131.30). AE, DC, MC, V.

Open: Lunch daily noon–2pm; dinner daily 7:30–10:30pm.

For lunch, you can dine in regal style at the Trianon Palace Hotel. Situated in a 5-acre garden, the hotel became world-famous in 1919 when it served as headquarters for the signers of the Treaty of Versailles. It still retains its old-world splendor, its dining room decorated with crystal chandeliers and fluted columns. The chef, Gérard Vié, is, it is conceded, the most talented and creative chef feeding visitors to Versailles these days. He attracts a discerning clientele who don't mind paying the high prices. The cuisine moderne is subtle, often daringly inventive and conceived, the service smooth. Specialties are likely to include roast pigeon in a garlic-and-cream sauce, a celery terrine with duck liver, and veal with sea urchins, along with ravioli stuffed with lobster, truffles, and spinach.

LE RESCATORE, 27 av. St-Cloud. Tel. 39-50-23-60.

Cuisine: SEAFOOD. **Reservations:** Required.

$ Prices: Appetizers 85F–135F ($14.90–$23.60); main courses 110F–220F ($19.30–$38.50); fixed-price lunch 255F ($44.60); fixed-price dinner 375F ($65.60). AE, MC, V.

Open: Lunch Mon–Fri 12:30–2pm; dinner Mon–Sat 7:30–10pm.

The decor is classic and conservative, within a pink-hued, high-ceilinged room, the tall French doors of which overlook ornate wrought-iron balconies and the busy avenue in the center of town below. The chef de cuisine, Jacques Bagot, creates an illusion of living near the sea with his cassolette of fish, his perfectly prepared turbot sweetened with mild garlic, and his pot-au-feu of seafood. Occasionally he offers a selection of grilled exotic fish.

LE POTAGER DU ROY, 1 rue du Maréchal Joffre. Tel. 39-50-35-34.

Cuisine: FRENCH. **Reservations:** Required.

$ Prices: Appetizers 65F–145F ($11.40–$25.40); main courses 95F–150F ($16.60–$26.30); fixed-price menu 170F ($29.80). MC, V.

Open: Lunch Tues–Sat noon–2pm; dinner Tues–Sat 7:30–10pm.

Philippe Le Tourneur used to work for another Versailles chef, Gérard Vié, before setting up his own attractive restaurant on a busy street corner in a commercial part of town. Set behind a maroon facade, in a modern decor of several warmly decorated rooms, he offers a fixed-price menu or comparably priced à la carte meals. You might begin with a lamb terrine with raisins and pistachio nuts, then follow with duckling with baby turnips or steamed fillet of sole with summer vegetables. You might also try roast lamb en papillote.

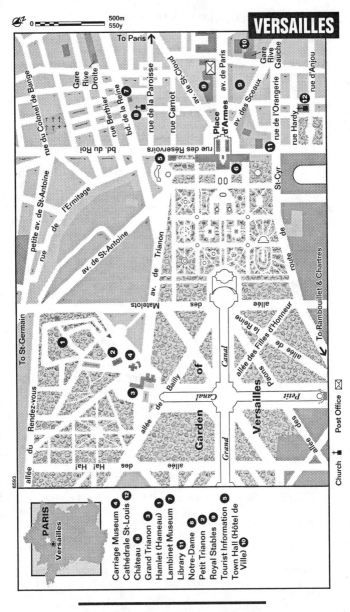

VERSAILLES

To Paris ↑

Gare Rive Droite
Gare Rive Gauche
rue du Colonel de Bange
rue Berthier
bd. de la Reine
av. de St-Cloud
rue de la Paroisse
rue Carnot
av. de Paris
av. des Sceaux
rue de l'Orangerie
rue d'Anjou
rue Hardy
Place d'Armes
rue des Réservoirs
St-Cyr
bd. du Roi
Petite av. de St-Antoine
rue de l'Ermitage
av. de St-Antoine
av. de Trianon
route de Rambouillet & Chartres
To St-Germain
Matelots
To Rambouillet & Chartres
allée des Filles d'Honneur
allée de la Reine
allée des Matelots
allée de Bailly
allée du Ha! Ha!
allée du Rendez-vous
Grand Canal
Garden of Versailles
Petit Canal

Church ✝   Post Office ⊠

0 ⊨⊨⊨⊨ 500m
      550y

Carriage Museum ❹
Cathédrale St-Louis ⓬
Château ❻
Grand Trianon ❸
Hamlet (Hameau) ❶
Lambinet Museum ❼
Library ⑪
Notre-Dame ❽
Petit Trianon ❷
Royal Stables ❾
Tourist Information ❺
Town Hall (Hôtel de Ville) ❿

PARIS
Versailles

6593

2. FONTAINEBLEAU

37 miles S of Paris, 46 miles NE of Orléans

GETTING THERE By Train Trains to Fontainebleau depart from the Gare de Lyon in Paris and take from 35 minutes to an hour. The Fontainebleau station is just outside the town in Avon. The town bus makes the 2-mile trip to the château every 10 to 15 minutes on weekdays (every 30 minutes on Sunday).

ESSENTIALS Dominated by its château, the town is surrounded by the dense **Forêt de Fontainebleau.** The main squares are place du Général-de-Gaulle and place d'Armes. The **Office de Tourisme** is at 31 place Napoléon-Bonaparte (tel. 64-22-25-68).

Napoléon called the **Palace of Fontainebleau** the house of the centuries. Much of French history has taken place within its walls, perhaps no moment more memorable than when Napoléon I stood on the horseshoe-shaped stairway and bade a loving farewell to his army before his departure to Elba and exile. That scene has been the subject of countless paintings, including Vernet's *Les Adieux* of the emperor.

Napoléon's affection for Fontainebleau was understandable. He was following the pattern of a succession of French kings in the pre-Versailles days who used Fontainebleau as a resort and hunted in its magnificent forests. François I tried to turn the hunting lodge into a royal palace in the Italian Renaissance style—he brought several artists, including Benvenuto Cellini, to work for him.

Under the patronage of François I, the School of Fontainebleau, led by painters Rosso Fiorentino and Primaticcio, gained prestige. The artists adorned the 210-foot long **Gallery of François I.** Stucco-framed panels depict such scenes as *The Rape of Europa*, and the monarch holding a pomegranate, a symbol of unity. The salamander, the symbol of the Chevalier King, is everywhere.

Sometimes called the Gallery of Henri II, the **Ballroom** is in the mannerist style, with the interlaced initials H&D in the decoration. This referred to Henri's mistress, Diane de Poitiers. You can also see the initials H&C, symbolizing Henri and his wife, Catherine de Médicis. At one end of the room is a monumental fireplace supported by two bronze satyrs, made in 1966 (the originals were melted down during the French Revolution). At the other side is the balcony of the musicians, with sculptured garlands. The ceiling displays octagonal coffering adorned with rosettes. Above the wainscoting is a series of frescoes, painted between 1550 and 1558, which depict such mythological subjects as *The Feast of Bacchus*.

An architectural curiosity is the richly and elegantly adorned **Louis XV Staircase.** The room above it was originally decorated by Primaticcio for the bedroom of the duchesse d'Etampes, but when an architect was designing the stairway, he simply ripped out her floor. Of the Italian frescoes that were preserved, one depicts the Queen of the Amazons climbing into Alexander's bed.

When Louis XIV ascended to the throne, he neglected Fontainebleau because of his preoccupation with Versailles. However, he wasn't opposed to using the palace for house guests—specifically such unwanted ones as Queen Christina, who had abdicated the throne of Sweden. Under the assumption that she still had "divine right," she ordered one of the most brutal royal murders on record—that of her companion Monaldeschi, who had ceased to please her.

Louis XV and, later, Marie Antoinette also took an interest in Fontainebleau.

The château found renewed glory—and shame—under Napoléon I. You can walk around much of the palace on your own, but some of the **Napoleonic rooms** are accessible by guided tour only. His throne room and bedroom (look for his symbol, a bee) are equally impressive. You can also see where the emperor

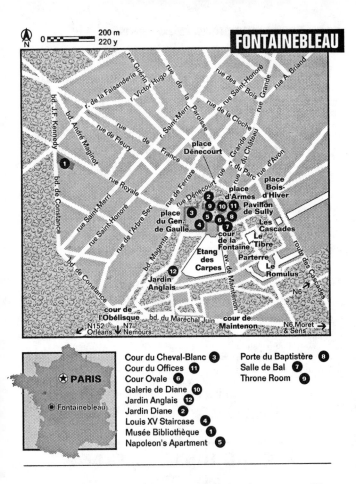

FONTAINEBLEAU

A 0 ⊢⊢⊢⊢⊣ 200 m
N   220 y

place Dénecourt

place
d'Armes
Pavillon
de Sully
place
Bois-
d'Hiver
Les
Cascades
Le
Tibre
Parterre
Le
Romulus

place
du Gen.
de Gaulle
cour
de la
Fontaine
Etang
des
Carpes

Jardin
Anglais

cour de
l'Obélisque   bd. du Maréchal Juin   cour de
Maintenon

★ PARIS

● Fontainebleau

Cour du Cheval-Blanc ❸	Porte du Baptistère ❽
Cour du Offices ⓫	Salle de Bal ❼
Cour Ovale ❻	Throne Room ❾
Galerie de Diane ❿	
Jardin Anglais ⓬	
Jardin Diane ❷	
Louis XV Staircase ❹	
Musée Bibliothèque ❶	
Napoleon's Apartment ❺	

signed his abdication—the document exhibited is a copy. The furnishings in Empress Joséphine's *petits appartements* and the *grands appartements* of Napoléon evoke the imperial heyday.

After your long trek through the palace, visit the **gardens** and, especially, the carp pond; the gardens, however, are only a prelude to the Forest of Fontainebleau.

The apartments (tel. 64-22-27-40) are open Wednesday through Monday from 9:30am to 5pm (9:30am to 6pm in July and August). Entrance to the Grands Appartements is 30F ($5.30); to the Petits Appartements and Chinese Museum, 12F ($2.10).

WHERE TO STAY & DINE

LE BEAUHARNAIS, in the Hôtel de l'Aigle Noir, 27 place Napoléon-Bonaparte. Tel. 64-22-32-65.

Cuisine: FRENCH. **Reservations:** Required.

$ Prices: Appetizers 95F–160F ($16.60–$28); main courses 140F–165F ($24.50–$28.90); fixed-price menus 180F–290F ($31.50–$50.80). AE, DC, MC, V.

Open: Lunch daily noon–2pm; dinner daily 7:30–9:30pm.

One of the leading restaurants is Le Beauharnais. Although it's been completely renovated, it still retains its old charm. Opposite the château, the building was once the home of the Cardinal de Retz. It dates from the 16th century, but was converted into a hotel in 1720. The restaurant, the most beautiful in town, was installed in a former courtyard. The interior is filled with Empire furniture and potted palms. Specialties include roast duckling in the style of Rouen, sweetbreads with foie gras served pot-au-feu, and grilled pigeon with pistachio nuts. There is a changing variety of other dishes, depending on seasonal availability.

The hotel has 57 bedrooms and 6 suites, all with private baths and such modern conveniences as color TVs, radios, minibars, direct-dial phones, double windows, and electric heating. Each is individually decorated, often with antiques and pleasantly tasteful colors. Singles or doubles range in price from 1,000F ($175), suites from 1,300F ($227.50).

LE CAVEAU DES DUCS, 24 rue de Ferrare. Tel. 64-22-05-05.

Cuisine: FRENCH. **Reservations:** Recommended.

$ Prices: Appetizers 38F–90F ($6.70–$15.80); main courses 80F–130F ($14–$22.80); fixed-price menus 95F–230F ($16.60–$40.30). AE, MC, V.

Open: Lunch daily noon–2pm; dinner daily 7–10pm.

Located deep underground, this reasonably priced restaurant occupies what was originally built in the 1600s as a storage cellar for the nearby château (a five-minute walk). Candles flicker against the vaulted stone ceiling; the decor is traditional and the staff helpful. Menu specialties include snails in garlic butter, a platter of sole and salmon on a bed of pasta, fillet of rumpsteak served with Brie sauce, and roast leg of lamb with garlic and rosemary sauce. An excellent dessert is tarte fine aux pommes.

---

3. EURO DISNEY RESORT

20 miles E of Paris

GETTING THERE By Train The resort is linked to the RER commuter express rail network (Line A), which maintains a stop within walking distance of the theme park. Board the RER at such inner-city Paris stops as Charles de Gaulle–Etoile, Châtelet–Les Halles, or Nation. Get off at Line A's last stop, Marne-la-Vallée/Chessy, a 45-minute ride from central Paris. The round-trip fare from central Paris is 85F ($14.90). Trains run every 10 to 20 minutes, depending on the time of day.

By Bus Each of the hotels in the resort is connected by shuttle bus to and from both Orly airport and Roissy–Charles de Gaulle. Buses depart from both airports at intervals of between 30 and 45 minutes, depending on the time of day and day of the year. One-way transportation to the park from either of the airports cost 75F ($13.10) per person.

By Car Take the A-4 highway east from Paris, getting off at Exit 14 where it's marked PARC EURO DISNEYLAND. Guest parking at any of the thousands of parking spaces costs 30F to 50F ($5.30 to $8.80), depending on the size of the vehicle. An interconnected series of moving sidewalks speeds up pedestrian transit from the parking areas to the theme park's entrance. Parking for guests at any of the hotels within the resort is free.

ESSENTIALS   Information   All hotels listed below provide general information about the theme park, but for specific theme park information in all languages, contact the Euro Disney Guest Relations office, located in City Hall on Main Street, U.S.A. (tel. 64-74-30-00).

Fast Facts   Coin-operated lockers can be rented for 10F ($1.80) per use, and larger bags can also be stored for 15F ($2.60) per day.   Children's strollers and wheelchairs can be rented for 30F ($5.30) per day, with a 20F ($3.50) deposit.   Babysitting is available at any of the resort's hotels if 24-hour advance notice is given.

After evoking some of the most enthusiastic as well as negative reactions in recent French history, the Euro Disney Resort opened its doors in 1992 to one of the most lavish theme parks in the world. Situated on a 5,000-acre site (about one-fifth the size of Paris) in the Paris suburb of Marne-la-Vallée, the park incorporates the most successful elements of its Disney predecessors—but with a European flair.

WHAT TO SEE & DO

The resort was designed as a total vacation package; included within one enormous unit are the Euro Disneyland Park with its five different entertainment "lands," six large hotels, a campground, an entertainment center (Festival Disney), a 27-hole golf course, and dozens of restaurants, shows, and shops.

One of the attractions, **Main Street, U.S.A.,** features horse-drawn carriages and street-corner barbershop quartets.   From the "Main Street Station," steam-powered railway cars leave for a trip through a Grand Canyon Diorama to **Frontierland,** with its paddle-wheel steamers reminiscent of the Mississippi Valley of Mark Twain's era.

The park's steam trains chug past **Adventureland**—with its swashbuckling 18th-century pirates, the treehouse of the Swiss Family Robinson, and reenacted legends from the *Arabian Nights*—to **Fantasyland.**   There, one can see the symbol of the theme park, the Sleeping Beauty Castle (Le Château de la Belle au Bois Dormant), whose soaring pinnacles and turrets are an idealized (and spectacular) interpretation of the châteaux of France.

Visions of the future are displayed at **Discoveryland,** whose tributes to human invention and imagination are drawn from the works of Leonardo da Vinci, Jules Verne, H.G. Wells, the modern masters of science fiction, and the *Star Wars* series.

Disney also maintains an entertainment center—**Festival Disney**—whose layout somewhat resembles a mall in California. Illuminated inside by a spectacular gridwork of overhead lights, the complex accommodates dance clubs, shops, restaurants, bars for adults who want to be away from children for a while, a French Government Tourist Office, a post office, and a marina.

Admission: Admission to the park for one day costs 175F to 250F ($30.60 to $43.80) for adults, and 125F to 175F ($21.90 to $30.60) for children under 12. Children 2 years and under enter free. Admission to the park for two days ranges from 335F to 475F ($58.60 to $83.10) for adults, and from 240F to 335F ($42 to $58.60) for children. Admission prices vary according to the season; the peak season is from mid-June to mid-September, as well as Christmas and Easter weeks. Entrance to Festival Disney, the resort's consortium of shops, dance clubs, and restaurants, is free, although there's usually a cover charge for the dance clubs.

Open: June 12–Sept 12 daily 9am–11pm; Sept 13–June 11 Mon–Fri 9am–7pm; Sat–Sun 9am–11pm. Opening and closing hours, however, vary with the weather and the season. It's usually a good idea to phone the information office (see above).

Tours: Guided tours can be arranged for 45F ($7.90) for adults and 35F ($6.10) for children ages 3 to 11. Lasting 3½ hours and including 20 or more people, the tours offer an opportunity for a complete visit. *Note:* Whether or not you participate in a guided tour, you will still have to wait in line (wherever necessary).

WHERE TO STAY

The resort has six hotels, each of which offers a different theme and shares a common reservations service. For more information call 407/W-DISNEY (934-7639) in North America, or 071/753-2900 in London. For information or reservations in France, contact the Central Reservations Office, Euro Disney S.C.A., B.P. 105, F-77777 Marne-la-Vallée Cedex 4 (tel. 49-41-49-10).

EXPENSIVE

DISNEYLAND HOTEL, Euro Disney Resort, B.P. 105, F-77777 Marne-la-Vallée Cedex 4. Tel. 60-45-65-00. Fax 60-45-65-33.479 rms, 21 suites (all with bath). A/C MINIBAR TV TEL

$ Rates: 1,400F–1,950F ($245–$341.30) for one to four persons; 2,900F–12,500F ($507.50–$2,187.50) suites. Continental breakfast 75F ($13.10) for adults, 35F ($6.10) for children. AE, DC, MC, V.

Located at the entance to the park, this flagship hotel is Victorian in style, with red-tile turrets and jutting balconies; some observers have likened it to the town hall of a major European city. The bedrooms are plushly and conservatively furnished. On the "Castle Club" floor, there are free newspapers, all-day beverages, and access to a well-equipped private lounge.

Dining/Entertainment: Three restaurants (the California Grill is recommended separately; see "Where to Dine," below) and two bars.

Facilities: Health club with indoor/outdoor pool, whirlpool, sauna, private dining and banqueting rooms.

Services: Room service, laundry, babysitting.

HOTEL NEW YORK, Euro Disney Resort, B.P. 105, F-77777 Marne-la-Vallée Cedex 4. Tel. 60-45-73-00. Fax 60-45-73-33. 537 rms, 36 suites (all with bath). A/C MINIBAR TV TEL

$ Rates: 1,090F–1,480F ($190.80–$259) for one to four persons; from 2,100F ($367.50) suite. Continental breakfast 75F ($13.10) for adults, 35F ($6.10) for children. AE, DC, MC, V.

Inspired by the Big Apple at its best, this hotel was designed around a nine-story central "skyscraper" flanked by the Gramercy

Park Wing and the Brownstones Wing. (The exteriors of both of these wings resemble the row houses of their respective Manhattan neighborhoods.) The bedrooms are comfortably appointed with art deco accessories and New York–inspired memorabilia.

Dining/Entertainment: The hotel has a diner, a cocktail and wine bar, and a jazz club.

Services: Room service, laundry, babysitting.

Facilities: Indoor/outdoor pool, two outdoor tennis courts, health club.

MODERATE

NEWPORT BAY CLUB, Euro Disney Resort, B.P. 105, F-77777 Marne-la-Vallée Cedex 4. Tel. 60-45-55-00. Fax 60-45-55-33. 1,083 rms, 15 suites (all with bath). A/C MINIBAR TV TEL

$ Rates: 650F–990F ($113.80–$173.30) for one to four persons; from 1,700F ($297.50) suite. Continental breakfast 55F ($9.60) for adults, 35F ($6.10) for children. AE, DC, MC, V.

This hotel was designed with a central cupola, jutting balconies, and a blue-and-cream color scheme, reminiscent of harborfront New England hotel. Each nautically decorated bedroom offers closed-circuit TV movies. The upscale Yacht Club and the less formal Cape Cod restaurants are the dining choices. Facilities include a lakeside promenade, a croquet lawn, a glassed-in pool pavilion, and outdoor pool, and a health club.

SEQUOIA LODGE, Euro Disney Resort, B.P. 105, F-77777 Marne-la-Vallée Cedex 4. Tel. 60-45-51-00. Fax 60-45-51-33. 997 rms, 14 suites (all with bath). A/C MINIBAR TV TEL

$ Rates: 590F–950F ($103.30–$166.30) for one to four persons. Continental breakfast 55F ($9.60) for adults, 35F ($6.10) for children. AE, DC, MC, V.

Built of gray stone and roughly textured planking, and capped with a gently sloping green copper roof, this hotel resembles a rough-hewn but comfortable lodge in a remote section of the Rocky Mountains. The hotel consists of a large central building with five additional chalets (each housing 100 bedrooms) nearby. The rooms are comfortably rustic. The Hunter's Grill serves spit-roasted meats carved directly onto your plate. Less formal is the Beaver Creek Tavern. There is an indoor pool and health club.

INEXPENSIVE

HOTEL CHEYENNE AND HOTEL SANTA FE, Euro Disney Resort, B.P. 105, F-77777 Marne-la-Vallée Cedex 4. Tel. 60-45-62-00 (Cheyenne) or 60-45-78-00 (Santa Fé). Fax 60-45-62-33 (Cheyenne) or 60-45-78-33 (Santa Fé). 2,000 rms (all with bath). TV TEL

$ Rates: Hotel Cheyenne, 475F–790F ($83.10–$138.30) for one to four persons. Hotel Santa Fé, 375F–590F ($65.60–$103.30) for one to four persons. Continental breakfast 55F ($9.60) for adults, 35F ($6.10) for children. AE, DC, MC, V.

Located next door to one another, these are the least expensive hotels at the resort. Both are situated near a re-creation of Texas's Rio Grande and evoke different aspects of the Old West. The Cheyenne accommodates visitors within

14 two-story buildings along "Desperado Street," while the Santa Fé, sporting a desert theme, encompasses four different "nature trails" winding among 42 adobe-style pueblos.

Tex-Mex specialties are offered at La Cantina (Hotel Santa Fé), while barbecue and smokehouse specialties predominate at the Chuck Wagon Café (Hotel Cheyenne).

WHERE TO DINE

Within the resort, there are at least 45 different restaurants and snack bars, each trying hard to please millions of European and North American palates. Here are a few recommendations:

AUBERGE DE CENDRILLON, Fantasyland. Tel. 64-74-30-00.

Cuisine: FRENCH. **Reservations:** Not required.
$ **Prices:** Appetizers 35F–80F ($6.10–$14); main courses 95F–125F ($16.60–$21.90); fixed-price menus 110F–260F ($19.30–$45.50). AE, DC, MC, V

Open: Fri–Tues 11:30am–11pm.

⭐ This is a fairy-tale version of Cinderella's sumptuous country inn, with a glass couch in the center. It is the major French restaurant at the resort. A master of ceremonies, in a plumed tricorne hat and wearing an embroidered tunic and lace ruffles, welcomes you. For an appetizer, try the warm goat cheese salad with lardons or the smoked salmon platter. If you don't choose one of the good fixed-price meals, you can order from the limited but excellent à la carte menu. Perhaps you'll settle happily for poultry in a pocket (puff pastry), loin of lamb roasted with mustard, or sautéed médaillons of veal.

THE CALIFORNIA GRILL, in the Disneyland Hotel. Tel. 60-45-65-00.

Cuisine: CALIFORNIAN. **Reservations:** Required.
$ **Prices:** Appetizers 55F–95F ($9.60–$16.60); main courses 160F–265F ($28–$46.40); children's menus from 85F ($14.90). AE, DC, MC, V.

Open: Dinner only, daily 6pm–midnight.

⭐ Focusing on the new and lighter recipes for which the Golden State has achieved recognition, this airy and elegant restaurant features such specialties as maple-glazed salmon roasted on a wooden plank with a mushroom and beer ragoût; assorted field lettuce with sun-dried tomatoes, farmer's bread croutons, and lemon-chive dressing; seared and spiced tuna fillet served rare with a bean sprout salad and soy vinaigrette; and such desserts as a warm feuilleté of mango with caramel sauce. A children's menu is also available. The wine cellar is heavily stocked with California vintages. Jackets are required for men.

KEY WEST SEAFOOD, in the Festival Disney Building. Tel. 49-32-40-15.

Cuisine: SEAFOOD. **Reservations:** Required.
$ **Prices:** Appetizers 30F–55F ($5.30–$9.60); main courses 95F–250F ($16.60–$43.80); children's menus 65F ($11.40). AE, DC, MC, V.

Open: Lunch daily 11:30am–3:30pm; dinner daily 6pm–midnight.
Resembling a seafood restaurant in the Florida Keys, this restaurant features exposed beams, a raffish hint of salt spray, and an amply stocked oyster bar. Drinks include a spice-laden Bloody Mary or a

margarita made with a mixture of tequilas. Your meal might consist of a sand-digger's bucket brimming with steamed mussels; crabs served either steamed or fried with garlic; Islamorada clam chowder; garlic crabs; heaping platters of shrimp, oysters, and clams; and either a Key lime or southern pecan pie.

WALT'S, AN AMERICAN RESTAURANT, Main Street, U.S.A., Tel. 64-74-30-00.
Cuisine: AMERICAN. **Reservations:** Not accepted.
$ Prices: Appetizers 25F–80F ($4.40–$14); main courses 80F–125F ($14–$21.90); fixed-price menu 145F ($25.40); children's menu 75F ($13.10). AE, DC, MC, V.
Open: Daily 11:30am–11pm.

A popular family restaurant, this one honors Walt Disney. On the ground floor is a well-decorated bistro, and upstairs there's a restaurant divided into small dining rooms. The decor consists, in part, of photographs tracing the career of Disney. Each dining room upstairs evokes one of the theme-park lands. Begin your meal with an appetizer such as seafood in a pastry shell and follow it with veal Oscar, grilled breast of chicken with barbecue sauce, or grilled New York steak. A hot apple cobbler with ice cream is among the dessert offerings.

EVENING ENTERTAINMENT

Although you might find it hard to escape the presence of children and the props that were designed to entertain them, Euro Disney offers hideaways for adults as well. Here are a few of the most visible.

BUFFALO BILL'S WILD WEST SHOW, in the Festival Disney Building. Tel. 60-45-71-00.
This nightly stampede of entertainment recalls the show that once traveled the West with Buffalo Bill and Annie Oakley. All the corn-pone elements are here—sharpshooting, a runaway stage coach, a shoot-'em-up showdown. You're also treated to a Texas-style barbecue. Two shows are staged nightly at 6pm and 9pm costing 300F ($52.50) for adults and 200F ($35) for children.

HURRICANE'S BEACH CAFE, in the Festival Disney Building. Tel. 60-45-70-00.
Skilled at entertaining adults as well as children, Disney offers electronic music, a dance floor designed as a tropical beach, and an amply stocked bar for adults who want to get away from their offspring for a while. At regular intervals, artificial hurricanes add to the shake, rattle, and roll. Admission is free before 9pm. After 9pm, admission is 50F ($8.80) for hotel guests; 75F ($13.10) for non-guests, including your first drink. Open daily from 1pm to 1am.

ROCK 'N' ROLL AMERICA, in the Festival Disney Building. Tel. 60-45-70-00.
Occasional presentation of live rock 'n' roll bands are staged here, and the best recorded music of the 1950s and 1960s is presented. Hamburgers and milk shakes on the menu help re-create America in the '50s.

After 9pm, admission is 50F ($8.80) for hotel guests; 75F ($13.10) for nonguests, including your first drink. It's open daily from 7am to 1am.

MENU SAVVY

Alsacien/à l'alsacienne Alsace-style (usually with sauerkraut, foie gras, or sausage)

Aiguillettes Long thin slivers, usually of duck

Aïoli Garlic-laced mayonnaise

Andouillette Chitterling or tripe sausage

A point Medium rare

Assiette du pêcheur Mixed seafood plate

Baguette The famous long loaf of French bread

Ballottine Deboned, stuffed, and rolled poultry

Basquais/à la basquaise Basque-style, usually with tomatoes, red peppers, and ham

Béarnaise Sauce made with egg yolks, shallots, white wine, vinegar, butter, and tarragon

Béchamel Buttery white flour sauce flavored with onion and herbs

Beurre blanc "White butter" sauce with white wine, butter, and shallots

Bigarade Bitter orange sauce, often served with duck

Blanc de volaille Breast of hen

Blanquette Stewed meat with white sauce, enriched with cream and eggs

Boeuf à la môde Marinated beef braised with red wine and served with vegetables

Bordelais/à la bordelaise Bordeaux-style; usually accompanied with a wine-laced brown sauce flavored with shallots, tarragon, and bone marrow

Bouillabaisse Mediterranean fish soup, made with tomatoes, garlic, saffron, and olive oil

Bourguignon/à la bourguignonne Burgundy-style, usually with red wine, mushrooms, bacon, and onions

Bourride Mediterranean fish soup with aïoli, served over slices of bread

Breton/à la bretonne Brittany-style, often with white beans

Brunoise Tiny cut-up vegetables

Canard à la presse Duck killed by suffocation, then pressed to extract the blood and juices, which are simmered with cognac and red wine

Carbonnade Beef stew, originally from Flanders, often cooked with beer

Carré d'agneau Crown roast or loin of lamb

Cassolette Dish served in a small casserole

Cassoulet Toulousien specialty of white beans cooked with preserved goose or duck, pig's trotters, sausages, carrots, and onions

Céleri rémoulade Shredded celery root with a tangy mayonnaise

Cèpes à la bordelaise Large, meaty wild boletus mushrooms cooked with oil, shallots, and herbs

Choucroute garni Alsatian sauerkraut garnished with pork products and boiled potatoes

Confit Meat (usually duck or goose) cooked and preserved in its own fat

Coq au vin Chicken stewed with mushrooms and red wine

Côte d'agneau Lamb chop

Côte de boeuf Rib steak

Court bouillon A broth with white wine, herbs, carrots, and soup greens in which poultry, fish or meat is cooked

Crème brûlée Thick custard dessert with a caramelized topping

Crème chantilly Sugared whipped cream

Crème fraîche Thick, heavy cream

Crème pâtissière Custard filling for cakes

Croque-monsieur Toasted sandwich containing cheese and ham; if prepared with a fried egg on top, it's called *croque-madame*

Darne A slice of fish steak, usually salmon

Desmoiselles de Cherbourg Small Norman lobsters in court bouillon

Diable Deviled and peppery

Dijonnais/à la dijonnaise Denotes the presence in a dish of mustard, usually Dijon

Duxelles Chopped shallots and mushrooms sautéed and mixed with rich cream

Eau-de-vie "Water of life"— brandy distilled from fruit or herbs

Ecrevisse Freshwater crayfish

Escabèche Provençale dish of small fish (often sardines) browned in olive oil, marinated and served cold

Escargots de Bourgogne Land snails prepared with garlic, parsley, and butter

Estoficado Purée of dried codfish, tomatoes, olive oil, onions, and herbs; a specialty of Nice

Faisan Pheasant

Farci Stuffed

Française, à la Garnish of peas with lettuce, pearl onions and herbs

Fricassée Braised meat or poultry stew; any medley of meat, even fish, that is stewed or sautéed

Friture Fried food

Fromage blanc White cheese (like cottage cheese)

Galantine Classic dish of cooked meat or fowl, served cold in jelly aspic

Galette Flat round cake or pastry; in Brittany, a crêpe of buckwheat flour

Gâteau Cake

Gelée Jelly or aspic

Gigot Haunch (or leg) of an animal, almost always that of lamb or mutton

Glaces Ice in general; ice cream in particular

Glaçons Ice cubes

Gratin Brown crust that forms on top of a dish when it's oven-browned; a dish that is covered with bread crumbs and melted cheese

Grenouilles Frogs' legs

Hollandaise Yellow sauce of egg yolk, butter, and lemon juice whipped into a smooth blend

Homard à l'armoricaine Lobster browned and simmered with shallots, cognac, white wine, and onions

Ile flottante "Floating Island," a rich dessert of a kirsch-soaked biscuit dressed with maraschino cherries and whipped cream

Jambon de Bayonne Salt-cured ham from the Basque region

Jardinière Garnish of freshly cooked vegetables

Julienne Cut into thin strips

Jus Juice; *"au jus"* means, with natural, unthickened gravy

Landais/à la landaise Landes-style—a garnish of goose fat, pine nuts, and garlic

Langouste Clawless spiny lobster or rock lobster

Langoustine Clawed crustacean (in Britain, a prawn)

Lardons Cubes of bacon, often served with soups and salads

Léger/légère Light in texture, flavor, and calories

Legume Vegetable

Limande Lemon sole

Lotte Monkfish or angler fish

Loup de mer Wolffish, a Mediterranean sea bass

Lyonnais/à la lyonnaise White wine sauce with shredded and sautéed onions

Macédoine Medley of diced vegetables or fruits

Marchand de vins Wine-merchant; it also implies a rich sauce made from shallots and red wine

Marmite A thick soup made from beef and vegetables, simmered for hours over a low fire; the pot in which the soup is cooked

Ménagère, à la "Housewife style"—accompanied with potatoes, onions, and carrots

Meunière, à la "In the style of the miller's wife"—rolled in flour and sautéed in butter

Meurette A red wine sauce, often served with poached eggs and freshwater fish; any wine sauce

Mignonette Food (usually beef) cut into small cubes

Millefeuille A napoleon

Mirepoix Minced onions, ham, and carrots sautéed in butter and flavored with herbs

Mornay Béchamel sauce flavored with cheese

Moules à la marinière Mussels in herb-flavored white wine with shallots

Nage, à la An aromatic court bouillon used for poaching

Nantua Pink sauce made of white wine, crayfish, and tomatoes

Navarin Mutton prepared with potatoes and turnips

Normande Sauce of eggs, cream, and mushrooms, Norman-style; meat or fish flavored with calvados

Oeufs à la neige "Eggs in snow"—beaten egg whites poached in milk and served with a vanilla-flavored custard

Omelette norvégienne Baked Alaska à la française

Pain Bread

Pamplemousse Grapefruit

Panaché Any mixture

Papillote, en Cooked in parchment paper

Parisienne, à la With leeks and potatoes

Parmentier A dish with potatoes

Pâté Minced meat that is spiced and baked in a mold and served either hot or cold; sometimes made from fish or vegetables

Pâté feuilletée Puff pastry

Paysanne Chicken or meat braised and garnished with vegetables

Périgourdine, à la Sauce usually made with foie gras and truffles

Pipérade Classic Basque dish of scrambled eggs with onions, tomatoes, peppers, and ham

Piquante Tangy sauce made with shallots, vinegar, herbs, small pickles, and white wine

Pistou Sauce of garlic, fresh basil, and olive oil, from Provence

Poêlé Pan-fried

Poisson Fish—*de mer* is from the ocean; *de lac* from the lake; *de rivière* from the river

Poivrade Peppery brown sauce made with wine and vinegar

Pomme Apple

Pommes de terre Potato; frequently shorted to *pommes*, as in *pommes frites* (french fries)

Pot-au-feu "Pot on the fire"—meat stew cooked in an earthenware pot

Poulet, poularde Chicken—*poulet fermier* is free-range; *poussin* is a chick

Pré salé Seaside meadow whose grasses are said to be especially beneficial for the pasturing of lambs or sheep

Pressé Pressed or squeezed, as in fresh orange juice

Profiteroles Small cream puffs of chou pastry with a filling of whipped cream or custard

Provençal/à la provençale In the style of Provence, most often with garlic, tomatoes, onion

Quenelles Rolls of pounded and baked fish, often pike, usually served warm; can also be made from chicken or veal

Ratatouille A Mediterranean medly of peppers, tomato, eggplant, garlic, and onions

Ravigote Sauce made with vinegar, lemon sauce, white wine, shallot butter, and herbs

Rémoulade Cold mayonnaise flavored with mustard

Ris de veau Veal sweet-breads

Rognons Kidneys, usually veal

Rosé Meat or poultry cooked medium rare

Rôti Roasted

Rouille Olive-oil based mayonnaise, with peppers, garlic, and fish broth, served with bouillabaisse in Provence

Roulade Meat or fish roll, most often stuffed

Sabayon Egg custard flavored with Marsala wine

Salade lyonnaise Green salad flavored with cubed bacon and soft-boiled eggs

Salade niçoise Made with tomatoes, green beans, tuna, black olives, potatoes, artichokes, and capers

Salade verte Green salad

Sandre Pickerel; a perchlike river fish

Saucisse French pork sausage

Sommelier Wine steward

Sorbet Sherbet, usually flavored with fresh fruit

Soubise A béchamel sauce with onion

Steak au poivre Pepper steak, covered with fresh peppercorns, with a cognac flambé

Suprême White sauce made with heavy cream

Table d'hôte A fixed-price, preselected meal

Tartare Any preparation of cold chopped raw meat flavored with piquant sauces and spices (including capers and onions)

Tartare (sauce) Cold mayonnaise spiced with herbs, vinegar, and mustard

Tarte Tatin Caramelized upside-down apple pie

Tartine Open-faced sandwich, or bread slathered with jam and butter

Terrine Potted meat in a crock

Timbale Fish or meat dishes cooked in a casserole

Tournedos Rossini Beef fillet sautéed in butter with pan juices, served with a foie gras garnish

Tripes à la môde de Caen Beef tripe cooked in calvados with carrots, leeks, onions, herbs, and spices

Truite au bleu Fish that is gutted moments before being plunged into a mixture of boiling vinegar and water, which turns the flesh blue

Vacherin Ice cream in a meringue shell; a rich cheese from eastern France

Velouté Classic velvety sauce, thickened with a roux of flour and butter

Véronique, à la Garnished with peeled white grapes; usually applies to fillet of sole

Vichy With glazed carrots

Vichyssoise Cold creamy potato-and-leek soup

Vinaigrette Oil-and-vinegar dressing flavored with herbs and perhaps of hint of mustard

Vol-au-vent Puff pastry shell

Zeste Citrus peel without its white pith, twisted and used to flavor drinks, such as vermouth

Please Send Me the Books Checked Below:

FROMMER'S COMPREHENSIVE GUIDES
(Guides listing facilities from budget to deluxe,
with emphasis on the medium-priced)

	Retail Price	Code		Retail Price	Code
☐ Acapulco/Ixtapa/Taxco 1993–94	$15.00	C120	☐ Morocco 1992–93	$18.00	C021
☐ Alaska 1994–95	$17.00	C131	☐ Nepal 1994–95	$18.00	C126
☐ Arizona 1993–94	$18.00	C101	☐ New England 1994 (Avail. 1/94)	$16.00	C137
☐ Australia 1992–93	$18.00	C002	☐ New Mexico 1993–94	$15.00	C117
☐ Austria 1993–94	$19.00	C119	☐ New York State 1994–95	$19.00	C133
☐ Bahamas 1994–95	$17.00	C121	☐ Northwest 1994–95 (Avail. 2/94)	$17.00	C140
☐ Belgium/Holland/ Luxembourg 1993–94	$18.00	C106	☐ Portugal 1994–95 (Avail. 2/94)	$17.00	C141
☐ Bermuda 1994–95	$15.00	C122	☐ Puerto Rico 1993–94	$15.00	C103
☐ Brazil 1993–94	$20.00	C111	☐ Puerto Vallarta/ Manzanillo/Guadalajara 1994–95 (Avail. 1/94)	$14.00	C028
☐ California 1994	$15.00	C134	☐ Scandinavia 1993–94	$19.00	C135
☐ Canada 1994–95 (Avail. 4/94)	$19.00	C145	☐ Scotland 1994–95 (Avail. 4/94)	$17.00	C146
☐ Caribbean 1994	$18.00	C123	☐ South Pacific 1994–95 (Avail. 1/94)	$20.00	C138
☐ Carolinas/Georgia 1994–95	$17.00	C128	☐ Spain 1993–94	$19.00	C115
☐ Colorado 1994–95 (Avail. 3/94)	$16.00	C143	☐ Switzerland/ Liechtenstein 1994–95 (Avail. 1/94)	$19.00	C139
☐ Cruises 1993–94	$19.00	C107	☐ Thailand 1992–93	$20.00	C033
☐ Delaware/Maryland 1994–95 (Avail. 1/94)	$15.00	C136	☐ U.S.A. 1993–94	$19.00	C116
☐ England 1994	$18.00	C129	☐ Virgin Islands 1994–95	$13.00	C127
☐ Florida 1994	$18.00	C124	☐ Virginia 1994–95 (Avail. 2/94)	$14.00	C142
☐ France 1994–95	$20.00	C132	☐ Yucatán 1993–94	$18.00	C110
☐ Germany 1994	$19.00	C125			
☐ Italy 1994	$19.00	C130			
☐ Jamaica/Barbados 1993–94	$15.00	C105			
☐ Japan 1994–95 (Avail. 3/94)	$19.00	C144			

FROMMER'S $-A-DAY GUIDES
(Guides to low-cost tourist accommodations and facilities)

	Retail Price	Code		Retail Price	Code
☐ Australia on $45 1993–94	$18.00	D102	☐ Israel on $45 1993–94	$18.00	D101
☐ Costa Rica/Guatemala/ Belize on $35 1993–94	$17.00	D108	☐ Mexico on $45 1994	$19.00	D116
☐ Eastern Europe on $30 1993–94	$18.00	D110	☐ New York on $70 1994–95	$16.00	D120
☐ England on $60 1994	$18.00	D112	☐ New Zealand on $45 1993–94	$18.00	D103
☐ Europe on $50 1994	$19.00	D115	☐ Scotland/Wales on $50 1992–93	$18.00	D019
☐ Greece on $45 1993–94	$19.00	D100	☐ South America on $40 1993–94	$19.00	D109
☐ Hawaii on $75 1994	$19.00	D113	☐ Turkey on $40 1992–93	$22.00	D023
☐ India on $40 1992–93	$20.00	D010	☐ Washington, D.C. on $40 1994–95 (Avail. 2/94)	$17.00	D119
☐ Ireland on $45 1994–95 (Avail. 1/94)	$17.00	D117			

FROMMER'S CITY $-A-DAY GUIDES
(Pocket-size guides to low-cost tourist accommodations and facilities)

	Retail Price	Code		Retail Price	Code
☐ Berlin on $40 1994–95	$12.00	D111	☐ Madrid on $50 1994–95 (Avail. 1/94)	$13.00	D118
☐ Copenhagen on $50 1992–93	$12.00	D003	☐ Paris on $50 1994–95	$12.00	D117
☐ London on $45 1994–95	$12.00	D114	☐ Stockholm on $50 1992–93	$13.00	D022

FROMMER'S WALKING TOURS
(With routes and detailed maps, these companion guides point out the places and pleasures that make a city unique)

	Retail Price	Code		Retail Price	Code
☐ Berlin	$12.00	W100	☐ Paris	$12.00	W103
☐ London	$12.00	W101	☐ San Francisco	$12.00	W104
☐ New York	$12.00	W102	☐ Washington, D.C.	$12.00	W105

FROMMER'S TOURING GUIDES
(Color-illustrated guides that include walking tours, cultural and historic sights, and practical information)

	Retail Price	Code		Retail Price	Code
☐ Amsterdam	$11.00	T001	☐ New York	$11.00	T008
☐ Barcelona	$14.00	T015	☐ Rome	$11.00	T010
☐ Brazil	$11.00	T003	☐ Scotland	$10.00	T011
☐ Florence	$ 9.00	T005	☐ Sicily	$15.00	T017
☐ Hong Kong/Singapore/			☐ Tokyo	$15.00	T016
Macau	$11.00	T006	☐ Turkey	$11.00	T013
☐ Kenya	$14.00	T018	☐ Venice	$ 9.00	T014
☐ London	$13.00	T007			

FROMMER'S FAMILY GUIDES

	Retail Price	Code		Retail Price	Code
☐ California with Kids	$18.00	F100	☐ San Francisco with Kids (Avail. 4/94)	$17.00	F104
☐ Los Angeles with Kids (Avail. 4/94)	$17.00	F103	☐ Washington, D.C. with Kids (Avail. 2/94)	$17.00	F102
☐ New York City with Kids (Avail. 2/94)	$18.00	F101			

FROMMER'S CITY GUIDES
(Pocket-size guides to sightseeing and tourist accommodations and facilities in all price ranges)

	Retail Price	Code		Retail Price	Code
☐ Amsterdam 1993–94	$13.00	S110	☐ Montréal/Québec City 1993–94	$13.00	S125
☐ Athens 1993–94	$13.00	S114	☐ Nashville/Memphis 1994–95 (Avail. 4/94)	$13.00	S141
☐ Atlanta 1993–94	$13.00	S112	☐ New Orleans 1993–94	$13.00	S103
☐ Atlantic City/Cape May 1993–94	$13.00	S130	☐ New York 1994 (Avail. 1/94)	$13.00	S138
☐ Bangkok 1992–93	$13.00	S005	☐ Orlando 1994	$13.00	S135
☐ Barcelona/Majorca/ Minorca/Ibiza 1993–94	$13.00	S115	☐ Paris 1993–94	$13.00	S109
☐ Berlin 1993–94	$13.00	S116	☐ Philadelphia 1993–94	$13.00	S113
☐ Boston 1993–94	$13.00	S117	☐ San Diego 1993–94	$13.00	S107
☐ Budapest 1994–95 (Avail. 2/94)	$13.00	S139	☐ San Francisco 1994	$13.00	S133
☐ Chicago 1993–94	$13.00	S122	☐ Santa Fe/Taos/ Albuquerque 1993–94	$13.00	S108
☐ Denver/Boulder/ Colorado Springs 1993–94	$13.00	S131	☐ Seattle/Portland 1994–95	$13.00	S137
☐ Dublin 1993–94	$13.00	S128	☐ St. Louis/Kansas City 1993–94	$13.00	S127
☐ Hong Kong 1994–95 (Avail. 4/94)	$13.00	S140	☐ Sydney 1993–94	$13.00	S129
☐ Honolulu/Oahu 1994	$13.00	S134	☐ Tampa/St. Petersburg 1993–94	$13.00	S1
☐ Las Vegas 1993–94	$13.00	S121	☐ Tokyo 1992–93	$13.00	S0
☐ London 1994	$13.00	S132	☐ Toronto 1993–94	$13.00	S
☐ Los Angeles 1993–94	$13.00	S123	☐ Vancouver/Victoria 1994–95 (Avail. 1/94)	$13.00	
☐ Madrid/Costa del Sol 1993–94	$13.00	S124	☐ Washington, D.C. 1994 (Avail. 1/94)	$13.00	
☐ Miami 1993–94	$13.00	S118			
☐ Minneapolis/St. Paul 1993–94	$13.00	S119			

SPECIAL EDITIONS

	Retail Price	Code		Retail Price	Code
☐ Bed & Breakfast Southwest	$16.00	P100	☐ Caribbean Hideaways	$16.00	P103
☐ Bed & Breakfast Great American Cities (Avail. 1/94)	$16.00	P104	☐ National Park Guide 1994 (Avail. 3/94)	$16.00	P105
			☐ Where to Stay U.S.A.	$15.00	P102

Please note: if the availability of a book is several months away, we may have back issues of guides to that particular destination. Call customer service at (815) 734-1104.